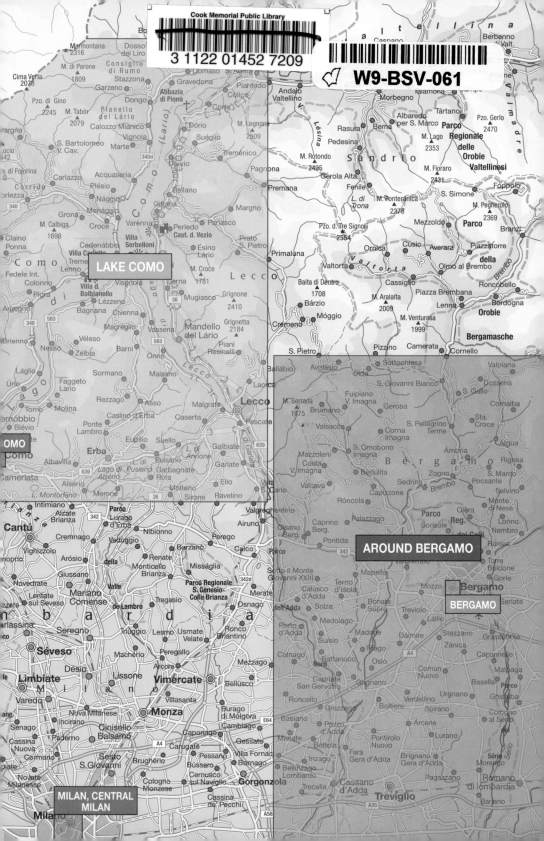

LAKE COMO

OMO

COMO

AROUND BERGAMO

BERGAMO

MILAN, CENTRAL MILAN

INSIGHT ⊙ GUIDES

ITALIAN LAKES

www.insightguides.com/Italy

⊙ Walking Eye App

YOUR FREE DESTINATION CONTENT AND EBOOK AVAILABLE THROUGH THE WALKING EYE APP

Your guide now includes a free eBook and destination content for your chosen destination, all for the same great price as before. Simply download the Walking Eye App from the App Store or Google Play to access your free eBook and destination content.

HOW THE WALKING EYE APP WORKS

Through the Walking Eye App, you can purchase a range of eBooks and destination content. However, when you buy this book, you can download the corresponding eBook and destination content for free. Just see below in the grey panels where to find your free content and then scan the QR code at the bottom of this page.

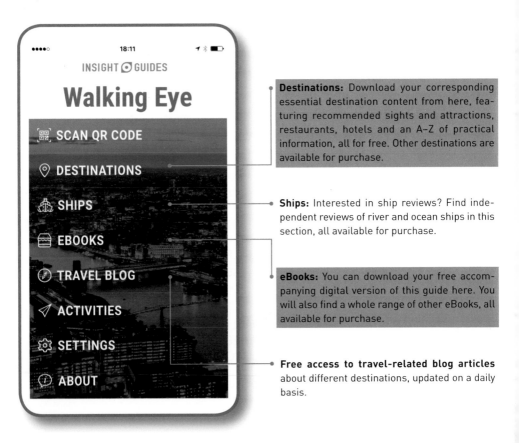

Destinations: Download your corresponding essential destination content from here, featuring recommended sights and attractions, restaurants, hotels and an A–Z of practical information, all for free. Other destinations are available for purchase.

Ships: Interested in ship reviews? Find independent reviews of river and ocean ships in this section, all available for purchase.

eBooks: You can download your free accompanying digital version of this guide here. You will also find a whole range of other eBooks, all available for purchase.

Free access to travel-related blog articles about different destinations, updated on a daily basis.

HOW THE DESTINATION CONTENT WORKS

Each destination includes a short introduction, an A–Z of practical information and recommended points of interest, split into 4 different categories:
• Highlights
• Accommodation
• Eating out
• What to do
You can view the location of every point of interest and save it by adding it to your Favourites. In the 'Around Me' section you can view all the points of interest within 5km.

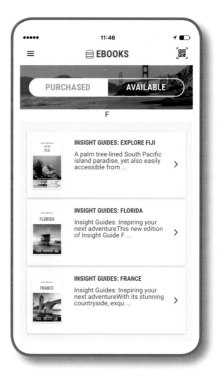

HOW THE EBOOKS WORK

The eBooks are provided in EPUB file format. Please note that you will need an eBook reader installed on your device to open the file. Many devices come with this as standard, but you may still need to install one manually from Google Play.

The eBook content is identical to the content in the printed guide.

HOW TO DOWNLOAD THE WALKING EYE APP

1. Download the Walking Eye App from the App Store or Google Play.
2. Open the app and select the scanning function from the main menu.
3. Scan the QR code on this page – you will then be asked a security question to verify ownership of the book.
4. Once this has been verified, you will see your eBook and destination content in the purchased ebook and destination sections, where you will be able to download them.

Other destination apps and eBooks are available for purchase separately or are free with the purchase of the Insight Guide book.

Contents

THE BEST OF THE ITALIAN LAKES: TOP ATTRACTIONS

Here, at a glance, are the region's must-sees and must-dos: art, ancient and inspirational; extraordinary buildings, from the strange Vittoriale to the dramatic Arco castle; grand opera in the Verona Arena; and of course, stunning scenery.

◁ **Castles.** Armies of crenellated castles march down the valleys of Trentino, protecting the ancient boundaries between Austria and Venice. Arco, near Lake Garda, is one of the most dramatic. See page 139.

▷ **Milan's shopping district.** Whether it's black-sequinned underpants or a diamond-encrusted watch, the place to spend your money is in the aptly named Quadrilatero d'Oro (Golden Square), a network of narrow streets from Via della Spiga to Piazza Duomo filled with high fashion from the fabulous to the ridiculous. See page 260.

▽ **Bellagio.** Tree-lined walkways and grand hotels line Bellagio's waterfront on Lake Como, an imposing sight best viewed from the deck of a private yacht. See page 199.

△ **Wines.** Choose your tipple from a rich red Bardolino or Valpolicella, a smooth Soave, light-headed Trentino or bubbly Franciacorta. See page 116.

◁ **Isola Bella**. Sculpted to look like a ship, named after a countess and planted with towering terraces, there is nothing natural about Isola Bella, but it is still a magnificent island garden. See page 226.

◁ **Parco Adamello-Brenta**. Spanning the border between Brescia and Trentino, this is a haven of wildlife, from edelweiss and chamois to bears and golden eagles. See page 61.

▽ **Il Vittoriale**. The warrior poet and Fascist supporter Gabriele D'Annunzio was an Italian hero – and probably barking mad. The fantasy villa he built for himself on Lake Garda is a place of strong emotion and strange decor. See page 128.

△ **Verona's Arena Festival**. Where lions once roared, sopranos now soar as grand opera fills the ancient Roman arena. Unmissable, spectacular and with glorious music in one of Italy's most imposing monuments – a perfect package. See page 98.

▽ **Orta San Giulio**. A legendary island, brightly painted fishing boats, and frescoes painted on the walls of a medieval piazza, make this village on the shores of little Lake Orta almost impossibly romantic. See page 242.

△ **Riva del Garda**. A stunning setting, graced by a castle, a Venetian fortress and the impressive cliffs of Monte Rocchetta. Nearby, visit the Grotta Cascate Varone, a waterfall cascading through a canyon. See page 138.

THE BEST OF THE ITALIAN LAKES: EDITOR'S CHOICE

The finest views, prettiest villas and gardens and best family outings – here are suggestions for the best of what to do and what to see, at a glance.

Leonardo's Last Supper, Milan.

WHERE TO SEE

Leonardo da Vinci. Leonardo's faded masterpiece, *The Last Supper*, at the Church and Convent of Santa Maria delle Grazie in Milan, is one of Italy's most visited sights. See page 256.

Giuseppe Verdi. The great composer lived and worked for most of his adult life in Milan, premiering all his great operas at La Scala. See page 252.

Gaetano Donizetti. Born in Bergamo and a prolific operatic composer, Donizetti worked all over Europe before returning to his home town to die. See page 182.

Romeo and Juliet. They may be fictional, but they supposedly lived and died in Verona. Both the famous lovers have houses and Juliet has a tomb, carefully chosen by the tourist office. See page 97.

George Clooney. Gorgeous George owns the Villa Oleandra at Laglio on Lake Como and is a regular visitor, along with many A-list pals. See page 194.

The Versaces. Gianni Versace chose to be buried at his beloved Villa Le Fontanelle at Moltrasio on Lake Como. The family are still regular visitors. See page 194.

Hermann Hesse. The Nobel prize-winning writer and painter lived in tower rooms in Montagnola near Lugano from 1919 to 1931. They are now a museum to his life and works. See page 210.

SACRED SIGHTS

The Sacri Monti. Now a Unesco World Heritage site, these sacred mountains in Orta (see page 241), Varese (see page 217), Ghiffa, Lake Maggiore (see page 228) and Ossuccio, Lake Como (see page 194) form a glorious procession of chapels leading pilgrims to hilltop churches.

Santa Caterina del Sasso, Maggiore. Getting to this cliffside hermitage requires strong knees, with a choice of 80 steps up or 267 steps down. See page 232.

Milan Duomo. A fabulous Gothic confection of a cathedral where you can dance among the gargoyles. See page 249.

San Tomé, Bergamo. An enchanting medieval round chapel in the woods. See page 184.

Sacro Monte, Varese.

FAMILY FAVOURITES

Go for a ride. Head to Gardaland, Italy's largest theme park. See page 120.

Make a splash. Choose a waterpark near Lake Garda or Milan. See page 121.

Go on safari. Parco Natura Viva is one of Europe's best animal parks – complete with dinosaurs! See page 120.

Get wet. Take a towel and head down to the lake for a swim. Choose from hundreds of kilometres of shoreline and hundreds of lakes.

Go fast. Hire a speed-boat by the hour or day or from any of the main resorts.

Reward yourself. Sample the delicious delights of Italian ice cream at a local *gelateria*.

Chill out with the chimps at Parco Natura Viva.

Gardaland thrills.

WATERFRONT WANDERING

Lugano City. An Art Nouveau horseshoe crescent of glittering glamour beneath towering mountains. See page 207.

Salò. The longest waterfront on Garda and the most pleasant to walk. See page 127.

Sirmione. Shuffle along behind the rest of the world in this charming but overcrowded tourism jewel on Lake Garda. See page 123.

Pallanza. Stroll in the gardens, then admire the sunset in this quiet resort on Maggiore. See page 227.

Varenna. Oleanders line the path in this prettiest of Como towns. See page 198.

Lugano waterfront.

ART – ANCIENT AND MODERN

Petroglyphs, Val Camonica.

Mart. Rovereto is an unlikely place to find world-class modern art from Warhol to Rauschenberg. See page 144.

Villa Panza, Varese. Perfect painting if you like your canvases monochrome – modern art in an 18th-century setting. It works. See page 216.

Pinacoteca di Brera. Superb Milan collection of grand masters from Tintoretto and Titian to Canaletto.

See page 254.

Val Camonica, Brescia. One of the world's greatest and oldest art collections, some 140,000 petroglyphs carved over 8,000 years. See page 170.

Arcumeggia, Varese. Since the 1950s, many artists have been adding murals to the streets of this mountain village, creating an extraordinary outdoor gallery. See page 218.

HIGH POINTS

Monte Brè, Lugano. Take the funicular or drive up seemingly endless hairpin bends for staggeringly beautiful views over Lake Lugano and the city. See page 207.

Monte Generoso. Since 1890, a cog railway has been hauling tourists up to the top of this mountain near Lake Lugano with unparalleled 360° views from the top. See page 213.

Monte Baldo. Expect long queues to get up the cable car near Malcesine on Lake Garda, with its spectacular views and mountain biking in summer, and ski slopes in winter. See page 115.

Monte Mottarone. This picturesque ridge between Lake Maggiore

and Lake Orta boasts superb views up into the Alps – sadly the cable car has been out of order for a while but there are walks to the top for those keen and fit. See page 225.

Rocca di Manerba. Much shorter and harder work than the cable-car runs, you need to climb this rocky promontory that towers over the Manerba coastline of Lake Garda, with lovely views and wild flowers as the prize. See page 126.

Monte San Primo, Lake Como. On a clear day they claim you can see from Mont Blanc to Milan Duomo from this peak, which is prime ski territory in winter. See page 201.

Villa Carlotta.

GARDENER'S WORLD

Sigurtà. Hire bikes or take the little train to get round the huge park south of Lake Garda without wearing your feet out. See page 111.

Isola Madre. An idyllic island garden on Lake Maggiore, with lush tropical planting and English design. See page 226.

Giardino Botanico Fondazione Andre Heller, Gardone. An imaginative small garden on the west shore of Lake Garda, borrowing themes and planting from around the world. See page 128.

Giardino Alpinia. Huge mountains and tiny plants combine to make this Alpine garden on Monte Mottarone above Stresa one of the most unusual in the region. See page 225.

Villa Melzi. This stunning 19th-century garden on Como combines English informality with oriental exoticism. See page 200.

Villa Taranto. A magnificent Scottish dream of a garden at Pallanza, Maggiore. See page 227. See also Gardener's Glory photo feature, page 236.

There are 360° views from the summit of Monte Baldo, on Lake Garda.

Giardino Botanico blooms, Gardone.

PICK A PALAZZO

Villa Carlotta, Como. This elegant 17th-century mansion set in lush formal terraced gardens was given to Albert of Prussia's daughter Carlotta as a wedding present. See page 197. **Villa del Balbianello, Como.** An 18th-century villa that has featured in *Star Wars* and James Bond films, housed monks, military and explorers. See page 195. **Villa Cicogna Mozzoni, Varese.** A seamless Renaissance villa with formal gardens kept much as they were over 400 years ago. See page 211.

The World Fireworks Championships on Lake Orta.

DIARY DATES

Milan Fashion Week. Twice a year the fashion caravan lands in Milan. This is really for the trade and is invitation only, but there is a real buzz in the air and celeb-spotting is rife. See page 260. **World Fireworks Championships**. Omegna, on Lake Orta, goes one further than most towns to celebrate its local saint's day with a two-week pyrotechnics championship. See page 247. **Sounds of the Dolomites.** Several weeks of free music from June to August, from symphony orchestras to world music, in inspirational settings in the Trentino mountains, reached by cable car. See page 141. **Mille Miglia**. Italy's oldest and most prestigious car rally, from Brescia. See page 154. **Centomiglia**. The biggest regatta on Lake Garda and the most important regatta on any lake in Europe. See page 271. **Estival Jazz**. A long-established free, open-air jazz festival in Lugano and Mendrisio, attracting the biggest international names. See page 271. **Palio del Baradello**. Como's colourful two-week historic celebrations of the defeat of Milan by Frederick Barbarossa in 1159. See page 271. **Arena Festival**. A sensational summer-long opera season in Verona's Roman amphitheatre. See page 98.

MONEY-SAVING TIPS

Budget Beds. Stay in wine estates (on a B&B basis or in self-catering apartments) or choose farm stays (*agriturismi*) just off the lake. These are generally friendly, family-run and in peaceful locations.

Sightseeing. The cities all offer excellent-value sightseeing saver cards; enquire at tourist offices. See page 275.

Lake Passes. Buy the right lake navigation pass: it sounds obvious, but only buy the (often pricey) day pass if planning to cover the whole lake that day. Otherwise, choose the (cheaper) more restrictive pass, and take the slower ferry instead of the hydrofoil. See pages 265 and 266.

Shopping. If you must have your Prada or Armani, head for the city's discount stores or one of the out-of-town outlet malls where you can buy the hottest Milan fashions at a fraction of their high-street price. See page 260.

Rural Lunches. For lunch, the bigger wine estates often have not just wine-tasting rooms but an inexpensive inn serving wonderful fresh produce and estate wines (you generally need to book). See key websites for the individual wine routes.

Lake Garda, a perfect blend of
Alpine and Mediterranean scenery.

Cycling on the lakeside at Toscolano-Maderno.

Approaching Isola dei Pescatori,
Lake Maggiore.

Isola di San Giulio, the pearl of Lake Orta.

A GLORIOUS LOCATION

Having emerged from the crash of tectonic plates
and the grinding of glaciers, then endured the
thunder of war, the waters of the Italian Lakes
have now mellowed into perfect tranquillity.

*Inspiration strikes as yet another artist
falls in love with Lake Garda.*

The Italian Lakes are a place between – caught between the frowning ice-capped crags of the Alps and Dolomites and the lazy flatlands of the Po River Valley, between the Goths and Romans, the Venetians and the Austro-Hungarians, the Allies and the Germans, between the financial firms of Zurich and the industrial giants of Milan.

Spread across the north of Italy and into southern Switzerland, most people know the four largest lakes – Garda to the east near Verona, Lugano, Como and, in the west, closest to Milan, Maggiore. Explore their waters by ferry, zigzagging between the windsurfers and dinghies to tiny fishing harbours and marinas fringed by geranium-clad *gelaterie*. But there are other lakes as well – literally hundreds of them, some such as Orta, Varese, Iseo and Idro still large, others as small as glacial ponds. Between them twist the tortuous sinews of the Prealps, their steep mountain roads always beautiful and dangerous and giddy, although motorways blasted through tunnels help speed you on your way.

Laglio, Lake Como.

Nearby lie great historic cities – überchic Milan to the southwest, Bergamo and Brescia in the south, Verona to the southeast, Trento to the northeast and Lugano to the north. Throughout most of their history, the people of the lakes have kept their heads down as the cities around them roared and postured, squabbling amongst themselves, and hoping that the bigger battles would pass by leaving them to get on with earning a living and enjoying the good things in life. These they have in abundance, from the vineyards of Garda to the snowfields of Trentino, scenery and food that have drawn poets and painters, dropouts and dictators to share in the good life, and moved hardened cynics to flights of eulogy. After all the paeans of praise sung to the beauty of the lakes, there are no adjectives left – none are needed.

Torbole, Lake Garda.

THE MODERN LAKES

The French writer Stendhal famously pitied "those who are not madly in love with them", and even Sigmund Freud was quite potty about them. The sparkling Italian Lakes continue to seduce and bewitch, but beneath the glamorous wrapping beats the economic and political heart of Italy.

Life around the lakes is sweet enough with the three surrounding capitals Milan, Turin and Venice each exerting its distinct influence. From the sophistication of Como, with its vibrant cultural life and excellent restaurants, to the independent enclave and tax haven of Campione d'Italia on Lake Lugano, each lake has its own identity. Perennially popular with readers of British and German newspapers, Lake Garda is also the weekend haven for the land-locked residents of Brescia and Verona. Como is the favoured weekend retreat of the Milanese, who happily rub shoulders with the glitterati and celebrity-seekers. Little Orta is quieter, mystical and low-key. Yet all are effortlessly beautiful. "*La figura*" in Italian life always take precedence over "*la sostanza*" – the substance of things.

Along with the pleasures of *dolce vita* conviviality and gastronomy, all the lakes are awash with music, opera and film festivals. And in an area where it's possible to water-ski in the morning, lunch at a sun-drenched lakeside café and snow-ski in the afternoon, life doesn't get much sweeter than in this richly endowed corner of Italy.

Everyday life

Yet what is life like for the ordinary people who live and work here, whose ancestors have grown olives and grapes on these shores for centuries and who now spend their working lives pampering the tourists? The underlying, uniting characteristics of the region are conformity, sense of ritual, food and wine and *campanilismo* – the attachment to one's own bell tower, described by Stendhal as the "*patriotisme d'antichambre*". Life in the lake district revolves around a clear sense of community. The sovereign appeal of the family remains paramount, and many of the most prosperous businesses are family-run.

Café in Varese.

Even in Lombardy, the most prosperous of Italian regions, there is a local-centred social and cultural life – Sunday lunch for 20 with three generations, ages seven to 70. It still continues, although many of the bigger towns have become very cosmopolitan. Brescia has the highest per capita number of immigrants in Italy. The influx has added a new, often vibrant dimension, with new restaurants mushrooming and horizons widening, as well as creating a degree of discord amongst locals fearful for their jobs and houses.

Local industry and economy

Italy's economic strength has always been in the processing and the manufacturing of goods, especially in small- to medium-sized family firms – inevitably, it is these businesses that have suffered the most in the economic crisis that has seized Italy over the last few years.

The major industries in the region are precision machinery, motor vehicles, chemicals, pharmaceuticals, electric goods, fashion and clothing. The powerhouse is Lombardy, which has become a world leader in design, textiles and machine tools. Milan is the main money-earner, but each lake has its own source of income.

Tourism is a vital part of the economy of the region, with Lake Garda alone accounting for more than five million foreign tourists a year.

every fine house – Armani, Chanel, Ferré, Ungaro, Valentino and Versace, to name just a few – rely on silk from Como. The Mantero family and Antonio Ratti are the two giants. Mantero alone has a yearly output of 8–10 million metres (9–11 million yds) and boasts a starry client list that includes the French couture house Chanel, for whom they are the exclusive makers of their signature scarves.

But the Faustian pact with the Far East has caused lengthening shadows. The outlook for the textile and clothing industry is not bright. Until the beginning of the 21st century, Italy

Big glasses, big hair and black leather are super cool in Como.

Religious tourism is also increasingly popular, centred on the nine Sacri Monti, which were developed for pilgrims in the 15th and 16th centuries as an alternative to travelling to the Holy Land.

Milan may be the design showcase but Como is *the* city of silk (see page 192). Silk has been processed here since the 16th century, and today the annual production totals 3,200 tons with exports of around $1,000 million a year. Italy produces 80 percent of Europe's silk, of which Como now produces 90 percent. The costly business of raising silkworms was discontinued in Italy after World War II, and today the fibres are imported from China ready to be woven, dyed and finished. Designers from virtually

FURBIZIA

As Italy faces a serious economic crisis, there have been calls for an increased focus on solidarity, social responsibility and community spirit. However, in a country that has long prized the quality of 'furbizia' (roughly translatable as 'cunning'), and in which family comes first, community second, this might take some time. As Tobias Jones comments in *The Dark Heart of Italy*, "Stay in the country long enough and you simply have to become 'cunning' in order to survive. With a shrug of honest admission, everyone in Italy will admit to having broken the law at some point (it's hard not to if being 'an accessory to tax evasion' involves leaving a shop without the till receipt)".

had been Europe's leading textile and clothing producer for a quarter of a century. Then, in 2001, China joined the World Trade Organisation and foreign direct investment poured into the country. In 2004 alone, EU imports from China increased by almost half, prices fell by a third and imports of some products grew sixfold. In the 1970s, the clothing giant Benetton, based near Venice in Treviso, used to outsource clothes-making to home workers throughout the district. By 1990, about 90 percent of its garments were still made in Italy, but in the mid-2000s the proportion dropped to 30 percent and dropped right down to 10 percent in 2010. Benetton opened a Hong Kong office in 2006 to supervise the burgeoning supply chain in mainland China. Many mid-market Italian clothing brands followed suit and moved production to lower-cost countries such as Bulgaria, Turkey and Romania. There are currently around 1,500 clothing and textile firms owned by Italians in Romania.

In 2014 there were some good news however. After more than 50 years the Italian textile industry returned to growing silk worms – and in 2015 around 100 silk worm factories were operating in the Veneto region. The industry's ambitious plan is to create 1,000 more factories in the next five or six years.

Other survival strategies have been adopted by upmarket fashion houses, like chic menswear designer Ermenegildo Zegna, which has a factory near Biella (also known as "textile valley"). Ten years ago, Zegna gave serious thought to taking its production to China, but decided that its home-grown Italian skills and production systems were of greater value than making wages savings. Zegna is now selling rather than producing in China and has opened shops in 36 cities.

Keen to reinvent itself, in recent years the Italian textiles market has found origin labelling a useful sales tool: the 'Made in Italy' tag – a proud reminder of many centuries of craftsmanship – has attracted many luxury brands willing to pay the extra for the quality and prestige of Italy-made goods.

Design icons

The valleys of the mountainous province of Belluno may not always be sunny, but shades are probably every Italian's most important fashion accessory, and it is around here that the vast majority of the world's sunglasses are crafted by a coterie of family-controlled firms including Safilo, De Rigo and Marchon. The biggest of all, the Luxottica group, had net sales of $9 billion in 2015.

Matchless Italian design also has a home on the shores of Lake Iseo, where Riva began making boats at the beginning of the 19th century. Soon they acquired and perfected the Italian lust for speed, and in 1934 set a world speed record on water with one of their 1,500cc racers. The crowning achievement came in 1962 with the wooden-hull, sleek Aquarama, which

Ermenegildo Zegna store, Via Montenapoleone, Milan.

retailed for £250,000. Plastic boats started to dominate the market, and Riva was sold to Vickers in 1996. But the reclaimed Aquaramas are still regarded as the Rolls-Royce of sports boats. The late Gianni Agnelli, the jet-set head of Fiat, was once asked to try one out. He was told that if he could turn it over, he could have it. Gianni tried, but, for once, he failed.

Around Lake Orta, the southern suburbs of Gozzano and San Maurizio d'Opaglio, known as "tap city", have everything for bathroom delights and are the site of Giacomini, the area's largest tap company. Omegna is especially known for household goods and designer kitchenware in Alessi's Dream Factory. The original Alessi-design icon coffee pot was produced here along with female corkscrews, funky fly swats and all kinds of beautifully crafted – yet useful – domestic jewels. As Alberto Alessi has famously said, "I don't think people buy an Alessi kettle to boil water," but he concedes, "I prefer it if they work."

Politics

In the 16th century, the writer and philosopher Machiavelli recognised even then that Italy is ever "waiting to see who can be the one to heal her wounds". In modern times, there has been Fascism under Mussolini, communism,

Prime Minister of Italy. In the wake of his resignation, amid the disbelief and, for many, euphoria that the 17-year tenure of "Il Cavaliere" had finally come to an end, there was fury at the rapidly emerging picture of a seriously ailing national economy. Until the last, Berlusconi had presented a glossed-over view of his country's economic woes, protesting "the restaurants in Rome are always full"; in fact, Italy's economy had been at a virtual standstill since the turn of the century – corresponding almost exactly with Berlusconi's ascendancy – and in the last years of his tenure his failure to imple-

An afternoon in the sun with the paper.

socialism and the longest-surviving government in Italy's republican history, led by Silvio Berlusconi. Perhaps a dubious distinction as he more than most betrayed freemarket economics. In *La Bella Figura*, Beppe Severgnini opines that "Italy is the only workshop in the world that could turn out both Botticellis and Berlusconis". He continues, "Silvio Berlusconi promised that he would be the captain who would turn the ship around but instead he concentrated on making his own cabin more comfortable and ran aground".

On 16 November 2011, following a litany of scandals – from his involvement in the infamous "Bunga Bunga" orgies to corruption on a grand scale – Silvio Berlusconi resigned as

ment fiscal reforms in time to stem the crisis was the final nail in the coffin.

Berlusconi's successor, Mario Monti, a former European Commissioner, was appointed to preside over a cabinet of technocrats until the economic conditions stabilised and new elections were held.

Looking to the future

The financial crisis succeeded where Italy's liberal parties had failed to remove Berlusconi from power, but the country is no stranger to economic crisis. In the late 1990s, Italy's manufacturing was overtaken by Asian competitors; lazy political leadership did little to boost growth, but the introduction of the euro helped bolster the economy. The advent of the global financial crisis in 2007, however, knocked Italy's economy by more than 6 percent. Investors feared that Italy could not manage its mountain of debt and a further decade of stagnation loomed.

Mario Monti's first move was to devise a radical package of spending cuts and tax increases. Particular focus was given to tax evasion, a widespread problem. His proposals were met with protests from both left and right. The core reforms, however, based on tax increases, were pushed through, marking a new age of austerity for an already cash-strapped country.

to keep the budget deficit at a safe level and in 2015 a hopeful economic growth of 0.3 percent was reported. Expo 2015, hosted by Milan for the second time in the event's history, also gave a boost to the economy of the city and the entire region.

For all his achievements, however, Italy's youngest ever prime minister is faced with ever-persistent social woes and a financial crisis aggravated by waves of immigrants flooding the country. In October 2016, a referendum is planned to approve the constitutional reforms put forward by Renzi.

Saturday market, Salò.

One of the most significant signs of Italy's steady decline has been the emigration of its young people: in the past decade around 600,000 have left Italy's shores in search of brighter prospects elsewhere. The country's two-tier labour market is largely to blame for the exodus: while older workers enjoy the benefits of fixed contracts and generous pensions, younger Italians – often highly educated – struggle to find even poorly-paid temporary work.

Following the 2013 general elections, Enrico Letta succeeded Monti as prime minister – albeit for a short while. In 2014, he was replaced by the Democratic Party's Matteo Renzi. With an ambitious package of reforms, the young and energetic former mayor of Florence managed

WINE LAKES

Italy exports more wine than any other country; its export value was estimated at $5.4 billion in 2015. The fertile land and warm climate of the lakes produces a great diversity of wines, from the rich reds of Barolo to sparkling, white Prosecco. Nebbiolo is the finest red grape in northern Italy, from which both Barolo and Barbaresco are made, and flourishes around the western shore of Lake Maggiore. Fruity Valpolicella and fine red Bardolino come from Lake Garda, dry Soave is produced east of Verona, and the wines of Franciacorta, produced around Lake Iseo, have been praised since Roman times.

DECISIVE DATES

Pictographs, Capo di Ponte, Val Camonica.

c.12000 BC
Neanderthals living in Trentino mountains.

c.6000–5000 BC
The first pictographs are carved in Val Camonica by Camuni hunter-gatherers. Neolithic farmers settle in Po Valley.

c.3300 BC
The Copper Age is well under way by the time Oetzi the Iceman sets out north from Trentino and is murdered en route.

c.1200–400 BC
The south of the region is colonised by the Etruscans, while the Ligurians inhabit the western Alps, the Oribi the centre and the Veneti the eastern Alps.

c.400 BC
The Celts cross the Alps, seizing Etruscan territory and sacking Rome in 390 BC. They found the cities of Milan, Bergamo and Como.

222–191 BC
The Romans drive out the Celts, and northern Italy becomes the Roman province of Gallia Cisalpina.

218–202 BC
Second Punic War between Carthage and Rome. Hannibal and his elephants cross the Alps in their march on Rome.

15 BC
Augustus reorganises the Transpadania region and makes Mediolanum (Milan) its capital.

AD 292
Diocletian divides the Roman Empire in two, taking the east for himself, while his co-emperor, Maximilian, rules from Milan.

313
Emperors Constantine the Great and Licinius write a joint Edict of Milan granting freedom of worship to Christians and making

Christianity the state religion of the Roman Empire.

330
Constantine moves the capital of the empire to Byzantium. With Rome a spent force, Milan becomes the effective capital of the Western Empire.

402–3
Without the protection of Rome, northern tribes pour south. The Visigoths besiege Milan and Verona.

452
Milan, Verona and the Po Valley are ransacked by Attila the Hun.

476
End of the Western Roman Empire comes officially as Germanic war leader, Odoacer, is elected king in northern Italy.

539
Milan is virtually destroyed during the Gothic Wars between the Ostrogoths and Byzantium.

Statue of Emperor Maximilian.

Roman Capitoline Temple, Brescia.

568–72
The Germanic Lombards invade northern Italy and take control of the lake district and northern Po Valley, with their capital at Pavia.

756
Frankish King Pepin the Short grants several Lombard provinces to the Pope, setting up centuries of future squabbles between Church and state.

774
The Pope asks the Frankish

Charlemagne.

king, Charlemagne, to stop the Lombard advance. He conquers the Lombard kingdom, and creates a Frankish state in north Italy.

800
Charlemagne is proclaimed Holy Roman Emperor by the Pope.

9th–10th centuries
Bishops of some cities obtain effective independence; other areas of northern Italy are fought over by French and German Franks.

962
German Otto I retakes Italy. His successors officially hold the area for nearly 200 years, but once more it disintegrates into a series of *comuni* (city states), marked by Milan's first popular assembly *(parlamento)* in 1024.

1118–27
The Ten Years War between Milan and Como is one of many violent local squabbles as the cities vie for position and wealth.

1155
The German Prince Frederick Barbarossa is crowned Holy Roman Emperor and tries to enforce his authority over the Italians.

1167–1250
The Lombard League of city states is founded with the support of the Pope to oppose Barbarossa. In an uneasy truce, the cities have effective autonomy but pay lip-service to the crown.

12th–14th centuries
Cities thrive on trade, but power shifts from several hundred small communes to a few large cities and families such as the Scaligeri in Verona and the Visconti and Sforza in Milan, who become aristocratic rulers *(signori)*.

Lion of St Mark.

1405–1521
Brescia, Verona and Lake Garda are conquered or hand themselves over peacefully to the Venetian Republic, symbolised by the lion of St Mark.

1496–1500
Modern-day Ticino is annexed by Switzerland.

1525–56

After the last Sforza duke dies, Milan is claimed by France, but following a scrap, is taken by the Habsburgs then, in 1556, by Spain.

1545–63

The Roman Catholic Church convenes several times for the Council of Trent (Trento), an ultimately unsuccessful attempt to fight the Reformation.

Council of Trent.

La Scala, Milan.

1701–14

The War of the Spanish Succession revives French claims to Lombardy before the Treaty of Utrecht gives the region to the Austrian Habsburgs.

Battle of Solferino, 1859.

1778

Opera house in Milan (La Scala) opens.

1796–1805

Napoleon conquers Lombardy and the Veneto in 1796 and is crowned "king of Italy" in Milan's Duomo. The puppet Cisalpine Republic is formed by the Treaty of Campoformio in 1797, becoming the Italian Republic in 1802 and the Kingdom of Italy in 1805.

1814–15

After Napoleon's defeat, the Congress of Vienna awards Lombardy and the Veneto to Austria.

1842

Amidst growing calls for Italian independence in Piedmont, Garibaldi names his movement after a local newspaper, *Il Risorgimento* (The Awakening).

1848–66

The Risorgimento fights against Austrian rule.

1859

Backed by France, the Risorgimento wins a decisive victory at the Battle of Solferino. Milan joins the kingdom.

1861

Garibaldi formally declares the new Kingdom of Italy, ruled by King Vittorio Emanuele II. Austria hands over Lombardy and the Veneto.

1915

Italy joins the World War I Allies.

1919

The Treaty of Saint-Germain gives Trentino to Italy. Mussolini creates the blackshirt Fascist brigades in Milan.

1922

Fascists under Benito Mussolini seize power in Italy.

1936-40
Mussolini supports Franco in the Spanish Civil War, conquers Ethiopia, invades Albania and enters World War II as a Nazi ally in 1940.

1943–5
Italy's northern front collapses. Mussolini retires to Lake Garda and founds the Republic of Salò. Italy joins the Allies, and a heroic resistance struggle against the Germans is fought in the mountains.

Benito Mussolini and Adolf Hitler, 1943.

1945
On 27 April 1945 Mussolini is captured and executed in Como the following day.

1946
Italy becomes a republic; the Savoy royal family is exiled.

1949
Italy joins Nato.

1958
Italy joins the Common Market, the forerunner of the European Union, as a founder member.

1960s–70s
Political unrest and violence by far-right and left groups, including the Red Brigade. Bombs in Milan (1969) and Brescia (1974), and the kidnapping and murder of former premier Aldo Moro in 1978.

1987
The industrial north powers Italy to a place in the G7.

1992
Tangentopoli ("Bribesville") scandal leads to a supposed overhaul of public life, although corruption scandals continue to rock the economic and political heart of Italy.

1994
Media tycoon Silvio Berlusconi creates a right-wing party, Forza Italia, and goes on to lead the longest-serving government in the republic's history.

1997
Political playwright Dario Fo, from Milan, wins the Nobel Prize for Literature.

2002
Italy adopts the euro.

2003
The Savoy royal family are allowed to return to Italy for the first time.

2006
A centre-left coalition, led by Romano Prodi, takes power in parliament.

2008
Berlusconi is re-elected as prime minister in April, with a large majority.

2011
Scandals rock Berlusconi's government, highlighting the premier's shady dealings and illicit liaisons. After losing his majority in parliament, Berlusconi officially resigns as prime minister on 16 November and is replaced by Mario Monti.

2012
Earthquakes hit the region of Emilia-Romagna in May with aftershocks felt as far as Milan.

2014
Matteo Renzi from the Democratic Party forms a new government.

2015
Milan hosts Expo 2015.

2016
Referendum to approve constitutional reforms proposed by Prime Minister Renzi.

Prime Minister Matteo Renzi.

*Catullus wrote forlorn love poems
to Lesbia in this villa in Sirmione.*

THE MAKING OF THE LAKES

Situated at the gateway to the Italian peninsula, the Italian Lakes have long been a geographical prize, colonised – and contested – by a bewildering range of peoples. This is a landscape that bears the fingerprints of everyone from the Gauls to Garibaldi.

It was glacial action that carved out the rugged beds of the Italian Lakes. And it was not long after the last ice sheets retreated, around 14,000 years ago, that early man began to colonise the region. Mesolithic hunter-gatherers were followed by Neolithic farmers, who carved delicate images into the rocks of the Val Camonica, near Lake Iseo (see page 170).

Around 2,500 years later, there was what amounted to a social revolution: stone tools were replaced by ones made from metal – first copper, then bronze. These prehistoric people were outward-looking, making use of Alpine passes to travel and trade with other parts of continental Europe and, as the discovery of Oetzi the Iceman (see box) showed, had some knowledge of natural medicines.

Bronze Age advances in agriculture led to the growth of more permanent villages. Lavagnone, near Desenzano del Garda, was continuously settled for around 1,000 years. An oak plough found

Petroglyphs, Capo di Ponte, Val Camonica.

> Once a vast bay of the Adriatic, the northern plains gradually filled with nitrate-rich silt from the Po, the Adige and other rivers and became the most fertile region in Italy drawing prehistoric clans to the area.

there (c.2000 BC) boasted a shrewdly designed replaceable ploughshare – and was probably pulled by oxen. Other Bronze Age finds in the area around the lakes include a spoked wheel, a dugout canoe and that sartorial survivor, the sprung safety-pin (a "fibula" in its earliest incarnation).

Iron Age people

With the Iron Age (c.1000 BC), the people of the lakes, such as the Camuni of Val Camonica, came into contact with new colonisers, notably the Etruscans and the Veneti, as well as the Liguri tribe, which had founded Brescia. By the 4th century BC, more belligerent Gauls (Celtic tribes) had swept across the Alps, driving out the Etruscans and putting their stamp on the landscape. They expanded Brescia, and founded Milan, Bergamo, Como and probably Trento, in modern-day Trentino. The Gauls then headed south and sacked Rome. The stage was set for conflict.

Roman province

The expansion of the Roman Republic had already led to war with Carthage, in modern Tunisia. In the First Punic War (264–241 BC),

Rome took Sicily and Sardinia from Carthage, then turned its attentions north and drove the Gauls from what is now Milan (222 BC). The Romans named their newly conquered city Mediolanum. The Second Punic War (218–202 BC) saw the Carthaginian commander Hannibal lead his army – and elephants – over the Alps, establishing control over much of the lakes with the help of the Gauls. Rome, however, was not to be resisted and eventually destroyed Carthage, seized its vast empire and drove the Gauls from the lakes and fertile Po Valley. The Romans now controlled a vast northern Italian province – Gallia Cisalpina, literally "Gaul on this side of the Alps". They began building the Via Aemilia, which linked Rimini on the Adriatic to Piacenza, and later extended the highway all the way to Milan. New settlements were founded, marshy ground drained, and Roman culture and language became dominant.

The boundary separating Gallia Cisalpina from Italic Rome was the Rubicon. Julius Caesar returned victorious from conquering Gaul, crossing this now legendary river with his army to seize control of the Republic. He wasted no

Oetzi the Iceman.

FROZEN IN TIME

In 1991, high in the mountains of northern Italy, two hikers discovered the body of a man who had died thousands of years earlier in the Chalcolithic (Copper) Age. Preserved almost intact by the ice, Oetzi as he was named offered a unique glimpse into an ancient world. Analysis of his body and belongings allowed scientists to build up a detailed picture of his life and death.

Oetzi was well prepared for his mountain journey, dressed in a fur hat, thick coat, thigh-high leggings and leather lace-up shoes. He also had on a woven grass cloak and a backpack. Propped on a rock beside his body was a finely worked yew axe with a copper blade. He had a quiver, arrows and a bow. Of most interest was his medical kit – balls of a birch fungus with antibiotic properties, possibly to ease stomach-ache (parasitic worm eggs were found in his gut). Pollen analysis shows it was spring when Oetzi set out on his final journey. He never reached his destination as someone shot him in the back; a stone arrowhead was still in his body. More clues in this prehistoric murder mystery emerged with recent studies of Oetzi's full genome which revealed that he had brown eyes, was blood type "O" and predisposed to heart disease.

Oetzi now resides in the South Tyrol Museum of Archaeology in Bolzano (Tue–Sun 10am–6pm; www. iceman.it).

THE MAKING OF THE LAKES ♦ 33

time in developing the lakes, and had soon moved the original centre of Como to its current location, laying out a new town (Novum Comum) that had the status of a municipality. Mark Antony later "promoted" Gallia Cisalpina from a mere province to an official part of Italic Rome. This laid the foundations for the Italy of today.

Imperial era

The 1st century BC saw the Roman Republic segue into the Roman Empire, with Caesar's chosen heir Octavian taking the title Emperor

The empire remained stable until the 3rd century AD, when invaders began to breach its boundaries. The northern lakes were at the heart of much of the fighting – Lake Garda was the scene for the Battle of Lake Benacus (AD 268), in which Rome successfully beat off a vast Germanic army. Collapse was averted when Emperor Diocletian split his unwieldy empire in two. He went to Turkey to take control of the east (Byzantium), and co-emperor Maximilian was given control of the west – which he ruled from Milan.

Diocletian had persecuted Christians with

The Roman columns in Milan.

Augustus. He developed Brescia as an important trading centre and, recognising the strategic importance of the location of Mediolanum ('Middle of the Plain', which became Milan), made it the capital of Transpadania (15 BC), a region that included Como and Bergamo. The north began to make both an economic and a cultural contribution to the empire (the Plinys, Elder and Younger, came from Como, and the legacy of the poet Catullus, who was born in Verona, is also significant). Imposing structures such as the Forum in Brescia and Amphitheatre in Verona were erected, and wealthy Romans established the area as a rich man's playground, building themselves luxurious lakeside villas – such as that at Desenzano on Lake Garda.

brutal enthusiasm, but Constantine – who later converted – was more tolerant. After he met his co-emperor (and new brother-in-law) Licinius in Milan (AD 313), the Edict of Milan was issued. This allowed freedom of religious worship and effectively made Christianity the state religion of the empire. Milan soon became a jewel in the Christian crown.

When Licinius died, Constantine became sole emperor, reuniting both halves of the Roman Empire. He moved the capital from Rome to the city of Byzantium, building himself an imposing imperial city named Constantinople. Strategically situated between the Alps and the Po Valley, Milan assumed the role of second imperial centre.

The Lombards swiftly conquered most of what is now Lombardy, the Veneto and Tuscany, replacing the centralised Roman political system with locally governed "duchies".

Barbarians and Byzantines

At the end of the 4th century, the empire was divided once again. Western Emperor Honorius initially made Milan his capital, but after it was attacked by barbarians, he moved the imperial capital southeast to Ravenna (in Emilia-

the Ostrogoth leader Theodoric to seize power. Theodoric's forces took Verona in 489 and besieged Ravenna for an astonishing three years. Eventually, he and Odoacer agreed that they would both rule Italy. However, in a move worthy of a fictional villain, Theodoric held a celebratory banquet, toasted his new compatriot, then murdered him.

Theodoric became the new king of Italy, spending a great deal of time in Verona, but the threat from the east remained. Justinian became ruler of Byzantium (527–65) and embarked on a mission to retake the former Western Empire.

Ostrogothic King Theodoric.

Romagna), as its malarial swamps made it easier to defend. It was a disastrous decision, leaving much of Italy prey to raids. Rome was sacked and the lake settlements were continually harried. As the Western Empire crumbled, Como, Milan and Verona were besieged, and eventually Attila the Hun stormed the region, razing Milan in 452.

The later years of the 5th century saw further instability, with an uprising of mixed Teutonic invaders led by Odoacer, the son of a chieftain in Attila the Hun's court. Odoacer took Ravenna and was eventually proclaimed *rex Italiae* – king of Italy, by the Eastern Emperor Zeno. He was crowned in Pavia.

Zeno came to see Odoacer as a threat and cunningly engineered his downfall by encouraging

The northern lakes became a battleground between Byzantium and the Ostrogoths during the Gothic Wars (535–54). Milan was besieged (again) and was eventually starved into surrender in 539. Many were massacred, and the city was virtually destroyed. Byzantine influence spread across Italy, and political instability allowed the Church to assume more authority.

The Lombard era

The later years of the 6th century ushered in a welcome period of relative peace for northern Italy. In 568, the Lombards (or Longobards), an industrious Germanic people, began their invasion (568–72) and soon had control of the lakes and much of the Po Valley. The Lombard era lasted until the 8th century and, as the name suggests, they wielded their greatest influence in what is now Lombardy. They established various duchies, the most important of which was at Pavia, which they intended to rival Ravenna (still under Byzantine rule). Other important centres were Brescia, Milan and Verona, and they also controlled Trento, Como and Bergamo.

Lombard rule is traditionally seen as a Dark Age for Italy. However, they left a linguistic but also an architectural legacy. They began to build churches and monasteries, frequently incorpo-

power of the Pope. In the Donation of Pepin (756), he granted land that had belonged to Ravenna, plus several Lombard duchies, to the Pope – effectively creating Papal States.

Perhaps as a way of ensuring a powerful Frankish–Lombard alliance, Pepin's son and successor Charlemagne married one of the daughters of Desiderius, the Lombard king. It was a brief liaison: Charlemagne soon had the marriage annulled and married someone else. Such ungentlemanly behaviour provoked Lombard anger, and Desiderius seized a number of newly gifted papal lands. The Pope requested

Pope Zachary asking Pepin the Short for help against the Lombards.

rating earlier Roman structures and ushering in the Romanesque style. Sant'Ambrogio in Milan, San Zeno Maggiore in Verona and the Monastery of Santa Giulia in Brescia all bear the Lombard hallmark.

Pepin and the Pope

Around the middle of the 8th century, the Germanic Franks invaded Italy. Led by their king, the memorably monikered Pepin the Short, and with the blessing of the Pope, who had been increasingly worried by the strength of the Lombard kingdom, they grabbed Lombard territory and ushered in the Carolingian era. Pepin then unwittingly laid the foundations for generations of future conflict by strengthening the

that Charlemagne get them back. Charlemagne duly invaded Italy (774) and conquered the Lombards (he was pointedly crowned with the Lombard crown in Pavia), creating a Frankish state. He went on to establish a mighty territory, across Italy and other parts of Europe, and was crowned emperor by the Pope in 800 – the first of the Holy Roman Emperors.

Carolingian rule continued after Charlemagne's death, with control of northern Italy switching between French and German Franks (while the south began to succumb to the Arabs and then the Normans, creating a distinct cultural difference between north and south). The line died out in the late 9th century, and the ensuing power struggle allowed several cities in the north to assume autonomy. Even the imposition of order by German Otto I, who was crowned Holy Roman Emperor in 962, failed to quell their rise.

Enter Redbeard

Otto, his son and grandson (rather predictably Otto II and Otto III) ruled until the year 1002, establishing a strong link between Germany and Italy. When Otto III died, his cousin, the extremely devout Henry II, assumed control. Henry empowered the Church, and ecclesiastical buildings sprang up around the lakes.

Frederick Barbarossa invades Italy, 1154, from a 15th-century manuscript.

Cities such as Milan and Como were now almost separate city states (*comuni*), ruled by councils of clergy and powerful merchants. The relationship between Church and state, popes and emperors, became increasingly uncomfortable, especially when, in 1076, Emperor Henry IV decided to flex his political muscles by investing as archbishop of Milan a man he knew was unacceptable to Pope Gregory VII. Henry deposed Gregory, who promptly retaliated by excommunicating the emperor. The struggle continued until Henry V took the crown and diplomatically conceded to most papal claims.

As the *comuni* grew in wealth and power, so did rivalries between them. Early in the 12th

> *Pavia's location on the Via Francigena brought in a valuable income from pilgrims on their way to Rome, who needed places to stay, eat, buy souvenirs and change money.*

century, the so-called Ten Years War (1118–27) broke out between Como and Milan – Como was eventually defeated and badly damaged. Then Arnold of Brescia led a reform movement against the Church, eventually moving to Rome and establishing a "republic" in defiance of the Pope. In 1154, Swabian ruler Frederick I (named "Barbarossa" because of his red beard) stormed into Italy, ostensibly to defend the papacy, but in reality to stamp his authority on this increasingly unruly region. He was crowned king of Italy at Pavia in 1154, and later Holy Roman Emperor. He rampaged across northern Italy and destroyed Milan in 1162 – an act that unexpectedly united the competitive *comuni* against this aggressive intruder.

The Lombard League

Barbarossa's belligerence led to the formation of an alliance of cities in the lakes. In 1167, at the village of Pontida, near Bergamo, Cremona, Mantua, Bergamo and Brescia united in an attempt to limit the emperor's influence. They were later joined by other cities, including Milan and Verona. Pavia and Como, however, sided with Barbarossa while Trento, governed by prince-bishops since 1027, kept aloof. The league built a fortified settlement, named Alessandria (after Pope Alexander III). Relations between the Pope and the league got closer, especially after Barbarossa attacked Alessandria. It should have been an easy victory – Alessandria was known as "Straw City" as its roofs were made of straw – but the assault was unsuccessful. There was then another blow to imperial pride when the league defeated Barbarossa at Legnano, near Milan, in 1176.

An uneasy truce began, and eventually Barbarossa granted most demands. After he died, the Lombard League had to be revived more than once as his successors (members of the Hohenstaufen dynasty) made more attempts to extend imperial authority. Barbarossa's grandson Frederick II declared war but was beaten back from Brescia in 1238 and he – and Hohenstaufen rule – died in 1250. But a distinct division had been established between supporters of the emperor – who felt he had the right to sanction popes (Ghibellines) and supporters of the Pope – who felt he had the right to crown emperors (Guelphs).

Southern Italy had now been opened up to French rule. In the north, the *comuni* became self-governing states ruled by secular councils (communes) made up of wealthy merchants and lawyers. This autonomy allowed cities such as Milan, Pavia and Verona to take full advantage of their location on lucrative European trade routes and increasingly busy pilgrimage paths. Banking, trade and commerce flourished, and the astute northern communes also encouraged agricultural innovation, fully exploiting the potential of the flat, fertile Po Valley.

Stellar Signori and La Serenissima

Freed from the need to fight against imperial powers, the cities now had the time to fight amongst themselves. Not only were there rivalries between cities (often based on Guelph or Ghibelline allegiances), there were also internal wranglings for control of the ruling councils. Cities began to look to members of powerful families for leadership, and control became centralised, wielded by *signori* (ruling lords).

In Milan, it was the archbishop, Ottone Visconti, who grabbed power. He became *signore* in 1278, and the city began to flourish as never before. By the early 14th century, the Visconti dynastic powerbase (aided by some enthusiastic violence and double-dealing) was decidedly impressive: Bergamo, Cremona, Como and Brescia were all ruled by Milan. Although the Black Death of 1348 inevitably slowed progress, the lakes survived the crisis. When ruthless Gian Galeazzo Visconti became duke of Milan in 1395, the city became the predominant power in northern Italy. You can still see reminders of the Visconti era today in monuments such as Milan's stunning Duomo (see page 249).

Visconti rule ended in 1447 with the death of Filippo Maria and passed to his son-in-law, Francesco Sforza, whose dynastic control lasted nearly 100 years. This was the time of the Renaissance, and the family's wealth allowed them to harness this intellectual and artistic luminescence. They built the Castello Sforzesco and Ospedale Maggiore (Ca' Granda) in Milan and, in an inspired move, brought Leonardo da Vinci to the city, where he painted the glorious *Cenacolo* (Last Supper; see page 256).

It is worth noting that the *signori* effected not just cultural but also economic change on the Italian Lakes. They dug canals, began growing rice on the marshes and planted thousands of mulberry trees – so developing Como's lucrative silk industry (see page 192).

However, they did not have it all their own way: the Republic of Venice, La Serenissima, which had originated during the years of Lombard rule, also trailed its elegant fingers across the lakeland landscape. Its influence was first felt in Verona – the snake-pit of power struggles and family feuds that inspired *Romeo and*

The walled town of Brescia, from the 16th-century Book of Privileges.

Juliet. Government was initially dominated by the Scaligeri (aka della Scala) family, who also ruled Lake Garda, scattering its shores with castles at Malcesine, Lazise and Torri del Benaco. But eventually they lost pole position to the seemingly unstoppable Viscontis. In 1405, the Venetians, fearing that expansion of Milan could threaten lucrative trade routes, seized Verona, followed by Brescia and much of Lake Garda (1426) and Bergamo (1428).

Spanish possession

The trouble with the *signori* was that they were unable to resist scheming. An alliance between Francesco Sforza and Cosimo de' Medici had

Medieval Master Builders

The master builders of Lake Como and Lugano were the equal of any in medieval Europe. These skilled and patient craftsmen passed on their art from father to son.

The Maestri Comacini

The Maestri Comacini were a school of gifted stonecutters, sculptors, masons and master

The Gothic-Renaissance spire of Como's cathedral.

craftsmen who were responsible for the decoration of pulpits, portals and facades from the late 11th to 13th centuries. They have left their mark in Como's churches of Sant'Abbondio and San Fedele, as well as in the slender bell-towers that grace the lake shore.

The Maestri's sculptural techniques were influenced by the geometric designs of Lombard ironwork, which featured intricate interlacing patterns and mythical beasts. Given that the Lombards were inveterate travellers, some scholars have looked further afield for their sources of inspiration, citing the distant influences of Byzantine silks, Islamic sculpture and Coptic reliefs. Sant'Abbondio lends weight to these theories, as the bands of stone

bas-reliefs reflect the patterns and design of Middle Eastern damask. Whatever the truth behind such cross-fertilisation, the school's influence spread to southern Italy, Spain and Languedoc.

The Maestri Campionesi

The Maestri Campionesi were the Lugano version of the Como master builders. Based in Campione d'Italia, an Italian enclave in Switzerland, the school was active throughout Lombardy, Veneto and beyond Italy's borders. In the Middle Ages, the notion of the individual artist did not exist: sculptors simply worked in the service of God and the community and left their works unsigned. Although theoretically anonymous, many sculptors scattered their creations with clues, featuring themselves and their colleagues in their craft, and sometimes leaving masons' marks inscribed in the stonework.

The earliest document identifying masters from Campione by name is a 1244 contract between Ubaldino, director of the Cathedral Works of Modena (1230–63), and Enrico di Ottavio da Campione who agreed, on behalf of himself and his family, to work for the cathedral "for ever."

In the second half of the 13th century, the style of the Campionesi master builders lost its distinctiveness, while their interest in early French Gothic sculpture became evident. By the 14th century, in Lombardy, Romanesque structural elements were gradually combined with Gothic details. The most eminent of the Maestri Campionesi in the first half of the 14th century was Giovanni da Campione, who mainly worked in Bergamo and Bellano.

Masters of the mysteries

The Maestri belonged to confraternities, brotherhoods which some dub Masonic and link to the long-lost skills of Roman architecture. A fanciful theory holds that the Maestri Comacini were secret heirs to the legendary Roman builders. Allegedly, the building techniques of antiquity were never truly lost but merely held in safekeeping, passed down within brotherhoods.

The Maestri cultivated the air of mystery about their craft. Fans of medieval architecture should be able to join fans of the best-selling novel The *Da Vinci Code* in deciphering arcane stonework and statuary in Lombardy's lake district.

The architectural legacy of La Serenissima is still evident in northern Italy: a bas-relief of a lion at Salò, a Venetian customs house at Lazise and Brescia's Venetian-style Piazza Loggia.

kept peace between Milan and its powerful southern neighbour Florence. But, at the end of the 15th century, Ludovico Sforza, hoping to garner an ally to counteract Venetian power, suggested that Charles VIII of France invade Italy and take Naples from the incumbent Spanish rulers. Although Charles (once cruelly described as "small... ill-formed... with an ugly face... and thick lips which are continually open") could not hold Naples, it set the scene for strife.

The French attempted to take the duchy, but when François I took Milan in 1515, he came up against a powerful opponent, Charles of Spain. Charles was not just king of Spain, he was heir to the Austrian Habsburg lands, had claims to Naples, possessed vast territories in Europe – and was soon to become Charles V, Holy Roman Emperor (1519). Though physically unprepossessing, with a misshapen jaw, gout and chronic indigestion, he was not a man to cross.

Charles's troops defeated the French at Pavia in 1525, but although he allowed the Sforzas to resume their rule, the family had died out by 1535 and Milan was again contested. It was not until 1559 that the French eventually recognised Spanish possession and the Italian Lakes were reduced to the status of a heavily taxed Spanish province for the next 170 years. The only exceptions were Bergamo, Brescia and Verona (which Venice had just managed to retain), and Trento (still governed by Catholic prince-bishops).

The lakes also became the setting for ecclesiastical, as well as international, power struggles. The exuberance of the Renaissance had sparked the Reformation, and the papacy was determined to resist this Protestant challenge. From 1545–63, at sessions of the Council of Trent, the Catholic Church condemned Protestantism, and set the stage for persecution of "heretics" and "witches" (burnings at the stake frequently occurred in the Val Camonica). Attending this influential council was Carlo Borromeo (1538–84), whose family later left a flamboyant Baroque imprint on Lake Maggiore.

Habsburg rule

The economy declined during the first part of the 17th century, not helped by outbreaks of plague. In 1700, the last of the Spanish Habsburgs died and the French king laid claim to his – not inconsiderable – European possessions. It sparked the War of the Spanish Succession (1701–14), in which the French and the Austrians fought for the Spanish spoils. The outcome, decided at the Treaty of Utrecht (1713), granted Naples, Sardinia, Mantua and most of the Duchy of Milan to Austria. Power in the lakes was now largely in Austrian Habs-

Castello Sforzesco, Milan.

burg hands – and they soon put in place some energising reforms, influenced by Enlightenment thinking.

Brothers Alessandro and Pietro Verri worked with the Austrians to introduce reforms in education, promoted ideas of free trade and published a lively journal; their friend Cesare Beccaria (1738–94) published a book on crime and punishment that condemned the use of torture. In Milan, the Accademia di Brera was founded and La Scala was built (1778).

The 18th century also saw the start of the Grand Tour. Italy became a fashionable destination for young European men of means and Romantic poets, painters and imaginative thinkers were soon bringing their money and ideas to the lakes, especially Como and Maggiore. But in the midst of all this great thought, revolutionary France went to war against the Austrian imperialists – and Napoleon invaded Italy.

Napoleon's puppet

In 1796, Napoleon took Milan (where he was received with enthusiasm), Bologna and Verona. He then established the Cisalpine Republic (1797) in the north: it included the Duchy of Milan and the western parts of the Venetian territories, and had Milan as its capital. In the same year, he declared war on Venice. The Venetian Republic was finished – Napoleon granted the parts he didn't want to Austria in return for other territories.

The Cisalpine Republic was a French creation and remained under French control. Napoleon renamed it the Italian Republic in 1802 with himself as president. In 1804, he promoted himself again – this time to emperor. He converted the Italian Republic to the Kingdom of Italy in 1805 and was crowned in Milan's Duomo.

Napoleon directs troops in the Battle of Rivoli.

GIUSEPPE GARIBALDI AND THE RISORGIMENTO

After the restoration of Austrian rule, secret societies, such as the Carbonari, fermented revolution. In their newspaper *Il Risorgimento*, Cesare Balbo and Count Cavour, prime minister of Piedmont, campaigned for a constitution and gave a name to the movement for Italian unification.

In 1848, there was an uprising in Milan, and Carlo Alberto, the king of Piedmont, declared war on Austria. Giuseppe Garibaldi (1807–82), who had made his name as a swashbuckling fighter in South America, had returned to Italy to support the Risorgimento cause and fought in Milan and Rome. Although the early battles were lost, Cavour was soon able to engineer an alliance with the French and, with their support, finally defeated the Austrians in Lombardy in 1859. Uprisings in Tuscany and Emilia led to their union with Piedmont, meaning that much territory was now in Italian hands. With the support of the British, Garibaldi collected a force of 1,000 men (the Expedition of the Thousand) and sailed to Sicily. Together with Naples, Sicily was under Bourbon rule, and Garibaldi managed to seize both. By 1860, unification was largely complete, but Garibaldi, who had fallen out with Cavour, had no political office and retired to the island of Caprera, off Sardinia.

Napoleon's quest for absolute power was eventually halted by his defeat at Waterloo in 1815, and at the Congress of Vienna in the same year, Austria was awarded Lombardy and the Veneto, as well as Trento. The old rule returned. But Napoleon had left an enduring legacy: revolutionary ideas and the concept of an all-embracing "Italian" state.

An Italian kingdom

From the Congress of Vienna in 1815 to the taking of Rome in 1870 by the troops of King Victor Emmanuel II, the history of Italy was one continuous struggle for reunification. The people of Lombardy hated the reimposition of Austrian rule. Although the region became relatively prosperous, the Austrians clamped down on freedom of expression. Secret societies grew and revolution fermented – the Risorgimento had begun. In 1848 the Milanese took to the streets for five days (the *Cinque Giornate*) and ousted their rulers, and in 1849 Brescia held out against Austrian troops for 10 days, giving it the nickname the "Lioness of Italy". In 1859, Risorgimento forces decisively defeated the Austrians at the battles of Solferino (a village between Milan and Verona) and Magenta (just west of Milan). Casualties were so appalling that they prompted the founding of the Red Cross in 1864.

Lombardy was finally ceded to the Savoy monarch Vittorio Emanuele II, the Bourbons were removed from the south, and in 1860, the Kingdom of Italy was born. Complete unification came after the Austrians were finally ousted from Venice and the Veneto (1866) and Rome (much to the fury of the Pope) was taken and annexed to the kingdom in 1870.

Lombardy prospered. Grand buildings, such as the Galleria Vittorio Emanuele II, were erected in Milan; the Gotthard rail tunnel through the Alps opened in 1882, facilitating trade with northern Europe; agriculture flourished in the fertile Po Valley and industrialisation proceeded apace. The Belle Epoque was a party time throughout the lakes – then war broke out once more.

The world at war

To some, especially the Irredentists, Italy was still not unified. The area around Trento, for example, was Italian-speaking yet remained an Austrian territory. When World War I broke out in 1914, Italy was neutral, but there were voices (including that of Benito Mussolini) in favour of war. In 1915, lured by the promise of gaining land, Italy joined the Allies and was rewarded with Trieste and Trentino. Reminders of the Alpine campaign can be seen at the Museo della Guerra Bianca in Adamello (see page 173).

Immediately after the war, there was immense social unrest, with demonstrations and strikes in cities like Milan. In reaction, Mussolini formed his Fascist league of blackshirts and seized power in 1922. In 1940, Italy joined World War II allied to Nazi Germany

Risorgimento forces clash with Austrian troops in Brescia, 1849.

but later switched sides. At the end of the war Mussolini was killed and his body strung up in Milan.

Post-war enterprise – and unrest

After the war, the king abdicated, and Italy became a republic in 1946. A close alliance was formed with America, and Lombardy led an economic boom. The old enterprising spirit, rooted in the autonomy of the medieval *comuni*, was revived. Milan, badly bombed in the war, grew into a slick financial and media centre. At a national level, the country was increasingly portrayed as divided between the

Mussolini

The jackboot of Benito Mussolini, one of the central figures of the fascist movement, left a firm imprint on northern Italy.

Born into a socialist family, Mussolini (1883–1945) showed no early dictatorial leanings, even moving to Switzerland in an attempt to dodge the Italian draft. His first job was in Trento (which at

Mussolini, by popular demand.

the time was part of Austria-Hungary), but he was expelled for political agitation. Back in Italy, he began editing the official Socialist newspaper *Avanti*, in Milan, opposing Italian entry into World War I, before changing his mind, influenced by the Irredentists.

Rise to power

Expelled by the Socialist Party, he founded his own pro-war paper *Popolo d'Italia*, but was himself conscripted. Wounded by a mortar bomb explosion in his trench, he was discharged from service in 1917. Mussolini returned from the front a violent anti-socialist. In 1919, he formed the *Fasci Italiani di Combattimento* (Italian Combat Veterans' League) in Milan. Black-shirted

members began rampaging across the country, even setting fire to the *Avanti* offices. In 1922, he marched on Rome, intimidating the king so much that he was invited to form a government. When politician Giacomo Matteotti dared to condemn Fascism he was murdered. Mussolini publicly declared: "I, and I alone assume the political, moral and historical responsibility for all that has happened."

Ill-fated alliances

By 1925, Il Duce had absolute control. He cannily formed an alliance with the Pope, making the Vatican an independent state in return for papal acknowledgement of the Kingdom of Italy. He then imposed censorship of the press, drained the Pontine Marshes, invaded Ethiopia (assisted by liberal use of poison gas) and helped Franco in the Spanish Civil War. Mussolini supported Hitler's annexation of Austria and in 1940 entered the war as a Nazi ally.

However, the war was not popular in Italy, and in 1943, after Allied forces landed in Sicily, Mussolini's colleagues (who included his son-in-law) condemned his conduct and demanded that he go. After an audience with the king, Il Duce was arrested and imprisoned in the Abruzzi. The Germans spirited him away to Lake Garda, where he was made head of a puppet state, the Republic of Salò (see page 127). Mussolini settled comfortably into the elegant lakeside Villa Feltrinelli with his mistress, Clara Petacci, conveniently ensconced nearby in the Villa Fiordaliso.

Downfall

On 25 April 1945, *Il Duce* delivered his last public speech at the Teatro Lirico in Milan and although he was no more than just a failed puppet ruler at this moment he was still very heartily applauded by the gathered crowds. On the same day, Mussolini and Clara tried to escape to Switzerland hidden in a German military transport. They were hoping to board a plane there to escape to Spain. They were captured, however, by communist partisans on 27 April 1945 in Dongo, Lake Como, and taken to a farmhouse. The next day, partisan commander Colonel Valerio drove them to Mezzegra, where they were lined up against a wall and shot. On 29 April, their bodies, with those of 15 other executed Fascists, were taken to Milan and hung, upside down, from meat hooks in the Piazzale Loreto.

wealthy, urban north and the poor, rural south.

Political unrest characterised the 1960s and 1970s, as protesters voiced their dissatisfaction with the government. Acts of terrorism, carried out by the far left and far right, shook the country during these Years of Lead *(Anni di Piombo)*. There were assassinations, and bombs in Milan (1969), Brescia (1974) and Bologna (1980).

Yet the economy in the north was resilient, and with Giorgio Armani, Gianni Versace and Miuccia Prada in the city, Milan became a fashionable as well as a financial force.

party. Berlusconi's business empire gave him almost complete control of the Italian media. No stranger to charges of underhand dealing, he was frequently accused of using his political office to further his business interests. He stayed in power until 2006, and was re-elected in 2008, but in 2011 one scandal too many finally ousted him from power for good. Berlusconi was succeeded by economist and academic Mario Monti. In 2013, Enrico Letta replaced Monti for a short while before being ousted by Matteo Renzi of the Democratic Party in 2014.

Lega Nord gathering in Pontida, Bergamo Province.

Scandal, success and separatism

The 1990s saw a series of political scandals strike Italian society. Politicians, it emerged, were receiving backhanders *(tangenti)* for awarding lucrative business contracts. The Tangentopoli ("Bribesville") investigation began in Milan, spearheaded by judge Antonio di Pietro. A tangled web of corruption was revealed, and the Christian Democrat Party, which had dominated Italian politics since the formation of the republic, collapsed. It opened the way to the election of Milanese media tycoon Silvio Berlusconi in 1994, who romped to power on an anti-corruption card with his right-wing Forza Italia

The lakes continue as the engine of the Italian economy – albeit one that has suffered the effects of a global economic decline. Tourists flock to their romantic shores, gasp at their beauty, look for a glimpse of a celebrity – but there are iron- and steelworks, hydroelectric plants and silk factories here too. The area considers itself very different from the south (which it views as lazy and corrupt), and there is even a separatist party – the Lega Nord. Much of its support comes from Lombardy. A notable boost to the region's economy came from the Milan Expo in 2015. Lombardy alone contributes about 20 percent of the Italian GDP, making it the richest region in the country and one of the richest in Europe.

Piazza delle Erbe, Verona.

ART AND ARCHITECTURE

Beyond a northern Italian aesthetic, there are few obvious unifying strands running through the bewildering array of art and architecture found in the Italian Lakes. From Gothic cathedrals to Venetian art, all styles are represented.

As a crossroads between the Alpine and Mediterranean worlds, the lakes have dipped into a dressing-up box of architectural styles, from Roman to Rococo, and Baroque to Belle Epoque – occasionally all at once, when wealthy owners have turned their residences into kingdoms of kitsch. The lure of the lakes continues to attract waves of outsiders, eager to buy a neoclassical villa or shape a home in their own eclectic image.

Artistically, the lakes have been influenced by Venetian and Lombard schools of art, depending on the vagaries of the patrons of art and the creative powerhouses of the day. One can tease out a love of colour and light, the legacy of effervescent Venetian art, and a passion for realism and veracity, the legacy of the more sober Lombard tradition.

Underlying this is a deep affinity for the Romanesque, a natural bond for any area so steeped in the grandeur of Roman civilisation. Yet any shared aesthetic is diluted by regional

Fresco from Santa Trinità, Torri del Bonaco, Lake Garda.

> The cosmopolitan nature of this corner of Italy has produced an alluring hybrid of architectural styles: from Romanesque to Rococo, Baroque to Belle Epoque.

diversity, reflecting the historical power shifts in the lakes. Add to the mix the progressive, cosmopolitan nature of this northern corner of Italy and the result is a melting pot of styles: austere Romanesque segues into pinnacled Gothic and princely Baroque, before pausing for breath for florid Art Nouveau or Fascistic Monumentalism. In essence, the lakes represent one of the most beguiling architectural hybrids in Italy.

The Venetian legacy

Regional rivalries and separate histories are reflected in the local architecture and shape broad differences between Lombardy and Piedmont, or Trentino and the Veneto. This is not a clear-cut regional divide that reflects modern-day boundaries: the Venetian Empire once ruled much of the lakes and has left a Venetian imprint on modern-day Lombardy, particularly in Bergamo and Brescia, including a fondness for balconies and astronomical clocks. The Venetian Republic marked the territory with stone lions, which symbolised the might of La Serenissima. (The symbol was in honour of St Mark, traditionally represented by a lion.)

Modern Veneto is far smaller, but the Venetian spirit, along with the odd lion, survives on the eastern shore of Lake Garda. The port of Lazise has a 16th-century Venetian Customs House, while Peschiera lies snug in Venetian bastions. Elegant Verona remains Venetian, even if its architecture owes as much to the preceding Scaligeri dynasty, which left the city and lakeside resorts with battlemented castles and bridges. The legacy also lingers on in the regional art galleries, where Giovanni Bellini's luminous Madonnas remind us that the Venetians were the supreme artists of colour and light.

If Verona is the standard-bearer for Venice, Milan represents Lombardy, and Brescia is caught between the two. When Brescia fell under the sway of the Venetian Republic in 1427, the new rulers created the symbol of Renaissance Brescia, Piazza della Loggia, which was graced with loggias, porticoes and an astronomical clock. The centrepiece, La Loggia, was the town hall started by Sansovino and completed by Palladio in 1562. This public building thus bears the imprint of two of the Venetian Republic's greatest architects.

Mosaics from the Roman villa at Desenzano.

ROMAN PLAYGROUND

The Romans established colonies in Brescia, Como, Milan and Verona, but Lake Garda was their playground, especially the spa resort of Sirmione. Evocative ruins of a villa associated with Catullus, Rome's greatest lyric poet, are visible (see page 123), matched by Desenzano's mosaics from a 3rd-century AD villa.

As Brixia, Brescia was a prominent Roman city and still has the greatest concentration of remains north of Rome, with new villas recently unearthed. The Amphitheatre stands close to the Forum and the Capitolium, with the Capitoline Temple erected by Emperor Vespasian in AD 73.

Several Pompeian-style Roman villas are incorporated into Brescia's exceptional Santa Giulia Museum, which displays busts, statuary and mosaics from lakeside villas, as well as the *Winged Victory*, the greatest Hellenistic sculpture in Lombardy.

The finest Roman remains are visible in Verona, where the Arena is second only to Rome's Colosseum. Designed to hold the entire 20,000-strong population, it is the third-largest in the world and the best-preserved. Even if critics decry the Amphitheatre as a place where the frame outshines the picture, the site has resonance, and the rosy pink marble steps will survive us all.

Lombard longevity

Lombardy has exerted even more influence. Medieval merchants who grew rich on silk and weaponry, the astute Lombards built to last, from Romanesque abbeys and monasteries to Gothic town halls and cathedrals, culminating in the pinnacled splendour of Milan's Duomo.

If the Lombard work ethic and ingrained Catholicism manifested themselves as cathedrals and monasteries, Piedmontese religiosity often took the form of shrines and statuary. On Lake Orta, Piedmont has one of the finest Sacri Monti, the devotional shrines and Marian sanctuaries

clear legacy from the era of the Austro-Hungarian Empire.

Architecturally, the lakes come together in the Renaissance, Baroque and neoclassical eras when villa-building flourished, with ever-grander bucolic residences built on the shores of lakes Como, Maggiore and Garda. The lakes then returned to being a sought-after retreat, much as they had been in their original Roman heyday.

From Roman to Romanesque

If the Romans treated Lake Garda as prime real estate, with the spa resorts a favoured

Piazza della Loggia, Brescia.

that add an air of spirituality to this corner of the lakes (see page 241). Lake Maggiore, the principal patch of Piedmont on the lakes, is a shrine to a living dynasty, the princely Borromean clan, who created palaces on the Borromean Islands, a vast monument to the sainted Charles Borromeo (1538–94) in Arona, and a magnificent castle on the far bank (see page 232).

In mountainous Trentino, north of Lake Garda, the rugged, borderlands nature of the region deems that castles are the greatest legacy, along with grand palaces linked to the prince-bishops who once treated Trentino as their personal fiefdom. The further north one goes from Lake Garda, the greater the sense of an Alpine spirit, with a Tyrolean stamp on the villages, a

location for their villas, the Longobards treated Lombardy, particularly Brescia and Pavia, as their power base and spiritual home. The Longobard era (6th–8th centuries) and the Caroliningian era (8th century to the early 10th century) were a golden age for Brescia and Lake Garda, even if many churches were incorporated into later medieval structures, as with San Severo in Lazise or San Zeno in Bardolino. Brescia's Santa Giulia displays Italy's most precious artwork from the Longobard era which, in true Italian fashion, recycles earlier treasures: The *Cross of Desiderius*, created for the last king of the Lombards, is a glittering 8th-century masterpiece, studded with Roman gemstones and cameos.

In the former Roman colonies of Brescia, Milan, Como, Bergamo and Verona, the imprint of Roman architecture was reinterpreted as Romanesque. Sant'Ambrogio in Milan, dating from the 9th century, is the prototype of the Lombard Romanesque, and spawned a rash of similar churches all over the Lombardy side of the lakes. Set on a colonnaded quadrangle, the church is characterised by a triangular facade, porticoes and decorative blind arcading, known as Lombard bands. Capitals carved with mythical beasts reflect a love of sculpture that reached its apogee with

Cross of Desiderius, Museo di Santa Giulia, Brescia.

GROTESQUES AND GIANTS

The lakes are dotted with memorable statues, from the grotesque Baroque creatures on Isola Bella to Canova's neoclassical couple, *Cupid and Psyche*, in Villa Carlotta. In Val Camonica, the church of Santuario di Via Crucis displays a series of distinctly kitsch Stations of the Cross, with 200 life-size 18th-century statues. Strangest of all is a huge bronze statue of St Charles Borromeo, the *éminence grise* of the Counter-Reformation, in the lakeside town of Arona. Known as San Carlone (Big Saint Charlie), the statue invites visitors to climb the stairs inside and peer out at the lake through the eyes of the saint.

the Maestri Comacini and Maestri Campionesi, the lakes' travelling confraternities of master builders, stonemasons and sculptors (see page 38).

The Romanesque phase was one of the most glorious eras, especially in Lombardy and Verona. Como has always been an aspirational city, beginning with its early prominence as a Roman town. As a result, the Romanesque style is woven into the warp and weft of the city fabric, from facades and fortified towers to the simplicity of the church of San Fedele. By comparison, Verona's San Zeno Maggiore stands out as the most elaborate Romanesque church in northern Italy, with its rose window encased in a superb facade, matched by a magnificent sculpted porch and ornate bronze door panels. But the strength of the Romanesque style is that its architectural vigour extends to the smallest churches in Val Camonica, which stand as stark beacons above the valley.

Gothic glories

The Gothic style, imported from France, has less resonance in the lakes, with several stunning exceptions. Milan's Sant'Ambrogio might be the blueprint for Lombard Romanesque churches, but the city's Duomo, Europe's largest Gothic cathedral, is more eclectic. A Milanese expression, *"lungo come la fabbrica del Duomo"* (as long as the building of the cathedral), speaks volumes for the Milanese sense of urgency. This daring, unfinished masterpiece was started in 1386 and seamlessly blends Gothic, Baroque, neoclassical and neo-Gothic styles. Flying buttresses and soaring pinnacles contrast with the excessive width preferred by native Lombard builders. Unlike French Gothic, which strived for spirituality through towering verticality, Lombard Gothic stresses width and solidity, sense over sensibility, and power over principle – the solid values of the merchant class.

In Como, the Duomo, begun in 1396, has an intricate gabled facade and spans the transition from late Gothic to Renaissance, with a richly sculpted main portal. Flanking the cathedral is the bell tower and magnificent Broletto, the former town hall, an arcaded Gothic affair with triple-arched windows.

In the early 15th century, many cities were under Venetian sway, which can be seen in

Brescia's graceful Renaissance squares and an astronomical clock tower. The Serene Republic also fortified its trading posts on Lake Garda, including the walled port of Lazise. Most charming of all is the Venetian influence on Bergamo, from the Gothic windows to the heraldic lions, the symbol of La Serenissima. Bergamo, a perfectly preserved medieval hilltown, retains its Venetian soul: 400 years of rule have left their mark in the elegant architecture and symbols of the Serene Republic. The Renaissance masterpieces extend to sculpture, notably in the Cappella Colleoni,

As fears of invasion faded, feudal castles were transformed into luxurious villas. Near Lake Iseo, Castello di Bornato is a crenellated medieval castle which opens onto a Renaissance villa and Italianate gardens. On Lake Garda, Riva is dominated by the Rocca, a moated medieval castle that typifies the transition from feudal fortress to patrician residence.

Although still framed by corner towers, the original fortress, complete with arsenal and barracks, gave way to a Renaissance pleasure palace for the ruling prince-bishops of Trento,

The Duomo in Milan.

designed as a funerary monument to the legendary *condottiere* Bartolomeo Colleoni, a rich mercenary leader, blessed with a jewel box of a mausoleum, swathed in Lombard Renaissance finery.

Castles and convents

As a gateway to Alpine Europe, the lakes are also castle country, with most medieval ports possessing a hulking fortress. Two imposing medieval castles stand above the fray: Sirmione's Rocca Scaligera, a moated 13th-century fortress crowned by swallow-tailed battlements, and Angera's Rocca Borromeo, a brooding Borromean stronghold on the quieter side of Lake Maggiore.

with the residence further domesticated in Austro-Hungarian times.

Despite a flurry of building, the Renaissance was far from being the coherent, revolutionary force that it was in Tuscany. Although the region possesses pure Renaissance churches, far more are hybrids, the result of changing tastes and gradual accretions. Whether in convents or villas, the Renaissance was constrained to accommodate other styles. Santa Caterina, overlooking Lake Maggiore, is typical, one of the finest monastic complexes in Lombardy, and a harmonious mixture of periods, from the Gothic bell tower and frescoes to the Renaissance porch looking across to the Borromean Islands.

In Brescia, Santa Giulia Museo della Città, set in a former convent, is both the best history museum in northern Italy and a beguiling complex showcasing Brescia's past that embraces Roman villas, a Byzantine basilica, a nuns' choir and a Romanesque oratory, all built on the same site.

Landmark villas

As for palatial residences, many were orignally built as convents. On Lake Como, the lovely Villa Balbianello is a prime example. It started out as a Franciscan foundation before taking the secular path to paradise. Many of the 16th-century waterside villas have lost their Renaissance spirit, but Villa Cicogna Mozzoni, outside Varese, remains a true Lombard Renaissance villa. Another Lake Como landmark, Villa d'Este, is part authentic, part hybrid: although transformed into a palatial hotel, this 16th-century former royal residence is still framed by Mannerist gardens enlivened by statuary, secret grottoes and a grand water stairway.

Baroque extravagance

The Baroque style found its truest expression in Turin, rather than Milan, but on the

"The Poor Man's Sistine Chapel", by Romanino, a Brescian painter, in Santa Maria della Neve.

THE WALLS OF DEATH

Gothic and Renaissance art is well represented in the region, particularly in the form of frescoes, which depict a wider range of subject matter than found in most of Italy. North of Lake Garda, Trento's Renaissance facades are surpassed by the Gothic frescoes in the city's Castello del Buonconsiglio, depicting the agricultural calendar.

On Lake Maggiore, the monastery of Santa Caterina is home to a chilling Gothic *Danse Macabre*, a Dance of Death complete with a very grim Grim Reaper. Other scenes depict the vanity of human wishes: both a merchant engrossed in his accounts and a courtier in love with his lady are faced with their own mortality.

Clusone, in Bergamo's Valle Seriana, displays even more disturbing Dance of Death frescoes, which decorate the facade of the Chiesa dei Disciplini. Held up as a moral lesson, the Gothic frescoes compare the different attitudes towards death held by the wealthy and the poor.

On Lake Iseo, Santa Maria della Neve is a showcase to Renaissance painter, Girolamo Romani, known as 'Romanino' (c.1484–1559). The Brescian-born painter is renowned for his realistic and dynamic portraits of contemporaries. Known as a poor man's Sistine Chapel, the church is frescoed with peasant-like faces that are still found in Val Camonica.

lakes is best represented by the Borromean follies. Although Isola Bella began as little more than a rock with a view, it became both a Baroque masterpiece and a hollow exercise in one-upmanship. Somewhat ironically for a family whose motto is humility, the turreted Borromean palace is a bombastic affair. From the gilded throne room to the Empire-style ballroom, ostentatious salons are encrusted with stuccowork and emblazoned with heraldic crests. Lapses in taste are redeemed by the genuine grandeur of the cantilevered spiral staircase and by an art collection of 16th–18th-century Venetian and Lombard artists. If the overwhelming impression is of an official residence, the Rococo palace on the adjoining Isola Madre represents a warmer, more private side to the princely clan. Outside the major cities, true Baroque works are rare. On Lake Orta, the lofty sanctuary of Madonna del Sasso, perched on a granite outcrop, is a frescoed Baroque church with stunning views over the mountains and lake.

Although a stifling, passionless form, the neoclassical spirit found its greatest expression in lakeside villas and in Milan's covered galleries, which are a triumph of engineering. Galleria Vittorio Emanuele remains the quintessential Milanese shopping mall. On Lake Como, the austere neoclassical Villa Melzi is set in the first "English" gardens on the lake, while Villa Olmo is a grandiose gem, matched by formal gardens and a lakeside promenade.

Villa Carlotta may be a Baroque villa with a theatrical staircase, but the exuberance acts as a foil to the cool neoclassical interior, which is bursting with statuary, including Canova's celebrated *Cupid and Psyche*.

Lombard and Venetian art

The lakes are particularly rich in Renaissance and Mannerist art in the Venetian and Lombard traditions, though individual geniuses such as Leonardo da Vinci, Andrea Mantegna and Caravaggio transcend neat categories. Works by the Lombard masters can be admired in churches and galleries all over the region, especially in Milan's Pinacoteca di Brera, the finest collection of northern Italian art.

Venetian art is the most prestigious affair, with greater influence and more brilliant masters, ranging from Giovanni Bellini to Veronese, Titian and Tintoretto, all of whom

are represented in the lakes. Venetian sensibility reflected a shimmering, watery world. While lacking the purity and perspective of Florentine art, it embodies a poetic, painterly sensibility at odds with the rational, monumental and sculptural Florentine style. Giovanni Bellini (*c*.1430–1516) is considered the founder of the Venetian school, the painter who freed art from its Byzantine stiffness, creating luminous Madonnas, and infusing his art with light, literally seen as a medium of grace. His work is on display in Castelvecchio in Verona, along with other late Gothic and

Madonna with Child (1475, detail) by Bellini, from the Castelvecchio in Verona.

Renaissance Venetian art, including works by Pisanello, Tintoretto, Veronese and Jacopo Bellini.

In the same gallery is *The Holy Family* by Mantegna, Giovanni Bellini's Paduan brother-in-law and the artist from the Venetian school who most influenced him. Also in Verona, San Zeno Maggiore is home to Mantegna's *Virgin and Child*, an altarpiece that echoes the shape of the rose window. Instead, Mantegna's *Dead Christ* (*c*.1480) is one of the masterpieces in Milan's Pinacoteca di Brera. This disturbingly brilliant work, an exercise in bold foreshortening, was found among the artist's possessions after his death. The Brera displays masterpieces from all Italian schools, including works by Caravaggio as well as by Piero della Francesca, depicting the duke of Urbino in Milanese armour in his *Montefeltro Altarpiece* (1475).

It is invidious to single out Renaissance artists who most shaped the lakes, but Leonardo da Vinci stands out. Invited by the duke of Milan, Leonardo used his Milanese sojourns to develop his *sfumato* technique, the smoky shading that accentuated his mystique. In Milan, *The Last Supper (Cenacolo Vinciano)* is one of the world's most evocative paintings, set in the

its muscular realism portrayed in a vivid style, greatly influenced the Brescian school.

Home-grown genius

Although not in the same league as the Florentine or Venetian schools, the Lombard Renaissance flourished with the works of Vincenzo Foppa (1427–1514), leader of the Brescian school, whose *Mercanti Altarpiece* is a highlight in the city's Martinengo gallery. Girolamo Romanino (d. 1561) is one of the finest home-grown Renaissance artists, with his pioneering realism and common touch

Accademia Carrara, Bergamo.

monastic refectory it was designed for. After a controversial restoration, the masterpiece has regained its lustre. Leonardo chose to use the techniques of oil painting rather than the more durable techniques of fresco-painting, but against all the odds the fragile work has survived both the passage of Napoleonic troops and Allied bombing, which destroyed the rest of the monastery in 1943.

Given Venetian rule over much of the area, combined with La Serenissima's artistic preeminence, the Lombard/Venetian distinction is often blurred. Titian, very much a Venetian artist, created the *Averoldi Altarpiece* (1522) for Brescia's church of Santi Nazaro e Celso. The poignant depiction of St Sebastian, with

seen in memorable works throughout Lombardy, particularly around Lake Iseo and Val Camonica. Bergamo's Accademia Carrara, a repository of Venetian and Lombard art, displays works by the Gothic master Pisanello, as well as luminous paintings by Giovanni and Jacopo Bellini. It is matched by Brescia's Martinengo gallery, showcasing the Brescian masters, including Moretto, the most grandiose and classical of artists, who presages Caravaggio in his muted colour palette and brooding sense of chiaroscuro.

The most celebrated Lombard artist is Caravaggio (1573–1610), often called "the master of chiaroscuro" and a founder of modern painting. As a force of nature, an anarchic rebel of an artist, Caravaggio created works of unparalleled drama and intensity. His paintings on display in Milan's Pinacoteca di Brera and Pinacoteca Ambrosiana include *A Basket of Fruit*, deemed one of the earliest Italian attempts at still life.

The march to modernity

For all its love of the past, the region is not marooned in an artistic time warp. Architecturally, the Mussolini era left a disquieting imprint on the lakes, especially in the public squares of Milan, Varese, Brescia and Ber-

and is a bold venture aspiring to "the Guggenheim effect". The MART showcases modern European artists, including Picasso, Dalí and Miró, and covers Symbolism, American Pop Art and Italian Arte Povera. The strongest collection features the Futurists, an Italian-centred movement that emphasised dynamism, revolution and constant change, led by Marinetti, Boccioni and local artist Depero. The Futurist Manifesto decried the bourgeois past – "We will destroy museums and libraries" – but fortunately their works are on display here, in true bourgeois fashion.

Triennale Design Museum, Milan.

gamo. But such ponderous Monumentalism also produced the masterpiece that is Milan Central Station.

As the most forward-looking region in Italy, Lombardy claims the greatest spoils in terms of modern art and design, rivalled by Piedmont. In Varese, Villa Panza is a showcase of American Abstract art and contemporary installations, while Bergamo's modern art gallery displays works by Kandinsky and Graham Sutherland. Milan, the modern design mecca, boasts the Triennale exhibition hub, with the alluring new Design Library and Design Museum.

In Rovereto, north of Lake Garda, the Museo de Arte Moderna e Contemporanea (MART) is one of Italy's finest modern art museums,

As for domestic architecture, the lakes' enduring appeal to wealthy outsiders has encouraged a new wave of eclecticism, particularly on Lake Como, Italy's Beverly Hills, but also on Lake Maggiore and Lake Garda. Not that lavish tastes are new to the lakes. Just as 19th-century composers and opera divas fell for Moorish follies and neoclassical gems, contemporary movie stars and media moguls opt for pastiches of French Norman châteaux, Scottish baronial castles, Belle Epoque villas and Palladian piles. The marriage of money and bad taste means that a Swiss mountain chalet, a miniature Versailles or a glorified hunting lodge are equally probable. The Italian Lakes have seen it all.

Glacier in the Ortler Alps, Alto Adige.

WILDLIFE OF THE ITALIAN ALPS

The immense 965km (600-mile) rampart of the Alps determines the geography of northern Italy. Its national parks protect a diverse range of flora and fauna, including animals that were hunted until recently, such as lynxes, wolves and bears.

The Alps were formed when the sea bed was lifted up by the movement of the Earth's tectonic plates, then moulded and sculptured by the movement of glaciers during the Ice Age. About 90 million years ago, a large tropical ocean, the Tethys, which separated the African and European continents, began to close. Forty million years later, the two tectonic plates collided beneath the Tethys and a fragment of Africa locked with the European landmass. The sediments of the sea were subjected to enormous pressure which gave rise to massive sheet-like folds of rock – or nappes – that rose out of the sea and pushed northwards, sliding and breaking over one another to form massive thrust faults.

In the final stage, as the ocean disappeared, a large mass of material which was originally far to the south was pressed onto and over the deep ocean layers. Thus, younger sediments are overlaid by more ancient material in some areas, and in valleys it is possible to see the crystalline rocks of the original proto-continent, some 400 million years old.

Gentian are just one of many species of flower found in the Italian Alps.

> *The Italian Lakes were created during the last Ice Age, the result of glaciers thrusting down from the Alps and gouging out deep valleys. As the ice melted in the valley bottoms, the lakes were formed.*

The Ice Age

The landscape we see today is only around two million years old, dating to the Quarternary Period (which was also the Ice Age), which did so much to remodel the region. At that time, it was glaciers rather than rivers that flowed south from the Alps, and all was enveloped in a vast mantle of ice. Engulfing the surrounding land up to 1,000 metres (3,280ft) deep in icy masses, the slow enormity of the glaciers' force gouged out the bottoms of the valleys, depositing moraine – the debris plucked from the valley floor, from silt to large boulders. The characteristic V-shape appearance of the glacial valleys deepened, producing gigantic basins that, once the glaciers' tongues of ice had retreated, left vast lakes of fresh water.

At a depth of 410 metres (1,345ft), Como is one of Europe's deepest lakes. Its northern end is reminiscent of a fjord showing the characteristic V-formed cross-section of ridges. Lake Garda, the largest lake, is 346 metres (1,135ft) deep, and the moraine deposits contribute 149 metres

(489ft) to that depth. The sheer thickness of the moraine allows its extension into the plain far out of its valley, making it unique among the lakes in having almost a third of its length outside its confining ridges. The rich deposits of the moraine have also given Garda's shoreline a fertility hardly matched by the other lakes. Yet, like the others, the northern reaches are confined by high ridges with a similar fjord-like appearance.

The coral mountains

Named "the most beautiful natural architecture on earth" by the famous French architect Le Sciliar dolomite – the core of the western massif. During that period, erupting volcanoes spewed lava into the sea, which cooled in the gaps between the "tropical" islands, leaving behind the dark-brown volcanic rock still visible today in places such as Val di Fassa and Val Gardena.

By the time of the late Triassic period, the area was a huge tidal flat covered with marine sediment which, when compressed, became the Dolomia Principale – the rock that characterises the eastern Dolomites. More and more layers of marine detritus were embedded, which remained undisturbed until around 60 million

The Dolomites at sunset.

Corbusier, the Dolomites are geologically very different from the main body of the Alps. The crenellated spires, soaring towers and jagged peaks of these spectacular pink-tinged mountains lend a surreal quality to the landscape.

It was the 18th-century French mineralogist Dolomieu who gave the name "Dolomite" to these mountains. The massifs divide into the eastern and western Dolomites, each formed under slightly different conditions. The western massif rose as a more or less single block from former tropical islands. When the region was covered by the tropical sea some 230 million years ago, the accumulation of marine invertebrates, coral and algae created islands and mudflats. These deposits became the rock known as

> The towering peaks of the Alps and the Dolomites preside over forested wilderness, Alpine pastures, meadows carpeted by wild flowers, vineyards in the foothills and orchards in the valleys.

years ago in the Tertiary Period when Europe and Africa collided. Unlike the western massif, which was supported by layers of ancient rock and rose as an undeformed block, the eastern, less protected side, had severe buckling and folding, and rose as elongated humps. Tofane, Cristallo and the Dolomiti di Sesto are all good examples of these vast banks of rock. The characteristic pink appearance of the Dolomites today is a result of erosion by water and ice which has revealed the original Triassic coral.

The *enrosadira*, when the jagged pinnacles and peaks of the Dolomites turn pink and then fiery red as the sun sinks, is one of the world's most magnificent spectacles.

Piedmont peaks

Apart from Western Europe's three tallest mountains, Monte Bianco (Mont Blanc), Monte Rosa and Monte Cervino (the Matterhorn), many are spread across Piedmont, literally at "the foot of the mountains", peppered with numerous parks. The Valsesia is Europe's highest nature conservation area, while the Gran Paradiso was Italy's first national park and is one of the finest.

Close to Lake Maggiore, the Val Grande, with its barren peaks, lonely valleys and untracked paths, is the largest uninhabited and most extensive wilderness area in the Alps. The mountains may be low in comparison with the soaring peaks of Monte Rosa to the west, but they are nonetheless extremely impressive, with the Val Grande River at the heart of the park fed by waterfalls and rivulets crashing through steep-sided gorges.

There are well-known legends in the Alta Valsesia of hidden lakes brimming with liquid silver. The spring waters above Macugnaga are said to come from a lost valley that was once home to the Valle d'Aosta's early tribes. But, below ground, real gold glistens, and the area around Macugnaga was once famous for its mines. The Guia Gold Mine was the first in the Alps to be opened to the public, and the guided tour shows the veins of shimmering iron pyrite (tantalising fool's gold).

Standing at 4,633 metres (15,200ft), the Monte Rosa range is the second-highest in the Alps after Mont Blanc. Famous for its "Himalayan rock face", Monte Rosa is named not after the colour pink, but rather from the local patois *roisa or roese*, which means "ice-covered". Its extensive glaciers are honeycombed with crevasses, and it is one of the few remaining major glaciated areas in the Alps.

Receding glaciers

Glaciers produced the magnificent lakes of the Alpine foothills – Garda, Iseo Maggiore, Como and Lugano – fashioned from above by tongues of ice and dammed below by terminal moraines. But the pattern of rising temperatures, believed to be caused by global warming, means that glaciers are receding. Between 1990 and 2000, underground temperatures had risen nearly 1°C – three times faster than at any other time during the 20th century. After the Marmolada glacier in the Dolomites shed 2 metres (6.5ft) of ice in only two days, revealing remnants of bunkers, barracks and storage areas built by Austro-Hungarian troops during World War I, it is now closed to summer skiers. A report on climate change by the Organisation for Economic Co-operation and Development is predicting the disappearance of 75 percent of Alpine gla-

The Marmolada glacier in the Dolomites.

ciers within 45 years, a surge in avalanches and floods, and the closure of all but the highest ski resorts. Walter Maggi, a geologist at Milan University, said that the closures had come after low rainfall in the spring and very high temperatures in June and July. "But there are deeper causes," he said. "The finger of suspicion points at global warming." Time will tell.

Lake vistas

The most romantic of the lakes must be Como, an amazing wishbone shape surrounded by rugged limestone mountains. This fabled lake is a voluptuous blend of the Alpine and the exotic, of cool, lofty mountains and Mediterranean-style warmth. After the expansive beauties of Lakes Como and Maggiore, Lake Lugano is more untamed and wild. Sir John Lubbock, in *The Scenery of Switzerland*, comments that it "owes its complex form to the fact that it consists of two longitudinal and two transverse valleys dammed up by moraines". John Addington Symonds, in his *Sketches in Italy*, depicts its great beauty as being coloured with "the changeful green and azure of a peacock's breast".

Reminiscent of Lugano, long and narrow Lake Iseo does, however, have less forest and more blue in its mountain shadows. At the upper end, where the stream of the Oglio

But those very peaks and pinnacles protect the flourishing olive trees, oleanders, camellias and citrus in this extraordinarily mild climate, known to the Romans as Lake Benacus, the "beneficent".

To the south of the lakes, the silts from rivers and moraines, before and after the Ice Age, formed the richly fertile Lombardy plain which is still the most productive area in Italy.

Orchids and edelweiss

Vines, olives, palms and citrus trees are sprinkled among horse chestnut, pine and conifer trees, and little Alpine wild flowers peep out

The northern end of Lake Garda at Torbolé.

brings down melted snow from the great Adamello range, the water in early summer takes on a pale opaque-blue colour. Its shores, although sub-Alpine, are almost Neapolitan in parts. Little Orta, lined by its snowy mountains at the north and low hills at the south enclosed in pearly mists, is magical and blue.

Lying apart from the others, Garda is the largest lake and the most scenically diverse. It stretches from the Lombardy plain to the foot of the Trentino Dolomites in the north, where mountains rise straight from the shoreline. Every afternoon in summer the cooling breeze of the Ora funnels down on to Lake Garda. The northern reaches resemble a deep Norwegian fjord, enclosed between towering mountain ranges.

from their snowy mantles in high pastureland, while lakeside exotic blooms don their glory in the warm microclimates.

The high wilderness of Alta Valsesia on the Swiss border has numerous species of plant below the snowline and an extraordinary 57 species above the snowline. Although much of the area is scree, ice and boulder-covered pasture, it is still a nursery for rare high-altitude plants and the most famous of all Alpine wild flowers – the edelweiss. This delicate white flower blooms in late summer and grows in limestone pastures up to 3,400 metres (11,000ft).

The Stelvio national park has an extraordinary diversity of plants, with over 1,200 species recorded. A member of the primrose family, the chickweed wintergreen thrives in the coni-fer woodland and displays its attractive star-like white flower. Splendid too are the sweetly scented black vanilla orchids, purple Alpine clematis and members of the gentian family, from the rare yel-low gentian to the azure trumpet variety.

The Val Grande area is cloaked with maple, beech, chestnut and yew trees, and the plenti-ful spring water ensures that the Alpine flowers flourish – including gentian, edelweiss, moun-tain tulip and the rare white alpenrose.

The Adamello-Brenta is one of Italy's key wild places. Soaring peaks, razor-edged pinnacles, jumbled screes and vast rock faces oversee splen-did paths – such as the Via delle Bocchette, the most famous of Italy's *vie ferrate*. Crimson-red lichen cloaks the granite boulders in autumn, and the fir and pine trees are interspersed with beech, birch, hazel and wild cherry trees. Among the cracks in the rock grows the deep-blue bell-flower, *Campanula raineri*, and the primrose *Primula spectablis* puts on a spectacular show, covering the rocks with its large reddish-pink flowers. Other varieties of Alpine flora include the edelweiss and the rare lady's orchid.

"The terraces of the garden are held up to the

Climbing above a via ferrata.

VIE FERRATE

Literally "roads of iron", *vie ferrate* mountain paths had their origins in the 1860s but date mainly from World War I, when they were constructed as a way of transporting troops and equipment over difficult ter-rain. Especially prevalent in the Trentino-Alto Adige area, some have rusted away, but many have been adapted to access free climbs. Vertical ladders, foot-holds into the rock, metal brackets and even bridges allow climbers to move across steep, sometimes vertical cliffs.

In the Brenta Dolomites, *vie ferrate* were con-structed during the 1930s purely to access difficult climbs of the dramatic and beautiful rock faces.

These classic routes include the famous Via delle Bocchette in the Parco Naturale Adamello Brenta.

The *vie ferrate* in this area differ widely in length and level of difficulty. Climbers must be equipped with a sit harness and a *vie ferrate* kit, which can be bought or rented from most climbing shops. This includes two karabiners tied on each end of a lanyard – or shock-absorbing rope. A helmet is also essential together with fitness, caution and a good head for heights. "Exposure" in *vie ferrate* parlance means proximity to a large vertical drop – which are both frequent and potentially terrifying. They are graded from A–G and all require good climbing skills.

Victorian Trailblazers

While the Dolomites were named after a Frenchman, it was the exploits of Victorian mountaineers that put these majestic mountains firmly on the map.

In 1837, John Murray Publishers produced a guide to the Alps which mentioned the Dolomites in print for the first time. This was the spur that

Mountaineers scale a peak c.1900.

sent so many British mountaineers to explore the peaks, and led to the founding of the Alpine Club of London (now Great Britain), the first Alpine association in the world.

Club members' exploits

The club members included aristocrats and better-off middle classes, the only Victorian social layers that could afford spending much money and time on quite a romantic hobby – climbing Alpine peaks. The British mountaineers would emphasize membership of their Alpine Club by writing "AC" next to their names when registering at Alpine inns and shelters. Rock climbing became an important activity of Victorian mountaineers in the Dolomites, and elsewhere in the Alps.

In 1852, Dublin-born John Ball, the first President of the club, was also the first to scale the Brenta Dolomites, using a route that is still considered the safest today. Ball's *Guide of the Eastern Alps* (1868) confirmed his status as an intrepid, trailblazing mountaineer.

Douglas Freshfield and Francis Fox Tuckett also led expeditions, and have had passes and Alpine refuges named after them. In 1864, they crossed the San Martino Dolomites, a feat that stunned the mountaineering community as the team eschewed maps and equipment for intuition, stamina and skill.

Even Tuckett's sister, Elizabeth, was a seasoned Alpine traveller: her *Alpine Journal* includes sketches of the ascent of the Cimon della Pale made by Edward Robson Whitwell in 1870. Known as "the Matterhorn of the Dolomites", this was the last major British conquest.

Leslie Stephen, the father of novelist Virginia Woolf, was a keen mountaineer and President of the Alpine Club (1866–1888) who explored the Pale di San Martino group in 1869, crossing Passo di Ball, the pass named after John Ball. Instead, a lasting memorial to Tuckett is the striking Alpine inn named after him, Rifugio Tuckett, set above the chic resort of Madonna di Campiglio.

Women pioneers

Victorian women were equally passionate about the mountains. Elizabeth Fox Tuckett was the first illustrator to turn her Alpine adventures into children's stories.

Amelia Edwards recounted the exploits of her peers in *Untrodden Peaks and Unfrequented Valleys* (1872). A tireless traveller herself, she explored the peaks on horseback and warned against the hardships of the crags: "The passages are too long and too fatiguing for ladies on foot, and should not be attempted by any who cannot endure eight and sometimes ten hours of mule-riding." Edwards was particularly fascinated by the tall peaks of Cimon della Pale in the San Martino group. She found the massif similar to a Pharaonic pyramid.

Although the British legacy lives on, in the form of such fine mountaineers as Chris Bonington, the baton has passed to Italian mountaineers of the stature of the great Reinhold Messner. Even so, the British Alpine journals still make inspiring reading.

sun, the sun falls upon them, they are like a vessel slanted up, to catch the superb, heavy light." So wrote D.H. Lawrence on Lake Garda in *Twilight in Italy* (1916). Along the eastern coast of Lake Garda are the high ridges of Monte Baldo. The scenery is spectacular, but perhaps even more important is the extraordinary botanical diversity which gave this area the name "Hortus Italiae" – the garden of Italy – back in the 16th century. The Alpine climate on the highest peaks, which are both snow-covered in winter and sun-scorched in summer, contrasts dramatically with the lower slopes, which are sheltered by Lake Garda.

Maggiore has the famous Kashmir cypress tree, Europe's single largest specimen which is over 200 years old. Camellias, rhododendrons and azaleas bloom in profusion, and lemon trees are confined not just to Garda, but also to Lugano, Como and Maggiore in the deliciously warm microclimate.

Alpine wildlife

After the Ice Ages, many animals sought refuge and migrated to the Alpine regions. The ptarmigan – or snow grouse – and mountain hare were originally inhabitants of Central Asia. Many species persecuted here in the 19th and 20th cen-

Anemone baldensis.

The lake has frozen over only once in recorded history, in 1701, and the microclimate allows citrus, olive and palm trees to flourish. During the Ice Ages, the highest ridges were unaffected by the vast glacier that covered the area and plants survived and flourished. Endemic species evolved bearing the epithet *baldensis or baldense*, such as the distinctive sedge *carex baldensis*. One of the best-known flowers to be first discovered on Monte Baldo is the Monte Baldo blue-white anemone, *anemone baldensis*. In spring, the grassy flanks are carpeted with alpine flowers and medicinal plants which attract herbalists worldwide.

Subtropical exotic plants flourish on the frost-free lake shores, and some of Europe's finest gardens are here. Isola Madre in the midst of Lake

turies, such as the lynx, wolf and bear, are once again on the increase.

In the Alta Valsesia, the predatory stoat, at home in the high mountains, matches its coat in winter to its snowy habitat, foxes roam and majestic golden eagles rear their young on inaccessible crags. Agile chamois race up and down the precipitous slopes and whistling marmots snuggle into their burrows.

Often called "the park of rock, ice and snow", the Stelvio is the largest protected area on the Italian Alpine ridge, and a tenth of it is permanently covered in ice. Remnants of the Great War such as barbed wire and guns are still entombed in the glacial ice. But wild as it is, chamois, and red and roe deer still roam, joined by brown bear from the Adamello. The long-horned ibex is here too, usually well above the tree line on craggy mountain ridge tops, migrating in winter to the warmer south-facing slopes.

The area is also home to more than 130 species of birds. Tiny pygmy owls hunt by day and night as do eagle owls – the largest of their species in Europe. Woodpeckers are common too, with five different species successfully breeding here – the great spotted, the grey-headed, the black, the three-toed and the wryneck (so named because of its dexterity in twisting its head supposedly through 360°). Above the treeline, in the shadow of the golden eagles and majestic bearded vultures, once thought to be extinct in the Alps, but now successfully reintroduced – little alpine choughs and accentors take their lives in their wings.

The Adamello-Brenta park is home to the eagle and pygmy owls and to the black, three-toed and grey-headed woodpeckers. In the barren uplands also lives the mountain hare, whose coat turns from brownish grey to snowy white in winter. Chamois, deer and marmots are also residents, along with the shy brown bears who leave behind tell-tale signs such as disturbed

A chamois in Gran Paradiso National Park.

RETURN OF THE BROWN BEAR

In 1999, it was realised that the Alps were in danger of losing their native brown bears for ever. Uncontrolled hunting and the intrusion of man into their natural habitats meant that bears were threatened with extinction: only five remained in the wild and mountainous Adamello-Brenta park, and no new cubs had been born since 1990.

Researchers found that the Slovenian brown bears were genetically virtually the same as the Italian brown bear *(Ursus arctos)*. In 2002, bears began to be reintroduced with the aim of creating a population of 40–60 bears, which is considered the minimum viable population (MVP) to sustain the species.

The bears reside in Trentino's Adamello-Brenta Nature Park, a protected area some 50km (31 miles) north of Lake Garda, but roam as far as the provinces of Bolzano, Sondrio, Brescia and Verona, an area of about 6,500 sq km (2,510 sq miles).

So far it seems that the Slovenian bears have adapted well to their new environment and are perfectly well integrated with their Italian cousins. Twenty baby bears were born between 2002 and 2006 from the six or seven "founder" Slovenian bears, and according to all forecasts, the bears which were reintroduced have adapted easily to their new Italian life.

bees' nests. Although the indigenous brown bear became extinct in the Brenta area, bears still exist elsewhere in the Dolomites, with numbers boosted by the introduction of Slovenian bears (see box).

In the Prealps of the Veneto, the highest reaches of Monte Baldo are home to rock partridge, black grouse, Alpine choughs and many other mountain birds, including golden eagles. On the lower reaches, songbirds congregate in the warm spring sunshine, tawny owls and nightjars nest in the conifer woods and, during migration, clouds of swifts swoop over Lake

Alpine adventures

Outside the ski season, meadows full of Alpine flowers recall a vision of Heidi heaven. But in summer those same ski lifts transport walkers up to wilder pastures in the lee of soaring peaks. Tunnels, trenches, embrasures and forts were constructed at strategic locations, linked by iron ways, *vie ferrate*, some of which can still be climbed today to see open air "museums" of restored defences.

There are plenty of adrenalin sports on offer, too, such as white-water rafting, canyoning and paragliding. Around the lakes there are numer-

Brown bear (Ursus arctos) in the Dolomites.

Garda. Brown bears are sighted occasionally, but more common are the herds of roe deer taking cover in the thick vegetation, while in the higher, exposed ridges marmots and chamois can often be spotted.

The lakes and rivers teem with coarse fish. Lake Iseo is especially well known for its perch (*persico*), while Lake Como is renowned for its shad (*missoltino*), and trout (*trota*) is especially good in lakes Orta and Maggiore. Eels (*anguille*) and chub (*cafvedano*) are widely found in Garda and Como. The Alpine char, *Salvelinus alpinus*, is a small fish which reached the Alps thousands of years ago with the glaciation. But lost in the mists of time are the serpents and dragons once thought to have inhabited Lake Orta's Isola San Giulio.

ous opportunities for swimming, boating, water-skiing and windsurfing, and for golf and tennis. Mountain biking is very popular, especially around the Mottarone above Lake Maggiore and on Monte Baldo above Garda. Pocket-sized Lake Orta also has itineraries such as the "Girolago" – a leisurely scenic tour around the lake.

Horse riding is also becoming very popular. In winter, the Scandinavian sport of skijoring is celebrated in Val di Fiemme – one of few places in the Alps to have this kind of fast and furious combination of skiing and horsemanship. A skier is pulled behind a horse at full gallop along a snowy track. During the Skijoring Grand Prix of Predazzo, teams race around a track in a frenzy of hooves and snow flurries.

ON THE PISTE

Great snow, great scenery and great style make the Italian ski scene seriously cool.

Getting a lift.

Skiing Italian-style is not just about designer equipment, skiwear and shades, but the combination of atmosphere, great skiing and snowboarding, fabulous food and dramatic scenery. Resorts tend to hug the borders between France, Switzerland and Austria, making it possible to ski in two different countries in one day. Many of the slopes may seem best-suited to beginners and intermediates, yet this is often less to do with gradient and more to do with excellent piste-grooming and snow-making facilities. And in the Dolomites, there is access to 1,220km (760 miles) of pistes – one of the world's largest ski areas.

West of Lake Maggiore, sharing the border with Switzerland, Monte Rosa is Europe's second-highest mountain after Mont Blanc. Dominated by the "pink mountain", Piedmont's **Monterosa** ski area is often referred to – in wintersports speak – as "Europe's best-kept secret". The three main resorts, Champoluc, Gressoney and Alagna, are charming, traditional villages set amid gorgeous scenery. Alagna has cult status as an off-piste paradise bristling with cornices and cliffs – strictly for the experts in some of the toughest terrain in the Alps. A 100-person cable car from Alagna gives access to a piste to Gressoney: an option for less intrepid souls. Both Champoluc and Gressoney have long, cruising intermediate runs that are usually very quiet and blessed with good snow.

To the east of Monterosa is a sprinkling of small villages, such as the pretty former Walser settlement, Macugnaga, covering 37km (23 miles) of pistes served by 12 lifts. Closest to Lake Maggiore

is **Monte Mottarone** at 1,200m (4,000ft); it has no village, but its ski area of 25km (15 miles) is popular with weekend visitors during the winter season.

In Brescia province, the **Adamello** ski area covers 100km (62 miles) of pistes spanning the Val Camonica in Lombardy and the Val di Sole in Trentino. Purpose-built and snow-sure, Passo Tonale perched above the treeline at 1,885m (6,200ft). It caters well for beginners and early intermediates and is popular more for its good-value accommodation and boisterous bars than for its charm. However, a new gondola lift and high-speed chairs link Tonale with the pretty, quieter area of Pontedilegno with attractive tree-lined runs. It is now possible to ski very varied terrain from the Presena glacier (3,000m/9,800ft) to Tonale, Pontedilego and right across to Temù (1,150m/3,800ft).

Nearby, Pejo, in the heart of the Stelvio national park, is a purpose-built ski resort with a cable

There are numerous snow parks for snowboarders to enjoy.

Dolomite peaks make a dramatic backdrop to the pistes.

Time out for hot chocolate, Madonna di Campiglio ski area.

car. Access to other areas in the Val di Sole (Valley of the Sun) such as Folgarida-Marilleva are also straightforward, thanks to a gondola link. Already linked to these pretty resorts is the larger **Madonna di Campiglio** ski area. Affluent, exclusive, very Italian and ultra-chic, Madonna's ski area covers 120km (75 miles) of pistes.

For the best snow-making and piste-grooming in Italy, the **Dolomites** have an unequalled record. In the northeast of the South Tyrol, this area is a delightful blend of Italian charm and Austrian efficiency. A vast network of 464 state-of-the-art lifts and 745 immaculately groomed, mostly intermediate pistes is on the doorstep – all covered by the single Dolomiti Superski lift pass. At the heart of the Val Gardena, Selva is cradled by Mediterranean-style warmth and the spectacular peaks and pinnacles of the dramatic pink-tinged Dolomite mountains. Selva, with a lively Tyrolean atmosphere, is the best place to stay on the famous **Sella Ronda** circuit. This is a 22km (14-mile) circular tour around the picturesque Gruppo Sella mountains, passing through the villages of Selva, Colfosco, Corvara, Canazei and steep and deep Arabba.

In the Veneto, über-chic Cortina d'Ampezzo is known as the "Queen of the Dolomites". Here, it is hard not to be seduced by the most stunningly beautiful mountain scenery in Italy. Cortina has skiing for all abilities, and the runs tend to be quiet during the week and at the sacrosanct lunchtime – with a choice of more than 50 mountain restaurants. As the sun sinks in a fiery glow during the *enrosadira* and all the Dolomiti peaks turn pink, the evening *passeggiata* gets under way, when everyone parades up and down in the Corso Italia. This is Italian skiing and après-ski at its most stylish.

Skiing on the Sella Ronda circuit.

The lakes were advertised in many elegant early 20th-century posters.

CELEBRITY PLAYGROUND

Long before the Côte d'Azur came into vogue, the
Italian Lakes were the haunt of the European elite and
a staging post on the Grand Tour – the appeal lingers
on, even if Byron, Bellini and Goethe have given way
to George Clooney and the celebrity set.

The Italian Lakes, nestling in the southern foothills of the Alps, have long cast a spell over jaded visitors. Virgil, Pliny and Catullus lavished praise on their homeland, whose villas and gardens represented Roman rest and recreation in an era which celebrated similar pleasures to our own. Henry James rightly praised the lakes for making urbanites feel "out of the rush and crush of the modern world".

The uptight Victorians loosened a few buttons on the lakes: the Murray guidebook to the area, published in 1842, swept enraptured visitors around the sights, from the Borromean Islands on Lake Maggiore to Villa Carlotta and Villa d'Este on Lake Como, creating a Grand Tour of the lakes that remains popular today, admittedly lacking the grumpy innkeepers and unreliable ferrymen of yore. The lakes only fell out of fashion in the 1950s when beach holidays became a badge of sophistication. But now the lakes are again a celebrity magnet, their charms sufficient to lure movie stars and media moguls to seek permanent moorings on the waterfront.

The Grand Tour

The lakes first became fashionable wintering grounds in the early 19th century thanks to their mild climate, the opening of the Simplon Pass and the growth of ferry services.

The Simplon was barely passable in 1800, when Napoleon blasted a trailblazing route through the ravines and chasms to Italy. While Wordsworth had been consigned to perilous mule-tracks in 1790, Napoleon's route made the lakes a migration path for the Grand Tourists, like swallows heading south. Byron and Shelley flew this way, delighted to leave the highwaymen behind. English carriages, reported Byron,

The first train to go through the Simplon Tunnel, 1905.

CROSSING THE SIMPLON PASS

The Simplon afforded a breathtaking descent into the Lombardy lakes but, for many Grand Tourists, crossing the pass to the lakes was a journey from purgatory to paradise. The French writer Théophile Gautier, who made the crossing in 1850, reported: "Travelling from the cold air of the high Alps into the warmth of Italy, carriages lurched and lumbered along vertiginous routes carrying travellers clutching their Baedeker, Bradshaw or Murray guidebooks, which hastened to reassure them that the world ahead was free of the 'perils of precipices and robbers' presently surrounding them."

were regularly "stopped and handsomely pil-fered of various chattels".

Among the early travellers came Caroline of Brunswick, later Queen Caroline, wife of George IV. As the estranged wife of the Prince Regent, she sought a fresh start on Lake Como, in the palatial Villa d'Este, where, in 1814, she installed her Italian lover, a Napoleonic general, and scandalised polite society before dying in England.

Artists in residence

A clutch of writers and artists soon followed, from a youthful Henry James, who walked

> The composer Franz Liszt wrote his Dante Sonata on the shores of Lake Como, supposedly inspired by a statue of Dante and Beatrice in Villa Melzi, one of the finest villas on the lake.

a Mediterranean hothouse, the northern part of the lake flourished under Austrian rule, between 1815 and 1918, when Riva became a stylish resort, attracting such intellectual heavyweights as Kafka, Nietzsche and Thomas

The Villa d'Este became Queen Caroline's new and happier playground.

part of the way in 1869, to Turner, who painted and sketched his way through Italy. Turner, the master of atmospheric effects, lapped up the lakes, which inspired his dreamlike landscapes, such as *Sun Setting over a Lake* (1840). The critic John Ruskin visited the lakes in 1844, the same year Charles Dickens swept in, accompanied by his wife, five children, their servants and even the family hound.

As for continental writers, French novelists such as Stendhal tended to prefer Lake Como, although Balzac loved Lake Orta, whose soft, dreamy landscape was likened to "a grey pearl in a green casket". For the Austrians, Lake Garda was the fashionable choice. Considered

Mann. The aristocracy and bourgeoisie of *Mitteleuropa* flocked to the sanatoria around Lake Garda, while Lake Lavarone, just north, was where Sigmund Freud sought inspiration every summer, using his therapeutic lakeside strolls for psycho-analytical musing.

Operatic Lake Como

The musical links on the lakes resemble the "five degrees of separation" game. On Lake Como, Bellini composed *Norma* and *La Sonnambula*, Rossini *Tancredi*, and Verdi Act II of *La Traviata*. The composers looked no further than their neighbours: Giuditta Pasta, the Maria Callas of her day, and her husband, the tenor Giuseppe Pasta.

Villa Melzi, one of Como's finest waterside villas, captivated singers and composers, including Franz Liszt, forced into Italian exile after a troubled love affair. What first inspired him was the Moorish coffeehouse standing sentinel to the lake, a bold folly with lofty vistas edged by banks of camellias. Fittingly, it was on Lake Como, on Christmas Day 1837, that Liszt's daughter Cosima was born, the future wife of Richard Wagner, to whom Isola Bella conceivably conjured up Kundry's enchanted garden in his opera *Parsifal*. Also on Isola Bella, "La Grissina" sang for Napoleon, the lake's aristocratic heyday.

Lake Garda's musical revival was left to Maria Callas, *"La Divina"*, who lived in Sirmione at the height of her powers in the 1950s. The diva, married to an Italian but besotted with Aristotle Onassis, became as celebrated for her operatic affairs as for her lyrical perfection. As in the finest operatic scores, her love affairs had tragic endings, a poignancy at one with the spirit of Sirmione. Villa Cortine, opposite Maria Callas's villa, became a battlefield hospital, Nazi High Command and Allied headquarters before becoming a hotel

The romantic gardens of the Villa Cortine Palace, Sirmione.

who conducted a tempestuous affair with the celebrated diva. In the 19th century, the atmosphere on Lake Como was so operatic that even the unlyrical Henry James found himself "fairly wallowing in a libretto".

Grand dukes and divas

Ostensibly less operatic, Lake Garda's northern resorts became winter watering holes for the musical Austrian grand dukes in the 1870s, including Emperor Franz Joseph and his cousin Albert. The resorts of Riva and Arco revelled in Belle Epoque balls, interspersed with health cures and carriage rides to exotic villa gardens and olive groves. It took the outbreak of World War I to put an end to

where Princess Diana's mother, Frances Shand Kydd, retreated after the death of her daughter, seeking the solace she failed to find on her small Scottish island.

Como and the A-list

Despite Garda's operatic grandeur, Lake Como, in mood, if not in reality, is the lake most swept up in the days of grand dukes and dowager empresses, of *fin de siècle* balls before the chill winds of democracy swept away the doomed, cobweb-encrusted carapace. As the most glamorous lake, it has been a retreat for weary urbanites for several thousand years. Pliny the Younger, poet, orator and senator, sang the praises of his two waterside villas, retreats from the cares of the world. Named Comedy and Tragedy, the porticoed villas saved him from the stress of life in ancient Rome. If Villa Comedia is traditionally sited in Lenno, where the young poet fished from his bedroom window, Villa Tragedia straddled a ridge in Bellagio and boasted superlative views of the Alps. Here, as in most of the lakes, the sights are subordinate to the mood. Bellagio is a summation of all the clichés, yet somehow rises above it.

Como's icing on the cake comes in the form of Villa Carlotta and its gorgeously

wives of other gentlemen to fly with them and ignore the restrictions of public opinion." Ever wise, James was the first to sanction snatching happiness where you may: "Lake Como is the place to enjoy *à deux* – it's a shame to be here in gross melancholy solitude."

Princes and potentates

By contrast, Lake Maggiore has long been a mecca for potentates, politicians and plantsmen. Still fabulously wealthy, the powerful Borromean dynasty have produced patrons of learning, cardinals, popes and even a saint,

Detail from Leonardo da Vinci's Virgin of the Rocks, inspired by the landscape near Varenna.

saccharine gardens. This central stretch of the lake, embracing Bellagio, Tremezzo and Varenna, is the most seductive. Near Varenna, the brooding woods and wild limestone peaks inspired Leonardo da Vinci to use the shadowy landscape as the setting for his *Virgin of the Rocks*. Stendhal, based in Milan, partly set his masterpiece *The Charterhouse of Parma* on these shores, which offered a clear-sighted look at love and the pursuit of happiness.

Naturally, the locals claim John Kennedy romanced Marilyn Monroe on Lake Como. But even in Henry James's day, it had a reputation for seduction: "It is commonly the spot to which inflamed young gentlemen invite the

> *Longfellow immortalised the resort in verse in 1872: "The hills sweep upward from the shore, with Villas scattered one by one upon their wooded spurs, and lower Bellagio blazing in the sun."*

and have had their powerbase on the Borromean Islands since medieval times. Their Isola Bella was the picturesque setting for the doomed 1935 Stresa Conference at which Italy, Britain and France failed to agree a strategy in the face of Hitler's rearmament. Stresa itself is still considered the noble part of the lake, and commands a place in the hearts of former heads of state of a certain vintage, from Winston Churchill to Margaret Thatcher and Helmut Kohl.

Snobbery certainly plays a part, as the residents are delighted to have hosted royalty. Carlo Pisoni, archivist for the princely Borromean clan, detects a keen sense of history among lake-dwellers: "If you mention Queen Victoria to people in Baveno, they'll talk about her as though she was here yesterday." Although well past its prime, this dowager resort once found favour with the crowned heads of Europe. In 1879, Queen

to the ornateness and sumptuousness which struck many a British and American visitor.

The simple (celebrity) life

In the past, romantic lakeside views and lush Mediterranean vegetation drew visitors of a certain sensibility. Their dreams were fulfilled by the profusion of villas and gardens set amid azaleas, giant palms, camellias and rhododendrons. Whether rich, rakish or rebellious, their concerns were scenery, climate, a release from social responsibility and a sense of surrender.

Laurence Olivier and Vivien Leigh on holiday in Lake Garda in 1955.

Victoria visited Baveno, staying in the turn-of-the-century Villa Clara, which Edward Hutton dismissed as "a replica of the Wimbledon or Putney residence of a retired tradesman". Yet on the neighbouring shore, in Villa Taranto, a Scottish soldier, Captain Neil McEachern, turned his back on social climbing to devote his life to planting his exotic gardens.

Thinking of this lake, Henry James noted: "The most striking feature of Italian scenery seems to be this same odd mingling of tawdriness and splendour – a generous profuse luxuriance of nature and the ludicrous gingerbread accessories of human contrivance." In his inimitable way, James may be referring

Historian John Pemble describes the typical Victorian and Edwardian exiles as "eccentrics with oversize personalities, whose voices, gestures and passions required high ceilings, strong light and stupendous views". Little has changed, except that the ceilings have got higher and the staff quarters bigger. The curious point about contemporary stars is that their motivations remain unchanged: the lakes represent a realm of enchantment and repose, where they can potter in privacy. Today's movie star seeks simplicity and, like Pliny, wants to feel he can fish from his bedroom window or enjoy what Liszt called "the melancholy murmuring of the waves lapping against the boat".

The Literary Lakes

The sight of sluggish steamers and snow-clad peaks stirs something deep in most visitors, but especially in the souls of poets.

Henry James's heart lifted as he left Switzerland for the Italian Lakes: "On into Italy we went – a rapturous progress through a wild luxuriance of corn and olives and figs and mulberries and chest-

The Romantic English poet Shelley.

nuts and frescoed villages and clamorous beggars and all the good old Italianisms of tradition."

Romantic inspiration

It is little coincidence that two of the most romantic Roman poets, Virgil and Catullus, came from the lake region, and were inspired by the seductive setting. Virgil lavished praise on the lakes, while Catullus chose Sirmione as the place from which to write lovesick verse to Lesbia, his fickle lover.

"This lake exceeds anything I ever beheld in beauty," declared Shelley of Lake Como. Shelley, exploring the lake in 1818, was stirred by Villa Pliniana, a Renaissance palace linked to a site beloved by Pliny. Like the Roman poet, Shelley waxed lyrical over the vast waterfall, "broken by the woody rocks into a thousand channels to the lake", but, with typical British acquisitiveness, wanted to rent the crumbling pile.

Novelist Edith Wharton, visiting in 1903, was intoxicated by the Romantic poets' visions of brooding lakes, especially Shelley's "glens filled with the flashing light of the waterfalls".

The German poet Goethe was drawn to Lake Garda by its classical resonance, even if it was the lemons rather than the literature which won his heart: "What I enjoy most of all is the fruit," he wrote in his journal in 1786. Goethe had less fondness for Malcesine, where the Austrian police, spotting the poet sketching the castle, arrested him on suspicion of being a spy.

D.H. Lawrence and Italy

Since the 18th century, Lake Garda's summer villas have lured such luminaries as Byron and D.H. Lawrence, who lamented a way of life that was passing, with the shift from plucking lemons to plucking tourists. Lawrence adored Limone, overlooking "a lake as beautiful as the beginning of creation". In 1912, having left England for the first time in his life, he travelled to northern Italy and spent almost one year at various picturesque localities on the shores of Lake Garda. *D.H. Lawrence and Italy*, published in 1916, is his nostalgic collection of travel essays on his Italian journey, with one of its parts "Twilight in Italy" solely devoted to Lake Garda. This is a very specific travel book in which the author of *Women in Love* ponders not only landscapes and nature, but also – on a more philosophical plane – mankind, human fate and religion.

Ibsen and Vladimir Nabokov concurred, even if their preference was for grander Gardone Riviera, where the latter enjoyed catching butterflies. This was also Winston Churchill's favoured resort, where he combined painting watercolours with journal-writing. They all stayed at the pastel-coloured Grand Hotel Gardone Riviera.

"One can't describe the beauty of the Italian lakes, nor would one try if one could," wrote Henry James, on catching sight of Lake Maggiore. Such outpourings of purple prose, particularly from writers fleeing northern climes, are part of the lakes' legacy, but look elsewhere for great literature.

Villas for the rich and famous

For all its cultivated simplicity, Lake Como could claim to be Europe's tightest power nexus: Rupert Murdoch owns a waterside estate in Blevio and, ironically, has Silvio Berlusconi, his rival media magnate, in the villa opposite. Fellow tycoon Richard Branson has plumped for a property in nearby Lenno, not far from several secretive Russian billionaires and Michael O'Leary, the Irish owner of Ryanair.

Footballers have now caught the Lake fever: Lionel Messi has bought a house on Como

Hollywood star George Clooney loves the laid-back lifestyle of his Lake Como home: "Italians have taught me how to celebrate life," he once said.

on his Harley motorbike. The star's popularity was briefly dented after his purchase of the neighbouring villas and beach provoked a local backlash, resolved by Clooney smoothly presenting Como with a new public beach.

George Clooney boards a yacht on Lake Como.

and both Cristiano Ronaldo and David Beckham are rumoured to be looking for their own houses in the area, too. Paradoxically, the common quest for privacy could degenerate into a deal-making frenzy of snappy power brunches on the powerboat.

Many Milan-based Italian fashion designers also own villas in the lakes, but since film star George Clooney bought Villa Oleandra, Lake Como has been bathed in Hollywood glamour and it has featured in such films as *Ocean's Twelve* and *Casino Royale*. Villa Oleandra is where Clooney entertains friends, from Brad Pitt to Matt Damon and Julia Roberts, when not playing tennis with the locals or roaring round the hills

The waters are calm once more, as Como strives to provide camouflage for publicity-shy residents. Hollywood stars are also regular guests at Donatella Versace's villa retreat in Moltrasio, Villa Fontanelle, where Gianni Versace is buried, and where extravagant fashion shoots are staged. The 18th-century mansion, a dreamy affair with a lily pond and dancing fireflies, is now owned by Russian millionaire restaurateur Arkady Novikov.

The lakes is where celebrities come for peace and quiet, keener on gossip and grilled lake fish than on fashionable column inches. It is hardly surprising that Clooney prefers sleepy Lake Como to the hip Hollywood Hills.

THE GRAND HOTELS

Some of Europe's grandest hotels line the lakes, a legacy of their importance on the Grand Tour.

The western shore of Garda was the first to embrace modern tourism when splendid lakeside villas were built in the 18th century. Long before, in Roman times, lovers and writers were seduced by its charms, and Catullus wrote many of his explicit amorous poems from his villa at Sirmione, which he referred to as his place of contented homecoming. D.H. Lawrence described Gargnano as "one of the most beautiful places on earth", and even Friedrich Nietzsche temporarily forgot nihilism in favour of the lake's beauty.

Gargnano's **Grand Hotel Villa Feltrinelli** was once a hideout for the infamous Mussolini and his wife, Rachele. Although more interested in her pet hens than the villa and her domineering husband, she could not have failed to be entranced by the glorious views. Now transformed into one of the world's best hotels, this luxury bijou residence has sweeping terraces, parquet floors, gilt-framed mirrors, sumptuous antiques and palatial bathrooms.

Nearby, Gardone Riviera was once the magnet for everyone, including heads of state and European royalty, and is lined with huge Belle Epoque hotels, including the pink-and-white **Villa Fiordaliso** – the convenient love-nest for Mussolini and his mistress, Clara. Now also an elegant boutique hotel, (although not quite in the same pecking order as the Feltrinelli), four of the rooms are named after flowers, the fifth after Clara.

Lake Maggiore was on the Grand Tour map by the late 18th century, and as the former fishing villages mushroomed into elite towns graced with Belle Epoque hotels and casinos rivalling those of Venice's Lido and Monte Carlo, it became a favoured retreat for Europe's nobility and glitterati. The **Grand Hotel des Iles Borromées**, overlooking the jewel-like Borromean Islands, has been home to well-heeled guests since 1861. Ernest Hemingway was a regular visitor who loved the hotel so much that he featured it in his book *A Farewell to Arms*. Like Hemingway, his eponymous suite is king-size in every way, with vast marble bathrooms. Recent lavish renovations have restored the hotel to its glory as the grande dame of lake hotels.

Near Lake Iseo, **L'Albereta** is set in the Franciacorta wine-growing area. The former country seat of a noble family, this ancient hunting lodge has been imaginatively restored into an elegantly furnished hotel-restaurant.

On Lake Orta, the **Villa Crespi** is an opulent Moorish fantasy, also boasting a superb two-star

Villa Crespi, Lake Orta.

Villa Fiordaliso, Lake Garda.

Grand Hotel des Iles Borromées, Lake Maggiore.

The grounds of Grand Hotel Villa d'Este, Cernobbio, Lake Como.

Michelin restaurant.

In Lugano, Switzerland, the decoratively Art Nouveau **Hotel Splendide Royal** overlooks the shoreline of one of the most enchanting Prealp lakes, its rooms a sumptuous mix of gilded tassels and silken stripes. Both rooms and views more than live up to the hotel's ambitious name.

Dramatic, deep and romantic, Como continues to bewitch everyone. Often named as Italy's most beautiful town, Bellagio is graced by the lavishly ornate **Grand Hotel Villa Serbelloni**, set in huge lakeside grounds. The star-studded guest book has signatures from royalty to a galaxy of actors and heads of state including Winston Churchill, who painted from his suite at the top of the marble staircase. Murano crystal, marble halls, glorious vistas and a nightly string quartet are all part of the elegant and spacious opulence.

Enjoying equally magnificent lake views, the luxurious **Grand Hotel Tremezzo Palace** stands next to the botanical gardens of the 18th-century Villa Carlotta. Built in 1910 and recently renovated, its lavish Liberty charm is complemented by the glamorous T Spa and the renovated Terrazza restaurant. Outside, a floating pool on the lake provides the ultimate setting for a swim amid glorious views.

On any list of the world's grand hotels, Como's **Villa d'Este** always ranks near the top. A former 16th-century princely residence and once the riotous retreat of Princess Caroline, the estranged wife of Britain's Prince Regent, it was transformed into a grand hotel in 1873. It has continued to be the opulent retreat of countless dignitaries, celebrities and royalty from all over the world. Latter-day fashionistas from Brangelina to Sharon Stone have joined musicians from Verdi to Mick Jagger amid the precious marble walls of this pleasure palace. This is a true Renaissance villa, reflecting a magnificent bygone era – yet with the most up-to-date of facilities. Set in its own 10-hectare (26-acre) lakeside park, it is still the most fabled, luxurious and expensive hotel in the whole lakes region.

Grand Hotel Villa d'Este statuary.

Trentino speck for sale, Saturday market, Salò.

A TASTE OF THE LAKES

Look in your supermarket trolley, and whether it's risotto rice from Verona, polenta from Bergamo, Gorgonzola from Milan, or even a bottle of San Pellegrino water – chances are something will have come from the Italian Lakes.

With the Po Valley to the south and the Alps to the north, the location of the Italian Lakes means that there is almost nothing that isn't produced in this glorious region, and its specialities are alive and well. Fertile river valleys are ideal for fruit-growing, and mellow climates produce ideal conditions for vineyards and olive-growing. Lombardy is one of the richest agricultural regions in Italy. The arborio rice paddies in the southern regions and the cornfields of Bergamo not only provide the key ingredients for the local staples – risotto and polenta – but also help to feed the thousands of cows and pigs which help to create the wonderful cheeses, hams and sausages with which they are flavoured.

Alla Milanese

For such a grand city, Milan has some very simple specialities – *minestrone alla Milanese*, a huge full-meal soup of vegetables, rice and bacon, and *osso buco*, braised veal shanks slow-cooked in a white wine and vegetable stew, traditionally served with *risotto alla Milanese*, with saffron and ham. It is said that the recipe was invented by an apprentice glazier working on the Duomo in the 16th century. The lad was so fond of the expensive yellow saffron that he put a handful into every batch of stained glass he mixed. His colleagues joked that he would even put it into his food. At his wedding, he did just that – and so the golden risotto was born.

> "The cooking of Italy is really the cooking of its regions, regions that until 1861 were separate, independent and usually hostile states" – Marcella Hazan.

Osso buco.

The *cotoletta alla Milanese*, a simple, breaded veal escalope, is better to known to most of the world as the Vienna Schnitzel, but was first mentioned in a Lombard cookbook in 1134. It was discovered here by Austrian Field Marshal Radetsky in the 19th century and taken back to the imperial court, where it was renamed.

Milan's other great export is *panettone*, somewhere between a bread and a cake, flavoured with dried fruit and candied citrus peel. It is usually served over the Christmas season with a sweet wine or *crema di mascarpone*, made from mascarpone cheese (originally a speciality of the region), eggs and a sweet liqueur such as *Disaronno Amaretto*, the almond liqueur which comes from Saronno, a few kilometres outside

Milan. Legend has it that it was invented in 1525 by a beautiful local innkeeper who fell in love with the great artist Bernardino Luini while posing for him as the model for the Madonna in his fresco of the *Adoration of the Magi* in the Basilica of Santa Maria delle Grazie, Saronno. She is still on view in the church, and her concoction is now the world's best-selling Italian liqueur – success all round.

The valleys of Varese

Up the road, in Varese province, Cantello, near the Swiss border, is renowned for its white aspara-

e buoni (ugly and good), made of egg whites, almonds, hazelnuts, sugar and vanilla, created in 1878 by a confectioner in Gavirate on Lake Varese. These became so essential that luminaries from Queen Elena to Giuseppe Verdi would make a detour to buy them.

The Venetian influence

Across the centre of the region, the historic influence of Venice is strong, and appetites are hearty. Bergamo and Brescia specialise in the sort of food that fills you up: *casconcelli* (ravioli with bacon and melted butter) and *foiade*

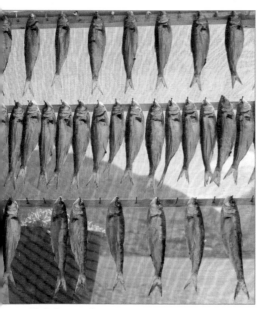

Fish drying on Lake Como.

Risotto ai funghi (mushroom risotto).

gus with a rosy tip. Laveno Mombello on Lake Maggiore specialises in honey, producing delicately scented *millefiori* honey, from the pollen of many flowers, acacia honey, perfect for eating with sheep's cheeses and fresh fruit, and strongly perfumed, dark chestnut honey, ideal for eating with goats' cheese or for use in cooking.

In the mountains of the Val Veddasca area, they produce "violins" – hams made from the thighs of semi-wild goats or sheep, salted and flavoured with garlic, red wine and juniper and hung for up to six months, which end up shaped roughly like a violin, with the knife held like a bow for slicing.

Possibly the best-known local delicacy is a roughly hewn little pastry known as *brutti*

FRESHWATER FISH

All of the lakes provide an excellent source of freshwater fish, particularly shad *(agonia)*, often salted and dried as *curadura*, and then soaked in vinegar as *missoltini*; perch *(persico)*; whitebait *(lavarelli)*; eel *(anguilla)*, traditionally served with dried mushrooms and anchovy fillets; pike *(luccio)*; chub *(cavedano)*, frequently used for pâtés; tench *(tinca)*, often oven-baked *(al forno)*; and trout *(carpione)*.

Fish also comes grilled, fried and stewed, in soup or risotto, or with polenta or pasta. The coast is just over an hour's drive away, so there is also plenty of excellent seafood nearby.

(pasta with porcini mushrooms). Above all, this is where you eat polenta – great buckets of it, served with everything, including *cotechini* (spiced sausage). In the ultra-rich *polenta taragna*, it is mixed with butter and cheese; in *polenta e uccelletti*, it is served with kebabs of small birds (possibly larks and thrushes) threaded onto a skewer, head and all, with sage, pork and pancetta. Polenta is also served with the less alarming *uccelli scappati* (pork wrapped in sage leaves) – check which you are ordering – and even with horse (*cavallo*) or donkey (*asino*). Both appear on the menu increasingly

(see page 116) leading into the lighter wines of Trentino. But the land around Lake Garda is ideally suited to olives. Garda oil is greeny-gold and delicately scented, that of Valpolicella darker with a slightly lemony aftertaste. Both merit DOP status and are taken seriously enough that you can do olive oil tastings.

Food is taken so seriously that even the radicchio (red-leaf chicory) gets its own DOP, while the top-quality Vialone Nano rice, grown on the plains around Verona, has a dedicated route (www.stradadelriso.it) and a fair. The 20-day Fiera del Riso at Isola della Scala (www.isolafiere.it)

Myriad ice cream flavours at a gelateria.

frequently as you work your way east towards the Veneto, so watch out if you are squeamish.

If that hasn't filled you up, follow it with *polenta osei* – sweet sponge cakes, coated with sugar and polenta and topped with chocolate birds. After all that, you may need something to help the liver, such as the medicinal waters of *San Pellegrino* (see page 184), just up the road from Bergamo, which now also find their way onto restaurant tables around the world.

Around Lake Garda

Heading east, more and more of the land is given over to vineyards – with the great wines of the Franciacorta (see page 164), Garda (see page 132), Bardolino, Valpolicella and Soave

began life as a village festival in 1967. Today, it attracts around 500,000 people, and around 350,000 risottos are cooked along with a great deal of other food, wine and merrymaking.

Verona itself has more than its fair share of gourmet restaurants, but look for its traditional dishes and they are not for the faint-hearted – or the vegetarian. The city's flagship sausage, *soppressa*, is made from roughly minced pork aged for up to a year with spices, garlic and red wine. Another traditional dish, *bollito misto* (mixed boiled meats), is served with *peará* sauce, made from bone marrow, beef stock, Parmesan, breadcrumbs and black pepper. According to legend, a medieval tyrant killed his father-in-law and forced his wife, Dona Lombarda, to drink from

Founded in Piedmont in 1986, Italy's Slow Food Movement now has over 100,000 members in 150 countries. Its aim is "to rediscover the flavours of regional cooking and banish the degrading effects of fast food".

her father's skull. She was totally unable to eat until the court chef tempted her back to health with this delicious sauce. Once fully back to strength, she had her husband assassinated. The meat comes with plenty of stodge – gnocchi

pickles, sauerkraut and bean salads. The local *speck*, unlike the slices of fat common further south, is small square pieces of pork, cured with garlic, bay, juniper, pepper and herbs, then lightly smoked. It is eaten for breakfast, as a lunchtime antipasto or just as a snack. *Stinco* doesn't really live up to its name – this is simply a shank of meat. For some reason, gnocchi with spinach, served with sage and butter, are known locally as *strangolapreti* ("strangled priests"). There are wonderful forest mushrooms, while the warmer areas of Lake Garda are perfect fruit- growing territory, providing apples, figs and even the famous lem-

A selection of local cheeses at Salò's Saturday market.

(potato dumplings), served to the whole city during carnival (see page 104), *bigoli* (a hefty pasta, often served with anchovies or duck) and *pasta e fagioli* (pasta and beans).

The Austrian legacy

To the north, in Trentino, the food changes yet again, the mountains supplying game, from partridge and pheasant to wild boar and venison, while the region's long Austro-Hungarian heritage has left its mark on the kitchen with dishes such as *canederli*, large dumplings made with bread, stuffed with liver or even prunes, and served with *brood* (broth) or *goulasch* (a rich, meat-based sauce); and *wurstl*, sausages similar to frankfurters.

Smoked meats are common, served with

ons that gave Limone sul Garda its name.

With a Germanic heritage, Trentino really wins out when it comes to desserts. Italian ice cream may be the best in the world, but here you have all the benefit of the *gelaterie* alongside Austrian *strudels* (spicy apple pie) and *sacher torte* (chocolate cake), and home-grown delicacies such as *fregolotta* (a light crispy cake made from flour, sugar and almonds).

Local cheeses

The rich green grass of the whole lakes region makes for perfect dairy country and a huge variety of local cheeses. Although incredibly famous, Bel Paese, meaning "beautiful country", is a relative newcomer, created by Egidio Galbani in

1906. He wanted to give Italy a light soft cheese similar to those he had tasted in France, and named it after a book by Abbot Antonio Stoppani, published in 1875 and popular amongst the nationalist middle classes. Made in Melzo, near Milan, its mild flavour has assured its popularity in nurseries across the world.

Something with a little more bite and age is the local rich and creamy blue cheese, Gorgonzola, made from whole cows' milk, that has been produced in the region since at least the 9th century. Now named after the area in which it is produced, it was originally known as *stracchino*

Across in the Veneto, Grana Padano serves much the same purpose and is used locally instead of Parmesan which it closely resembles, although a little sweeter. Made of unpasteurised cows' milk and formed into 36kg (80lb) wheels, it is aged for about 20 months before eating.

Add to these less well-known but equally delicious cheeses such as formai de Mut and Branzi from the Brembana Valley of Bergamo, Monte Veronese from the Verona region, which comes in three strengths, and the soft goats' cheese, formaggella del Luinese, from Luino on Lake Maggiore, and you have a cheeseboard to die for.

Grappa, the Trentino hooch.

after the word for "tired", as it was made after the long journey back from the summer pastures in the high Alps.

North of Bergamo, Val Taleggio has also been producing a cheese for about 1,000 years that has now burst out into the factories and supermarkets. Taleggio is a soft cows' cheese that strangely smells much stronger than it tastes. There are several strengths – all of them utterly delicious.

Probably the most famous cheese to come out of the Brescia region is Bagòss, a deep-yellow, hard cows' cheese that is rubbed with linseed oil and develops some holes and a slightly grainy texture. It can be eaten raw but is mainly used for cooking, as its rather strong, rather harsh flavour mellows as it melts and is perfect for the pot.

GRAPPA

The regions of the Veneto and Trentino are the foremost producers of the famous firewater known as *grappa*. It is made by distilling the *pomace* (grape skins, stems and seeds) that remains after pressing wine. A true grappa is clear, aged in the bottle for about six months *(giovane)*, although some, aged in wood *(affinata)* for up to 18 months, take on a faint tinge of colour from the barrel. A good grappa should be served chilled, in a long-stemmed flute or tulip glass. At 80 to 140 percent proof, it was traditionally drunk as an after-dinner digestive, sometimes added to coffee in a *caffè corretto*, although it is now also drunk like vodka, icy cold in shots.

The rooftops of fair Verona.

On the boat to Isola di San Giulio.

ORIENTATION

In this detailed guide to the region, the principal
sites are cross-referenced by numbers to the maps.

*Vineyards in Tonale,
Val Camonica.*

While most visitors choose to stay on one of the
Italian Lakes, one of the joys of the region is that
it is small enough for you to visit the others, the
great historic cities and the beautiful countryside between
the lakes on easy day trips. It is only an hour by train from
Desenzano del Garda to Milan.

Fabulous Verona, the city of Romeo and Juliet, grand
opera and medieval mansions, makes an ideal base.
Through the winelands of Valpolicella, you arrive at Lake
Garda, the largest and most touristy of the lakes and a
place of vineyards, lemon trees and olive groves, thanks to
its balmy Mediterranean climate. North of here, a change
of scene is provided by the mountains of Trentino, home of brown bears,
hearty Germanic cuisine, gleaming ski slopes and the charming walled city
of Trento. Further west are two appealing cities:
Brescia boasts a clutch of excellent museums
and is within reach of wild Lake Iseo, the Franciacorta winelands and the fascinating ancient
pictographs of Val Camonica; while clifftop Bergamo is all Venetian walls and cobbled alleys.

Porta Brà, Verona.

Heading slightly northwest, the stars and
their comet tail of celebrity spotters regard Lake
Como as the jewel in the crown. Como, Bellagio
and Menaggio are the biggest draws, but little-
explored towns such as Varenna also offer vistas
to swoon over. West again is pretty Lake Lugano,
much of which is actually in Switzerland: carry
your passport with you on forays into the glorious mountainous landscape around the lake.

Wedged in the triangle between Como, Maggiore and Lugano is Varese,
with its gardens, hillside chapels and quiet charm. The shores of magnificent Lake Maggiore offer further treats for garden-lovers, not to mention
an abundance of peaceful, palm-lined promenades and serene natural
beauty. Nearby, magical little Lake Orta is well worth exploring, low-key
and relaxed, with a jewel of a town in Orta San Giulio. Finally, metropoli-
tan Milan provides an exciting start or finish to a Lakes trip: hole up in
a designer hotel, treat yourself in a swanky day spa, or do as the locals do
and shop till you drop.

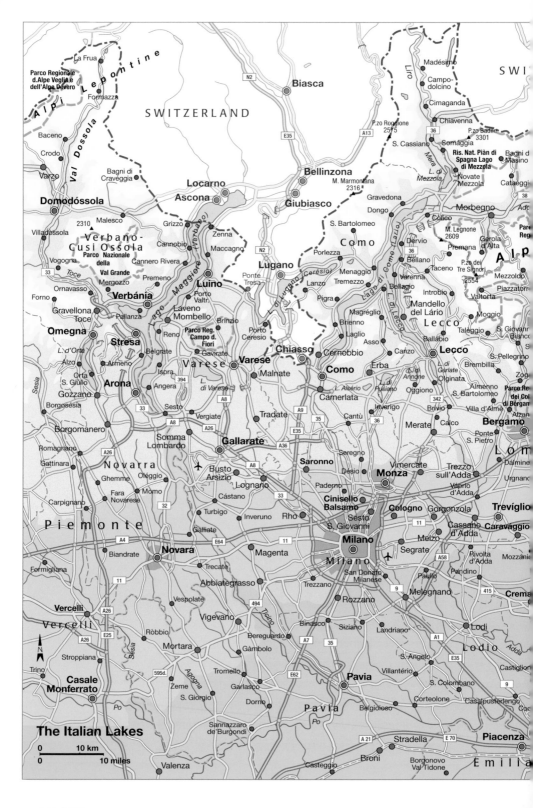

The Italian Lakes

0   10 km
0   10 miles

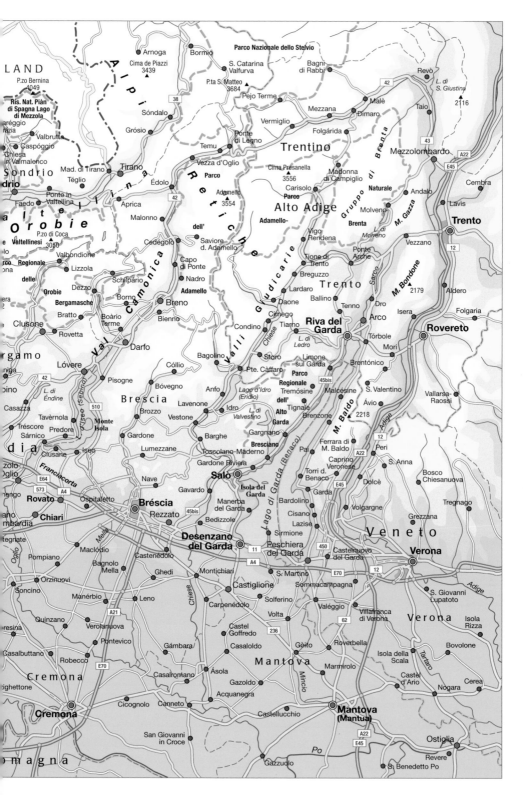

Verona on a winter's day.

VERONA

From its grand Roman amphitheatre to its elegant medieval and Renaissance palaces, Verona is an enticing city, with some of the finest piazzas and monuments in Italy, and great dining and nightlife.

Forget for a moment the lure of Romeo and Juliet and the appeal of a night at the opera in the famous Arena. Even forget a city that takes food so seriously that its surrounding restaurants have won a clutch of Michelin stars. And ignore the Valpolicella and Soave vineyards on the doorstep. Even without all that, Verona is special, one of the most beautiful cities in Italy.

Verona is thought to have been first colonised by Venetians in the 3rd century BC, becoming a Roman colony in 89 BC. Theodoric, king of the Ostrogoths, chose to make his home and capital here in the 5th century, and it remained the seat of power for the Carolingian King Pepin. In the 11th century, it came under German rule and in 1136 became a city state, with the Scaliger (della Scala) family taking control in 1277 and ruling until they were ousted by the Viscontis in 1387. In 1405, Verona voluntarily joined the Venetian Republic, remaining there until 1796 when Napoleon invaded. After his defeat, it came under Austrian rule until independence in 1866 but then sustained heavy damage during both world wars.

Today, all traces of the damage mended, contemporary Verona is an aesthetically pleasing swathe of pale pink stone curling along the banks

The much-loved Madonna Verona on Piazza delle Erbe.

of the River Adige, its streets paved with precious marble and lined with discreet restaurants and chic designer shops. It has a population of around 250,000 and lives on a mix of tourism and industry.

The Arena

Start your tour in the splendidly named **Piazza Brà** (meaning something big or wide), a huge open space surrounding the **Arena ❶** (Piazza Brà; tel: 045-800 5151; Tue–Sun 8.30am– 7.30pm, Mon 1.30–7.30pm). Built in

Main Attractions
Arena
Casa di Giulietta
Piazza delle Erbe
Torre dei Lamberti
Basilica di Santa Anastasia
Duomo di Santa Maria
  Matricolare
Castelvecchio
Basilica di San Zeno
  Maggiore
Tomba di Giulietta

TIP

Throughout the opera season, an optional extra is to book up for the early evening Anteprima Opera (Introduction to the Opera; www.anteprima opera.it) in the fabulous church of Santa Maria in Chiavica, where musicians from the opera company give you an introduction to the opera (in Italian and English) that is being performed that night, together with a tasting of local wines.

the early 1st century AD, this amphitheatre was designed to seat 22,000 – the city's whole population at the time. It is the third-largest in Italy (after the Colosseum and Capua), an ellipse measuring 152 metres (500ft) by 123 metres (400ft), and one of the best-preserved in the world, with two of its three rings of arches intact. Only the topmost tiers of seats have vanished into history, destroyed by a series of earthquakes in the 12th century, leaving the 31 metres (100ft) high "Ala" (wing), a series of four arches to show how it would have looked.

Unlike many, this amphitheatre has been used as a place of entertainment throughout its life, but the type of entertainment has been extremely varied, from gladiatorial combat in ancient Rome to trial by ordeal and public executions during the early Middle Ages – nearly 200 heretic Paterines were burned at the stake here in 1278. In 1276, an act was passed making it the city brothel for nearly 250 years, but by 1580 it was being used for tournaments. The last of these was held in 1716, and after

that there was a parade of circus and comedy, theatre and dance, horse racing and gymnastics, and even hot-air balloon flights and Buffalo Bill's Wild West Show. It is still the home of a summer-long opera festival and occasional rock concerts.

An arch between the restaurants along the side of the square leads to the **Museo Lapidario Maffeiano ❷** (Piazza Brà 28; tel: 045-590 087; Tue–Sun 8.30am–2pm), established in 1745 and one of Europe's oldest public museums, devoted to Greek, Etruscan, early Venetian and Roman inscriptions.

At the north end of the square, **Via Mazzini** is a narrow pedestrianised road, lined with designer boutiques and frequented by ladies wearing the latest Gucci or Armani. Great for window-shopping and also the route up to your next must-see destination.

The star-crossed lovers

As the setting for Shakespeare's *Romeo and Juliet*, Verona continues to attract lovers, unconcerned about the level of fiction in the story. There were no Montagues and Capulets, but there

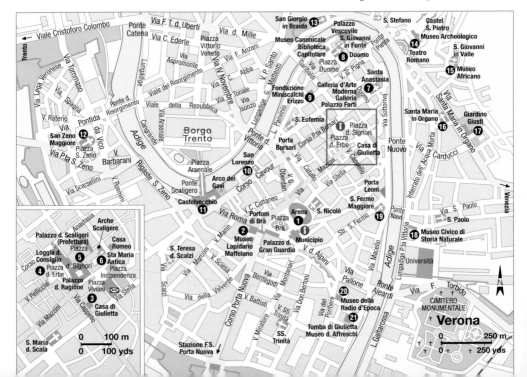

were Montecchi and Capuleti. Some say that the Montecchi supported the Guelphs (Pope) and the Capuleti the Ghibellines (Holy Roman Emperor) in the violent civil war during the 14th century; others say that they all got on perfectly well. Whatever the case, they are as close as anyone can come to a real-life prototype for *Romeo and Juliet*. In 1935, Antonio Avena, then director of the city's museums, realised that the city could be on to a good thing, following the success of the new Hollywood blockbuster version of the story, starring Norma Shearer and Leslie Howard, and doctored up the Capuleti House as the **Casa di Giulietta** ❸ (Juliet's House; Via Cappello 23; tel: 045-803 4303; Tue–Sun 8.30am–7.30pm, Mon 1.30–7.30pm, last entry 6.45pm), furnishing the house, adding a fake balcony (actually an old sarcophagus) and a bronze statue of Juliet by Nereo Costantini. It is eccentric to say the least – for some reason, it has become customary to rub Juliet's right breast if you are wishing for a new lover – and she is very shiny! The walls are covered in graffiti

declarations of love, the courtyard is heaving with people, but relatively few pay to go into the genuine 12th- (not 14th-) century townhouse, furnished with Romeo and Juliet costumes, bed, and so on. The Dal Cappello coat of arms (a cap) can be seen above the inner archway of the courtyard.

Piazza delle Erbe

Just along the road, the **Piazza delle Erbe** ❹ (Herb Market) has been the focus of the city's power and wealth since it was the Roman forum. With a small, touristy market in the centre and cafés round the edges, it is also surrounded by stunning old buildings, amongst the most important of which are the **Torre del Gardello** (on the left, closed to the public), an older tower restored with its clock added by the Scaligeri in 1363–70; the Baroque **Palazzo Maffei** with roof terrace and its row of statues of the gods; and the **Casa Mazzanti** with jolly 16th-century mythological frescoes.

First built in 1172, the brick-and-tufa **Torre dei Lamberti** (Via della Costa; tel: 045-927 3027; daily 9.30am–8.30pm,

The walls of Juliet's home are covered with declarations of love, some in graffiti, others on paper, some even on old chewing gum, while a team of lovestruck volunteers at the Juliet Club (www.juliet club.com) undertake to answer every one of the thousands of letters which pour in each year (addressed to Juliet, Verona).

Juliet's balcony.

ROMEO AND JULIET

In 1597, William Shakespeare wasn't the first or the last to tell this tale of teenage hormones gone mad (or the greatest love story ever told, depending on your point of view). He got the idea from Arthur Brooke, who wrote it in bad rhyme in 1562 in *The Tragical History of Romeus and Juliet*. He in turn probably translated Matteo Bandello's *Novelle* (1554) based on Luigi da Porto's *Istoria novellamente ritrovata di due Nobili Amanti* (1531). A captain in the Venetian guard, da Porto claimed it was a true story which he had heard from a Veronese bowman in his company, but it bore an uncanny resemblance to the story of Mariotto and Gianozza, told by Masuccio Salernitano, in *Il Novelino* (1476), and set in Siena.

Since then, of course, the tale has continued with George Cukor's film starring Norma Shearer and Leslie Howard (1935), Franco Zeffirelli's version with Leonard Whiting and Olivia Hussey (1968), hit Broadway musical West Side Story (1957) and its 1961 film version with Nathalie Wood and Richard Beymer in the lead roles, Baz Luhrmann's MTV-esque 1996 effort (roughly recognisable as Shakespeare) starring Leonardo DiCaprio and Claire Danes, and countless other adaptations. What they all have in common is that they are entirely fictional – whatever the Verona tourist office may say!

The Arena Festival

One of the greatest open-air music festivals in the world, in a 2,000-year-old stadium, based on some of the finest music ever written.

There are two hours to go, the doors are thrown open and the first eager opera-lovers begin to climb the worn stone steps to the highest rings of the Verona Arena. Outside, as crowds gather at the café tables in the Piazza Brà, the evening sun streams down onto the Arena, whose arches gleam as red as the blood once spilled on its sawdust-strewn floor. In the lowest tunnel, where lions once prowled in cages and gladiators stood in chains, opera singers stand, waiting to be transformed into Egyptian warriors. With 300 men and 80 women in the cast of *Aida*, it takes two hours to get them all through make-up.

In the summer of 1913, tenor Giovanni Zenatello and theatrical impresario Ottone Rovato decided to celebrate the centenary of the birth of Verdi in style by staging *Aida* in the Arena di Verona. To see it now, they would be astonished by what they had started. This is big business – the world's biggest open-air lyrical theatre festival – with around 550,000 people attending 50 performances each summer and an annual turnover of $500 million. There are 350 permanent staff and 1,400 hired for the season, with talent pouring in from around the world, led by names such as Franco Zeffirelli and José Carreras.

While the Arena could originally seat 22,000, these days numbers are pegged at 14,100 for security. *Aida* is performed every year, *Nabucco* every one to two years and *Carmen* every second year, with the rest of the programme made up of old faithfuls from the *Barber of Seville* to *Madame Butterfly*.

The opera festival runs from June to August, but the entertainment continues year-round, with a winter opera and ballet season at the Teatro Filarmonico and a concert season from October to April at the Stagione Sinfonica.

As the evening draws in, candles flicker into life around the arena and the dark-robed chorus slip onto the shadowed stage. Singing is without microphones, and even these superb acoustics struggle a little, but the atmosphere is electric and hours later, as Aida and Radames are walled up into the vault for the 90th season and the last tragic notes die away, the audience forgets the cold stone seats and chilly midnight air and wants it all to start again.

For tickets visit the website, www.arena.it.

A spectacular production of Aida keeps the audience spellbound.

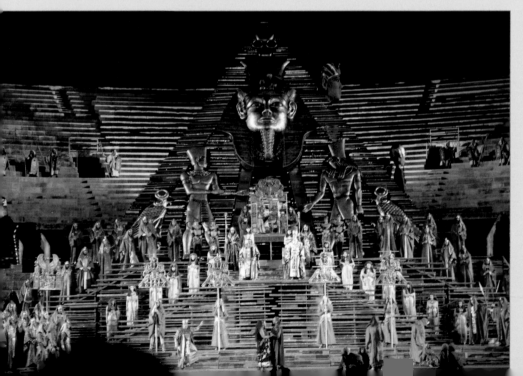

June–Sept Fri–Sat until midnight, Sun until 10pm) was struck by lightning in 1403 and restored between 1448 and 1464. Two bells were later added – one as a fire alarm, the other for calling meetings of the city council. The clock was added in 1779. You can climb up the stairs (the tower is 84 metres/276ft tall) or do it the easy way and take the lift, only walking the last couple of floors past the bell chamber. The views from the top are magnificent.

The Scaligeri legacy

When the Scaligeri first tightened their grip on the city in the 13th century, they set up their home and seat of government in what had been an insignificant piazza just to the north of the main square. It was soon transformed by fabulous architecture and became known as the **Piazza dei Signori 5**.

The rather formidable building with the battlements is the **Palazzo degli Scaligeri**, first built in the 12th century, but massively altered over the years and now home to the prefecture. The very pretty yellow building with the arches is the fine Renaissance **Loggia del Consiglio** (1476–93), probably built by Fra' Giocondo and topped by statues of Roman luminaries, including local boys Catullus and Pliny. It used to be the city's assembly hall.

The statue of Dante, by Ugo Zannoni, was erected in 1865 to celebrate the 600th anniversary of the writer's birth (he lived for a number of years in the piazza). The **Caffè Dante**, which opened in 1863, claims to be the city's oldest. It still has its 19th-century decor (but with 21st-century prices).

Excavations of the **Scavi Scaligeri** (Scaligeri Tombs; Cortile del Tribunale; tel: 045-800 7490; closed for restoration), in the basement of the Scaligeri palace, have uncovered a Verona timeline, from the Romans onwards. The ruins are also used for photographic exhibitions. Off the square, the **Cortile Mercato Vecchio** is the inner courtyard of the Palazzo del Comune, with a magnificent 15th-century Gothic staircase.

Around the corner, the Romanesque church of **Santa Maria Antica 6** (Via S. Maria Antica; daily 7.30am–12.30pm, 3.30–7pm; free) was the Scaligeri family chapel, built in 1185 over a smaller 7th-century church. Surrounding it are the **Arche Scaligere** (always open; free), the tombs of many of the Scaligeri rulers, including Cangrande I (died 1329), whose equestrian statue tops the church itself, the arch of Mastino II (1351) – his equestrian statue standing under a canopy surrounded by the Virtues – and the florid tomb of Consignorio by Bonino da Campione and Broaspini (1374), encircled by warrior-saints.

Nearby you come to the next spot on the Romeo-and-Juliet trail. Romeo Montague, for all the feuding and swagger, really was the boy next door – **Casa di Romeo**, also called **Montecchi House**, was supposedly on Via Arche Scaligere, just across the park from Juliet. The 13th-century house, once home to the counts of Cagnolo Nogarola, close followers of the Scaligeri, is in poor condition and closed to the public.

WHERE

Monuments in the Piazza delle Erbe include: the Madonna Verona, a statue dating back to 380 (the fountain was added in 1368); the Tribuna or Berlina, where all public officials swore their oath of office; and a Venetian lion of St Mark, actually a 19th-century copy – the column is original, but the statue was destroyed in the 18th century.

Lion of St Mark in Piazza delle Erbe.

Dante Alighieri lived in Verona for several years while on the run because of his political problems (he had been exiled from Florence during the Guelph-Ghibelline conflict). Parts of his masterpiece, Il Inferno, are based on the city and surrounding countryside.

The fountain in the Piazza delle Erbe can be a godsend on a hot day.

Basilica di Santa Anastasia

To the north is the **Basilica di Santa Anastasia** ❼ (Piazza Sant'Anastasia; tel: 045-592 813; Mar–Oct Mon–Sat 10am–6pm, Sun 1–6pm, Nov–Feb Mon–Sat 10am–1pm 1.30–4pm, Sun 1–5pm), which was funded by the Scaligeri family. Started in 1290 and completed in 1481, it is the largest church in Verona. Its bare facade was never completed, belying the glory of the art inside – each of its 16 chapels are lavishly adorned with fine altarpieces and frescoes, culminating in Pisanello's fragile fresco of *St George Saving the Princess from the Dragon*. Look out for the two holy-water stoups just inside the entrance: known as 'gobbi' (hunchbacks), each features a stooped figure bearing the weight on his shoulders.

By now you may want a breather. There are a couple of good cafés in Piazza Brà Molinari behind the church and more near the Duomo. Opposite the church, **Corso Sant' Anastasia** is an interesting shopping street that links back to Piazza delle Erbe. It also has a couple of excellent delis if you want to buy ingredients for a picnic.

The Duomo

A whole complex of buildings surrounds the **Duomo di Santa Maria Matricolare** ❽ (Cathedral, Piazza Duomo; tel: 045-800 8813; Mon–Sat 10am–6pm, Sun 1–6pm). The church itself was started in 1120, and rises in graceful stripes of tufa with white and rose-coloured marble, from the Romanesque in the lower section, to Gothic higher up, and into the 16th-century mid-section by Sanmicheli. The bell tower was never finished. Inside, the whole church was given a Gothic make over between 1444 and 1513, its sidewalls and chapels lush with frescoes and paintings.

Next door, the little church of **San Giovanni in Fonte** (same hours as the Duomo) was once the baptistery, founded in the 8th century, but dating mainly to the 12th, with a superb octagonal font (*c.*1200) carved from a single block of rose marble, showing scenes from the New Testament. Also nearby are the **chapterhouse and cloisters**, built in 1140. The arches on the east are original, those to the west were restored after World War II. Fragments

of the mosaic floor of the early Christian basilica have also been uncovered.

The cathedral treasures are all held in the **Museo Canonicale** (Piazza Duomo 29, entry from the cloister; tel: 338-902 4923; open for guided tours only; booking essential); highlights include a relief sculpture of *SS Ermagora e Fortunato* by a Como artist (1120), and several 15th–16th-century paintings. But the greatest items live in Europe's oldest surviving library, the **Biblioteca Capitolare** (Tue–Sat 9.30am–12.30pm, Tue, Fri also 4–6pm), founded in the 5th century AD, which contains many priceless early manuscripts including letters from Cicero to Brutus; the Capitolare Gospels, a 5th-century gospel written in silver and gold on parchment soaked in purple; and the 6th-century "Verona Riddle", the earliest written Italian (as opposed to Latin).

To the Castle

If you want to head back to the Arena the quick way, take the little road just in front of the Duomo, then turn left and right onto via San Mamaso. Here, the cavernous halls of the old Palazzo Miniscalchi now house the **Fondazione Miniscalchi Erizzo** ❾ (Via San Mamaso 2A; tel: 045-803 2484; Mon–Fri, 11am–1pm, 3.30–7pm; www.museo-miniscalchi.it), with archaeological remains, 16th-century drawings, Renaissance bronzes, marbles and ivories.

A little further south, the quietly elegant church of **San Lorenzo** ❿ (Corso Cavour 28; tel: 045-805 0000; Mar–Oct Mon–Sat 10am–6pm, Sun 1–6pm, Nov–Feb Mon–Sat 10am–1pm, 1.30–4pm, Sun 1–5pm) was built in the early 12th century over the remains of a 5th-century church. Typical of the local Romanesque style, it uses striped brick and tufa rock, while two round towers house stairs leading to a rare surviving women's gallery (a separate area where women used to pray).

As you walk south towards the castle, you pass the **Arco dei Gavi**, a 1st-century AD Roman triumphal arch that later became used as a city gate. Destroyed by Napoleonic forces in 1805, it was moved from its original site near the clock tower of the Castelvecchio and reconstructed where it stands now.

The Tribuna on the Piazza delle Erbe, looking towards the Palazzo Maffei.

The stripey facade of the Duomo.

Detail from the 12th-century font in the church of San Giovanni in Fonte.

Born out of the family squabbles of the Scaligeri, the **Castelvecchio** ⓫ (Corso Castelvecchio 2; tel: 045-806 2611; Tue–Sun 8.30am–7.30pm, Mon 1.30–7.30pm) was built by Cangrande II after his half-brother Fregnano headed a revolt against his tyrannical rule. Construction began in 1354, under the control of Guglielmo Bevilacqua, but the walls and the German mercenaries with which Cangrande surrounded himself proved useless. On 14 December 1359, he was killed by assassins working for his brother, Cansignorio, who took power over the city, moving into the urban fortress and ruling with an iron fist. It continued to be the seat of power throughout the Visconti and Venetian rules, eventually becoming a museum in the 1920s. Take time to explore the towers and tunnels of the castle itself before you enter the museum in the "royal" palace, the Scaligeri family residence.

Aerial view of the Castelvecchio.

The collection is extremely rich in medieval, Renaissance and Mannerist works, all beautifully presented, and deserves plenty of time to explore. Highlights include the Longobard

jewellery in Room 1, the International Gothic collection in Room 11, including the *Madonna of the Quail* by Pisanello, several glorious paintings by Andrea Mantegna in Room 19, and those by Veronese and Tintoretto in Room 23. And that's just the tip of the iceberg. Beside the castle, the castellated **Ponte Scaligero** is an exact replica of the bridge built as part of the castle defences in 1355 which spanned the river until blown up by the Germans in 1945. It was reopened in 1951.

Basilica di San Zeno Maggiore

Once you leave the heart of the *centro storico*, distances between sights grow, and it may be worth taking to the buses to save time and energy.

Bus no. 31 takes you to the **Basilica di San Zeno Maggiore** ⓬ (Piazza San Zeno; tel: 045-800 6120; Mar–Oct Mon–Sat 8.30am–6pm, Sun 12.30–6pm, Nov–Feb Mon–Sat 10am–1pm, 1.30–5pm, Sun 12.30–5pm), to the west of the Arena. San Zeno, the eighth bishop of Verona, died in 370, and the first church on the site was built over

his tomb. Between the 9th and 13th centuries, this grew into one of the finest and most powerful Romanesque abbeys in the region, but the community was devastated by plague in 1630 and the power of the abbey quashed by Venice in 1770. By 1831, only the basilica itself, sandwiched between the red abbey tower and free-standing campanile, remained standing. All three date back to the 12th century.

The relatively simple facade of the building is pierced by an elaborately sculpted porch and heavy bronze doors showing scenes from the Old and New Testaments, the miracles of San Zeno and the life of Theodoric. Above is a huge rose window, thought to be by Master Briolato, and also known as the "wheel of fortune". It is best admired from inside, under the sweeping keel-shaped wooden Gothic ceiling. Along the right wall are a number of fine 13th- and 14th- century frescoes. On the high altar stands a luminous *Triptych with Madonna and Saints* by Andrea Mantegna (1457–9). In the crypt, there are 49 11th-century columns, each with different highly imaginative capitals, leading to the shrine of St Zeno himself.

Across the river

North from the centre of town, near the Duomo, the **Ponte Pietra** (Stone Bridge) over the river is thought to have been named as early as 89 BC, when the original wooden crossing was replaced by a stone one. It has been replaced many times since, most recently in 1959, when much of the 1508 bridge has been blown up by the retreating Germans in 1945. The new version is a faithful copy.

On the far side, first turn left for the church of **San Giorgio in Braida** ⑬ (Lungadige San Giorgio; tel: 045-834 0232; daily; free), rebuilt by the Venetians in 1442 on the ruins of an 11th-century Benedictine monastery. The facade and bell tower were added in the 16th century, designed by Brugnoli, although some think it was designed by Sammicheli or even by Palladio. Inside, amongst many other paintings, there are two great treasures, *The Baptism of Christ* by Tintoretto above the main door and *The Martyrdom of St George* by Veronese, the city's greatest export.

TIP

The VeronaCard is an excellent money-saver, offering you free entry to most museums, churches and monuments in the city and free travel on local bus services within the city. There are 24- and 48-hour versions available (€18 and 22, respectively), on sale online (www.turismoverona. eu), at participating sights, the tourist office and some tobacconists and hotels.

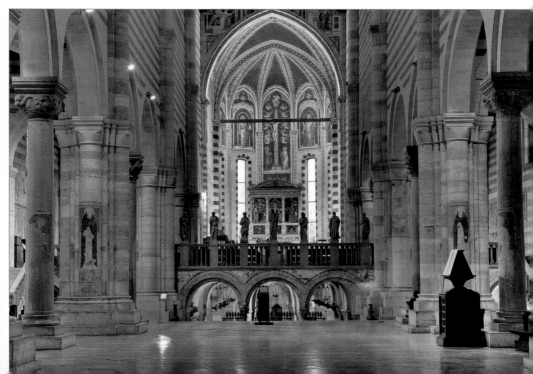

Basilica di San Zeno Maggiore.

Costumed participants at the Bacanal del Gnoco.

Roman Theatre

Now follow the river round to the **Teatro Romano e Museo Archeologico** 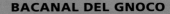 (Roman Theatre and Archaeology Museum; Rigaste Redentore 2; tel: 045-806 2611; Tue–Sun 8.30am–7.30pm, Mon 1.30–7.30pm), occupying a pleasing position on the hill. While the Arena was used for games and spectaculars, every Roman city would also have a theatre for plays and other cultural performances. Typically semicircular, they were often built into the hillside to save on the digging, and this one, constructed overlooking the river in the late 1st century BC, is no exception. It was lost under the city for years until a local archaeologist, Andrea Monga, purchased the site in 1830, demolished the houses on it and began the painstaking task of uncovering the Roman splendours beneath. It has been heavily restored and is back in use, staging concerts and performances during the summer.

At the eastern side of the theatre, the only building that Monga allowed to stand is the little 10th-century church of **SS Sirus e Libera**, heavily remodelled in the 17th century. Above the theatre, reached by a lift, the former Monastery of San Girolamo now houses the fully renovated **Archaeology Museum** (same hours and ticket as Teatro Romano), with a well-displayed collection of mosaics, statues and other bits of ancient Rome, while the church has some 15th- and 16th-century frescoes.

African art

Behind the theatre and rather out of context with the rest of the city, the **Museo Africano** 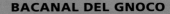 (Vicolo Pozzo 1; tel: 045-809 2199; www.museoafricano.org; Tue–Fri 9am–12.30pm, 2–5pm, Sat 9am–12.30pm, first and third Sun of the month 2–6pm) whisks you briskly across the continental divide to look at African art via its existential meaning and rites of passage – a very Italian way of dealing with it, and in stark contrast to the Renaissance frescoes and *gelaterie*.

To get back to the Italian mood, drop in next at the church of **Santa Maria in Organo** 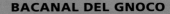 (Via Santa Maria in Organo; daily except Mass times; free), a Benedictine monastery first built during the Lombard era (still

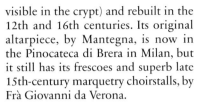
visible in the crypt) and rebuilt in the 12th and 16th centuries. Its original altarpiece, by Mantegna, is now in the Pinocateca di Brera in Milan, but it still has its frescoes and superb late 15th-century marquetry choirstalls, by Frà Giovanni da Verona.

Renaissance gardens

Nearby, the **Giardino Giusti** ⑰ (Via Giardino Giusti 2; tel: 045-803 4029; daily Apr–Sept 9am–8pm, Oct–Mar 9am–7pm) is generally regarded as one of the finest surviving Renaissance gardens in Italy, designed by Agostino Giusti in the late 16th century. Lawns surround the villa, while behind it a great avenue of cypress trees lead up the hill. To one side are wildly romantic woodlands leading to a cliff with mossy caves; on the other the formal bed and fountain pools of the Italian garden, with its panoramic views across the city and plethora of statuary between the flowers.

Natural history museum

Back down at the river, head south and just past the **Ponte Navi** (the Ships' Bridge) you will come to the **Museo Civico di Storia Naturale** ⑱ (Lungadige Porta Vittoria 9; tel: 045-807 9400; Mon–Thu 9am–5pm, Sat–Sun 2–6pm). Amidst the inevitable dead animals and insects, there is a particularly fine collection of plant and animal fossils, with many rare specimens from Bolca, on the slopes of the Lessinian mountains. The museum is housed in the 16th-century Palazzo Lavezzola-Pompei.

Benedictine church

Walk back up to the Ponte Navi and cross over the river to the church of **San Fermo Maggiore** ⑲ (20 Stradone S. Fermo; tel: 045-592 813; Mar–Oct Mon–Sat 10am–6pm, Sun 1–6pm, Nov–Feb Mon–Sat 10am–5pm, Sun 1–5pm), one of the most beautiful churches in Verona. The first church here dates back to the 8th century, but it was rebuilt by the Benedictines, starting in 1070 and only finished in 1313 by the Franciscans, while much of the interior is later still. Its chic stripey facade of white tufa and red brick blends the

WHERE

Tourist information: Via degli Alpini 9 (Piazza Brà), tel: 045-806 8680; Mon–Sat 10am–1pm, 2–6pm, Sun 10am–3pm; www.tourism.verona.it.

Teatro Roman e Museo Archeologico.

Juliet's tomb, another of the manufactured sights that have proved such a success for the city. The city celebrates Juliet's birthday on 16 September each year.

Giardino Giusti is one of Italy's finest surviving Renaissance gardens.

Romanesque and Gothic surprisingly harmoniously, while inside the fabulous wooden ship's-keel ceiling and rich 14th- and 15th-century frescoes around the walls miraculously escaped when the church was hit by a firebomb during World War II. Inside, note the 1495 Brenzoni Chapel behind the pulpit, Pisanello's magnificent fresco of *The Annunciation* on the left wall and the 11th-century capitals of the lower church.

Keep looking up at the fine aristocratic homes above the shop-fronts as you walk south along Stradone San Fermo and Stradone Maffei, then turn left and right.

There's one more little sidetrack for the mechanically minded. The **Museo della Radio d'Epoca 20** (Via del Pontiere 40; tel: 045-595 855; www.museo dellaradio.com; Mon–Fri 10am–6pm, Sat–Sun and holidays by appointment) is the passion of Alberto Chiantera. Designed as a homage to the radio, it has literally hundreds of sets, some of the equipment dating back to the days of Marconi, who was born in nearby Bologna in 1874.

Juliet's tomb

Most people, however, will make a beeline straight to the **Tomba di Giulietta e Museo degli Affreschi G.B. Cavalcaselle 21** (Via del Pontiere 35; tel: 045-800 0361; Tue–Sun 8.30am–7.30pm, Mon 1.30–7.30pm), set in the 13th-century convent of San Francesco al Corso. Here they will find a collection of 1st-century AD amphorae, medieval frescoes, 16th- and 19th-century sculptures, including two magnificent statues by Torquato della Torre, and some Renaissance and Baroque altar paintings. But the big draw is an empty red marble sarcophagus, said to have been Juliet's tomb. It is also here, according to legend, that the lovers were secretly married by Friar Lawrence. However, while the site was already being identified with Juliet in the 19th century, it was only in 1935 that it became part of the Romeo and Juliet trail. Today, romantics come to lay flowers, throw coins into the empty fountain, flowers into an empty grave, and sometimes to get married (civil weddings are conducted here).

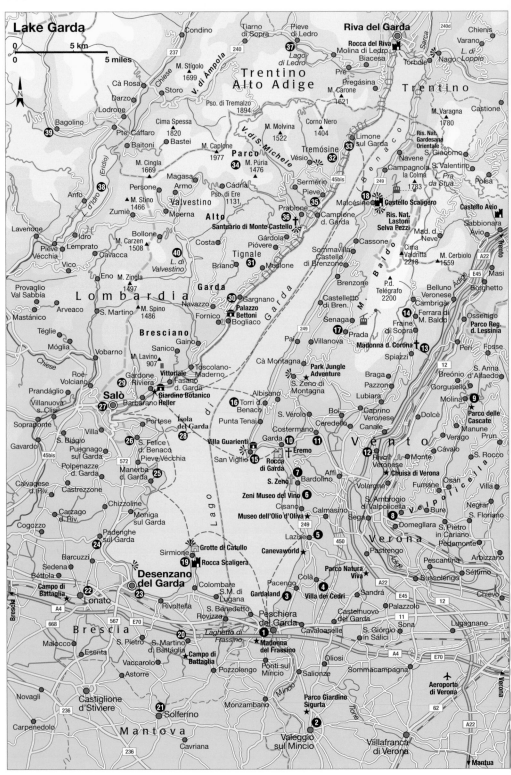

Lake Garda

0   5 km

0   5 miles

N

LAKE GARDA

Virgil wrote poems to Lake Garda, Kafka set a
novel here, Goethe got himself arrested,
Catullus and Mussolini set up house on its
shores – millions of tourists wish they could.

Cycling through Arco.

Garda was given its name in the Middle Ages,
a reference to the guardian rocks along its
fortress-like northern shores. To the ancient
Romans it was known far more benignly as Lake Benacus (the Beneficent); the alternative name Benaco is
still used to this day.

The largest lake in Italy, it is 51km (31 miles) long
(Riva to Peschiera) and up to 17km (10.5 miles) wide
at its widest point (Lazise to Moniga). It covers an
area of 370 sq km (143 sq miles), and stands at 65
metres (213ft) above sea level. The lake has a coastline
158km (98 miles) long.

Created by glaciers, Garda reaches a maximum
depth of 346 metres (1,135ft). It is effectively an
inland fjord, the high walls of the northern lake carved out by the action
of the ice, the great low, fertile bowl at
the southern end moulded by the erosion
that spilled out into a vast arc, building
a natural dam. The main river flowing
into the lake in the north, between Riva
and Torbole, is the Sarca. To the south,
the Mincio flows out from the lake at
Peschiera.

The mountains to the north protect the
lake's bowl from the chill Alpine winter,
creating a mini-Mediterranean climate
of indigo waters where lemon trees, olive
groves and vineyards can thrive.

Now, Garda is divided between three
provinces, which are based on historic
empires. Its eastern shore has now
become part of the Veneto province,
along with Venice, Verona and Valpolicella, while the western shore is
part of Brescia. The north shore is in Trentino, an area which was once
part of the Austro-Hungarian Empire until the end of World War I.

Soaking up the sunshine in Bogliaco.

The Monte Baldo cable car offers great panoramic views over Lake Garda.

EASTERN LAKE GARDA

Garda's eastern shore is a pleasure playground – whether you find your pleasure on a roller-coaster or a mountain bike, in a glass of Valpolicella or in the deep gold of the setting sun over old Venetian stone.

The drive towards Lake Garda's eastern shore from Verona or Brescia can be offputting and busy with traffic and superstores along the coast road, but don't be discouraged. You only have to drive a few kilometres to find an idyllic medieval village or a spectacularly crenellated castle covered in vines with a stunning view across the azure waters.

Peschiera del Garda ❶, in the far south, stands at the outlet of the lake. Although named as a fishing port, this has above all been a garrison town since Roman times, fortified by Venetian walls 2.3km (1.5 miles) long, later reinforced by Napoleon. The medieval Rocca Scaligera (castle), built on Roman foundations and turned into a Venetian dockyard, is joined by the Palazzina Storica (tel: 045-640 0600; closed at the time of writing, check website for re-opening times www.peschiera museo.it), built by the Austrians in the mid-19th century, and home to the official archives of the Risorgimento and World War I. The Battle of Solferino (see page 125) was fought nearby. The tourist office can advise on a walking tour of all the military buildings and battlements.

At the **Laghetto di Frassino**, a tiny glacial lake 3km (2 miles) out of town, the very elaborate **Santuario della Madonna del Frassino** marks

the spot where the Virgin miraculously appeared, enthroned in an ash tree, in 1510.

Parco Giardino Sigurtà

Further south, the small town of **Valeggio sul Mincio ❷** is renowned for its excellent restaurants, its Saturday market, and as home of one of the finest gardens in Italy, the **Parco Giardino Sigurtà** (Via Cavour 1; tel: 045-637 1033; www.sigurta.it; daily mid- to end-Mar, Oct–early Nov 9am–6pm, Apr–Sept 9am–7pm, last

Main Attractions
Parco Giardino Sigurtà
Gardaland
Lazise
Zeni Museo Del Vino
Monte Baldo
Castello Scaligero

Parco Giardino Sigurtà.

EAT

Give yourself over to the spirit of a jolly family night out at the Medieval Times banquet (Canevaworld; tel: 045-696 9900; www.canevaworld.it/ medievaltimes). Expect splendid court jesters, displays of horsemanship and other "medieval" entertainment.

entry one hour before closing). This huge park, now covering 56 hectares (138 acres), was first created in 1617 and was used by Napoleon III as his headquarters in 1859. As well as rolling parkland and great trees, the park is famous for massed flowerings of tulips, irises, roses, lilies and asters, and for its 40,000 topiary box bushes. If the walking gets too much, you can hire bicycles, golf carts or take the road train.

The Garda playground

Heading back up to the lake, there may be a moment when you think you have strayed from Italy into Orlando. The area just to the north of Peschiera has several theme parks. A forest of signboards directs you to large car parking areas, free shuttle buses run between Peschiera station, and all the parks and those on the water have their own jetties. **Garda-land ③** is the biggest, but others include **Canevaworld**, **Parco Natura Viva** at Bussolengo, a little further inland, and **Park Jungle Adventure** at San Zeno di Montagna, to

Lazise harbour.

the north (see page 120). Tucked among the big names are a multitude of smaller attractions offering arcade games and go-karts, medieval banquets, bouncy castles and slot machines – a great deal for families looking for entertainment.

The **Villa dei Cedri ④** (Piazza di Sopra 4, Colà di Lazise; tel: 045-759 0988; www.villadeicedri.it; Mon–Thu 9am–10pm, Fri, Sun 9am–11pm, Sat 9am–1am) is a great grown-up playground. It is a quiet thermal park with wonderfully landscaped grounds around two swimming lakes, one with a cave, with thermal water at a constant 37°C/98.6°F (body temperature). There are therapies and treatments, or you can just swim and sunbathe, and there are restaurants and accommodation on site as well.

Lazise

Only a few kilometres up the road, **Lazise ⑤** is a glorious little town – a sort of mini-Venice, its grandly crenellated town walls stamped by the Venetian lion. A Bronze Age village and a Roman *castrum*, it is a natural harbour

that became one of the most important towns on the lake in the Middle Ages. The beautifully preserved **castle** with five imposing towers was built in 1014, and restored by the Scaligeri in the 14th century. In the little harbour, the early 12th-century church of **San Nicolò** has some lovely frescoes. Next to it is the arcaded **Dogana Venezia** (Venetian Customs House). Above all, with the streets filled with cafés and the old stone glowing gold in the sunset, this is a wonderful place to spend a leisurely evening, drinking in the scenery and the fabulous local Bardolino wine. The local market day is on Wednesday.

There are several vineyards that you can visit for tastings nearby, along with the **Zeni Museo del Vino** ❻ (see page 116) up the road near Bardolino. In Cisano is the **Museo dell'Olio d'Oliva** (Olive Oil Museum, Via Peschiera 54, Cisano; tel: 045-622 9047; www.museum.it; Mon–Sat 9am–12.30pm, 2.30–7pm, Sun 9am–12.30pm, closed Sun Jan, Feb, closed first week and last two weeks in Jan; free). This started life as an olive mill, but has grown into a huge enterprise attracting thousands of visitors with its reconstruction of a 19th-century watermill, the possibility of a tasting, and the chance to buy olive oil, olive-based beauty products and local wines.

Bardolino

The next town up the shore, **Bardolino** ❼ is again an ancient one, its name known throughout the world for its wonderful wines (see page 116), which it celebrates during the Feast of Bardolino Chiaretto (Clear Bardolino) in May, the Bardolino Grape and Wine Festival in October, and the Festival of Bardolino Novello (New Bardolino) in November. Between visiting cellars and vineyards, allow time to wander around the pretty *centro storico*, where the lovely 11th–12th-century church of **San Severo** (daily 9am–6pm; free) has an imposingly huge campanile and some lively 13th-century frescoes of the Passion and the Apocalypse. The crypt, behind the high altar, is a surviving fragment of a far earlier Lombard

Olive grove above Lake Garda.

THE OLIVE RIVIERA

Garda's eastern shore is also known as the 'Riviera degli Olivi'. This 50km (31-mile) stretch of coastline is backed by cliffs which protect the world's most northerly olive groves from the harsh winters. Olive trees have been cultivated here since ancient times. Most of the olives are used for extra virgin olive oil which is made by cold pressing (without the use of solvents or heat). It is mostly produced in small family enterprises and available for purchase at producers' shops. Lake Garda olive oil is renowned for its delicate and fruity flavour, low acid content and deep golden green colour, due to a high chlorophyll content. This high-quality product even has its own DOP (*denominazione di origine protetta*). Vineyards, cypress trees, oleander and other Mediterranean plants also thrive in this area.

Checking boat times, Garda.

church. Nearby, the 8th-century chapel of **San Zeno** (Via San Zeno 13–15; daily 9am–6pm; free), with a simple barrel-vaulted nave and pillars of red marble, is one of the oldest surviving churches in Italy. Market day is on Thursday.

Valpolicella winelands

From both Lazise and Bardolino, roads head east from the lake across the Adige River to the villages of **Sant'Ambrogio di Valpolicella** ... and **San Giorgio di Valpolicella**, the villages at the heart of the Valpolicella winelands (www.valpolicella.it), where a number of vineyards open the doors of often stately mansions to those wishing to tour, taste and buy.

There are 80 patrician villas in the region, most built during the years of the Venetian Republic, some with architects as great as Sanmicheli and even Palladio. Most are still in private hands. Some open for limited hours or by appointment; ask the tourist office for details. The **Pieve di San Giorgio di Valpolicella** is a glorious little church, an almost intact early

Sant'Ambrogio di Valpolicella.

8th-century chapel, that has somehow survived war and earthquake.

Waterfall canyon

Mountain roads north from here lead to the remote **Parco Regionale della Lessinia** (tel: 045-679 9211), where the medieval village of **Molina** ❾ stands at the head of a canyon of waterfalls. The **Parco delle Cascate** (Via Bacilieri 1; tel: 045-772 0185; www.parcodelle cascate.it; Apr–Sept daily 9am–7.30pm, Oct daily 10am–6pm, Nov–Mar Sun 10am–3.30pm) has walking trails past the crashing spray, slabs of rock and caves, and some of the 300 species of plant found in the area. There are plenty of other sights worth investigating in the park, too.

Garda

North of Bardolino, on a curved gulf framed by olive groves and cypress trees, the town of **Garda** ❿, like the lake, takes its name from the Germanic (Longobard) word *Warte* (fortress). A suitably powerful example, built by Ostrogothic King Theodoric in the 5th century, once loomed from the top of the 294 metres (964ft) **Rocca di Garda**. It was here that Berengario II once imprisoned the widowed Queen Adelaide of Borgogna who managed to escape, and married Ottone I who promptly exiled Berengario. The castle was destroyed in the 13th century and only a few ruined walls now remain, but there are plenty of grandiose *palazzi*, such as the 16th-century **Palazzo Fregoso** (Via Spagna) in the town centre, to keep architectural sightseers happy, while the church of **Santa Maria Maggiore** has a fine 15th-century cloister. Try to make the Friday market, one of the biggest and best on this side of the lake.

Boats leave from Garda, as well as other points around the lake, to visit the lake's largest island, the **Isola del Garda** (tel: 328-384 9226; www.isola delgarda.com; late-Mar–Oct Tue, Wed, Thu, Sun, May–Oct also Fri; guided

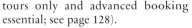
tours only and advanced booking essential; see page 128).

Just south of the town, **Monastero d' Eremo**, or Camaldolesi Hermitage, is a working monastery in an old clifftop fort. Women have only recently been allowed to visit. One of the monks responsible for the current building became Pope Alessandro VII in 1673. Beside it is the small Romanesque church of **San Pietro**.

Inland at **Costermano** ⓫ is Italy's **Cimitero Tedesco** (German World War II Cemetery), consecrated in 1967. There are 21,920 German soldiers, previously buried across northern Italy, who were transferred to this vast graveyard. It is full of heather and roses and marked with a dove of peace. East of Costermano, sandwiched between the autostrada and the Adige River, is the small town of **Rivoli-Veronese** ⓬, where history-lovers will enjoy the **Museo Napoleonico** (Napoleonic Museum; see box).

Madonna della Corona

If that doesn't appeal and you would prefer something more rural, take the twisting mountain road around the back of Monte Baldo to Cortelline, where the **Santuario della Madonna della Corona** ⓭ stands, with Madonna peering out across the Adige Valley from her lofty 774 metres (2,540ft) location since 1530. You can walk up the 450 steps to the church, but there is also a road for the less energetic.

Further along at **Ferrara di Monte Baldo** ⓮, the **Orto Botanico del Monte Baldo** (Botanic Gardens; tel: 045-624 7288; May–Sept daily 9am–6pm) showcase the many endemic species that have led geologists to speculate that Monte Baldo survived the Ice Ages. More than 60 species of orchid are found on the mountain along with gentians and edelweiss, and other wildlife includes chamois, martens and golden eagles.

Punta di San Vigilio

Situated at the neck of the lake, where the gentle bowl of the south abruptly gives way to the narrow mountainous drama of the north, about 3km (2 miles) from Garda, the **Punta di San**

The Napoleon Museum in Rivoli tracks the would-be emperor's Italian campaigns across the plain and up the side of Lake Garda.

Napoleon Bonaparte.

THE BATTLE OF RIVOLI

In September 1796, Napoleon Bonaparte's armies began a series of skirmishes and battles against Venetian and Austrian forces from Legnano and Arcole east of Verona to Borghetto near Valeggio sul Mincio, Castelnuovo del Garda, that decided the fate of Europe. In the 1797 Act of Campo Formio, the area north of the Adige River was given to Austria. After the Battle of Rivoli (14–15 January 1797), Napoleon erected a memorial (1806), later destroyed and replaced by an Austrian fort. Ironically, that fort has now become a Napoleon museum (Piazza Napoleone I 14; tel: 045-728 1309; Mar–Oct Tue, Thu–Sun 9.30am–noon, 3.30–6pm, Mon and Wed, and rest of the year by appointment), with memorabilia and documents from the corporal's Italian campaigns.

Wines of the Region

Whether you are a true aficionado or simply want a few bottles to take home, head for the hills of Eastern Garda – home to some of Italy's most popular wines.

There is a cluster of well-known wine varieties around the southeastern corner of Lake Garda. The sheltered climate, sunshine and rich, well-irrigated soil produce perfect grape-growing conditions.

Custoza (www.stradadelcustoza.com), to the south, produces soft, dry, intense and slightly bitter white *(bianco)* wines from grapes including Trebbiano Toscano, Garganega, Tocai Friulano, Malvasia Toscana, Riesling Italico and Cortese.

To the east of Verona, the rolling hills of **Soave** (www.stradadelsoave.com) produce popular white wines, based mainly on Garganega grapes. Look, too, for *spumante* (sparkling) and dessert wines.

Along the shore between the lake and the Adige River are *Bardolino* wines (www.stradadelbardolino. com). The growers claim the success of the mainly full-bodied reds *(rosso)* is due to St Zeno, who taught their ancestors to cultivate the grapes. His face is on

Bardolino vineyards in autumn.

many bottles. The wine is typically blended using Corvina, Rondinella, Molinara and Negrara grapes and comes in *classico*, *novello* and *superiore*. The *chiaretto* is a rosé, young and fresh with overtones of peach and apricot.

Valpolicella (www.stradadelvalpolicella.com), east of the Adige River, means "valley of many cellars". Its classic reds are some of Italy's most famous, created from corvina, molinara and rondinella grapes. A fruity, medium-weight wine, Valpolicella is usually drunk at about three years. Amarone-Valpolicella is made using sun-dried grapes aged in toasted oak to produce a deep-coloured, dry, fruity wine with flavours of liquorice and vanilla, tobacco and fig. It can be drunk young, but will age for up to 20 years. Recioto is a sweet, intense red dessert version.

North of Valpolicella, the wines take on the lighter, more perfumed characteristics of German wines. In the valley of **Terra dei Forti**, the local wine is the robust red L'Enantio, but the international success story is the fruity, elegant white Pinot Grigio.

A number of wineries offer tastings, but the best place to start is at the **Zeni Museo del Vino** (Via Costabella 9, Bardolino; www.museodelvino.it; free), a vineyard that has been run by the same family since 1870. It offers explanations of local wines, production methods and tastings. You can purchase the entire range of Zeni wines as well as local olive oil and vinegar at the shop.

Vigilio ⑮ is as near a piece of scenic perfection as you are likely to find, an avenue of cypresses leading down to the tiny harbour past Sanmicheli's elegant 16th-century Villa Guarienti and a rare surviving 17th-century *limonaia* (lemon house). With some fine hotels and restaurants, perfect views and one of the best beaches on the lake overlooking the Baia dei Sirene (Mermaids' Bay), it is pretty close to paradise.

Numerous celebrities, from André Gide to Laurence Olivier and Vivien Leigh, have been drawn to the area by the Hotel Gardesana just to the north at **Torri del Benaco** ⑯. This began life as a Roman town, *Castrum Turrium* (Camp of Towers). There are a few Roman remains in the piazza in front of the church, but the town's surviving towers belong to the squat **Castello Scaligero** (Viale Fratelli Lavanda 2; tel: 045-629 6111; Apr–mid-June, mid-Sept–Oct 9.30am–12.30pm, 2.30–6pm, mid-June–mid-Sept daily 9.30am–1pm, 4.30–7.30pm), with swallowtail battlements, built in 1383. These days, it is a wide-ranging local museum focusing on local fishing, olive and lemon cultivation and petroglyphs found in the nearby hills (see feature).

The Baroque church of **SS Pietro e Paolo** has a glorious organ, built in 1744, while the small church of **Santissima Trinità** (Piazza Calderini) has some fine early 15th-century frescoes worth a look. The little harbour, which was built on Roman remains, is surrounded by cafés that make a good place to chill out, and there are several local villages such as **Pai**, **Albisano** and **San Zeno di Montagna** where you can climb high up the slopes for panoramic views of the lake.

Monte Baldo

To the north, the little hamlet of **Prada** ⑰ is the proud possessor of the **Funivia Prada–Monte Baldo** (tel: 045-728 5662; www.funiviedelgarda.it; reopening in summer 2017), the chairlift which carries those not afraid of heights in open buckets up to a breathtaking terrace 2,218 metres (7,277ft) high, to take in exquisite views.

TIP

If you fancy going horse-riding there are several stables in the area and fabulous trekking routes along the lake and into the mountains.
Centro Ippico Rossar (Garda; tel: 045-627 9020).
Genziana SRL (Ferrara di Monte Baldo; tel: 045-722 0366).
Maneggio (Lazise; tel: 045-647 0577).
Gruppo Equibaldo (San Zeno di Montagna; tel: 045-728 5333).

Punta di San Vigilio, a little piece of paradise.

A ribbon of tiny villages collectively known as **Brenzone** connects Torri del Benaco with Malcesine 20km (12 miles) to the north. A lakeside walking and cycling route stretches much of the way, and parked cars are crammed into every available space as people swim from the rocks. Behind the road soars the bulk of **Monte Baldo**, actually a mountain chain, not a single peak.

Malcesine

Malcesine ⑱ stands at the gateway between Venetian and Austrian territory and at the northern end of the Riviera degli Olivi, in a fabulous setting with a distant backdrop of the Dolomites. Undoubtedly one of the most charming towns on the lake, it is always busy with tourists. **Castello Scaligero** (Via Castello; tel: 045-740 0837; daily 9.30–6pm), perched on a rock to the north of the town, was built by the Scaligeri in the 13th century. The view from the battlements is striking, but the castle is best seen from the water. Goethe was so taken with the look of the place in 1786

Malcesine viewed from its 13th-century castle.

that he took out a sketchbook to draw the scenery and was arrested as a spy, spending some time in the castle as a prisoner before he was identified and released. Some of his sketches are on show in the castle museum.

Down in the harbour area, the **Palazzo dei Capitani del Lago** (June–Sept daily 8am–7pm) was formerly the home of the Venetian governors. The weekly market is on Saturday.

The highlight (in every way) of a visit to Malcesine is the **Funivia Monte Baldo** (tel: 045-740 0206; www.funiviedelbaldo.it), the cable car that swings up the mountain from a station 2km (1.2 miles) north of town, reaching a stunning 1,760 metres (5,774ft). Queues can be long and queues for the car park even longer, but the 360° views are worth every minute. If you want to come down the hard way, mountain biking and paragliding are options, and there are 11km (6 miles) of ski runs in winter. There are also plenty of walking trails, with opportunities to spot wildlife, rare wild flowers and some petroglyphs.

HISTORICAL GRAFFITI

In 1964, on the remote slopes of Monte Luppia, behind San Vigilio, archaeologists uncovered pictograms similar to those at Val Camonica (see page 170). To date, around 3,000 inscriptions on 250 rocks have been uncovered, in an area of 40 sq km (15.5 sq miles) from Monte Luppia right up to Monte Baldo. Dating from the Bronze Age (1500 BC), they include religious symbols, games, battle scenes, mounted warriors, ships, captives and weapons – the Castelletto di Brenzone (in Verona Natural History Museum) shows 73 axes and eight daggers. They are best seen in early morning and are more visible if you wet the rock. Local tourist offices can provide maps, itineraries and details of walking and cycling tours.

TIME FOR THE KIDS

Lake Garda is undoubtedly the family holiday centre with the biggest cluster of theme parks, holiday homes and campsites.

Theme Parks

It's a thrill a minute at **Gardaland** (Casteluovo del Garda; tel: 045-644 9777, www.gardaland.it; late-Mar–Sept daily 10am–6pm, Oct–late-Mar Fri–Sun, check website for times; last entry 1.5 hrs before closing time), Italy's largest theme park, near Peschiera del Garda, with roller-coasters that loop the loop, wild water rides, the Fantasy Kingdom for littler ones, a dolphin show and plenty of other entertainment. Along the road, there's hot competition from **Movieland at Canevaworld** (Via Fossalta 1, Lazise sul Garda; tel: 045-696 9900; www.canevaworld.it; May–mid-Sept 10am–6pm, until 7pm mid-July–end Aug, weekends only Apr, mid-Sept–end Oct), where you can rock with Rambo, tussle and scramble with Lara Croft and fight pirates with Peter Pan.

Cable Cars

Give kids a tower or a mountain and up they have to go – there are both in bucketloads here. Be prepared to dig deep into your pockets for trips up cable cars and chairlifts. Once at the top there are wonderful walking trails. Take cold weather gear, binoculars and a book on wildlife as the flowers and birds are as lovely as the views. You may even see a marten or fox.

Animals

To see animals – alive, extinct or endangered – spend a day at **Parco Natura Viva** (Loc. Figara 40, Bussolengo; tel: 045-717 0113; www.parconaturaviva.it; Faunapark Mon–Sat 9am–5pm, Sun until

Giraffe at Parco Natura Viva.

Thrills at Gardaland.

6pm; Safaripark Mon–Sat 9.30am–3.30pm, Sun until 4pm), which has a drive-through safari park, walk-through fauna and dinosaur parks and a tropical greenhouse and aquaterrarium. Rated as one of Europe's top zoos, it works for the protection of endangered species.

Culture for Kids

This is the perfect place to give kids a love of history and art. Pace it out, research the horribl

Cable car over Lake Maggiore.

Screaming and sliding for all, Canevaworld.

WATER PARKS

Prefer things a little splashier? There are some watery rides at **Gardaland**, but you would probably be better off heading for Parco Aqua at **Canevaworld** (address, see left; mid-May– mid-Sept 10am–6pm, until 7pm July–Aug), with rides and slides, lagoons and pools. The rest of the advertised water parks are mainly overgrown pools with some slides. They include: **Parco Acquatico Cavour (Località Ariano, Valeggio sul Mincio; tel: 045-795 0904; www.parcoacquaticocavour.it)**, **Acquasplash Franciacorta (Via Generale della Chiesa 3, Corte Franca; tel: 030-982 6441; www.acquasplash.it)**, **Acquapark Altomincio (Località Torrente Valle, Salionze, Valeggio sul Mincio; tel: 045-237 3540)**, **Parco Acquatico Picoverde (Via Ossario 19, Custoza; tel: 045-516 025; www.picoverde.it)** and **Acquatica Park (Via Gaetano Airaghi 61, Milan; tel: 02-4820 0134; www.acquaticapark.it)**.

Touching heaven from Milan Duomo.

istories and get some real-life stories dripping with blood and gore; look at the way things were made and used and the next thing you know you will have a pint-sized archaeologist (or travel writer) on your hands.

Swimming in the Lakes

Who needs a pool when there are several hundred natural swimming pools with water of deepest blue to vivid tur- quoise, with hundreds of kilometres of (usu- ally rocky) shore to play on; whether you're paddling or snorkelling, this is the ideal playground for kids and grown-ups.

Eating Ice Cream

taly may have given the world Michelangelo nd Leonardo da Vinci, but for most children s greatest gift was food – pizza, pasta but above l, *gelato* – luscious ice cream in a rainbow array f flavours.

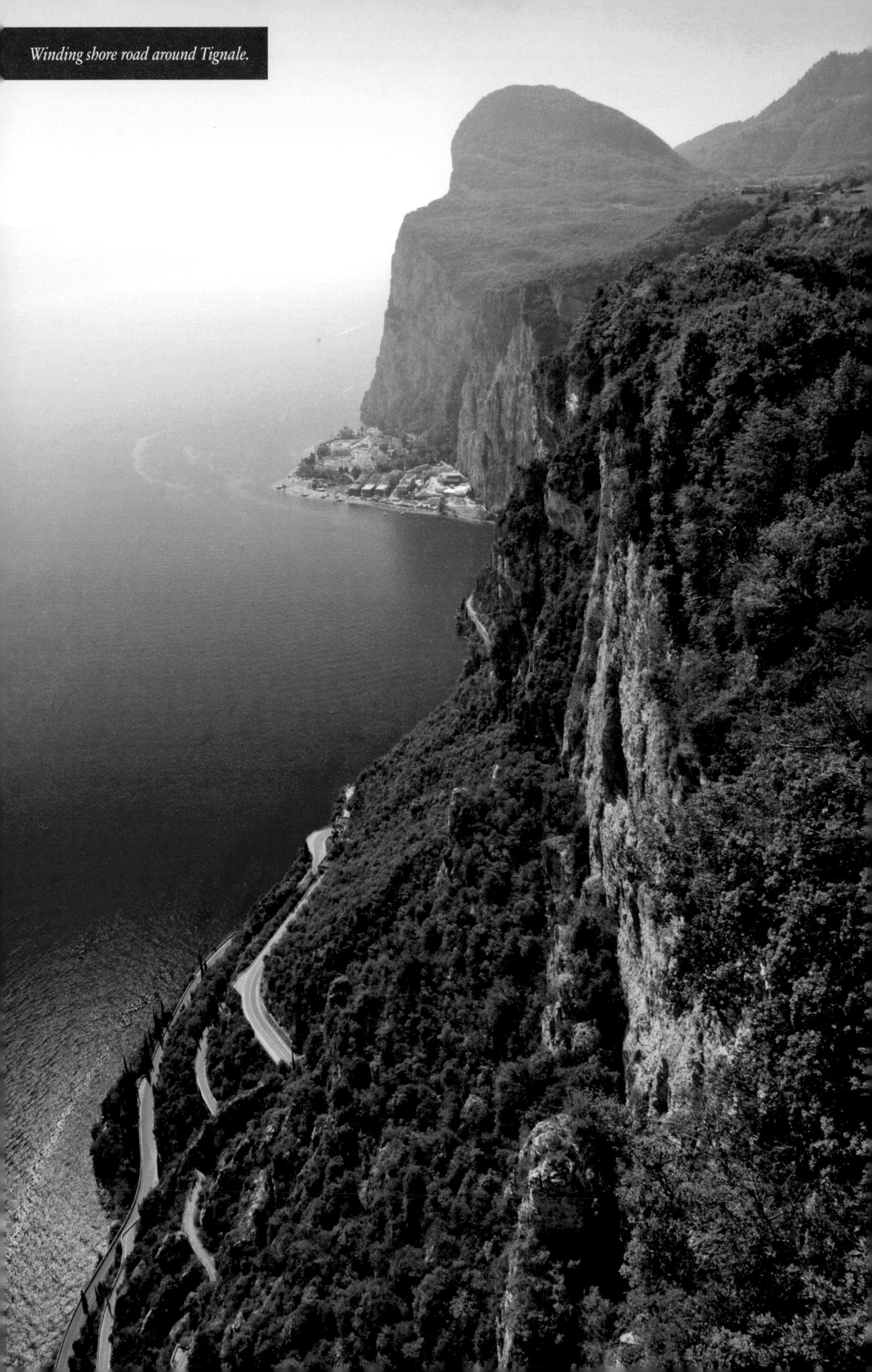

Winding shore road around Tignale.

WESTERN LAKE GARDA

The blend of Alpine and Mediterranean scenery, gorgeous villas and gardens, as well as wine-tasting forays into the hills, make this a beguiling region.

On Garda's dramatic western shore, the scenery ranges from soaring, snow-capped peaks and deep conifer forests to rolling vineyards and olive groves. Despite the Alpine glaciers to the north shelving down to the water's edge, the lake itself radiates Mediterranean warmth. Towards the north, the Alpine landscape is softened by glistening lemon and olive groves and heady scents. Magnolias and oleanders, figs and roses, palms and pomegranates all thrive in this mild climate, adding southern warmth to the chill of the Alps. Exotic plants, imported from Asia, the Americas and Australia in the late 19th century, were selected for the villas' gardens around the lake. Amazonian water lilies and lotus blossoms, Japanese maples and jasmine were all part of the grand design to combine art and nature in a harmonious scene.

Sirmione

Set on a peninsula at the southern end of the lake, **Sirmione ⑲** is a delightful spot, despite the waves of day-trippers. Only Limone is more besieged in summer but, unlike this more northern resort, Sirmione is adept at crowd dispersal. A most self-consciously charming resort, this is a place for pottering down alleys, wallowing in sulphurous hot pools or meandering through olive groves to Roman ruins.

The **Grotte di Catullo**, which crown the rocky tip of the peninsula, have ruins infused with heady romance because the villa belonged to Catullus, Rome's greatest lyric poet. It was here that the poet languished while suffering rejection from Lesbia, his fickle mistress in Rome. These lakeside hot springs have proved popular ever since. The steamy, sulphurous thermal baths of **Aquaria** (www.termedisirmione.it; see page 156) are Sirmione's best cure for stress.

Main Attractions
Sirmione
Solferino
Villa Romana, Desenzano
Salò Waterfront
Il Vittoriale
Giardino Botanico
  Fondazione Andre Heller
Valtenesi Wine Route
Limone Sul Garda

Dog-walkers in Sirmione.

The husband of the diva Maria Callas, Giovanni Meneghini, rationalised his wife's affair with the Greek shipping magnate thus: "Aristotle Onassis has his billions and wants to polish up his tankers, using the name of a great star."

Maria Callas's Villa Meneghini.

Rocca Scaligera (Scaligera Castle; Piazza Castello 34; tel: 030-916 468; Tue–Sat 8.30am–7.30pm, Sun 8.30am–2pm), a battlemented fortress complete with drawbridge and moat, dominates the centre of Sirmione. In medieval times, this fortress controlled the southern part of the lake. The Scaligeri built both the castle and the town walls in the 15th century when they were lords of Verona, using Roman foundations for their fortress. Today, these bastions tempt visitors into an unfolding parade of ice-cream parlours and craft shops. More charming are the walks through olive groves, the lapping of the lake, the public beach, and the faint mood of nostalgia that pervades Sirmione.

It was to the remoteness of the **Villa Cortine Palace** that Princess Diana's mother retreated after the death of her daughter – to seek the solace she couldn't find on her small Scottish island. **Villa Meneghini**, opposite, was where Maria Callas lived in her 1950s heyday. Here, she pondered the merits of her husband, an ageing Italian tycoon, and her lover, the ship-owning Aristotle Onassis. The diva embarked

on a turbulent affair with Onassis that took her on trysts all over the world – until Jackie Kennedy entered his life. Callas's ochre-coloured villa is not open to the public but the **Palace Hotel Villa Cortine** still serves the best Bellinis in town. From the terraces are views of Roman ruins and Monte Baldo, which reminded Callas of Mount Olympus.

Solferino

Military buffs will be drawn south to the battlefields of Solferino and **San Martino della Battaglia** ⑳, just inland from Lake Garda. This part of the lake became a theatre of war during the Risorgimento, the 19th-century patriotic struggle for nationhood, which was driven by Piedmont and the ruling House of Savoy. On Midsummer's Day in 1859, the combined Italian and French forces defeated Emperor Franz Joseph's Austrian army in these battlefields. A **circular tower** now dominates the skyline, while an **ossuary chapel** holds the bones of the slain.

The campaign's bloodiest battle came at **Solferino** ㉑, a few kilometres

to the south. Here, the combined forces, led by Napoleon III, crushed the Austrians in a victory commemorated by a bridge over the Seine in Paris. As one of the most decisive Risorgimento battles, Solferino has spawned a museum, military fort and ossuary, but the battlefield is also significant for more important humanitarian reasons. Appalled by the brutality of the conflict, with its 40,000 casualties, Swiss citizen Jean-Henri Dunant was spurred into founding the Red Cross.

Lonato

Further west, another intense experience awaits at **Lonato** ㉒, a slightly sombre medieval town nestling in low-slung hills off the lake. Dominated by the **Rocca**, a hulking Venetian fortress, the well-preserved town is of less interest than the fortress and the museum-residence that faces it.

The **Fondazione Ugo da Como** (Via Rocca 2; tel: 030-913 0060; www. fondazioneugodacomo.it; daily 10am–noon, 2.30–6.30pm) is a fitting memorial to its austere founder. Shaped by the will of a singular aesthete, Ugo da Como (1869–1941), this home is a convincing neo-Gothic folly that conveys a passion for medieval culture. In turning his back on his own times, Ugo da Como created a treasure-trove that, while not on the scale of Il Vittoriale, is still an enthralling invitation to a richly imagined world. The library contains over 30,000 volumes, including illuminated manuscripts dating from the 12th century. The original mansion, the medieval Podestà, the ruler's seat during Venetian rule, was not so much restored to its Gothic splendour as re-imagined as "essence of Gothic". Studded with Lombard art and medieval furniture, Ugo da Como's house feels more like a museum than a home. The glorious library was modelled on a medieval Lombard church. As a bookish politician, Ugo da Como retreated to his Gothic ivory tower as a satisfying retreat from the political fray.

Desenzano

Back in the modern world, **Desenzano** ㉓ feels more worldly than the rest of the lake, despite its undoubted charm. As the business capital of Lake Garda, the resort represents a transport hub, with a terminus for lake steamers, a station on the Milan–Venice line and a convenient A4 motorway exit.

As a wealthy commuter resort, Desenzano commands its share of designer boutiques, lively nightlife and gourmet restaurants. Yet a deeper identity harks back to Roman times, and is underscored by the discovery of a 3rd-century AD Roman villa close to the harbour. Set on Via Crocefisso, the **Villa Romana** (tel: 030-914 3547; Mar–Oct Tue–Sun 8.30am–7pm, Nov–Feb until 5pm) is northern Italy's finest late imperial villa. Although built in the 1st century BC, the multicoloured mosaics mostly date from the 4th and 5th centuries and bear comparison with those at Pompeii. Curiously, the Christianising effect of that era left its mark on the artefacts, which include a late 4th-century glass bowl engraved with an image of Christ.

The library of the Fondazione Ugo da Como.

In Roman times, Desenzano was an important trading town, and today's bustling Tuesday market evokes that entrepreneurial spirit. Built over a Roman fort, Desenzano's ruined castle stands in the lofty Capo la Terra district, close to the former grain market. Desenzano also flourished under Venetian rule and owes its quaint **inner harbour** to these times. Even if it feels city-like, the resort reveals a softer side in its tree-lined waterfront and scenic inner harbour. No visit is complete without a gluttonous seafood dinner in one of its lakefront restaurants, the place to see Desenzano at its greedy, bourgeois best.

Wine country

Padenghe sul Garda ㉔ has a split personality, part prosperous little wine town overlooking a pleasant marina, part medieval stronghold, once dominated by a 10th-century castle. Surrounded by rolling hills, vineyards and olive groves, Padenghe is at the heart of the **Valtenesi wine route** (see page 132). Neighbouring **Moniga sul Garda** boasts its own wine roots in

Desenzano waterfront.

the form of Chiaretto, an adaptable rosé. The village itself is a scenic spot, framed by a 10th-century crenellated castle. The road down to the shore winds through olive groves and vineyards, culminating in a harbour lined with restaurants and cafés.

Perched on a headland overlooking the lake, **Manerba del Garda** ㉕ is a cluster of hamlets bordering wine country. On the promontory, **Rocca di Manerba** is one of the loveliest spots on Lake Garda: the site dates back to the Stone Age but the castle, as such, was razed by the Venetians in 1575. No traces of the original Longobard castle remain, and there are few signs of later castles. On a sparkling summer's day, this pastoral setting conjures up balmy Sardinia rather than Alpine Lake Garda. When the crowds in the touristy lake resorts become tiring, clambering around the Rocca provides a perfect antidote, as does the orchid-studded nature reserve below the ruins.

San Felice del Benaco ㉖ is a low-key resort overlooking the Isola del Garda, an island which can be visited on a guided tour. In San Felice, the

Gothic parish church of **Madonna del Carmine** displays a Renaissance altarpiece by Romanino and, curiously, has recycled the castle tower as its church bell tower. It is just south of the village, on the road to Manerba.

Salò

The most elegant resort on Lake Garda, **Salò** ㉗ retains its sense of self, and resists the blandishments of the tour operators and trinket-sellers that have tarnished lesser resorts. Welcoming, yet supremely indifferent, Salò is the closest visitors will come to feeling how the lakes might manage without us. Perfectly well is the answer. Strolling along **Via San Carlo**, the arcaded shopping street, allows visitors to snoop on the sophisticated and self-contained lives of the inhabitants. This is a serious shopping street, such as those in Como, Verona and the bigger centres, and culminates in the quaint city gate. Chic matrons and yummy mummies browse the designer shoe stores before calling in for coffee and cake in **Vassalli Pasticceria**, a citadel of good taste since the 1930s.

After the world has been put to rights over an iced coffee and crunchy hazelnut biscuits, saunter along the **Lungolago**, the waterfront. This bracing promenade, which sweeps around the seductive bay, is the longest and best on Lake Garda. On the waterfront is **Piazza della Vittoria**, the showpiece square and the gateway to Salò's medieval heart. On Piazza Duomo, just off the lake, the handsome **Duomo** lacks grace, reflecting the heavy Baroque hand that descended with the reforming zeal of San Carlo Borromeo. The highlights are the Renaissance portal, a 15th-century altarpiece and works by Romanino. Tourists have impinged enough on the local consciousness for there to be a collection of scarves and veils "to cover better oneself" (sic) waiting by the cathedral door.

Salò is inevitably linked to Mussolini, who set up the Ministry of Foreign Affairs in the delightful **Hotel Laurin**, an Art Nouveau gem. Even so, Mussolini's puppet state, the Republic of Salò (see box), is a slight misnomer as most of the ministries were

It is possible to dine in the upmarket Villa Laurin in Salò or Villa Fiordaliso in Gardone, an Art Nouveau villa associated with Mussolini and his mistress.

Salò lights up at night.

THE REPUBLIC OF SALÒ

One of the most shameful episodes in Italian history took place in Salò's name. Between 1943–5, the Republic of Salò was a fig leaf of respectability used to disguise the brutality of the Nazi regime. Villa Feltrinelli in Gargnano was the seat of the puppet government, with major villas commandeered as embassies or propaganda offices. Mussolini's private residence was a secluded villa, where his wife devoted herself to her pet hens while Mussolini passed time discussing casualties with the German ambassador. His mistress, Clara Petacci, lived in Villa Fiordaliso. He took the opportunity to exact revenge on former colleagues, even executing his son-in-law, but failed to survive the vengeance of the partisans in 1945.

FACT

As a morbid hypochon-
driac with poor eyesight,
D'Annunzio preferred the
penumbra of light
filtered through stained
glass. When even the
half-light became too
much to bear,
D'Annunzio retreated to
the bier in "the death
chamber" (the spare
bedroom) in order to
think cosmic thoughts.

clustered around Gargnano, further along the coast.

Isola del Garda

Travel by boat from Salò, Garda, Bardolino and Gardone Riviera to **Isola del Garda** ㉘ (tel: 328-384 9226; www.isoladelgarda.com; island open late Mar–mid-Oct, booking required). The trip includes food and wine-tasting in the fee. In medieval times, Garda's largest island once supported a monastery that attracted a triumvirate of saints, including St Francis of Assisi; it is thought that Dante Alighieri also stayed here. The monastery was razed by Napoleon and replaced by a neo-Gothic Venetian-style villa and lush English and Italianate gardens. The down-to-earth owners of this palatial pile, including Countess Cavazza herself, also own campsites on Lake Garda.

Gardone Riviera

Gardone Riviera ㉙, a fabled resort that has fallen out of favour, is still home to the most famous villa-museum on the lake, Il Vittoriale, and to the arty botanical gardens. In Gardone's palm-court glory days, royalty, writers and heads of state filled the dowager-like hotels. The pretty lakeside **Villa Fiordaliso** (see page 76), formerly Mussolini's love nest, now a chic villa-hotel, remains an evocative tribute to those times.

Not that faded grandeur characterises the delightfully bohemian **Giardino Botanico Fondazione Andre Heller** (Via Roma 2; tel: 0336-410 877; www.hellergarden.com; Mar–Oct daily 9am–7pm). Alpine plants and Mediterranean vegetation grow happily on this rocky spur lying in the shadow of the Dolomite peaks. The gardens are enlivened by playful or surreal installations by the Austrian artist.

Il Vittoriale

A testament to the megalomania of two men, Mussolini and Gabriele D'Annunzio, stands **Il Vittoriale** (Via Vittoriale 12, Gardone Riviera; tel: 0365-296 511; www.vittoriale.it; Apr–Sept 8.30am–8pm, Oct–Mar 9am–5pm). The soldier-poet D'Annunzio transformed this unremarkable Art Nouveau villa and park into a

D'ANNUNZIO'S DESTINY

Cast in the heroic mould, the soldier-poet, war hero and founding Fascist occupies an odd place in Italian hearts, somewhere between reverence and bafflement.

D'Annunzio declared, "Destiny calls me towards Lake Garda." In fact, it was Mussolini who presented the villa of Il Vittoriale to the maverick patriot in 1925. Il Vittoriale is a decadent Disneyland, a shrine to one of Italy's most flamboyant pre-war figures. Gabriele D'Annunzio (1863–1938) was a poet, patriot, pantheist, dandy, daredevil, aviator, aesthete, maverick and megalomaniac.

As a right-wing nationalist who posed as the saviour of his country, D'Annunzio favoured Italy's entry into the war in 1915 and plunged into the fighting, carrying out derring-do missions, such as flying over Trieste in 1915 and Vienna in 1918. Believing that Italy had been cheated by the 1919 Treaty of Versailles, he led an unauthorised invasion of the Dalmatian port of Fiume, which he ruled until 1921, on the basis that it had been promised to Italy before the war. Such activities convinced Mussolini that the dangerous maverick should be pensioned off to Lake Garda.

The poet's home fails to solve the riddle of the man, but offers enough clues to keep legions of psychiatrists and biographers in business. D'Annunzio accepted the 18th-century villa as a monument to his massive ego, called it Il Vittoriale, in memory of Italy's victory over Austria in 1918, and remodelled it out of all recognition. The virtual recluse lived here from 1921 until his death.

Il Vittoriale is as crazily complex as its creator. The greatest contrast is between the loveliness of the grounds and the hideousness of the creations that inhabit them. There is the grandiose mausoleum, a magnolia grove housing a war memorial, while the Puglia battleship that featured in the Fiume fiasco is bizarrely beached amid cypresses. On display in a hangar are other vehicles from the escapade, the biplane used for the flight over Vienna and the Italian flag D'Annunzio flew over Yugoslavia. The mausoleum where the Italian "patriots" are buried is also a monument to kitsch, while an eerie museum contains the poet's death mask. Despite this disfiguring gloom, pockets of the former lemon gardens escape the philosophical straitjacket and even the Fascistic amphitheatre has fine views from the top tier.

bombastic folly, a kingdom of kitsch, which is his true memorial. His home, presented as a shrine, is a gilded cage fit for a *fin de siècle* poet who abhorred daylight. In every over-stuffed room, the decor reflects the delusions of a cigar-smoking aesthete who strutted around in silk dressing-gowns, declaiming verse and rearranging his reliquaries before snoozing in a coffin. Such self-aggrandisement led D'Annunzio to create a low entrance to his study so guests had to stoop, bowing to the poet's genius. His warped sense of humour is revealed in the gleaming Art Deco dining room where his embalmed pet tortoise, which died of indigestion, is displayed.

Given that the villa had been expropriated from a German art critic, D'Annunzio's first task was, as he put it, to have his new home "de-Germanised". Not that the result is remotely Italian. The once lovely **grounds** are scattered with symbols of wartime exploits and delusions of grandeur, from a battleship to vintage warplanes, a recreation of a Roman amphitheatre and a doom-laden mausoleum.

The **villa** itself has two waiting rooms, a faintly cheerful one for favoured guests and a gloomy temple for unwelcome guests, such as Mussolini. The mad aesthete and the brutalist dictator were never soulmates. In the parlour for undesirables, a cutting inscription above a mirror was apparently aimed at Mussolini: "Adjust your mask to your face and remember you are merely glass against steel." Mussolini's reaction is not recorded, but D'Annunzio lived to tell the tale.

Even if the maverick war hero and proto-Fascist started out as a supporter of Mussolini, he was swiftly walled up in this decadent Disneyland for ever. The coda, of course, is that despite his bombastic bohemianism, Mussolini's fellow megalomaniac had the sense to counsel his leader against a Faustian pact with Hitler. The rest, as they say, is history.

Windy shores

Toscolano-Maderno, with several distinctive churches, a rash of apricot and pink facades and an appealing sandy beach, is before **Bogliaco**, an erstwhile

Bougainvillea and romance, Gargnano.

Villa Fiordaliso.

Painted kitchenware, Limone sul Garda.

Giardino Botanico Fondazione Andre Heller.

fishing village which marks the beginning of the best windsurfing and sailing waters. Here, the lake narrows and attracts the "Ora del Garda", a local wind system which blows from the south with a very specific timetable.

Dominating the lakefront is **Palazzo Bettoni**, an impressive ochre-and-green Lombard Baroque mansion that belongs to Brescian aristocrats. More typical is the inviting beach at the end of Via Castello, and the bold view of Monte Baldo on the far bank.

Gargnano

Beyond is **Gargnano** ㉚. A favourite among sailing enthusiasts, it is arguably the least spoilt resort on the lake, and certainly the most understated. The lure here is the sumptuous **Villa Feltrinelli** (see page 76), built in 1892 by the sons of a lumber merchant, Faustino Feltrinelli, and now a luxurious hotel. With its crenellated roof and ochre-and-vanilla stripes, the villa has something of the look of an overblown wedding cake about it. In 1943 the Germans commandeered the villa and installed Mussolini in

this gilded cage. He was effectively under house arrest, guarded by German officers, until he escaped in 1945, ending in his capture and death at the hands of partisans.

By the harbour is the tiny Romanesque church of **San Giacomo** (pick up the key from fishermen next door), a pilgrimage chapel founded on the site of a pagan temple. This was the medieval harbour, when the steepness of the slopes forced pilgrims to arrive by boat. Fittingly, fishermen, admittedly a dying breed in these parts, still set sail from this harbour. They even stack their nets in the portico of a chapel frescoed with a St Christopher, patron saint of travellers.

Nearby, the 13th-century Franciscan foundation of **San Francesco** (8am–noon, 2.30–6pm) boasts Romanesque cloisters with citrus fruit sculpted on the capitals, proof that lemons were part of the landscape even then. D.H. Lawrence stayed just outside Gargnano while penning *Twilight in Italy*, an evocative account of a disappearing way of life. Touchingly, the old way of life has survived better in Gargnano than on other Lake Garda resorts.

Coastal wilderness

The coastal route then sweeps into **Tignale** ㉛ in a series of tunnels, revealing occasional flashes of lake and a tangle of olive groves and lemon trees. Tignale disentangles itself in a series of views that are more an introduction to the Upper Lake Garda Park than to the villages themselves. Olives and lemon groves give way to chestnut and pine groves on the higher slopes.

Rather like Tignale, the name **Tremosine** ㉜ is a notional one for 18 disparate hamlets, including the coastal village of Campione, set in an amphitheatre of cliffs. Tremosine, too, is less a specific place than a necklace of lakeside terraces, deep-wooded valleys and forgotten hamlets. The road up from Campione is truly terrifying to all but those with nerves of steel, so you would do better to continue on through

Limone and follow the Upper Lake Drive and enjoy lunch perched above the cliffs, as the best way to appreciate this wilderness.

Limone

Beyond lies quaint, lemon-scented **Limone sul Garda** ③. Even though the old fishing port beloved by Goethe, Ibsen and D.H. Lawrence has plenty of tourists, the place has charm enough. Bright southern light, a tiny port and pastel facades hide the pizza parlours. The steep, cobbled streets are self-consciously quaint, as is the inner harbour and the bustling promenade. Limone is as charming and sickly sweet as a Limoncello liqueur.

Still, visiting the authentic "lemon house" at the top of the hill restores a sense of what Limone once was. The **Limonaia del Castel** (Via Orti; tel: 0365-954 008; daily mid-Mar–mid-May, mid-Sept–Oct 10am–6pm, mid-May–mid-Sept until 10pm) reveals the secrets of lemon production, a crop that has flourished around the lake since the 13th century. The lemons were introduced by Franciscan monks

and, by the mid-19th century, there were over 400 *limonaie* (lemon houses), which produced the most northerly lemons and citrons in Europe.

These evocative lemon terraces, which can be seen from the lake, are complex structures, with stone pilasters topped by wooden latticework which was covered in winter to protect the fruit from frost. Growing lemons was a major undertaking, necessitating the creation of water channels and even the transportation of richer soil from the south of the lake. Yet the challenge clearly paid off: the local citizens enjoy incredible longevity, which some attribute to the healthy Mediterranean diet of lake fish, lake oil and fresh lemons. The more scientific view is that the presence of a "wonder gene" and cholesterol-beating protein (Apolipoprotein A1-Milan) in the gene pool has protected the locals against heart disease and other ills.

A drive around Upper Lake Garda

Stretching high above Limone and Gargnano is the wilderness area of

Lemons still grow on the terraces at Limone sul Garda, as they have for hundreds of years.

Gargnano waterfront.

Valtenesi's Wine & Oil Route

The Valtenesi or "Little Tuscany" is the most appealing drive on the lower lake, combining olive oil estates and vineyards with gourmet restaurants.

North of Desenzano stretches a patchwork of rolling hills, vineyards and olive groves, situated on the Strada dei Vini e Sapori (www.stradadeivini.it), that, after a few glasses of wine, can conjure up Tuscany. From Salò, this foodie circuit meanders through the hills behind Lake Garda and visits the most individualistic estates close to the western shore. (Vineyard visits and lunch stops are best booked beforehand.)

From **Salò**, follow the lakeshore on a circular route heading down to Desenzano and back. Towards the headland is the hamlet of **Portese**, overlooking the Gulf of Salò, and the first port of call: the wine and oil estate of **Le Chiusure** (tel: 0365-626 243; www.lechiusure.net). Enjoy the views from the ruined castle at **Rocca di Manerba** before considering lunch at chic Ristorante da Rino, overlooking the lake.

Continue to **Padenghe sul Garda**, calling in at the traditional **Zuliani** estate (Via Tito Speri 28; tel:

From vines to barrels.

030-990 7026; www.vinizuliani.it), tucked into a fortress-like interior and run by the indomitable Eleonora. Chiaretto, made with Groppello, Barbera, Marzemino and Sangiovese, is a rosé that suits light, uncomplicated dishes. Bianco Donna Eleonora, named in the owner's honour, is a classic Chardonnay.

Olive oil tasting

Heading south to **Desenzano**, visit the charming olive oil estate of **Frantoio Montecroce** (Montecroce, Viale Andreis, Desenzano; tel: 030-991 1504; www.frantoio montecroce.it). This award-winning olive oil producer gives the best presentation of how extra-virgin olive oil is made, using a traditional olive press. The artisan-style oils have no additives and, like the best Garda oil, tend to be delicate and fruity, or medium-fruity.

Inland at **Lonato**, stroll by the castle ruins before returning via **Padenghe** for a fish-inspired late lunch in AquaRiva at West Garda.

Towards **Salò** in **Puegnago**, **Comincioli** (Via Roma 10; tel: 0365-651 141; www.comincioli.it) is both the oldest and the most innovative wine producer in the area, where the Comincioli family have been making wine since 1552. The firm only produces wines made with native grapes, such as Gropello and Erbamat, which is threatened by extinction. It also produces award-winning olive oil. After a wine-tasting here, head south via the walled medieval town of **Polpenazze** – and more vineyards before returning to Salò.

the **Parco Alto Garda Bresciano** ㉞, a regional park including a clutch of hamlets and challenging hiking trails. The beauty of the park is in the desolate weight of the wilderness, ranging from deep pine forests to silvery olives, with oleander and bougainvillea on the lower slopes. Compared to eastern Lake Garda, the west commands the dramatic views, but with the mountains dropping direct into the lake and the lake road plunging into tunnels, the views are best seen on two mountain drives – a route from Limone to Gargnano that coils through the soaring wilderness of the park, and the much longer Four Lakes Drive, from Riva, also ending in Gargnano.

Begin in the main car park at **Limone sul Garda** and head for the coastal road south. Known as the **Gardesana Occidentale**, this exhilarating lakeside road is riven with tunnels and daredevil bends but rewards drivers with heady, partially glimpsed views of the lake. The switchback roads cut through Forra, a gorge en route to the Tremosine hamlets, centred on **Pieve di Tremosine** ㉟. Hotel Paradiso (Viale Europa 19; tel: 0365-953 012; www.terrazzadelbrivido.it) makes a good lunch or coffee stop, with its dizzying views from the vast terrace over cliffs down to the lake. Equally dramatic, but with a cosier terrace, is **Miralago** (Piazza Cozzaglio; tel: 0365-953 001; www.miralago.it).

At the hamlet of **Vesio**, go straight over the junction before crossing the river, Torrente Campione, deep in the wilderness above Lake Garda. A side turning leads to **Santuario di Monte Castello** ㊱, a Romanesque church with the finest views in the reserve. After retracing your steps to the main route at Vesio, head for Gardola, where the road meets the lakeshore.

The Four Lakes Drive

Rejoin the Gardesana Occidentale, the main coastal road heading north to Riva del Garda, gateway to Trentino and the **Four Lakes Drive**, one of the most adventurous driving routes from Lake Garda and a good way to loop back down to Gargnano. Dramatic twists and turns take in three Alpine lakes and the medieval village of Bagolino, before returning to Lake Garda via the rugged heights of the Parco Alto Garda Bresciano.

Begin at **Riva del Garda** (see page 138) and climb Val Ledro, turning off to the south onto the SS45bis and then right (onto the SS240) for rural **Lago di Ledro** ㊲, with its Bronze Age pile-dwellings, museum explaining the 4,000-year-old community, and the resort of Pieve di Ledro. At Storo, turn left onto the SS237, towards the deep-blue fjord-like **Lago d'Idro** ㊳, framed by woody crags and famous for its trout-fishing, making a detour right to atmospheric **Bagolino** ㊴. Retrace your steps to Lake Idro, the highest lake in Lombardy at 368 metres (1,207ft), pausing to swim at Anfo's beaches (in August only). Then wander down from Pieve Vecchia and Zumie via the forked tarn of **Lago di Valvestino** ㊵, which is actually a dam, back to Gargnano.

TIP

The Italian medical profession insists that the lake climate is beneficial for "the stressed and neurotic, the arthritic and the asthmatic, the elderly and young children". As a result, the spas in the region are highly valued, especially those in Sirmione.

Riva del Garda.

LAKE GARDA ON THE WATER

With its surreal blue waters and dramatic cliffs, there is something other-worldly about Lake Garda, and out on the water the magic is all the more intense.

Ferry loading at Limone sul Garda.

Ferries

There is no one "must do" tour of this huge lake – even on the high speed catamaran, getting from Riva del Garda in the north to Desenzano in the south takes over three hours. Instead, Garda boat tours are a splendid pick and mix from amongst the dozens of ferries and pleasure boats that criss-cross the water every day, linking towns along both shores, crossing the lake at key points and, in the south, converging like a spider's web on Sirmione.

Choose between standard ferries, historic paddle steamers, high-speed catamarans or hydrofoils (and pay a small premium for the privilege). Most of the boats carry passengers only, but there are some car ferries, from Riva to Desenzano, Limone to Malcesine and Maderno to Torri del Benaco. The number of services drops dramatically in winter (Oct–Mar).

Tickets are available by the journey, but if you want the freedom to roam, consider buying a day pass. These come in three versions – one covering the whole lake, one for the Upper Lake (Riva down to Bogliaco, just beyond Gargnano) and one for the Lower Lake (Desenzano, Peschiera up to Gargnano). There are adult and child fares available and ticket sales offices by all the quays. For more information, contact Navigazione Lago di Garda, tel: 030-914 9511 or 800-551 801 (freephone), www.navlaghi.it.

Taking a boat out

Rent a boat for an hour, an afternoon or a day and sail or motor where you like. There are boat-hire yards in most of the resort towns. Prices vary wildly and can be steep, so do your homework before setting out. Most of the boats have a ladde making it easy to swim off the back, so you ca take fins and snorkels, or a fishing rod, or simp take a picnic and some sunblock. Just rememb what your home harbour looks like, so you ca find it again.

Dinghies

The northern part of the lake in particula around Torbole, is known as perfect sailing te ritory, and the ferries have to thread their wa through flotillas of training dinghies whi windsurfers zip precariously under the bow There are plenty of places to hire equipment an schools where you can have lessons in safety you'd like to have a go.

Breezes to storms

While blessed with warm summers and mild winters, Garda is also known for winds and even savage storms. The *gardesana* is a pleasant cooling breeze on hot summer days – perfect for cooling down. The *vent de sora* is benign, blowing from the north in the early mornings in fine weather, ideal for windsurfers, while the *vesentina* blows in off the Bardolino hills. The *spisoca* whips up a stronger wind in the gulf. The *ora* is a hot, rising wind blowing in off the southern plain. Both give sailors a run for their money, but it is the *leva*, blasting down from Trieste, that can cause most damage onshore.

Fasano
d. Garda
Gardone
Riviera
Il Vittoriale
Barbarano
Salò
Isola
del
Portese
Pieve Vecchia
Manerba d. Garda
Dusano
Moniga
sul Garda
Porto di Moniga
Padenghe
sul Garda
Sirmione
Fabbrica
**Desenzano
del Garda**
Colomba
Rivoltella

Desenzano del Garda c.1900.

EARLY BOATS

Garda has had ferries for as long as it has had people living on its shores, but it got its first steam ferry, the *Arciduca Ranieri*, in 1827. More and more ships were added to the fleet, possibly the most interesting of them the *Amico a Prora*, known as "The Handlebar", which was powered by eight horses yoked to handlebars on deck, turning the paddle wheels, which sailed for 10 years until 1830. By World War I, around 30,000 visitors a year were travelling on the ferries. In the period between the wars, a new fleet of ships was carrying up to 400,000 a year, numbers not reached again until the 1980s. These days well over a million people a year take to Garda's waters.

Windsurfing in Torbole.

The waterfront at Toscalano Moderno.

Sailing off Bogliaco.

Riva del Garda.

NORTHERN LAKE GARDA AND TRENTINO

The culture of Lake Garda changes yet again as you reach the far north. Now part of the province of Trentino, this area remained part of the Austro-Hungarian Empire right up until 1918.

Trentino is a mountainous land where eagles soar in summer and skiers swoop down gleaming pistes in winter. It may be Italian-speaking, but its Germanic roots remain strong, with beer and *sacher torte*, sausage and sauerkraut on the menus, while the architecture is influenced by the Austrian court and by the steep rooflines necessitated by the winter snows.

People were living in the area by 12,000 BC – this was the home of the Neanderthals and Oetzi the Iceman (see page 32). It was largely ignored by the Romans, although officially part of the empire. Christianity arrived in the 4th and 5th centuries, followed by Goths, Longobards and Franks. In 1027, the region, by now part of the Holy Roman Empire, was given to the local bishop as a principality. In 1363, a deal brokered between the dukes of Austria and the prince-bishop left him as a virtual figurehead, while the dukes got on with running the country.

In 1545–63, faced with the growing threat of Protestantism north of the Alps, the Council of Trent convened to shake up the Roman Church, but it failed to agree on anything much other than a willingness to stamp out any sign of heresy.

Napoleon came and went before the Holy Roman Empire crumbled.

In his wake, the Austrians got their lands back, but the prince-bishops of Trento didn't, and Italian-speakers suddenly found themselves being directly ruled by a northern, German regime. Long before World War I, there was a move towards joining the newly formed Kingdom of Italy. In that war, thousands died in bitter fighting on the Trentino front. When it was over, on 4 November 1918, Italian forces moved into Trento.

Meanwhile, throughout the more peaceful periods of the 19th and

Main Attractions
Riva del Garda
Grotta Cascata Varone, Riva del Garda
Piazza Duomo, Trento
Castello del Buonconsiglio, Trento
Castel Avio
MUSE – Museo delle Scienze di Trento
MART, Rovereto
Parco Naturale Adamello-Brenta

View of Mount Cevedale, Parco Nazionale dello Stelvio.

early 20th centuries, the northern part of Lake Garda was considered a sanatorium for the bourgeoisie and aristocracy of *Mitteleuropa*. Today, local thermal spas are being reborn as "well-being spas", led by Levico Terme. For the healthy, the mountains provide challenges aplenty, from mountain biking to hiking, paragliding to birdwatching, and if you are very, very lucky, you may just catch a glimpse of one of the brown bears recently released into the wilds of the Parco Naturale Adamello-Brenta (see page 64).

The Lake

Riva del Garda ❶, a 19th-century Lido, is still the main resort in the north, its broad waterfront with its porticoed medieval **Piazza III Novembre** perfectly designed for strolling in the evening sun. The rest of the town is crammed into the small amount of available space before the massive cliffs of **Monte Rocchetta** at 1,575 metres (5167ft) soar skywards. The German influence is clear – in the solidly northern architecture, in the menus, in the sheer volume of German tourists who flock here. The 12th-century **Rocca** (Castle, Piazza C. Battisti 3; tel: 0464-573 869; mid-Mar–May, Oct Tue–Sun 10am–6pm, June–Sept daily 10am–6pm) at one end of the waterfront has the town's museum and art gallery, while a footpath leads up to the **Bastione**, a Venetian fortress (built 1508) that looms over the lake. In the cliffs behind the town, the **Grotta Cascate Varone** (tel: 0464-521 421; Mar, Oct 9am–5pm, Apr, Sept 9am–6pm, May–Aug 9am–7pm, remaining months Sun and public holidays only 10am–5pm; www.cascata-varone.com) is a dramatic waterfall that cascades through a narrow canyon, showering the rocks with opalescent spray.

Cycling is hugely popular, whether on the roads or off-track.

Riva del Garda waterfront.

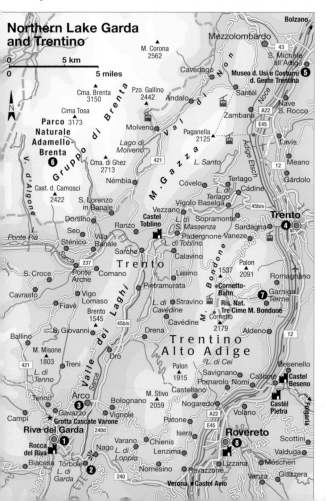

Northern Lake Garda and Trentino

Further east on the lakeshore, **Torbole ❷** is one of the lake's prettiest resorts, chiefly known for the winds which make it an ideal base for huge flotillas of windsurfers and dinghy sailors. You can see the full length of the lake on a clear day – though these are few and far between. A slight haze is the norm even in full sunlight. Goethe was most admiring when he stayed here in 1786, a visit commemorated by a statue in the main square.

A few kilometres inland, **Arco ❸** was the Austrian imperial resort and the most prestigious of the 19th-century spa resorts, a *kurpavilon*, a sanatorium with a spa, medicinal inhalations and therapeutic baths. Treatments centred on the curative properties of the Sarca river water, which was vaporised to produce steam scented with pine resin. These days, it is best-known for the dramatic medieval **Castello di Arco**, which clings to a rock on the outskirts of town (tel: 0464-510 156; Apr–Sept 10am–7pm, Mar, Oct 10am–5pm, Nov–Feb 10am–4pm, Jan Sat–Sun only).

Trento

Beyond Arco, a regiment of other villages with castles, including **Drò, Drena** and **Castel Toblino**, proceed up the Sarca Valley to the regional capital of **Trento ❹**, a startlingly beautiful walled city surrounded by the jagged peaks of the Dolomites.

Start in the **Piazza Duomo ⓐ**, which was founded on the site of the old Christian cemetery just outside the Roman **Porta Veronese**, a twin arch that controlled the road along the Adige Valley. These days the city has wrapped itself around the cathedral, with 15th–16th century arcades on three sides of the piazza and the beautiful **Fontana del Nettuno** (Neptune Fountain; 1767–9) by Francesco Antonio Giongo at the centre. Of the many painted houses in the city, two of the finest are in front of you – the **Casa Balduini**, probably the work of Francesco Verla from Vicenza (1510), and **Casa Cazuffi**, painted by Marcello Fogolino (1527–49) from San Vito in the Friuli region.

The **Basilica Duomo di San**

Playing on Torbole beach.

DRINK

In the northern part of Lake Garda, a legacy of Austro-Hungarian times is the bizarre grape cure known as the *traubenkur*, an autumn ritual involving the imbibing of large quantities of grape juice. Originally thought to cleanse one's body of toxins after the excesses of summer, the contemporary "cure" is more of an excuse to drink a fine range of regional wines and grappas.

Vigilio Ⓑ (Piazza Duomo; tel: 0461-980 132; daily 6.30am–noon, 2–6pm) was designed by sculptor-architect Adamo d'Arogno during the rule of Prince-Bishop Vanga (1207–18), although much was destroyed in adding the great galleried dome. Unusually, the side facing the piazza is more elaborate than the west front, which faces a small street.

Beneath the cathedral are the remnants of the early 6th-century **Basilica Paleocristiana di San Vigilio** (Palaeochristian Basilica of St Vigilio; Piazza Duomo 18; tel: 0461-234 419; Mon–Sat 10am–noon, 2.30–5.30pm), built over the tombs of Trentino's first evangelists, the martyrs Sisinio, Martirio and Alessandro and Bishop Vigilio (AD 400).

A few blocks away, in the **Spazio Archeologico Sotterraneo SASS Ⓒ** (Subterranean Archeological Area; Piazza Cesare Battisti; tel: 0461-230 171; Tue–Sun June–Sept 9.30am–1pm, 2–6pm, Oct–May 9am–1pm, 2–5.30pm), a timeline of the town is traced back 2,000 years from Roman buildings to a medieval quarter, a Renaissance palace, a 19th-century theatre and the modern day.

Back in the Piazza Duomo, the foundations of the **Torre Civica Ⓓ** (tel: 0461-234 419) rest on the former Roman gateway. Built in the 10th century, with many additions over the years, this was the keep of Palazzo Pretorio, used as a prison for a time. The Renga bell announced public meetings and executions.

The palace

The 13th-century **Palazzo Pretorio Ⓔ** (Piazza Duomo 18; tel: 0461-234 419; June–Sept Mon, Wed–Fri 9.30am–12.30pm, 2.30–6pm, Sat–Sun 10am–1pm, 2–6pm, Oct–May Wed–Sat 9.30am–12.30pm, 2–5.30pm, Sun 10am–1pm, 2–6pm; www.museodiocesanotridentino.it) holds the **Museo Diocesano del Trento** (Diocesan Museum of Trento), with the lavish collection of treasures, vestments, tapestries and art amassed by the prince-bishops over the centuries. On the other side of the Palazzo Pretorio is the austere **Castelletto dei Vescovi** (tel: 0461-234 419; visit to be

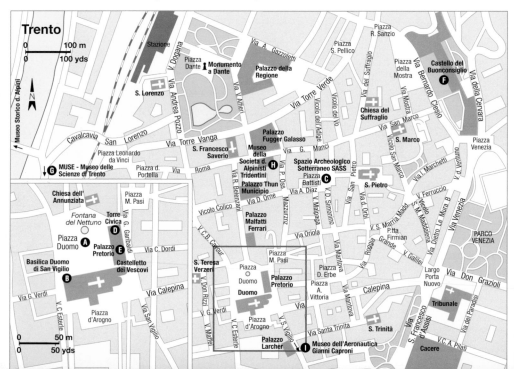

arranged with the Diocesan Museum of Trento). The basement contains the chapel of San Giovanni, the next floor the chapel of San Biagio, now used as the cathedral sacristy, while the impregnable top floor, fortified by Bishop Vanga in the 13th century, was the prince-bishops' home.

The castle

Their official seat was in the huge **Castello del Buonconsiglio ⓕ** (Via Bernardo Clesio 5; tel: 0461-233 770; www.buonconsiglio.it; Tue–Sun May– early Nov 10am–6pm, late-Nov–Apr 9.30am–5pm, also open Mon in Aug). Built on a rocky hill near the 13th-century city walls, over the centuries it has evolved, and today you can visit the 13th-century Palazzo Vecchio (Old Palace) and the luxurious 15th-century Magno Palazzo, built by Prince-Bishop Bernardo Clesio and liberally covered with his own heraldic symbols. Both are museums holding rich collections of archaeology, art and history, furniture and tapestries and musical scores dating back 1,500 years. Housed in

the castle carpentry workshops is the **Museo Storico del Trentino** (Museum of the History of Trentino; tel: 0461-230 482; www.museostorico. tn.it; closed for restoration).

The **Torre dell'Aquila** in the castle grounds is one of many along the 13th-century walls at the city limits. Bernardo Clesio (later prince-bishop 1514–39) housed his entourage here, and there are some magnificent 15th-century frescoes of the seasons by a Bohemian master. Several towers still stand, but only a couple can be visited.

Mountain museums

Anyone interested in mountain life should visit the **MUSE – Museo delle Scienze di Trento ⓖ** (MUSE Science Museum; Corso del Lavoro e della Scienza 3; tel: 0461-270 311; Tue–Fri 10am–6pm, Sat–Sun 10am–7pm; www.muse.it), formerly the Museo Tridentino di Scienze Naturali and now in a new location in a modern Renzo Piano-designed building next to Palazzo delle Albere. Along with the usual flora and fauna

TIP

Every summer the Sounds of the Dolomites festival brings open-air concerts to the mountains, with international musicians performing in breathtaking settings. For events listings, see www.isuonidelledolomiti.it.

Trento Duomo.

Castles in the Front Line

From ruined keeps clad in ivy to luxury chateau hotels, vast fortresses and walled cities – Trentino has a castle for everyone.

The motorway rolls invitingly down the Adige Valley, following the line of the Roman Via Claudia Augusta Altinate which connected the Adriatic Sea to the Danube – a vital trading route and also the obvious choice for any invading force, with a fork down the Sarca Valley to the lake.

Since Ostrogoths tramped south to end the Roman Empire, this region has seen far more than its fair share of armies on the march. Garrison towns and observation posts became dramatically sited, with splendidly crenellated castles, and the building continued even into the 20th century as the Austro-Hungarian forces strung World War I forts across the high ground to defend the borders of their empire.

The result is an extraordinarily rich collection of military history spanning over 1,000 years.

Castello del Buonconsiglio.

Some are still private property and not open to the public. Some are open as hotels and restaurants, others as museums.

Museum of Italy at war

Cream of the crop was the seat of the Prince-Bishops, **Castello del Buonconsiglio** in Trento (see page 141).

Rovereto's 15th-century Venetian castle, **Castello di Rovereto**, is home to the sombre **Museo Storico Italiano della Guerra** (via Castelbarco 7, Rovereto; tel: 0464-438 100; www.museodellaguerra.it; Tue–Sun 10am–6pm), which tells the violent local story of the Risorgimento and two world wars.

Built by the Castelbarco family in the 14th century, today it is considered to be one of the best examples of Venetian-type Alpine fortifications. It is a useful introduction if you wish to visit the plateaux that bore the brunt of the fighting. To do so, head back up north a short distance to Calliano, where the vast **Castel Beseno** (tel: 0464-834 600; www.buonconsiglio.it; mid-Mar–early May Sat–Sun 9.30am–5pm, early May–early Nov Tue–Sun 10am–6pm, early-Nov–early-Mar Tue–Sat 9.30am–5pm) encases the whole hilltop in rambling walls.

This, together with its smaller twin, **Castel Pietra**, marks the turn-off to **Folgaria**. The World War I front was along this area, which still bears the scars with forts, pillboxes, gun emplacements and trenches. The tourist office produces a detailed leaflet with a route map.

Castle of war and love

Castello di Avio (Sabbionara di Avio, 32km/20 miles south of Trento; tel: 0464-684 453; www.fondoambiente.it; Wed–Sun Mar–Sept 10am–6pm, Oct, Nov and second half of Feb 10am–5pm, also open Tue in Aug, last entry 30 minutes before closing; closed Dec–mid-Feb) stands at the back of protective Monte Baldo, an imposing 12th–13th-century complex of five towers, a palace and a keep commanding the Adige valley.

Inside are some vivid 14th-century frescoes – the guardhouse is decorated with scenes of war celebrating the military victories of the multiple-castle-building Castelbarcos, the historical owners of the castle, while the Hall of Love on the fourth floor of the keep is adorned in a more chivalric fashion with paintings on the theme of medieval romance.

displays, the museum explains the geology of the Dolomites and the prehistoric people of the mountains, including Neanderthals. Its tropical greenhouse showcases 132 African plant species.

The **Museo della Societa degli Alpinisti Tridentini**  (Museum of the Society of Trentino Alpinists; Via Manci, 57; tel: 0461-981 871; open on booking only; free) is a small museum of old documents, photos and climbing gear housed in the headquarters of the Trentino Alpinists Association, founded in Madonna di Campiglio in 1872.

On the edge of town, the **Museo Storico degli Alpini** (Museum of Alpine Troops; Doss Trento; tel: 0461-827 248; Tue–Thur 9am–noon, 1.30–4pm, Fri 9am–noon; free) is a national monument commemorating the role of the Alpine Troops in World War I. It is based in an Austrian powder-magazine near a 6th-century church.

There are twenty planes, some dating back to 1910, with various engines and parts as well as photographs and archives, on display at the **Museo dell'Aeronautica Gianni Caproni** ❶ (Aeronautics Museum; Via Lidorno 3, Trento Aeroporto; tel: 0461-944 888; Tue–Sun 10am–1pm, 2–6pm; www.museocaproni.it) on the outskirts of town.

The Adige Valley

A few kilometres north of Trento, the **Museo degli Usi e Costumi della Gente Trentina** ❺ (Folklore Museum; Via Mach 2, San Michele all'Adige; tel: 0461-650 314; www.museo sanmichele.it; Tue–Sun 9am–12.30pm, 2.30–6pm) is one of Italy's finest ethnographic museums, in a former Augustine convent, showing local customs, costume and traditions.

The road branches east into the wild high peaks of the Dolomites for the **Parco Nazionale dello Stelvio**, the largest park in the Alps, and the **Parco Naturale Adamello-Brenta** ❻, the last refuge of the brown bear (see page 64). For the Adige Valley castles.

South of Trento

Just south of Trento, on the slopes of Monte Bondone, the spa town of

The Renzo Piano-designed MUSE.

Garniga Terme ⑦ (tourist information tel: 0461-842586) specialises in hay baths (with curative grasses) said to cure osteoarthritis, rheumatism, muscle spasms and stiff joints.

Rovereto

Further down the valley, the medieval town of **Rovereto** is full of surprises, first among them a fabulous world-class museum of modern art in a stunning gallery designed by Swiss rationalist architect Mario Botta. The **MART** (Museo Arte Moderna e Contemporanea Trento Rovereto, Corso Bettini 43; tel: freephone 800-397760; www.mart.trento.it; Tue–Sun 10am–6pm, Fri until 9pm) has a collection which started in 1987 when the artist Fortunato Depero donated around 3,000 of his works to the town. Since then it has grown to include works from around the world, including Warhol, Roy Liechtenstein, and Bruce Naumann.

Rovereto itself reveals an engaging medieval and Renaissance heart, despite unprepossessing modern quarters. In the town centre, the River Leno is lined with silk-workers' tall houses. Silk-making was introduced in the 16th century and helped make Rovereto the region's chief industrial centre 200 years later. World War I caused great damage but the centre still has a faded charm, with frescoed facades, loggias and portals adorned with family crests.

The winding Via della Terra is the backbone of the picturesque medieval quarter, linking the church of San Marco with the Gothic civic tower and the **Castello** which houses the **Museo Storico Italiano della Guerra**. The castle came into being as a moated military fortress guarding the Adige Valley crossing. The crenellated bastion was remodelled by the Venetians but still follows the rugged contours of the rock. It has served as a poorhouse, a Napoleonic garrison and an Austrian barracks before becoming a war museum.

Until the 18th century, much of the surrounding countryside was given over to mulberry orchards and the silkworm breeding that supplied the local industry. Today, the slopes are covered in vineyards.

The stunning MART atrium.

ALPINE CLIMBING

The rugged individualists who opened up the Dolomites inevitably passed their baton to the Austrians and Italians, and the Alto Adige (South Tyrol) region now produces some of Italy's finest climbers, including Reinhold Messner, perhaps the greatest mountaineer of all time. This high-altitude Alpinist had scaled most of the Dolomites peaks by the age of 20, and inspired such climbers as Britain's Chris Bonington. Messner's mantra is still: "I am my own home and my handkerchief is my flag," but his latest mission is to create museums of mountaineering to preserve his legacy. Ironically, the greatest proponent of Alpine-style climbing now declares: "Alpinism is dead, though its spirit still lives on a little in Britain and America."

BRESCIA

Lombardy's "mini-Milan" is relishing its cultural renaissance, thanks to its revitalised city centre, restored Roman remains, the most rewarding historical museum in Italy – and the wine lakes in its back garden.

L ong overlooked, dignified Brescia strikes few chords with lovers of the lakes, but to envious Italians it means money and materialism, sparkling wine and Slow Food. To the locals, it means a hinterland of wine and lakes. The city itself is a Lombard workhorse – handsome rather than beautiful – though the multi-layered urban mix of Roman temples, Romanesque churches and Renaissance palaces is a draw for locals and visitors alike.

Once considered to be a philistine city that placed commerce before culture, Brescia has only recently woken up to its artistic goldmine. Often dubbed a "mini-Milan", Brescia has been reborn as an art city: Roman, Romanesque and Renaissance Brescia represent a true heritage trail. The rebranding came with the transformation of Santa Giulia into Italy's leading historical museum, followed by an ongoing series of blockbuster art exhibitions. Today, Brescia's reputation as a ploddingly industrious city is being buried under plaudits for its artistic flair.

The Longobard era

The city was always underrated, even in its early medieval heyday, when craftsmen created intricate stone sculpture, frescoes and jewellery that

defined the Longobard and Carolingian eras. The Longobards, a warlike Germanic people, conquered the lakes and colonised Brescia in the 6th century. Despite intermarrying with the natives and dutifully espousing Christianity, the settlers retained their stolid image. Perhaps this residual Teutonic work ethic, coupled with a lack of corruption, produced the resolve that paved the way for Lombardy's phenomenal industrial success. This murky period of the Longobard and Carolingian

Main Attractions
Piazza Della Loggia
Duomo Vecchio
Brixia
Museo di Santa Giulia
Il Castello

A picturesque cobbled backstreet.

WHERE

Tourist Offices: Via
Trieste 1; tel: 030-240
0357; Piazzale Stazione;
tel: 030-837 8559;
www.bresciatourism.it.

conquests is well presented in Brescia's stunning Museo della Città.

The lower city

Dominated by the medieval castle, the lower city is a reminder that Brescia was a stronghold of the Lombard League, and an arms producer since the Middle Ages. Long before that, **Brixia** (Brescia) was a prominent Roman base, which is easy to overlook as Lombard and Venetian palaces made their mark, along with the brutal stamp of Mussolini's boot. This multi-layering is clear in the interlocking squares of Piazza della Loggia, Piazza della Vittoria and Piazza Paolo VI, which form the heart of old Brescia. Here, a provincial mood prevails, with

neon-and-chrome bars losing out to cosy inns and quaint shopfronts.

The piazzas

Piazza della Loggia ❶ is the symbol of Renaissance Brescia, and the city's loveliest square, liveliest during the Saturday market. The space is dominated by **La Loggia**, the town hall, which combines Renaissance style with neoclassical sensibility: the facade was designed by Sansovino (1486–1570) and Palladio (1508–80) but only finished in 1575.

The square's harmonious mansions, gilded astronomical clocktower and graceful loggias are testament to the Venetian influence in the Renaissance era. Architecturally, the square is a poetic Venetian ensemble, in contrast

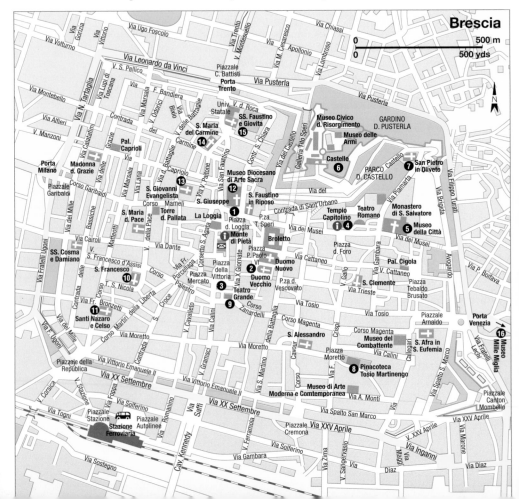

with the more prosaic Lombard style elsewhere. Even so, Brescia's love of recycling is seen in the facades, which are studded with Roman inscriptions, symbolically sited there by the Venetian rulers in 1480.

Under the porticoes, where Via dei Musei meets Piazza della Loggia, lie two chapels woven into the urban fabric of the city. The tiny frescoed chapel of **Santa Rita** is dedicated to the patron saint of lost causes, while the adjoining chapel of **San Faustino in Riposo** (Via dei Musei; Mon–Sat 8.30am–noon, 2.30–5.30pm; free), is a snug chapel hung with *ex-votos*.

Possessing rival cathedrals and the seat of the medieval city rulers, **Piazza Paolo VI ❷** represents the convergence of spiritual and temporal powers. The cylindrical **Duomo Vecchio** (Old Cathedral; daily 9am–noon, 3–6pm; free) is the star, one of the few such Romanesque churches in Italy. Its deep spiritual presence is picked up on by the head of tourism for the city, Massimo Ghidelli, who said, "Catholicism is in our DNA." But so too are ambition, art and commerce, as Massimo cheerfully admits.

Dwarfing it in size but not in spirituality is the **Duomo Nuovo** (New Cathedral; tel: 030-42714; daily 7.30am–noon, 3–7pm; free), a chilly concoction with a facade carved out of local white *botticino* marble. Beside it, the turreted **Broletto**, which incorporated Roman columns as a status symbol, was the medieval seat of power when Brescia was a city state, though its facade is caked in flouncy statuary.

Here you could sit and have a drink in one of the square's Latin-style outdoor cafés, and then enjoy the distractions of the elegant shops on the porticoed **Via X Giornate**; they are consolation for the somewhat soulless **Piazza della Vittoria ❸**. This ponderous tribute to Fascism, Mussolini's podium, fails to re-evoke the glories of ancient Rome. Instead, this "new" Fascistic forum, inaugurated by Mussolini in 1932, resembles a troubled De Chirico canvas, with its alienating geometrical dislocations.

Piazza della Loggia.

Roman Brescia

Far better loved is **Brixia**, the real **Roman Brescia**, represented by the remains of the Capitolium, Forum, Amphitheatre, Basilica and a cluster of villas, some of which were unearthed in the Santa Giulia complex. The grid-like Roman street plan has left a deep imprint on Brescia, influencing urban design to this day. Moreover, not only does Brescia boast the greatest concentration of Roman buildings north of Rome, but the discoveries continue; Unesco recognised its importance in 2011 by awarding it World Heritage Site status.

The latest archaeological excavations below the Capitoline Temple have revealed part of a Late Republican sanctuary decorated with geometric friezes and Pompeiian frescoes, which will eventually be on display.

Between Piazza della Loggia and Via dei Musei lie most of the visible Roman ruins, which are being incorporated into an archaeological park. Yet the medieval Via dei Musei runs across the Roman Forum, provoking the eternal Italian debate: can we justify destroying one ancient historical treasure to rescue another?

The most eye-catching site is the **Capitolium** or **Tempio Capitolino** ❹ (Piazza del Foro; tel: 030-240 0640; www.bresciamusei.com; mid-June–Sept Tue–Fri 10.30am–7pm, Oct–mid-June Tue–Fri 9.30am–5.30pm), which was preserved by a medieval mudslide that covered it until 1823. Above the ancient Forum loom the graceful Corinthian colonnades of this Capitoline Temple, erected by Vespasian in AD 73. The best Roman sculptures are already in the Museo della Città, including an arresting *Winged Victory*, a fitting symbol for such a warlike city.

Adjoining the Capitolium is the **Teatro Romano**, the partially restored Roman amphitheatre, one of northern Italy's largest, which was used for public meetings until well into medieval times.

Museo della Città

The **Museo della Città** ❺ (City Museum, Via dei Musei 81; tel: 030-297

The Duomo Nuovo and Duomo Vecchio.

7834; www.bresciamusei.com; mid-June–Sept Tue–Sun 10am–7pm, Oct–mid-June Tue–Sun 9.30am–5.30pm) is located in the nearby Santa Giulia monastic complex, which lies on the *decamanus maximus*. The museum is the broadest-ranging historical museum in Italy – also recently declared a Unesco World Heritage Site – covering Brescia's 3,000-year history in a compelling presentation that touches on most aspects of our common European heritage. Set in a former convent, itself built over Roman baths and Carolingian churches, the museum forms a labyrinth of buildings found *in situ*, including patrician Roman villas, a Byzantine basilica and a Romanesque oratory.

The convent was founded in AD 753 by Desiderius, king of the Longobards. Brescia was an 8th-century duchy under Desiderius, whose daughter was married to Charlemagne as part of the deal to crown him Holy Roman Emperor.

Given Brescia's artistic mining of its past, even the *Cross of Desiderius*, a bejewelled Carolingian gem, incorporates tiny Roman cameos. In an unspoken dialogue between generations to come, one cameo shows a Roman woman appearing to peer perplexedly into the descending Dark Ages.

However, there is nothing dry and dusty about this museum: Hellenistic goddesses, Longobard kings, Dionysus and his pet panther, and that cameo of a Roman noblewoman all speak to us across the ages. The city symbol, the powerful *Winged Victory*, was recently revealed to be Greek, dating back to the 3rd century BC, although the wings were added four centuries later to turn Aphrodite, the Greek goddess of love, into an avenging symbol of Roman military might. Even the nuns of Santa Giulia have left a sense of their cloistered lives. Mostly wealthy noblewomen, they were forbidden contact with the outside world but could at least spy on visitors from the gorgeously frescoed confines of the Nuns' Choir.

While the city's splendid Renaissance art gallery, the Pinacoteca Tosio Martinengo, is undergoing restoration, part of the collection is on view at the Museo della Città Giulia providing further reason to make a visit.

The castle

For the most atmospheric walk up to the castle, turn right out of the Museo della Città to the café-lined **Piazza Tito Speri**, sitting at the foot of the castle. On a sunny day, take the bucolic route via **Contrada di Sant'Urbano**, a succession of stairways winding up the hill. Even exploring the twisting back alleys below the castle will allow you to travel back in time.

Looming above the city, the **Castello ❻** (Via del Castello; grounds 8am–8pm; free) has a leafy feel, with the languid mood underscored by the haunting sounds of piano-playing that float through the windows of the music students. Inside

Beautiful fresco on display at Santa Giulia.

The Roman Capitolium.

TIP

In the city centre, Mariabruna Perfumery is a haven from urban stress run by Mariabruna Zorzi, Brescia's beauty guru. Here you can concoct new perfumes, get impartial advice on beauty products, or try a new beauty or spa treatment (Piazza Vescovato 1; tel: 030-45194; see recommended spas on page 156).

the castle, the **Museo delle Armi** (Arms Museum; tel: 030-297 7833; www.bresciamusei.com; mid-June–Sept Fri–Sun 11am–7pm, Oct–mid-June Thu–Fri 9am–4pm, Sat–Sun 10am–5pm) acts as a reminder that Brescia has been Italy's main arms producer since medieval times. The locals play down their deadly expertise, but are secretly proud that the FBI "buys Brescia", and that "their" Beretta pistols are the handguns of choice for the New York police.

Also housed in the castle, the **Museo del Risorgimento** (tel: 030-297 7833; same hours as Museo delle Armi) holds an array of artefacts relating to the Italian Risorgimento, including paintings, ceramics and sculpture.

Tucked into the wooded slopes, **San Pietro in Oliveto** ❼ (Via del Castello; tel: 030-41531/49264; Mon–Sat 7–11.30am, 4–7.15pm, Sun 9.30am–noon, 4–8pm; free) enjoys a tranquil setting. Today home to Carmelite friars, the harmonious complex conceals 16th-century cloisters and a Renaissance interior.

Brescia's castle.

Via Piamarta, one of the original Roman thoroughfares, lies below, and at the bottom of the hill is **Piazza Tebaldo Brusato**, an atmospheric, tree-lined medieval square that feels like it could belong in Provence. For a return to contemporary Brescia, join the cocktail circuit on **Piazzale Arnaldo**, the former grain market further to the south.

Nearby, one of the city's big attractions, the **Pinacoteca Tosio Martinengo** ❽ (Piazza Moretto 1; tel: 030-297 7834), is currently closed for large-scale restoration; the collection of Lombard Renaissance art is on display at the Museo della Città and the Museo Diocesano.

Corso Zanardelli

It is pleasant to window-shop along the arcaded boulevard of **Corso Zanardelli**, where cafés, boutiques and the colonnaded opera house await. The **Teatro Grande** ❾ (Corso Zanardelli 9; tel: 030-297 3333; www.teatrogrande.it) offers a dynamic mix of opera and classical music. Just north, **Piazza del Vescovato**, on Via Mazzini, is an

elegant square with lime trees around a monumental fountain.

Corso Matteotti and Corso Mameli

Further west, the church of **San Francesco** ❿ (Via di San Francesco d'Assisi; tel: 030-292 6701; Mon–Sat 7–11.30am, 3–7pm, Sun 3.30–7.30pm; free) is the most serene late Romanesque church, enhanced by Gothic cloisters and vaults frescoed by Romanino. **Santi Nazaro e Celso** ⓫ (Corso Matteotti; tel: 030-375 4387; Sat 3–7pm, Sun 8am–noon, 2–7pm; free) has a grand neoclassical facade but is best-known for Titian's *Averoldi Altarpiece*, a masterpiece that fuses Venetian mystery with Roman muscularity.

This atmospheric area of Corso Matteotti, Mameli and Garibaldi is gradually being renovated rather than gentrified. Bourgeois Brescians had abandoned their crumbling mansions and immigrant communities had moved in, but the tide may be turning. The regeneration of Corso Mameli reflects the new spirit, typified by the locals' pride in **Torre della Pallata**, a rough-hewn medieval gateway, and the restoration of a magnificent fountain.

Nearby, the **Museo Diocesano di Arte Sacra** ⓬ (Via Gasparo da Salò; tel: 030-40233; Thu–Tue 10am–noon, 3–6pm) displays religious art, including works by Moretto and Tiepolo; a few works from the Pinacoteca Tosio Martinengo are also being housed here.

The Carmine District

A short walk away is **San Giovanni Evangelista** ⓭ (Contrada di San Giovanni; tel: 030-240 0224; daily 7.30–11am, 3.30–6.30pm; free), with its 15th-century facade and Renaissance art by Romanino and Moretto. This is the vibrant Carmine district, the ethnic part of town which adds another interesting dimension to the city. Meandering around here dispels the myth of Brescia being a static, closed place. There are plenty of North African rugs and Ghanaian robes around, and some of the dilapidated *palazzi* are now being renovated.

The Cross of Desiderius, the Museo della Città's prized exhibit.

WHERE

The Mille Miglia (thousand miles) vintage car rally goes in a loop from Brescia's Piazza della Loggia to Rome and back. Held every May, this is Italy's most famous rally, and attracts over 20,000 people to line the streets in the section from Brescia to Desenzano on Lake Garda.

At the heart of the district is the handsome, barrel-vaulted Gothic church of **Santa Maria del Carmine**  (Contrada del Carmine; tel: 030-304 169; Fri–Sun 10am–noon, 3–6pm; free).

Santi Faustino e Giovita ⑮ (Via San Faustino; tel: 030-292 195; Mon–Sat 7.30–11am, 3–7pm, Sun 7.30am–noon, 3–7pm; free) is a Benedictine foundation with a facade carved out of *botticino* stone, and art by Tiepolo and Romanino.

At the southern end of the Carmine stands the 16th-century monastery of **San Giuseppe** (Vicolo San Giuseppe 5; tel: 030-40233; Mon–Sat 7.30–11am, 3–5.30pm, Sun 7.30–11am; free), its finely frescoed cloister (Mon–Sat 8.30am–noon, 3–6pm) squeezed between tall mansions.

Mille Miglia

Despite cobblestones and steep slopes, Brescia is overrun by cyclists, though it also manages to remain in thrall to cars. The city's Mille Miglia (Thousand Miles) rally has played its part in helping Italians fall in love with cars for ever. It's a short cab ride east to the

Vintage cars compete at Brescia's Mille Miglia.

Museo Mille Miglia ⑯ (Viale della Rimembranza 3; tel: 030-336 5631; www.museomillemiglia.it; daily 10am–6pm). Set in a Benedictine monastery, the Vintage Car Museum showcases the vintage rally cars in their racing colours. British racing driver Stirling Moss's record time of 10 hours 7 minutes to Rome in 1955 was a milestone in racing history.

La passeggiata

Back on the streets, Brescia is sometimes dismissed as a city of somewhat ponderous souls, characters as conservative as they are Catholic, but a ritual evening stroll reveals a less strait-laced side. Corso Zanardelli comes alive for *passeggiata*, the parade that lake-loving Brescians call "*le vasche*", as in "doing lengths" in a communal pool. These "Lengths" tend to end in trusty wine bars like Vineria, or hearty inns like Al Frate, where deals are clinched over Franciacorta wine, salami and cheese. As citizens who believe in working hard and playing hard, it seems that Brescians were born to mix business with pleasure.

The clocktower on Piazza della Loggia.

SPA HEAVEN

Brescia's sulphurous thermal waters, known since Roman times, are particularly appealing on cool days.

In keeping with Italian practice, most authentic thermal spas are clinical-looking medical spas that are mired in the past and manned by doctors in scary white coats. However, Aquaria, in the Terme di Sirmione, by Lake Garda, is a glowing exception. The setting is delightful, based around a succession of pools and water jets beside the waterfront.

Italians distinguish between thermal spas *(terme)* and well-being spas *(centri benessere)*, where water is not an intrinsic component of the treatment. As a rule, thermal spas are more suitable for specific cures and longer stays, while well-being spas are aesthetically pleasing, pampering, and offer a range of massages, facials and beauty treatments. But in the best thermal spas, such as Sirmione, the distinction is blurred. Swimming in the bubbling, cocooning pools is particularly soporific in winter, when the steam rises off the water and swimmers are transported into a dream-like state reminiscent of an Antonioni movie.

Italians swear by water therapy and the healing properties of specific types of water. **Aquaria** (www.termedisirmione.it) is a seductive, soothing thermal spa where you can idle away a morning slipping from one open-air plunge pool to another or being wrapped in mud, while the trace elements supposedly work on your cellulite. As for the science bit, the mineral-laden waters, rich in sodium chloride and trace elements such as iodine, potassium and magnesium, heated to 36–38°C (96–100°F) gently exfoliate the skin, and induce deep relaxation, but are especially beneficial for anyone suffering from respiratory complaints, vascular problems, rheumatism or arthritis.

The steaming outdoor pool at Aquaria.

Pool at Cappuccini, Franciacorta.

Lotions and potions.

Mud treatment at Aquaria.

Purely well-being treatments can be sampl in the region's boutique hotels. In Brescia itse **Il Santellone** resort (www.ilsantellone.it) is a tr spa journey, taking in the "Roman route", fro the Roman Baths, Caldarium and Tepidarium, a serene setting that reuses Romanesque colum and artefacts. Set in a stylishly converted monas complex, the spa embodies a mood of peace a harmony. But with delicious unguents slather over one's naked body, indulging in wine or choc late therapy can feel like dabbling in the Dark A

MILAN'S BEST SPAS

Best spa for glamour and professionalism: Club 10 in the Principe di Savoia is Milan's grande dame of spas, where you could swim in a rooftop pool before your treatment, and possibly spot Donatella Versace in her favourite hotel (www.dorchestercollection.com).

Best spa for Japanese expertise: **Le Terme di Kyoto** at the Enterprise Hotel with panoramic views of Milan that places emphasis on cutting-edge treatments (www.planetaria hotels.com).

Best spa for stylish shopping: **Bulgari Spa**, on a private street in the heart of the shopping district, is beautifully designed, exclusive and renowned for facials (www.bulgari hotels.com).

Closer to Lake Garda and Lake Iseo, **Palazzo zaga** (www.palazzoarzaga.it) combines a golfing eak with a spa escape, typically a his-and-hers tion; the spa complements the Clarins approach h its own exotic, oriental treatments. The radical ental-themed spa, **Centro Tao** (www.centrotao.it) Limone sul Garda, is based on balance, yin and g, Chinese medicine and oriental spa therapies. ar Lazise, the **Hotel Principe di Lazise** (www. telprincipedilazise.com) offers the Aquavitae spa, h an array of treatments using the luxe Culti oducts, and a focus on 'oriental paths', inspired by rvedic medicine. **Cappuccini** (www.cappuccini.it) 16th-century former monastery in Franciacorta h classic spa treatments Italian-style, meaning a ackage" including too many (potentially clash- g) "cures" at once.

Despite the decadent setting, in umante-producing Fran- corta, Henri Chenot's orous French spa is the tidote to pampering. The a's philosophy is pre- tious, but well inten- ned: a potentially e-changing "cure" to

Urban chic at Club 10, Principe di Savoia, Milan.

put the sinner on the straight and narrow. There is only one obstacle in the path of the Cartesian *grand projet*. Set in the countryside above Lake Iseo, **L'Albereta** (www.albereta.it) is a renowned gastro-hotel, with both an Italian chef and M. Chenot, the French celebrity spa guru. It seems wilfully cruel that one guru should be proffering gastro fare while the other punishes guests with strict "cures for weight loss, stress and anti-ageing". Possibly yin and yang, but definitely very French.

Hot stone therapy at Palazzo Arzaga.

Val Camonica winter scene.

LAKE ISEO, FRANCIACORTA AND VAL CAMONICA

Wild Lake Iseo is bordered by the cultivated wine country of Franciacorta and is a stepping stone to Val Camonica, where the rocks are carved with accounts of the lives of the Camuni people, the valley's prehistoric population.

Brescia's inhabitants think of the lakes as a summer playground, and as a reward for their hard work in banking, pharmaceuticals and the arms trade. Lake Iseo, located between Brescia and Bergamo, is also Bergamo's back garden, representing a restful weekend escape around one of the largest lake islands in Europe, called Monte Isola. Resolutely untouristy, Lake Iseo's charms reside in the peaceful hamlets fringed by mountains and the cosy local inns.

From Brescia, the short hop to the lake passes rolling countryside, wine estates and manor houses. This is the prosperous wine-growing district of Franciacorta, where gourmet cuisine is matched by Italy's finest sparkling wines. It is a place of gentle moraine hills scattered with grand villas, castles and parks.

North of Lake Iseo stretches Val Camonica, running from the shore to snow-capped Tonale, passing villages which have worked stone, wood and iron ore since antiquity. As the ancestral home of the Camuni civilisation, the valley is scored with prehistoric rock carvings, especially around Capo di Ponte, which present a vivid account of the lives and beliefs of these people.

Lake Iseo

Brescia is a perfect stepping stone to rural **Lake Iseo**, which is a short but

The town of Peschiera Maraglio on Monte Isola.

scenic train ride to Iseo itself. Lago d'Iseo, which measures 25km (15.5 miles) long by 5km (3 miles) wide, encloses one of the largest lake islands in Europe, and boasts wild scenery on the western shore, as well as wine-growing hills to the south. Thickly wooded slopes rise up from the waterfront. Iseo experiences a more Alpine climate than Lake Garda: olives and horse chestnuts flourish, rather than lemons and palms. Unfairly neglected in favour of the larger lakes, Lake Iseo is sweeter, quieter and less

Main Attractions
Santa Maria Della Neve
Iseo
Franciacorta Winelands
Abbazia di San Nicola
Franciacorta Outlet Village
Bienno
Val Camonica Rock Carvings
Parco dell'Adamello

self-consciously quaint. Unlike its rivals, the lake offers no heart-stopping set pieces but compensates with the slow burn of contemplative walks and a way of life not wholly based on tourism. Iseo, the natural base for exploring the lake, is a charming unspoilt historic town, while the hills around hide some of the region's finest inns.

Sarnico ❶, the Bergamo gateway to Lake Iseo, embodies the local attitude that this is a living, working community rather than a tourist trap. Set on the rugged western shore, Sarnico occupies the site of a prehistoric stilt village. Despite its delightful porticoes and medieval ramparts, Sarnico is best-known as a speedboat base, thanks to Riva, a company which produces the "Ferrari" of speedboats, which was founded here.

Torbiere del Sebino.

Tavernola Bergamasca ❷ signals the start of the wildest stretch of the lake, despite the blots of a cement works and over-quarried hills. Beyond here, the dramatic western shore is riddled with coves carved into limestone cliffs, and ravines running down to gnarled rocks.

At the northern end is **Lovere**, the capital of the Bergamo side of the lake and the starting point for expeditions into the Val Camonica. It is a good place to pause for a walk around the medieval village of **Qualino**, set on a hillside terrace with great panoramic views of the lake and the lower Camonica Valley.

Romanino frescoes

The rock carvings in **Val Camonica** (see page 170) are best reached via the valley road from **Pisogne ❸**. The village is famous for the frescoed church of **Santa Maria della Neve** (Via Antica Valeriana; Tue–Sun 9.30–11.30am, 3–6pm; free). Known as a poor man's Sistine Chapel, the church is frescoed by Romanino (c.1484–1559), a complex artist steeped in the

Lake Iseo and Franciacorta map

Venetian Renaissance tradition, but influenced by Michelangelo, and a precursor to Caravaggio. On display is his powerful *Passion of Christ* cycle which, rare for the times, makes little distinction between sacred and profane subjects, placing them both on the same level. As a typically Brescian painter, Romanino is renowned for his realistic portraits of his contemporaries, faces that can still be seen all over Lake Iseo. These expressive frescoes depict a typical Romanino scene peopled by bulky, peasant-like figures, typical of an artist praised as "painting in dialect".

The 'Pyramids of Zone'

Sheer lakeside cliffs frame **Marone**, where there is a turn-off to **Cislano** via Monte Marone and a tortuous route through chestnut woods to **Zone ❹**. From here, there are views of strange mushroom-shaped pinnacles of soft rock topped by comical boulders. Formed by the erosion of glacial moraine deposits, these weathered "pyramids" can be seen close up by following the hiking trail from Zone.

Monte Isola

To the south, and on the lakeside, **Sale Marasino** and Sulzano on the eastern shore offer crossings to **Monte Isola ❺**, an island forested with chestnut trees and olive groves. En route, the ferry passes a tiny private island belonging to the gun-making Beretta dynasty, whose fearsome reputation is enough to deter curious visitors; Beretta's industrial base is in the Brescian hinterland.

The ferry slips into Monte Isola, the highest lake island in Europe, and also the continent's largest inhabited lake island. This mountainous, heavily forested island supports a 1,700-strong community of fishermen, boat builders and net-makers. Despite its humble origins, Monte Isola's fishing hamlets reveal refined touches, from sculpted portals to tiny courtyards.

At **Peschiera Maraglio**, take the gentle walk from the jetty to **Sensole**, which covers the hamlets on the sunny side of the island, and allows for views of Iseo and the island of San Paolo. Above, tiers of olive groves merge into vineyards, chestnut groves and the

WHERE

Lake Iseo Tourist office
IAT Lago d'Iseo e Franciacorta (Lungolago Marconi 2/C, Iseo; tel: 030-374 8733; Tue–Fri 10am–12.30pm, 3–6pm; www.iseolake.info) is helpful, as is the Franciacorta wine route (www.stradadelfranciacorta.it) and, for an overview, Brescia tourism (www.bresciatourism.it).

Romanesque frescoes, Santa Maria della Neve, Pisogne.

Mending nets near Peschiera Maraglio on Monte Isola, an area famous for its net-making industry.

View over Marone.

occasional medieval tower, with the highest peak surmounted by a 16th-century sanctuary, built over a pagan shrine. The lakeside promenade is lined with fish restaurants, the best place for a scenic view of the mountainous terrain. It is hard to resist a waterfront inn for grilled sardines, perch risotto and lake scampi, washed down with a local wine.

On the shore, heaps of hammocks and fishing nets drying in the sun are the only clues that this has been a net-making area for 1,000 years. Cluniac monks built an industry which now embraces Wimbledon tennis nets and World Cup football nets. Look in at Retificio Architetti Paolo (on the waterfront), which sells serviceable hammocks.

Why not buy a picnic and consider the hike to the Gothic **Santuario della Madonna della Ceriola** (600 metres/ 1,970ft). It is a steep 90-minute climb past olive groves and walnut trees. Alternatively, the short (15-minute) route to the Marian sanctuary begins from Cure (and can be reached by bus).

Far gentler, and more in keeping with local tastes, is the lakeside promenade around the island. The pace of life is slow: cars are banned in favour of bicycles, mopeds or public minibuses (bicycles can be hired through the Peschiera tourist office). If in a hurry to return to civilisation, take the fastest ferry back to the mainland, which connects Monte Isola with **Sulzano**.

Iseo

Just south, the town of **Iseo** ❻ can also be reached on an attractive train journey from Brescia. Now the elegant lake capital, Iseo was a significant port until the 1870s, shipping grain from Val Camonica and steel from the industrial depots on the lake. Iseo is more irredeemably bourgeois and self-assured than its rival, Lovere, on the Bergamo bank, a town the locals dismiss as "provincial". Sandwiched between the waterfront and a feudal castle, Iseo retains its cosy medieval street pattern as well as a sweeping promenade and handsome squares. The bustling shops display a slice of local life with huge Parmesans, salamis and mounds of

fresh pasta. The clumsily remodelled church of **Sant'Andrea** boasts the finest Romanesque bell tower on the lake. Porticoed **Piazza Garibaldi** is the liveliest part of town, dominated by a statue of the patriot perched on a mossy rock, one of the few horseless statues of him in existence. The square's cafés, particularly Ariston, make an appealing spot for people-watching and wine-tasting. Shaded by plane trees, the waterfront promenade is a soporific spot from which to watch the lake traffic.

Iseo is not simply the most attractive town on the waterfront, but a stepping stone to lakeside beaches, including the **Lido di Belvedere**.

Franciacorta

Just inland from Lake Iseo is a neat green patchwork of villas, extensive vineyards and monasteries that makes this Lombardy's most mellow wine-growing area. It helps that **Franciacorta** produces the country's most prestigious sparkling champagne-style wines, a world away from supermarket Spumante.

The path to prosperity was set by the medieval monks who colonised this once desolate corner in return for privileges. In the 11th century, the nobility called on Cluniac monks to drain the marshes, resulting in a building boom and grand crenellated monasteries. From 1277, tax concessions caused the area to be known as Corte Franca ("free court") and spurred patrician families from Brescia and beyond to build castles in these low hills. During the Renaissance, these castles were converted into patrician villas and noble wine estates. Ambitious restaurateurs and wine-makers have since moved in, making Franciacorta the sought-after rural retreat for bons vivants it is today.

Monasteries and wine estates

Foremost among the monks who drained the lands were the Cluniac brothers from the **Monastero di San Pietro ⑦** (Via Monastero 5; tel: 030-982 3617; Sat–Sun Apr–Oct 10am–noon, 3–6pm, Nov–Mar 10am–noon, 2–5pm). Built over a Roman temple and enveloped by moody marshes close to Lake Iseo, the monastery still

TIP

The **Treno Blu** is a delightful train-bus-boat summer excursion from Bergamo to Lake Iseo, that takes in Palazzolo and Paratico, as well as a ferry crossing to Monte Isola on Lake Iseo (some Saturdays and Sundays in May, June, September; tel: 030-740 2851; www.ferrovieturistiche.it).

Piazza Garibaldi, Iseo.

Franciacorta Wine Trail

The blend of superb wines and harmonious landscape finds favour with foodies and wine buffs alike, making Franciacorta a sought-after spot for a lost weekend.

This prestigious wine-growing region produces sparkling champagne-style signature wines, which are subject to a slow fermentation process. Known as Franciacorta DOCG, the wines run from Pas Dosé (exceptionally dry) to Brut (classic dry), Sec (dry) and Demi-Sec (dessert wine).

Bearing in mind the connection between wine and wealth, the rolling countryside is dotted with wine estates spilling out of castles, villas and manor houses. While some estates have attached wine museums, sophisticated inns or simple farm-stays, virtually all producers offer wine-tasting. (Book directly, or through the Strada del Franciacorta association; www.stradadelfranciacorta.it; tel: 030-776 0477.) This

The Franciacorta wine district.

well-developed wine route proposes tours as well as a handy wine map.

Given the number of superb estates and the desirability of booking, the following is only a taster of the most emblematic estates.

Wine estates

Unassuming Erbusco lies at the centre of the wine district. **Bellavista** (tel: 030-776 2000; www.bellavistawine.it) is a highly rated estate of Brescian magnate Vittorio Moretti, now president of the Franciacorta Consortium. You can also browse Franciacorta wines in the village's **Cantine di Franciacorta wine shop** (Via Iseo 98; tel: 030-775 1116), which also sells local honey, cheeses and salami.

In neighbouring **Adro**, the **Contadi Castaldi** estate (tel: 030-745 0126; www.contadicastaldi.it) in a former brickworks is noted for sparkling Saten Brut, made from Chardonnay with a dash of Pinot Bianco. Nearby, the **Ricci Curbastro** estate in Capriola (tel: 030-736 094; www.ricci curbastro.it) offers tastings and a tour of the wine museum, as well as an antique shop in its farm-stay. Near Corte Franca, **Barone Pizzini** (tel: 030-984 8311; www.baronepizzini.it) is Franciacorta's first fully organic estate, in a castle with a small museum, tasting rooms and restaurant. In Borgonato, just over the hill, **Fratelli Berlucchi** (tel: 030-984 381; www.berlucchi.com) is one of the best-known producers, owned by five brothers.

In Monticelli Brusati, further east, the **Villa** estate (tel: 030-652 329; www.villa-franciacorta.it) occupies its own hamlet, with 16th-century cellars, a rustic inn and farm-stay apartments. In neighbouring Camignone di Passirano, **Il Mosnel** (tel: 030-653 117; www.ilmosnel.com) is a welcoming family-run estate run by the dynamic Giulio Barzano. A wine-tasting can be followed by lunch chosen to complement the wines.

If visiting Ome, be sure to try **Azienda Agricola Al Rocol** (Via Provinciale 79, tel: 030-685 2542; www.alrocol.com), a rustic inn on a family-run award-winning wine estate and farm. In autumn and winter order traditional spit with *polenta e osei*, washed down by a glass of the excellent local Grappa Chardonnay (Franciacorta DOCG). Also in Ome, stop by the Majolini winery (Via Manzoni 3, tel: 030-652 7378; www.majolini.it) run by the same family since the 15th century and producing excellent Brut and Demi-Sec Franciacorta DOCG wines.

feels aloof, but exudes a gentle charm, from the Romanesque bell tower to the tiny cloisters and school of Romanino frescoes. (An oddity of Franciacorta is that, while you can risk simply turning up, all places prefer booking, even churches; details available on www.stradadelfranciacorta.it.)

At the foot of the monastery is the nature reserve of **Torbiere del Sebino** ❽ (always open). This is birdwatching territory, as well as being the watery preserve of perch, trout and eel, and home to happy predators from herons to kingfishers. Paths wind through the peat bogs, providing sightings of white swans gliding between the water lilies, or the swoop of a marsh falcon onto its victim in a clump of ferns.

Provaglio d'Iseo, once part of the Cluniac estates, leads to **Monticelli Brusati** ❾, where vineyards stretch for as far as the eye can see. This is the delectable setting for the **Villa** wine estate (Frazione Villa; tel: 030-652 329; www.villa-franciacorta.it), complete with wine tours and a welcoming rustic inn.

Culture-lovers should call in at **Rodengo-Saiano** to see the restored

Abbazia di San Nicola ❿ (Via Brescia; tel: 030-610 182; Mon–Sat 9am–noon, 3–6pm, Sun from 12.30pm). Founded by the Cistercians in the **10th century**, but later Olivetan, this is one of the most impressive monastic complexes in northern Italy. The abbey displays 15th- and 16th-century frescoes by the greatest Brescian artists, including Romanino and Moretto. The monks still reside here and, in traditional monastic style, restore antiquarian books and manuscripts as well as concocting liqueurs, such as Sambuca, which you can buy. Fashionable visitors will also enjoy the designer boutiques at discounted prices in **Franciacorta Outlet Village** (www. franciacortaoutlet.it).

Passirano is dominated by Franciacorta's most striking crenellated castle, which conceals a Renaissance villa and wine estate. Another crenellated castle and Renaissance villa awaits at **Castello di Bornato** ⓫ (Via Castello 4, Bornato; www.castellodibornato.com; mid-Mar–mid-Nov Sun 10am–noon, 2.30–6pm). The Italianate gardens open onto the estate vineyards, providing a

TIP

To see frescoes by Romanino (1484–c.1559), the region's finest Renaissance painter, visit the churches of Santa Maria della Neve in Pisogne, Santa Maria in Bienno, Sant'Antonio in Breno, as well as the abbazia di San Nicola in Rodengo-Saiano and Brescia's best gallery, the Pinacoteca Martinengo (closed for restoration but some of its works are being hosted by the Museo di Santa Giulia).

Monastero di San Pietro.

TIP

These are the best
sources of information
on: Val Camonica rock art
(www.vallecamonicaunesco.
it); Adamello park
(www.parcoadamello.it);
summer sports and
skiing (www.adamelloski.
com); and the Francia-
corta wine route
(www.franciacorta.net). For
an overview, Brescia-
tourism (www.brescia
tourism.it) remains the
most useful.

Val Camonica.

pretext for another wine-tasting. In its previous incarnation as a medieval castle, Bornato once welcomed Dante, but the poet's views on divine Franciacorta wines are unrecorded.

Rovato

Rovato ⓬, Franciacorta's main centre, lacks the charm of the wine hamlets but has an impressive Servite convent. Clear your head by walking up Monte Orfano for sweeping views from the hilltop and a visit to **Sant'Annunziata** (tel: 030-772 1377; daily 9am–noon, 3–6pm), which displays a fine *Annunciation* by the Renaissance master Romanino (see page 165).

Back among the vineyards, **Erbusco ⓭**, the wine-production centre, is both earthy and elegant, much like sparkling Franciacorta itself. Despite the Romanesque church of **Santa Maria Assunta** and the Palladian Villa Lechi, Erbusco is indelibly associated with **L'Albereta**, the lovely villa-hotel and gastro-haunt. In gourmet Franciacorta, convents inevitably lose out to feasting.

Yet the good life also proved attractive to worldly prelates. The village of

Borgonato ⓮, near Corte Franca, even became the summer residence of the high-born sisters from Brescia's Santa Giulia nunnery. Today, Borgonato is better-known as the home of **Fratelli Berlucchi** (Via Broletto; tel: 030-984 381; www.berlucchi.it; daily; guided tours in English at 2pm), a renowned wine estate, slightly belittled locally as being "too industrial". Neighbouring **Nigoline** offers an escape from wine in the form of the **Franciacorta Golf Club** (tel: 030-984 167; www.franciacorta golfclub.it) which, unlike most clubs in the locality, accepts non-members.

Adro is bristling with churches, but the noted **Contadi Castaldi wine estate** (see page 164) is also worth visiting. **Capriolo**, named after the deer which once roamed here, is near the lake. Consider roaming around the **Ricci Curbastro wine estate** and museum located nearby (see page 164).

Fish-lovers should time any Franciacorta outing to finish with supper in **Clusane ⓯**, a foodie haunt, known for its baked tench. Crowned by an abandoned castle, Clusane overlooks a port full of bobbing boats setting out in search of fish including tench, pike, chub and lake sardines. If this all sounds too fishy for your tastes, head for the hills overlooking the lake, which offer a romantic, rural setting – and a sparkling mineral water.

Val Camonica

Unpolished, underrated Val Camonica is one of the least explored but most rewarding stretches of Lombardy. Traditionally, the region was known for its witchcraft. In 1510, hundreds of "witches" were burned at the stake, accused of "copulating with the Devil". Burning witches turned out to be a business, as their chattels were confiscated by the Church. More recent "sightings" of witches on broomsticks at Passo Tonale could be linked to the local grappa!

Today, the region's bewitching appeal lies in its complex mix of prehistoric rock art, frescoed Romanesque

churches, rural farm-stays and industrial archaeology. That's without mentioning skiing, hiking and the swathes of wilderness and majestic Alpine scenery. The welcome may be a bit brusque, but that's the nature of a valley only slowly coming to terms with tourism.

The Lower Valley, centred on Boario Terme, benefits from its closeness to Lake Iseo, while the Upper Valley draws the crowds to its ski slopes. The Middle Valley, centred on Capo di Ponte, has yet to reap the rewards of tourism, despite its magnificent rock art. Towards Lake Iseo, the views have been disfigured by a disregard for the environment. Green awareness is catching on but, given the valley's industrial bent since the Bronze Age, metalworking and light engineering are in the blood. Even so, Lovere has turned its back on heavy industry, while villages such as Bienno manage to combine sleepy medieval charm and a rich industrial heritage.

Lovere

The lakeside town of **Lovere** ⓰ is the stepping stone to Val Camonica,

the valley north of the lake, but has a rewarding Renaissance centre of its own, thanks to the legacy of Venetian rule. The town's transition from textiles and steel to tourism is not quite seamless, even though visiting boats bob on the marina and the appealing historic heart is well restored. The most impressive church is **Santa Maria in Valvendra**, with its majestic Baroque interior and Renaissance artwork. On the lakefront is the eclectic art collection of **Accademia Tadini** (Via Tadini 40; tel: 035-962 780; www.accademiatadini.it; May–Sept Tue–Sat 3–7pm, Sun 10am–noon, 3–7pm, Apr, Oct Sat 3–7pm, Sun 10am–noon, 3–7pm). Count Tadini, a local benefactor, left his collection to the city in 1828 after part of his palace collapsed, killing his son and heir. Apart from a swathe of madonnas, including one by Bellini, the pleasure of the palace lies in the quirkiness of the founder's personal tastes.

Stone Age theme park

Darfo-Boario Terme ⓱, an uninspiring spa town and the producer of

FACT

The *rosa camuna*, the Camunian rose, is the symbol of Lombardy and found all over Val Camonica rock art. Although one of the oldest representations of the rose ever found, its meaning is enigmatic; it is likely to refer to a solar symbol or a warrior-like aura of invincibility than to ideas of sacrifice, love and eternity.

Contemporary art at Accademia Tadini.

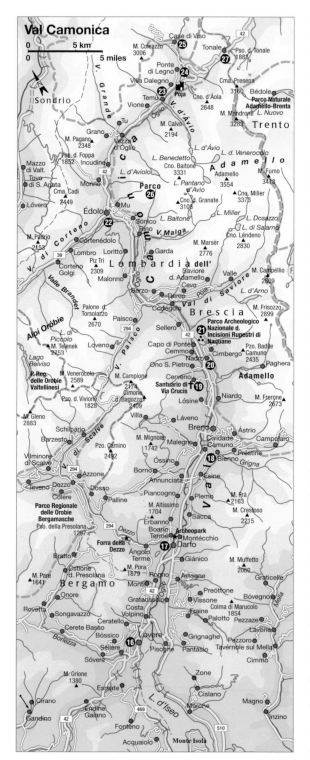

Ferrarelle mineral water, has yet fully to embrace tourism. Just outside town is **Archeopark** (Gattaro; tel: 0364-529 552; Mar–Nov daily 9am–5.30pm; www.archeopark.net), an entertaining Stone Age theme park. Wide-eyed children can experience the Camuni civilisation of 10,000 years ago, sampling life in rock shelters or stilt villages. After they have tried corn-grinding in the stilt village and tending to the smelly wild boar, there is rowing in Stone Age-style flat-bottomed boats on the reedy lake.

In the neighbouring hamlet of **Montecchio** stands the **Ponte Romano**, the "Roman" bridge, an early medieval tollbridge. Beside it is the parish church and the **Chiesetta dell'Oratorio**, covered by vivid frescoes attributed to Pietro da Cemmo, the greatest 15th-century painter from Val Camonica.

Bienno

Praised as one of the prettiest villages in Italy, **Bienno** ⑱ has forged its identity out of metal and water. Benedictine monks were responsible for channelling the river into the Vaso Re canal, which powered the mills and foundries. The water-mills, introduced by the monks in the 10th century, functioned until the 1960s, while forges and foundries have been in operation here since antiquity. Prehistoric Val Camonica rock carvings depict blacksmiths and an array of metal objects, from spades to daggers, a reminder of the valley's vocation for metalworking. Beretta handguns and hunting guns continue to be produced in a neighbouring valley. Today, several of the 60 original foundries still exist, even if the 150 watermills have shrunk to one functioning flour mill. You can call into **Il Mulino**, off Piazza Roma, to see a working flour mill, before strolling along medieval alleys, past tower houses and mansions with balconies trailing geraniums.

The Baroque parish church of **Santi Faustina e Giovita**, on via San Benedetto, incorporates a medieval tower, while the Gothic church of **Santa Maria**, on Piazza Santa Maria, is frescoed by Renaissance artists of the stature of Romanino and da Cemmo. **La Museo Fucina** (Via Artigiani; tel: 0364-300 307; Tue–Sun 9.30–11.30am, 2.30–4.30pm) is a gentle introduction to Bienno's industrial heritage. With its soot-blackened walls, the evocative foundry displays one of the original water-driven forges: a waterwheel powers the mallet to strike the anvil and work the molten metal; smaller forges refashioned the metal into the pots, buckets and tools which made Bienno's name.

Cerveno ⑲, halfway up the valley, demands attention for the **Santuario di Via Crucis**, which displays Lombardy's most memorable 18th-century woodcarvings. The distinctly kitsch *Stations of the Cross* present 200 life-size statues, which evoke the Passion with the familiar refreshing realism that typifies Val Camonica art.

The rock carvings

Nadro ⑳ is an intriguing hamlet, built around a medieval tower in a honeycomb of alleys overlying a prehistoric settlement. The compact **Riserva Regionale delle Incisioni Rupestri** (Regional Reserve of Rock Art; Località Nadro; tel: 0364-433 465; Mar–Oct daily 9am–5.30pm, Nov–Feb 9am–4pm) is a prelude to exploring the superb rock carvings, the prehistoric comic strips and the matchstick men known as *pitoti* (puppets), that have been drawn on these rocks for thousands of years. The magic of the landscape survives, enhanced by the mysterious symbolism of the rock art. Although clearly a sacred place, the site has no graves, so the supposition is that bodies were cremated and ashes scattered.

Foppe di Nadro

Just behind the museum is the short trail to the prehistoric rock art of **Foppe di Nadro** (daily 9am–6pm). It is best to visit in the morning, when the light is clearer, or in the late afternoon, when the light is at its most mysterious. The main trail reveals around 50 rocks, which focus on Stone Age to Iron Age art, with clear Etruscan

Il Mulino is still a working flour mill as well as a museum.

Fresco in Santa Maria, Bienno.

Reading Rock Art

"Rock art has been described before, but it has never been read," declared a triumphant Italian archaeologist recently, surveying a site which has obsessed him for 50 years.

Emmanuel Anati, the world's leading authority on the Val Camonica site, believes that the prehistoric rock engravings are not just artworks but an early form of writing. "The turning point was to consider the rocks as messages – messages, which are legible ten or fifteen thousand years after they were written."

Professor Anati (b. 1930), an Italian archaeologist of international renown, was the first to recognise the scale and richness of Val Camonica in the 1950s. Having compiled a chronological framework of the site's rock carvings, in 1961 he wrote *Camonica Valley*, a ground-breaking study of Val Camonica and in 1964 established the Centro Camuno di Studi Preistorici in Capo di Ponte (www.ccsp.it) with the aim to study

Val Camonica rock carvings.

prehistoric art. The centre has also founded the World Archive of Rock Art and was instrumental in having Val Camonica inscribed on Unesco's World Heritage list in 1971.

At once rural and industrial, Val Camonica, north of Lake Iseo, has been inhabited since the Neolithic era, when the Camuni tribal civilisation first etched itself into existence. For generations, these hunters and farmers recorded everyday life and their relationship with the other world. As a tribal record of a civilisation, the valley offers a span of creativity stretching from Stone Age culture well into Roman times, when the Camuni, hunters rather than warriors, were easily crushed and assimilated by the Roman imperialists.

Dubbed "stick men" by modern valley people, the primitive carvings of people and shamans have always had resonance locally. The rock carvings date back to 6000 BC, with the earliest images featuring rudimentary animal figures in static poses, usually deer and elk, which represented local deities. More sophisticated narrative art emerged during the Bronze and Iron Ages, while the Etruscans, Romans and Christians continued in their ancestors' footsteps: the practice was abandoned in the late Middle Ages. While there has always been respect for the art in modern times, ancient graffiti artists felt little compunction about erasing or embroidering their predecessors' work.

Deciphering the rocks

Archaeologists began to work out the "grammar" of this proto-writing system using the concepts of pictograms, ideograms and psychograms. Pictograms are pictures resembling what they signify, ideograms represent concepts, while psychograms symbolise psychological maps. By deciphering a number of rocks, Anati has more sense of the messages being conveyed: "After managing to decipher an Iron Age rock, we concluded that the majority of the inscriptions refer to mythological accounts and information about initiation rites." he explained.

The deciphering is ongoing, but the initial findings tap into a daring thesis: that there are universal themes in world prehistoric rock art: sex, hunting, food and the territorial imperative. The boldest conclusion is also the most mundane: that prehistoric peoples resembled each other; and our prehistoric ancestors were much the same as us.

influences. Even if the carvings span 6,000 years, running from the Stone Age to medieval times, it is the prehistoric scenes that captivate, blending mythology with the mundane.

Foppe di Nadro looks much as it did in prehistoric times: a crest of a hill, gentle terraces, wooded slopes, smooth rocks, megalithic walls and the remains of a prehistoric fortified village. Only the Iron Age homestead is a reconstruction. The Camuni were hunter-gatherers, then farmers, who settled amid these chestnut groves, lived in primitive farmsteads and cultivated their crops, respecting the rhythms of the seasons, studying the movement of the stars and worshipping the sun and animal deities.

Rock 1 celebrates the sun cult with prayers, while Rocks 4, 22 and 23 attest to local metalworking skills with the depictions of daggers, axes and halberds. Rock 27, which stands out for its size and imposing setting, is inscribed with Neolithic, Bronze and Iron Age scenes, running from Stone Age shamans and winged idols to Iron Age duels, by way of Etruscan script and symbols. Inscriptions in Latin and in Northern Etruscan appear mixed with scenes of farming, hunting and daily life on Rocks 1, 5, 6, 24 and 27. But Emmanuel Anati, the greatest living rock art expert, posits the theory of our shared linguistic roots, speculating that early *Homo sapiens* may have shared a "primordial mother language from which all the spoken languages developed".

Naquane Rock Art National Park

Capo di Ponte is the gateway to the greatest rock art but has little of intrinsic interest other than **San Siro**, a striking Romanesque church in the hamlet of **Cemmo**.

The prehistoric rock carvings over the Oglio River in the **Parco Archelogico Nazionale delle Incisioni Rupestri di Naquane ㉑** (Prehistoric Rock Art of Naquane National Park, Località Naquane, Capo di Ponte; tel: 0364-42140; daily 8.30am–1.30pm; www.parcoincisioni.capodiponte.beni culturali.it) make up for any disappointment. In this national park, also Italy's

Detail of rock carving, Capo di Ponte.

TIP

Siberian husky-trekking is available, winter or summer, in Ponte di Legno (Scuola Italiana Sleddog; www.scuola italianasleddog.it), where you can learn how to lead the pack on wild trails in the Adamello-Brenta and Stelvio national parks.

Parco Archeologico Nazionale delle Incisioni Rupestri di Naquane.

first Unesco World Heritage Site, over 300,000 rock carvings are etched onto glacier-seared sandstone in an area covering 8km (5 miles). Given the bewildering array, focus on the impressive boulders near the entrance of the archaeological park.

Big Rock 1 remains the most important surface in the valley, and is engraved with over 1,000 drawings, which run from the Neolithic era to the Iron Age. It is a cavalcade of warriors, women, shamans and riders wrapped up in deer-hunting, weaving, warmongering, initiation rites and appeasing the gods. This rock is humorously entitled: "when food is also a god", referring to the dual role of the deer as sacred symbol and venison snack. Nearby, the "horsemen of the rocks" is a common status symbol. But if civilisation is about progress, then look at Rock 23, with its four-wheeled wagon – a precursor to the car, or Rock 35, which depicts a blacksmith in his smithy, forging the definition of Iron Age man, and propelling the valley towards the industrial vocation that sustains it today.

Despite huge advances in deciphering the rocks, some remain a mystery. Rock 32 was probably selected for its soft, feminine contours. On these smooth surfaces, propitiatory rites merge into ploughing scenes, warfare and weaponry, all intercut with symbols of labyrinths, which may represent the passage from this life to the next. Hunting, praying, dancing, copulating, invoking the gods, indulging in sacrificial rites – all human life is here, but the key is still lost somewhere in these wild chestnut groves.

Although this open-air museum is linked by walkways, with numbered rocks and explanatory panels in English, a guide is still desirable to decipher a few of the mysteries.

Exploring the Upper Valley

Edolo ㉒, the main town in the Upper Valley, is notable for the church of **San Giovanni Battista**, a Renaissance church frescoed by remarkable Renaissance images depicting Adam and Eve and the life of St John the Baptist.

Temù ㉓, a slightly sombre greystone village surrounded by forest,

is home to the **Museo della Guerra Bianca** (World War I Museum; Via Roma 40; July–Aug Mon–Sat 3–7pm, Sun 10am–12.30pm, Sept–Oct Sat 3–6pm, Sun 10am–12.30pm, rest of the year times vary). In 1914, Europe's largest glacier became a battleground, the first conflict to be fought at such altitudes. On this forgotten front, the icy "White War" was waged in snowfields and glaciers above 3,000 metres (10,000ft), and cost the lives of several thousand Italian and Austrian soldiers. The modest museum still hits home with its machine guns, medals, sleighs, helmets, uniforms, flags and photos, all found around the glacier. Simply dragging one cannon up the mountain in conditions of -30°C (-22°F) cost 100 Italian lives. Today, keen hikers can explore the battlefields and inspect the artillery positions and trenches, including the secret Italian "ice tunnel", a 5km (3-mile) passageway that was lit by electricity.

Ponte di Legno

Villa Dalegno, an old-fashioned hamlet outside Ponte di Legno, is significant only for the Agriturismo Belotti, the place for a hearty rustic supper or overnight stay. **Ponte di Legno** ㉔ itself, perched on a sunny plateau, makes the most charming base for exploring the Upper Camonica Valley. With its quaint wooden bridge, geranium-hung balconies, ornate parish church and Alpine chalets, it resembles a Tyrolean village. While plotting a long walk, retreat to La Rasega (via IV Novembre 74), a cosy wine bar in a converted sawmill overlooking the river Oglio, which feeds Lake Iseo. Dine in the San Marco, the valley's finest restaurant. Even in summer, this is a lively resort, popular with the Milanese, who combine hiking with polenta dishes in rural inns. In winter, this is a ski area linking into Tonale via scenic runs through the trees, and is far prettier than its Trentino counterpart.

Case di Viso

The scenic hamlet of **Case di Viso** ㉕ to the north is arguably the loveliest spot in the Upper Valley. The stone-clad shepherds' huts have been turned

Marmot, a type of whistling ground squirrel, were originally endemic to Central Asia. They spend up to nine months a year in hibernation.

Ponte di Legno.

into summer homes, often by the former shepherds themselves. In winter, the devoted owners return on skis or snowshoes, drawn by the prospect of polenta and cheese rustled up in a cosy cabin. In summer, the sweeping Alpine valley views can be appreciated on a two-hour trail to **Rifugio Bozzi** (tel: 0364-900 152), a mountain hut open for rustic lunches, and the base for hikes to Alpine lakes, military outposts and the ruins of World War I forts.

Adamello park

Parco dell'Adamello 26, which embraces Ponte di Legno and Tonale, is a wilderness area itself stretching from Lombardy into Trentino, and forms part of the largest protected area in Europe. The Adamello park climbs to 3,500 metres (11,500ft), passing from reed-beds and prehistoric terraces to woods of chestnut, mountain maple and fir, which gradually lose out to larch groves, Alpine lakes, meadows, glaciers and the craggy peaks.

The Adamello appeals to sporty types, with summer mountain biking and horse riding giving way as the snows fall to husky-trekking, snowshoeing and skiing (www.adamello ski.com). For information on farmstays, hiking routes, mountain bike trails and wildlife, call into the Casa del Parco (Via Nazionale 132, Vezza d'Oglio; tel: 0364-76165; www.parco adamello.it).

Lofty **Tonale 27** marks the end of the valley, and is littered with Austrian and World War I fortifications. The trenches and tumbledown forts can be visited on summer trails, but only mountain bike fans choose to stay there. It is in winter when treeless, charmless Tonale comes into its own as a popular **ski resort**. Daredevils ascend to the **Presena glacier**, home to year-round skiing, while the rest opt for the wintry slopes of Ponte di Legno, Tonale and Temù, which make one seamless ski area, linked by a cable car. Beyond is **Passo di Tonale**, the windswept Tonale Pass, which surveys the Lombardy–Trentino border. Any low spirits are soon dispelled by an Alpine inn serving mounds of polenta oozing cheese.

The village of Tonale.

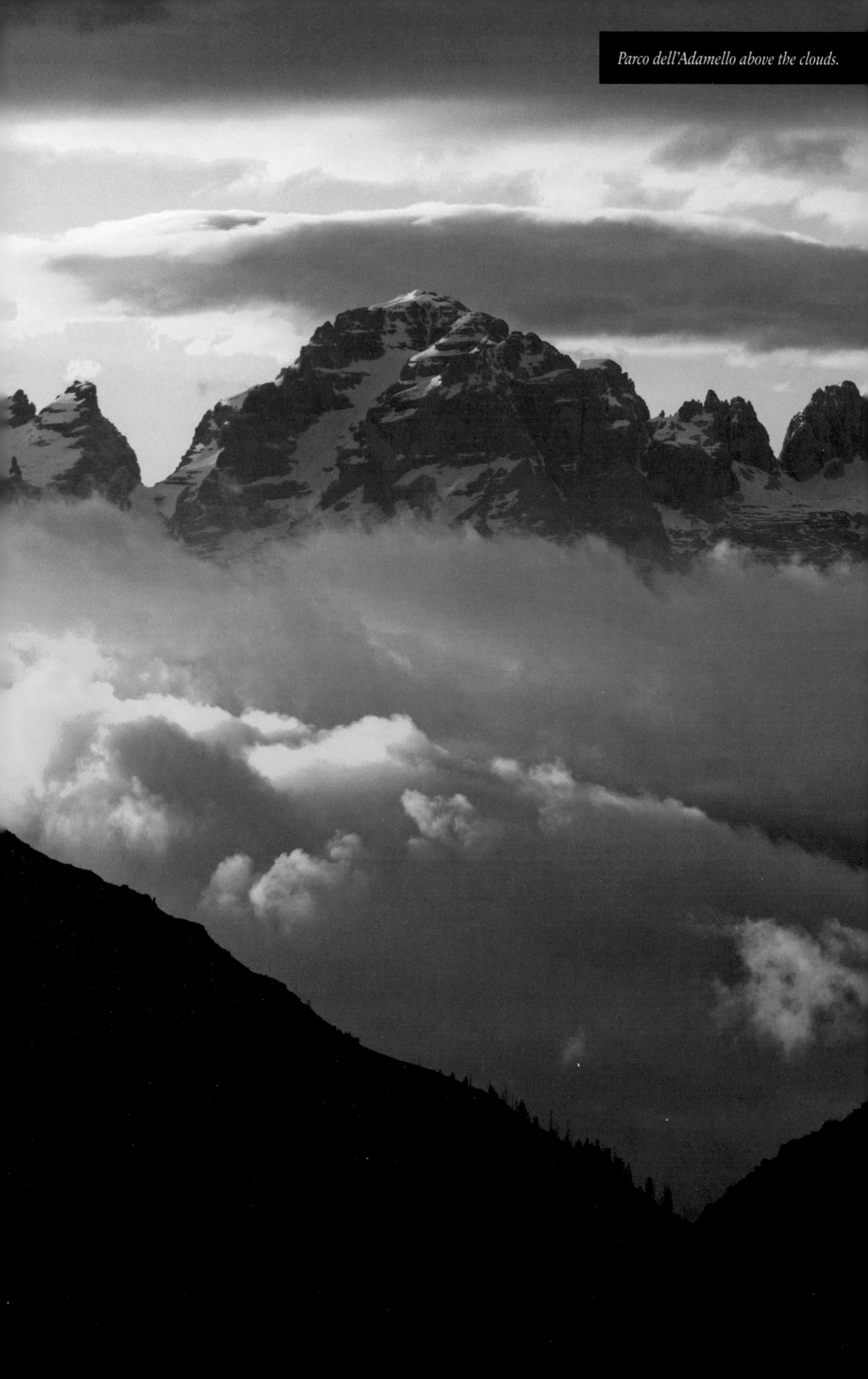

Parco dell'Adamello above the clouds.

The Colleoni Chapel.

BERGAMO

There are two distinct parts to the city – the Città Alta (the upper city), with its formidable city walls, and the Città Bassa (the lower city), the wider area below. The beautiful Piazza Vecchia and some exquisite churches are within the gates of the Città Alta.

Main Attractions
Accademia Carrara
 Collection
San Vigilio
Via Colleoni
Piazza Vecchia
Cappella Colleoni
Basilica di Santa Maria
 Maggiore
Rotonda di San Tomé
Valle Brembana
Crespi d'Adda

The combination of cobbled streets, cypress-clad hills and mountain air make the picturesque town of **Bergamo ❶** a refreshing diversion. Inhabited by the Ligurians around 1200 BC, fortified by the Etruscans in 600 BC and named Berg Hem (Mountain Dwelling) by the incoming Celts some 50 years later, Bergamo has a long and illustrious pedigree involving all the powers that swept through the region. There are two distinct parts to the city. At the centre, on the clifftop, is the Città Alta (upper city), the old city, reached by winding road or funicular. The Città Bassa (lower city) is the much larger area down below. With one or two notable exceptions, all the tourist sights and most of the best restaurants are in the Città Alta.

The Città Bassa

Although it had burst through its walls before then, with the construction of the suburbs (*borgos*), Bergamo began to sprawl across the plain with the coming of the railway in 1857. The road linking the station to the city split its name between two local heroes, hence Viale Papa Giovanni XXIII and Viale Vittorio Emanuele II. In the 1920s, a Roman architect, Marcello Piancentini, won the competition to design the grand buildings which process across the plain,

holding offices, banks and other institutions. In Piazza Matteotti, it passes a **Monumento alla Resistenza** (Monument to the Resistance) by Giacomo Manzù (1977), the **Teatro Donizetti** and **Donizetti monument**, built by Francesco Jerace in 1897 to mark the centenary of the composer's birth.

The only star attraction in the lower city is the fabulous art gallery, the **Accademia Carrara ❹** (Piazza Carrara 82; tel: 035-234 390; Tue–Sun 10am–7pm, in summer Fri until midnight; www.lacarrara.it) in the Borgo

View down over the Città Bassa.

TIP

Getting to Bergamo is exceptionally easy from "Milan" Orio Al Serio Airport (tel: 035-326 323; www.orioaeroporto.it). It is only 5km (3 miles) from the city, with excellent rail and motorway connections.

Santa Caterina. It was founded as an art school in 1796 by Count Giacomo Carrara, whose collections formed the core of what has become one of Italy's most important galleries. In 2015, the gallery reopened after a seven-year renovation. Its 1,800 paintings are now arranged in several themed trails. Highlights include works by Raphael, Botticelli, Titian, Mantegna, Lotto and Pisanello.

Across the road, a 16th-century convent houses the **Galleria d'Arte Moderna e Contemporanea** Ⓑ (Via S. Tomaso 53; Tue–Sun 9am–1pm, 3–6pm; www.gamec.it; free), covering works from the 20th century onwards, with a small permanent collection with works by Sutherland and Kandinsky and regular temporary exhibitions.

The Città Alta

There are still only five gates through the formidable, almost perfectly preserved **City Walls** of the upper city (plus the hole blasted through them for the funicular, which runs from near the Piazzetta San Giacomo in the lower town; tel: 035-236 026).

The first walls were probably Etruscan and there were Roman and medieval versions, but the elaborate fortress that surrounds the city was the work of the Venetians, whose lion lazes above the gates. They raised the barricades in 1561–88, destroying a few hundred homes and several churches in the process. The walls are designed so that no part of them is out of sight of the defenders and there is overlapping firepower at all points, while

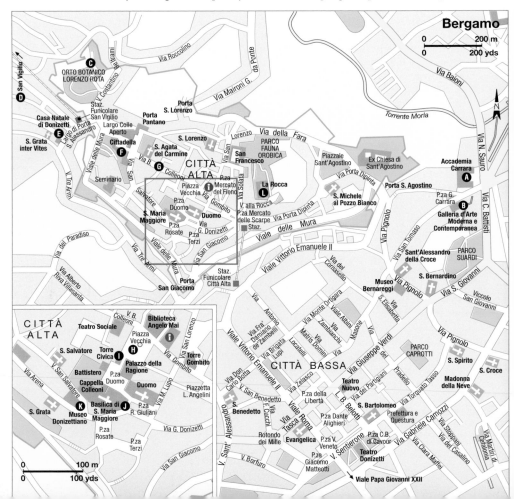

underground tunnels allow soldiers to run safely between the bastions. Free guided tours of the **Underground Levels** by le Nottole Caving Group are available in summer (groups only; tel: 333-258 8551; June–Sept).

Extra-mural activities

The road up to the Old City loops through the Porta San Agostino along the southern line of the wall. There is parking just inside the Porta San Alessandro, in the Largo Colle Aperto (where the bus stops) and in the Piazza Cittadella.

Before plunging into the heart of the Old City, take some time to admire it from the outside. On the left, Largo Colle Aperto loops around to the **Orto Botanico Lorenzo Rota C** (Scaletta Colle Aperto; tel: 035-286 060; Mar–Oct daily 10am–noon and Mar, Oct 2–5pm, Apr, Sept until 6pm, May, July, Aug until 7pm, June until 8pm; free), a fine botanical garden tucked into the ramparts, with great views from the battlements.

Next, it is possible to take a trip up to **San Vigilio D**. A second funicular,

just outside Porta San Alessandro, whisks you up to the top of the hill from where the Old City is laid out like a map. The best views are from the ruined **Castello di San Vigilio** (tel: 035-236 284; daily Apr–Oct 7am–9pm, Nov–Mar 8am–5pm), while the Baretto di San Vigilio is one of the city's best restaurants. The energetic can take the steps down the Via dello Scorlazzone back to the Città Alta.

Alternatively, go on down the Largo di Porta San Alessandro to the fairly humble **Casa Natale di Donizetti E** (Via Borgo Canale 14; tel: 035-244 483; Sat–Sun 10am–1pm, 3–6pm or phone for an appointment; free), where the great operatic composer was born in 1797, its rooms arranged as they would have been when he lived there. Round the corner, on via degli Orti, local artist, Paolo Vincenzo Bonomini (1756–1839) decorated the church of **Santa Grata inter Vites** (1591) with a graphic collection of Dance of Death frescoes.

The heart of the city

Back in Piazza Cittadella, the rather dour complex of the **Cittadella F**,

Strolling through the Città Alta.

WHERE

Bergamo tourist offices
Urban Center, Viale Papa
Giovanni XXIII 57, Città
Bassa;tel. 035-210 204.
Mon–Fri 9am–12.30pm,
2–5.30pm, Sat–Sun
9am–5.30pm
Via Gombito 13, Città
Alta; tel: 035-242 226.
Daily 9am–5.30pm
Airport, arrivals terminal;
tel: 035-320 402.
Daily 8am–9pm
www.visitbergamo.net

once a Visconti fortress, houses local government offices as well as two museums – the **Museo Civico Archeologico e Museo di Scienze Naturali** (both museums, Piazza Cittadella; tel: 035-286 070; Apr–Sept Tue–Fri 9am–12.30pm, 2.30–6pm, Sat–Sun 10am–1pm, 2.30–6.30pm, Oct–Mar Tue–Fri 9am–12.30pm, 2.30–5.30pm, Sat–Sun 10am–12.30pm, 2.30–5.30pm; combined ticket). The archaeology museum has prehistoric, Roman and Longobard collections from the local region. The natural history museum adds to the rocks and plants with a mammoth skeleton and a *Eudimorphon Ranzii Zambelli* (flying reptile dinosaur).

Through the arch in **Piazza Mascheroni**, used as a linen market by the Venetians and later as a place for funfairs and festivals, it is appealing to turn back to look at the **Torri di Campanella** above the arch, begun in 1355 and completed in the 19th century. Both piazzas also have fragments of 16th-century frescoes.

Across the piazza is the start of **Via Colleoni** **G**, the narrow cobbled main street of the Old City, lined by enticing

restaurants, delicatessens and patisseries. A short distance along on the left is the 15th-century church of **Sant'Agata del Carmine**, while further down on the right is the **Teatro Sociale**, designed in 1803 by Pollack. Closed as a theatre in 1929, its glamorous neoclassical interior is used for exhibitions.

Piazza Vecchia

Just beyond, the road comes out into the central square, the fabulous **Piazza Vecchia** **H**, purpose-built as a show-stopping, power-wielding centrepiece to the city by the Venetians in the 15th century.

On the left, with a white marble colonnade only finished in the 20th century, the Palazzo Nuovo was built in the early 17th century by Vincenzo Scamozzi, a pupil of Palladio. Once the town hall, it now houses the **Biblioteca Angelo Mai** (Piazza Vecchia 15; tel: 035-399 430/399 431; Mon–Fri 8.45am–5.30pm, Sat 8.45am–1pm, closed first two weeks in Aug; free), one of Italy's finest libraries, founded in 1768.

Opposite, stairs lead up beside the open arches to the **Palazzo della Ragione** (tel: 035-270 413; Mar daily 10am–noon, 2–6pm, Apr–Sept daily 9am–noon, 2–8pm, Sat closes 11pm, Oct Sat–Sun 10am–noon, 2–6pm, Nov–Feb Sat–Sun 10am–noon, 2–4pm). This is known to have been here in some form in 1199, but faced the other way. It was turned round by the Venetians, who added the loggia and Lion of St Mark (now a modern one, replacing a far more resplendent original).

Next to the palazzo, the 54-metre (177ft) high **Torre Civica** **I** (Piazza Vecchia; tel: 035-247 119; Apr–Oct Tue–Fri 9.30am–6pm, Sat–Sun 9.30am–8pm, Nov–Mar Tue–Fri 9.30am–1pm, 2.30–6pm, Sat–Sun 9.30am–6pm) took its present form in 1197 under the Suardi-Colleoni family, who used it as a prison. The bells were added later, and the clock arrived in 1407. The main bell, the **Campanone**, was hung in the mid-17th century and narrowly escaped being

Via Colleoni is the busy centre of the Old City.

melted down by the Germans in 1943. It strikes 180 times to mark the curfew and the locking of the city gates and strikes 12 times at noon. There is a lift, and the views are, of course, superb.

In the centre of the piazza is a monumental fountain donated by Alvise Contarini, the Venetian Podestà, in 1780.

A glory of churches

As you walk through the arches beneath the Palazzo della Ragione, look for the sundial on the paving. The **Piazza del Duomo** was the Roman Forum and the city centre until the Venetians shifted it sideways. On the left as you enter, clad in white marble is the **Duomo** (Piazza Duomo; tel: 035-210 223; Mon–Fri 7.30am–noon, 3–6.30pm, Sat–Sun 7am–7pm; free). The grandiose facade dates from 1886, but the church, once dedicated to San Vincenzo, goes back to 1100, and has been modified again and again through the ages.

Directly opposite, the delicate little octagonal building like an oriental birdcage is the **Battistero** (Baptistery). This was placed here in 1856, using fragments of a baptistery that stood inside Santa Maria Maggiore, and was designed by Giovanni da Campione in 1340.

At the far side of the piazza, Bergamo's two real crowning glories stand side by side. Standing on the left, the plainer Romanesque church with a Gothic portal (and lions) is the **Basilica di Santa Maria Maggiore ❶** (Piazza Duomo; tel: 035-223 327; Apr–Oct Mon–Sat 9am–12.30pm, 2.30–6pm, Sun 9am–1pm, 3–6pm, Nov–Mar Mon–Sat 9am–12.30pm, 2.30–5pm, Sun 9am–1pm, 3–6pm; free). The flamboyant Renaissance building immediately to its right is the **Cappella Colleoni** (Piazza Duomo; tel: 035-210 061; Mar–Oct daily 9.30am–12.30pm, 2–6pm, Nov–Feb Tue–Sun 9.30am–12.30pm, 2–4.30pm; free).

The first church on this site dates back to 774 and the end of a bout of plague. Work on the expanded version began in 1137, under the watchful eye of Maestro Fredo. The Gothic portal facing the Piazza Duomo was added by Giovanni da Campioni in 1351–3, who later added the southern portal.

TIP

Between April and October, there are two-hour guided walking tours of the Città Alta, in English and Italian, on Wed and Sun at 3pm and on Sat at 10.30am, meeting at the Funicular Upper Station, Piazza Mercato delle Scarpe. For tours at other times, contact the Gruppo Guide Turistiche Città di Bergamo, tel: 035-344 205, www.bergamoguide.it.

Palazzo Nuovo.

Detail of the exterior of the Basilica di Santa Maria Maggiore.

Inside, the basilica flowers into a full-blown Baroque extravaganza.

Inside, little sense of its Romanesque simplicity remains beneath the gilding and other overpowering magnificence, although there are some 13th-century frescoes amid the Baroque tapestries (1580–86), an elaborately carved confessional (Andrea Fantoni, 1705) and the marquetry choirstalls (by Lorenzo Lotto, with woodwork as delicate as an oil painting). At the back of the church, there is a monument by Vincenzo Vela to the composer Gaetano Donizetti (1797–1848), whose body was moved here in 1875.

The **Colleoni Chapel**, built by sculptor and architect Giovanni Antonio Amadeo in 1476 for the tomb of Bartolomeo Colleoni and his daughter Medea, and dedicated to St John the Baptist, is even more decorative than the main church. The work is mainly the vision of one man and it has a harmony and delicacy of touch that is truly charming. The ceiling frescoes are by Tiepolo.

Donizetti

From the back door of Santa Maria and to the left is the small round 11th-century **Tempietto di Santo Croce** (tel: 035-278 111; by appointment only) modelled, like so many of the period, on the Church of the Holy Sepulchre in Jerusalem. To the right, the **Museo Donizettiano** Ⓚ (Via Arena 9; tel: 035-247 116; June–Sept Tue–Sun 9.30am–1pm, 2.30–6pm, Oct–May Tue–Fri 9.30am–1pm, Sat–Sun 9.30am–1pm, 2.30–6pm) takes up two rooms in the 15th-century Misericordia Maggiore, lavishly frescoed in the 19th century by local artist Bonomini. The museum focuses on the highlights of Donizetti's career with manuscripts, first editions, letters and personal possessions, including his piano and other musical instruments. Domenico Donizetti (1797–1848) was born in Bergamo. His operatic debut was in Venice in 1818 with Enrico di Borgogna and he went on to enormous success as one of the giants of opera, working in Milan and Naples, where he premiered his finest work, *Lucia di Lammermoor*, in 1837. Named "Maestro di Cappella and Composer of the Imperial Court" by the Emperor

Ferdinand I of Austria in 1842, he became ill in 1845, returning to Bergamo to die on 8 April 1848.

La Rocca

Back in Piazza Vecchia, the main road continues down the hill to the right as Via Gombito, through Piazzetta Angelini to **Piazza Mercato delle Scarpe** and the top station of the **funicular**.

From here, Via alla Rocca leads up to **La Rocca** Ⓛ (park: daily June–Sept 9am–8pm, Oct–May 10am–5.30pm, tower: June–Sept Tue–Fri 9.30am–1pm, 2.30–6pm, Sat–Sun 9.30am–7pm, Oct–May Tue–Sun 9.30am–1pm, 2.30–6pm; charge for museum, park free). Perched on one of the highest points in the walled city, this castle was founded by John of Luxemburg, while its 23-metre (75ft) high tower was built in the 1330s by the Visconti. It houses a museum of 19th- and 20th-century history, covering Bergamo's role in the Risorgimento and two world wars. Outside is a war memorial garden with shrines to aviators, astronauts and the resistance.

Around Bergamo

Valle Seriana

Stretching northwest from the city, roughly parallel with the motorway, the **Valle Seriana** (www.valleseriana. bg.it), along the line of the Serio River, is a mix of rundown industry, development and mountain scenery. Stop in **Alzano Lombardo** ❷ to visit the little Sacred Art Museum in the sacristy of the Basilica di San Martino (Piazza Italia 8; tel: 035-516 579; Sun 3–6pm, tours at 4pm, or by appointment).

A little further on, the **Cene Parco Paleontologico** ❸ (Via Bellora, 17km/ 10.5 miles from Bergamo; tel: 035-729 318; www.triassico.it/parcocene; usually open Sat–Sun 2–6pm, check website for details; guided visits for groups on demand in the week) stands on 220-million-year-old Triassic fossil beds.

The real star of the valley is the little town of **Clusone** ❹, 34km (21 miles) from Bergamo, known as the *città dipinta* – the painted town. The main attraction here is the masterly 15th-century fresco depicting the *Danse Macabre* (Dance of Death) in the

Donizetti's piano has pride of place in his museum.

Oratorio dei Disciplini by the Basilica di Santa Maria Assunta. The **Museo Arte Tempo** (Via Clara Maffei 3; tel: 0346-25915; Fri 3.30–6.30pm, Sat–Sun 10am–noon, 3.30–6.30pm) also displays paintings and sculptures by local artists from the 15th century on, as well as a collection of rare clocks. Look out too for the fine **Orologio Planetario di Fanzago (Astronomical Clock)** on the south side of the town hall (Piazza dell'Orologio), designed and built by Pietro Fanzago in 1583. The town also hosts a major jazz festival in June and July.

Valle Imagna

Northwest of the city, the Valle Imagna is a traditional centre of fine woodworking, with a sideline in puppetry – this is where to buy your own Pinocchio. In the village of **Almenno San Bartolomeo ❺**, the **Museo del Falegname Tino Sana** (Via Papa Giovanni XXIII 3; tel: 035-554 411; Mon–Fri 9am–noon, Sat 3–6pm, Sun 9.30am–noon, 3–6pm; closed Aug) is a museum of carpentry, with a section on puppets and a World War I Ansaldo

Rotonda di San Tomé.

A1 biplane belonging to local war hero Antonio Locatelli. Nearby, the **Rotonda di San Tomé** (tel: 034-528 1132; May–Oct Tue–Fri 10am–noon, 2.30-5.30pm, Sat–Sun 10am–noon, 2.30–6pm, Nov–Apr Tue–Sat 10am–noon, 2.30–4.30pm, Sun 10am–noon, 2.30–5pm) is an enchanting late 11th–early 12th century chapel in the woods, with beginnings that stretch back to the early 8th century. Its tiers of Romanesque arches provide a rare upper women's gallery and an array of fantastic capitals. Only small fragments of the frescoes remain. The church of **San Giorgio** in nearby **Almenno San Salvatore** was first built in the 10th century, rebuilt in 1120, and has fine 14th-century frescoes.

Valle Brembana

Back on the main road and heading north along the Valle Brembana, a huge bottling plant across the river marks the entry to a town with a familiar name – **San Pellegrino Terme ❻**, 24km (15 miles) north of Bergamo.

Everywhere you look in this pretty little town filled with Art Nouveau

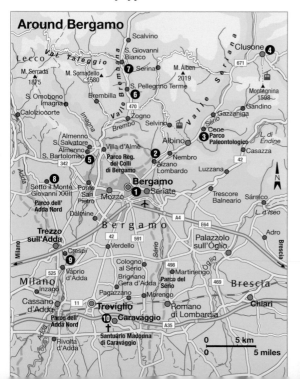

Around Bergamo

architectural treasures you will see the bottled water logo. This once fashionable resort has been neglected for many years, with its glamorous casino closed and the glorious old Art Nouveau Hotel Grande crumbling. However, hope is in sight: a multi-million-euro redevelopment plan is in the works which aims to turn the town into a resort of swish spa hotels – and restore some of its lost sparkle in the process.

A little further up the valley, a turning to the left leads to **San Giovanni Bianco ⑦** and the medieval village of **Oneta**, where the 14th-century Casa di Arlecchino (tel: 0345-43262; daily 10am–noon, 3–6pm), belonging to the aristocratic Grataroli family, is considered to be the home of Harlequin, the patchwork fool of the *commedia dell'arte*. Beyond is the spectacular scenery of **Val Taleggio**, which produces one of Italy's finest cheeses.

West of Bergamo

Pope John XXIII came from the village of Sotto Il Monte, 16km (9.5 miles) west of Bergamo. Born in 1881, the fourth of 13 children of a poor farming family, Angelo Giuseppe Mazzola studied and worked in Bergamo before going to Rome in 1921, moving as a bishop to Bulgaria, Turkey, Paris and Venice. He was elected Pope John XXIII in 1958. An ardent worker towards peace between nations and religions, he presided over the seminal Vatican II Conference in 1962. He died in 1963 and was beatified in 2000.

A statue of the Pope stands at the entrance to the village, now known as **Sotto il Monte Giovanni XXIII ⑧**. Opposite is a **tourist information office** (tel: 035-790 902). A monumental way processes up the hill to the church, near a gigantic picture of *il Papa*. Visit the **Casa Museo di Papa Giovanni XXIII** (Via Camaitino 12; tel: 035-792 956; daily 8–5.30pm, summer until 6.30pm; free) and **Pope John's home** (Missionari del pime, Via Colombera 5; tel: 035-791 101).

Further west, the **Adda River** broadens and slows, winding through a mix of picture-book countryside and derelict industrial development, including the 1906 hydro-electric plant at Trezzo sull'Adda. It is a popular place for

San Pellegrino Terme.

boating, walking and cycling holidays; passing ancient and modern bridges, churches, castles, and the marshy reed-beds south of **Trezzo sull'Adda**, which are a bird sanctuary.

Crespi d'Adda ❾ (tel: 02-9098 7191; www.villaggiocrespi.it) is an excellent example of a 19th-century 'company town'. It was founded in 1878 by the philanthropic Crespi family of industrialists to meet the needs of the workers at their cotton factory. They provided facilities that included schools, churches, shops and places of entertainment. The architecture of the village is extraordinary, with the trim grid of English-style houses, each with a garden big enough to grow some vegetables, surrounding the tiny proportions of the elaborate riverbank factory; there is also the battlemented castle that was the Crespi family home, and the vastly elaborate stepped pyramid in the cemetery. It was the first village in Italy to have electric lighting, and the village has a Milan area code thanks to the direct line between the family's homes in Milan and Crespi in the late 19th century.

Houses in the industrial village of Crespi d'Adda.

The village became a Unesco World Heritage Site in 1995 and is still lived in, mainly by descendants of the original workers, but the efforts to keep it perfect while the industry at its core has crumbled (the factory closed in 2004), makes it strangely unworldly. The family home is now a hotel and the village survives largely as a tourist sight.

South of Bergamo

Caravaggio ❿, 25km (15.5 miles) south of Bergamo, was the childhood home of one of the greatest artists of the Baroque era, Michelangelo Meresi, known as "Il Caravaggio".

At the **Santuario della Madonna di Caravaggio**, a miraculous statue of the Virgin is now housed in an imposing 18th-century shrine just outside the city, built on the spot where the Virgin is reported to have appeared to a local woman, Giannetta De'Vacchi, on 26 May 1432 and where a spring miraculously gushed from the earth. There is now an elaborate Holy Font at the site of the spring, with an even grander High Altar behind. Pilgrims come to bathe in the sacred pool.

IL CARAVAGGIO

Both Milan and Caravaggio claim to be the birthplace of Michelangelo Meresi (in September 1571), but what is certain is that by the age of six he was living in Caravaggio. Apprenticed to Titian at the age of 13, he moved to Venice, from where he escaped to Rome after murdering a shop assistant. By 1599, he was receiving important commissions, but again ran into trouble, jailed for rowdy behaviour, tried and convicted for defamation of character and eventually, in 1606, killing a man and fleeing to Naples, then Malta and Sicily. On 18 July 1610, friends at court had supposedly arranged a pardon and he was on his way back to Rome when word came of his death. No body was ever found.

Lake Como waterfront.

LAKE COMO

For over two millennia, the rich, the powerful, the artistic and the romantic have been drawn to Lake Como. The distinctively forked shores of the lake offer the quintessence of romantic Italy – opulent villas, glamorous hotels and absurdly pretty villages that tumble down the dark green mountain side.

L ombardy's Lake Como is the most dramatic of the lakes. In a prime position between the Alps and the Po Valley, it's rich in both natural beauty and man-made grandeur. Lario, as it is known locally (from its Latin name, Larius, named after the Roman household deities, the Lares), is shaped like an upside-down "Y" and is fed by the Mera River, while the Adda flows from the lake at its southeastern tip. Stretching 50km (32 miles) between Como and Sorico, it is at its widest (4.4km/3 miles) between Fiumelatte and Cadenabbia, and its surface area of 146 sq km (56 sq miles) makes it Italy's third-largest lake (after Garda and Maggiore). The Ramo (branch) di Como has more glamour and charm than its austere twin Ramo di Lecco, while its northern reach, Ramo di Colico (or Alto Lario) offers Alpine scenery and watersports. The Centro Lago, where the three branches meet, is by far the most beautiful part of the lake.

City of Como

The city of **Como ❶** (pop. 83,000) lies at the southern tip of the western branch. It draws the crowds largely because it is the perfect starting point for exploring the rest of the lake, but it is worth a quick visit for its atmospheric old quarter, and a remarkable cathedral. Climbing up the dark-green

wooded hillside behind the lake is a funicular leading to wonderful views. Beyond lies the industrial heart of Europe's greatest silk manufacturers.

Como began life in the nearby hills during the early European Bronze Age; it moved to its present waterside location when it was decreed a municipality by Julius Caesar and renamed Novum Comum. The Franks led by Charlemagne followed, and it became a centre of commercial exchange until it was partially destroyed during the Ten Years War with Milan (1118–27).

Main Attractions
Como's Duomo
Villa d'Este
Centro Lago
Villa Carlotta
Varenna's Gardens
Villa Cipressi and Villa Monastero
Bellagio Waterfront

Piazza Cavour, Como.

Basilica di San Fedele.

Rebuilt with the help of Frederick Barbarossa, it became part of the Ducato of Milan (1395–1797) and then flourished under Austrian rule as the silk industry got under way. The town became part of the newly-formed Kingdom of Italy under Giuseppe Garibaldi in 1895, an action commemorated in the many streets, museums and piazzas in the area bearing his name.

The Città Murata

To see Como at its best, arrive from the north by boat and enjoy the views of its horseshoe-shaped front, bounded on either side by Villa Olmo and Villa Geno. The rectangular old quarter spreads southeast from the promenade's rather pedestrian **Piazza Cavour**.

Starting at the centre of the bay, head southeast through the main square into the **Città Murata**, the old quarter still bounded in parts by its medieval walls. Within a minute or two's walk along busy **Via Plinio** (named after Como's most famous sons), you will arrive at the city's main draw, the busy **Piazza Duomo**. Dominating it all is the **Duomo Ⓐ** (Cathedral) (1396–1740), (Mon–Sat 7.30am–7.30pm, Sun until 9.30pm; www.cattedraledicomo.it; free) remarkable for its Gothic-Renaissance style. Designer Lorenzo degli Spazzi's original Gothic design was constructed over the next five centuries and was only completed when Filippo Juvara added the 20-metre (75ft) high cupola in 1744. Giovanni Rodari and his

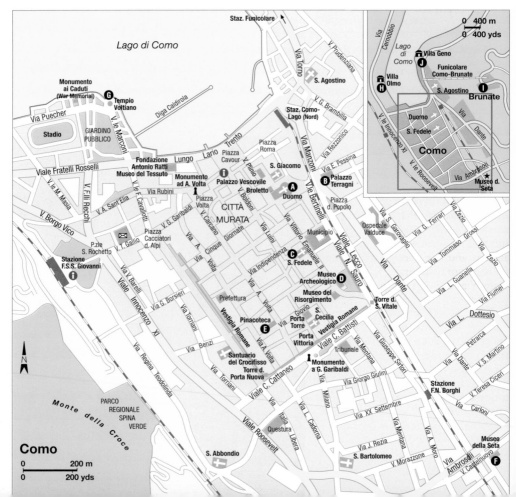

sons sculpted much of the statuary, including the two incongruous seated figures of the (non-Christian) Plinys framing the west door. Works by Bernardino Luini (*Adoration of the Magi*) and Guadenzio Ferrari (*Flight from Egypt*) brighten the dark interior, while two 9th-century lions support the fonts, paying homage to the church that once stood here, Santa Maria Maggiore.

Next to the Duomo, the grey-and-white-striped marble **Broletto**, the 13th-century town hall and campanile stand proudly above the throng of shoppers exploring the more commercial side of the piazza. Close to the cathedral stands the apricot-coloured church of **San Giacomo**, partly demolished to make room for the Duomo, and the 11th-century Bishop's Palace. Just beyond, on the other side of the railway tracks, stands what is considered a masterpiece of modern architecture, the functional rectangular block with loggia that is the **Palazzo Terragni ❸**. Named after the Rationalism pioneer and local architect Giuseppe Terragni, it was built by him in 1932 as the Casa del Fascio, or former Fascist party headquarters. Today, it is home to the Guardia di Finanza.

Back in the Città Murata, the **Basilica di San Fedele ❻** (daily 8am–noon, 3.30pm–7pm; free) stands in the Piazza San Fedele, the city's former marketplace. The 10th-century building houses Renaissance and Baroque artwork and Romanesque decorations in its gloomy interior. Continuing along Via Vittorio Emanuele II brings you to the Piazza Medaglie d'Oro and the **Museo Archeologico ❼** (Archaeological Museum; tel: 031-252 550; Tue–Sun 10am–6pm), which tells the story of Como's past with Iron Age finds, Roman glass and Risorgimento memorabilia. Head down Via Giovio to see the **Porta Torre** (1192), which formed part of the defensive system built under Frederick Barbarossa's rule, with Baradello Castle. Continue along the street to the **Pinacoteca ❺**

(Via Diaz 84; tel: 031-269 869; Tue–Sun 10am–6pm), with its medieval and modern paintings.

South and east of the city

Over on the southwest side of the city, a short walk from San Giovanni train station, stands the **Basilica Sant'Abbondio**, founded by Benedictine monks in 1013. Chances are you will have this church to yourself. The 14th-century frescoes of the *Life of Jesus* make it worth the trip.

Silk is Como's most famous contribution to industry, proudly commemorated in the **Museo della Seta ❼** (Via Castelnuovo 9; tel: 031-303 180; www. museosetacomo.com; Tue–Fri 10am–6pm, Sat 10am–1pm). The museum provides a unique look at the entire silk-making process with its large collection of weaving machinery and finishing equipment. The **Fondazione Antonio Ratti Museo del Tessuto** (Lungo Lario Trento 9; tel: 031-338 4976; www.fondazioneratti.org; Tue–Sun 2.30–5.30pm; by appointment only; free) has around 6,000 examples of antique textiles and sample books.

FACT

Born in Como, Pliny the Elder (AD 23–79), Roman naval and military commander, lawyer and scientist, wrote the Naturalis Historia, an ancient scientific encyclopaedia. His nephew and fellow author, Pliny the Younger (AD 61–13), wrote an account of his uncle's death while witnessing the eruption of Vesuvius. Also a lawyer and magistrate, the younger Pliny owned two villas at Bellagio and wrote about the lake's beauty in his Epistulae (Letters).

Piazza del Duomo, Como.

Silk

Como is to silk what Venice is to glass – *pura seta di Como* is a phrase known the world over.

Today, some 75 percent of Europe's silk comes from Como. Both the Duchess of Cornwall and the Crown Princess of Spain wore it on their wedding days, and leading ladies such as Penelope Cruz have sashayed down the red carpet in it at the Oscars.

The industry originated in 1510, introduced either by Friar Daniele or Pietro Boldoni from Bellano. It did, however, take a considerable time for the industry to develop. Rudimentary manufacturing only got under way in 1554, when wool producers, faced with stiff competition from Northern Europe, eventually embraced the new textile. However, since weaving was for centuries restricted to domestic use, the process became more refined only in the 19th century. By the second half of the 1800s, Como and its surroundings were filled with factories as the processes of weaving and dyeing expanded. But it was the production of power looms in the late 19th century that led Como to become the world leader in fabricating highly refined woven and printed silk.

Silk production

The production of silk is time-consuming and complex, which explains its appeal and high prices. The natural textile fibre is produced by silkworms, which are fed huge amounts of mulberry leaves for around a month. Today, the process is scientifically controlled and the mulberry leaf is being replaced by an easier substitute. Once satiated and at its full size, the silkworm spins a cocoon. It is the thread from this cocoon which is then reeled off, once done by hand-dipping the cocoons in basins of hot water in the spinning mills still found throughout the area. Several threads are joined together to make a yarn, which is cleaned, twisted ("thrown") and steamed. It takes 100 cocoons to weave one tie, and 630 cocoons to make a blouse.

As silk is rarely used in its natural colour (a yellowy-white), it is dyed, before or after weaving, and then printed by block, screen or roller, a process now controlled by computer. The final stage is the "finishing", a highly technical and specialised process for which Como companies are justly renowned. Known as "ennoblement" for its ability to improve the product's final look, the finishing processes were for decades a closely guarded secret, with specialised handmade machinery and rare chemical products used to give the fabric certain effects such as pleating, softness and veining.

Silk scarves for sale in Como.

Via Regina Teodolinda, which runs parallel to the **Regionale Parco Spina Verde**, eventually takes you back to the lake. Dedicated, along with several other monuments, to the local-born physicist Alessandro Volta, the temple-museum **Tempio Voltiano**  (Viale Marconi; tel: 031-574 705; Tue–Sun 10am–6pm) is home to the world's first battery. Further along the bay, you pass the Terragni-built **Monumento ai Caduti** (War Memorial), the stadium, strikingly odd in its modernity, and the seaplane club before reaching the magnificent park of the neoclassical **Villa Olmo** ⬤, named after a giant elm tree said to date from the time of Pliny the Elder. The ochre-coloured building is now a villa that hosts conferences, but its ground floor, gardens and lido are open (villa Tue–Sun 10am–6pm, gardens daily Apr–Sept 7am–11pm, Oct–Mar until 7pm; lido June–Sept daily 9am–7pm; villa and gardens free, lido charge).

A stroll along the promenade in the other direction takes you past busy Piazza Matteotti and its bus station to the **Funicolare** (Piazza de Gasperi 4; tel: 031-303 608; www.funicolarecomo. it; daily 6am–10.30pm, Sat until midnight, every 15–30 mins, until midnight daily June–mid-Sept), a delightful trip 500 metres/1,640ft up the hillside to **Brunate** ⬤, a 19th-century village with a distinctly Swiss atmosphere – and fabulous views. From here, you can head on a number of excursions, notably a two to three-day hike or cycle to Bellagio along the "Backbone of the Lario Triangle". Back on the corniche, a 10-minute stroll further round takes you to a headland occupied by the **Villa Geno** ⬤ and its grounds (tel: 031-306 127; daily 9.30am–7pm summer, until 6pm winter; free), with a lido, restaurant and lovely views back to Como.

Ramo di Como

As you leave the city to explore the rest of the lake, head north for the stars – this bottom-left branch of the lake has been dubbed "Comowood" by some.

The best way to see both shores is to hop on a boat and zig-zag between the two quite different shores (see page 204). Heading up, the western side, with its collection of charming villages such as Cernobbio, Laglio and Cadenabbia and the prestigious villas in between, is more popular, which can make wandering through the quieter towns on the eastern shore such as Torno, Nesso and Lezzeno all the more attractive in high summer.

The western shore

Cernobbio ❷ is an attractive town made up of a cluster of 16th-century houses and prominent villas. Hugging the slopes of Monte Bisbino, whose summit marks the Swiss border, Cernobbio's chief attractions are two sumptuous villas standing aloof from the compact lakeside piazza and centre. The 19th-century former home of film director Luchino Visconti, **Villa Erba** (www.villaerba.it) is now a conference centre (closed to visitors).

Close by is the 16th-century **Villa d'Este** (see page 77), one of the grandest – and certainly most famous

FACT

Smuggling over the Swiss border has long been a cause for concern to the *finanzieri* (customs officers). Two museums, one in Como's Customs Police headquarters, the other in the Val d'Intelvi's Erbonne (Piccolo Museo della Guardia di Finanza e del contrabbando, San Fedele Intelvi; tel: 333-238 4179), explore the time when bags of sugar, coffee and cigarettes were loaded into bags and sneaked into the country by *spalloni* (smugglers).

Como centre.

– hotels on the lake. Commissioned as a home for Cardinal Tolomeo Gallio in 1568, its magnificence has been attracting royalty, heads of state and the very wealthy ever since. Acquired by Caroline of Brunswick in 1815, it was converted into a hotel in 1873 and has since changed little of its extraordinary interior lavishness and glorious 10-hectare (25-acre) gardens. If your bank balance is not quite that of pop-star proportions, then you can content yourself with a visit to its dining room or grand cocktail bar.

Passing though the pretty villages and hamlets of **Moltrasio, Carate-Urio, Laglio** and **Brienno**, you may glimpse some resplendent villas among the old balconied houses that fringe the shoreline. These are home to the Italian elite and international celebrities, including George Clooney, the Versaces and Sir Richard Branson.

It is between the small town of **Argegno** on the western shore and Nesso on the eastern shore that the lake bed drops to the greatest depth (410 metres/1,345ft) of any lake in Europe. There is a road from here marking the start of the **Val d'Intelvi**, a high valley with lovely walking and driving up to the Swiss border; the "Balcony of Italy" at Lanzo d'Intelvi has dramatic views over Lake Lugano and the Alps. For magnificent views of Lake Como, take the cable car from Argegno to **Pigra** (800 metres/2,624ft).

Another small detour, this time 400 metres/1,312ft into the hills above Ossuccio, is the **Sacro Monte di Ossuccio** ❸ (see page 217), one of a group of 15–17th-century chapels and now a Unesco World Heritage site, reflecting its architectural and artistic importance. Opposite Ossuccio and Sala Comacina is the lake's only island, **Isola Comacina** ❹. Separated from the west shore by a stretch of water so smooth it is known as the Zoca de l'Oli (basin of oil), the island's wooded wilderness hides a fascinating history amongst its ruins and olive trees. One of the earliest settlements in the area, it was sacked in 1169 in retaliation for allying with Milan in the Ten Years War (1118–27). It was then abandoned until the 20th century, when local Augusto Caprani bequeathed

Villa d'Este.

it to King Albert of Belgium, who returned it to Italy in 1920 to use as a retreat for Belgian and Italian artists. Today, it is home to a few artists and an exclusive restaurant.

The eastern shore

The rugged eastern shore along the Lariana, the coast road from Como to Bellagio, is much sleepier and less visited; this is reflected in the quietness of the narrow roads and the intermittent boat services – check the timetable carefully.

Standing out from the steep shores, **Villa Pliniana**, in **Torno** ❺, has hosted many distinguished guests since 1575, including Stendhal, Rossini, Byron and Shelley. Torno has a pretty medieval centre overlooked by the Romanesque church of San Giovanni.

Nesso ❻, with its cluster of stone houses jostling for space on top of one another, is the largest town between Como and Bellagio. The former fortified town is divided into the pretty hamlets of Castello, Vico and Careno and is home to some spectacular scenery, notably the Nesso Gorge and the Masera grotto, with its inner lake, one of several caverns in the area. Further towards the tip of the Triangolo Lariano is **Lezzeno** ❼, directly opposite the Isola Comacina, which has Celtic and Ligurian origins and some notable churches. Its main attraction, however, is the **Carpe Grotto**, also known as the Bulberi or Blue Grotto for the remarkable colour beneath the walls of the Sassi Grosgalli.

Centro Lago

The spot where the three branches of the lake meet is home to the popular towns of Tremezzo, Bellagio, Menaggio and Varenna. The luxuriant Mediterranean gardens, alluring villages and mild climate make it hard to leave at any time of year. A frequent triangular boat service running between Bellagio, Varenna and Menaggio reflects their popularity.

On the Lavedo promontory just outside Lenno is the breathtaking **Villa del Balbianello** ❽ (tel: 0344-56110; www.fondoambiente.it; mid-Mar–mid-Nov Tue, Thur–Sun 10am–6pm). Facing Isola Comacina and Tremezzo,

FACT

Diners at the Locanda dell'Isola Comacina take part in an "exorcism of fire" at the end of their meal. Drinking flambéed liqueur coffee is said to ward off a curse laid on the island in 1169 by the Bishop of Como during the Ten Years War between Milan and Como: "The bells will ring no more, stone will not be placed upon stone, no one will ever play host, on pain of violent death". A dazzling annual firework display is held here on the Saturday following St John the Baptist's Day.

Isola Comacina.

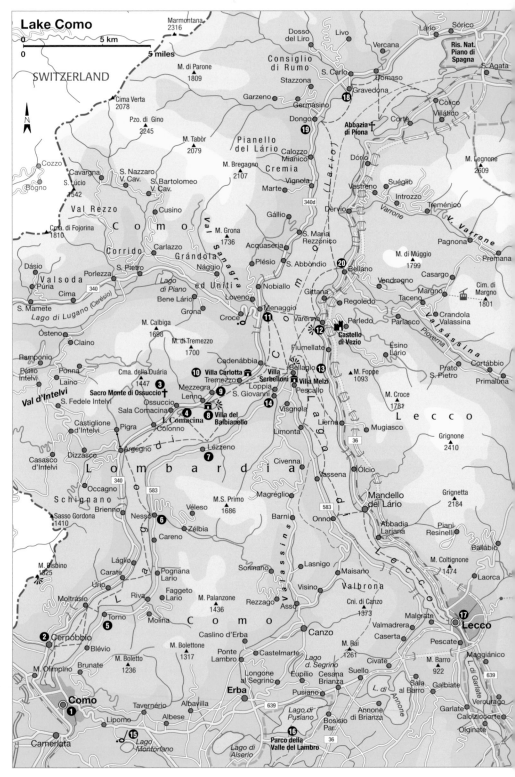

Lake Como

its glorious panoramic views and fairytale villa complete with towers and a portico have drawn visitors and film-makers alike (parts of *Star Wars Episode II* were filmed here). Built in the 18th century, the house and its valuable art collection and sumptuous gardens were donated to the FAI (Italian National Trust, see page 218) by the famous explorer Count Guido Monzino. Access is by boat from Lenno, but on Tue, Sat, Sun and public holidays you can walk the kilometre (just over half a mile) from Lenno.

Inland from here is **Mezzegra ❾**, best-known as the town where Benito Mussolini and his mistress Clara Petacci were shot dead by partisans on 28 April 1945. A cross marks the place of their execution.

Tremezzo and its neighbour **Cadenabbia** just north of Lenno are filled with grand hotels from the Belle Epoque, attracting famous guests such as Giuseppe Verdi, Stendhal and Queen Victoria. A large English community soon followed, resulting in one of Italy's first Anglican churches. Today, visitors from all over the world are drawn to the sedate area by the renowned **Villa Carlotta ❿** (Via Regina 2; tel: 0344-40405; www.villacarlotta.it; daily Apr–mid-Oct 9am–7.30pm, first half of Mar, mid-Oct–late-Oct 10am–6pm), an exceptionally photogenic majestic villa with glorious gardens. It was built in the late 17th century by Marquis Giorgio Clerici, the heir to a fortune made in the silk trade. In the 19th century, businessman Gian Battista Sommaria lavishly filled it with precious works of art, including sculptures by Canova and Thorwaldsen. In 1843, his heirs sold it to Princess Marianne of Nassau, who gave it as a wedding present to her daughter Carlotta. Its 6-hectare (14-acre) formal terraced gardens are as big a draw as the startlingly white house and its art, with fountains and statues carefully arranged among 150 types of rhododendron, camellia and azalea.

Menaggio

Menaggio ⓫, where the Via Regina forks west to Switzerland and northwards up the lake, is bustling. The

The languid charms of Villa del Balbianello stretch even to the painted nymphs who frolic on the walls and ceiling.

Picture-perfect Tremezzo.

WHERE

Como is home to the oldest seaplane school in the world (founded in 1913). Tourist planes leave from the town's lakefront to wherever you choose – making virtually every bit of the lake accessible. Aero Club Como, Via Masia 44; tel: 031-574 495; www.aeroclubcomo.com.

Every garden was designed to frame the view and every building designed to enhance nature.

19th-century waterfront is lined with cafés, bars and hotels. Its beach and lido (late June–mid-Sept daily 9am–7pm) make it a popular stop with tourists, as can be seen by the excellent and frequent boat links. Watersports, golf and hiking are particularly good here; the **tourist office** (Piazza Garibaldi 3; tel: 0344-32924; www.menaggio.com; 9am–12.30pm, 2.30–6pm, closed Sun, Wed) has details of walking routes, including some into the beautiful **Parco Naturale Val Sanagra** and to **Rifugio Menaggio** (1,400 metres/4,593ft), the "balcony", with views over Lake Como, Monte Legnone, Corni di Canzo and the Grigne peaks.

If you want to get away from the throng, head up the narrow cobbled streets of the medieval town, once a major military stronghold; you can still make out the remains of a 10th-century castle and the fortifications that once encircled the hill down to the harbour.

From the centre stretch three charming hamlets: Nobiallo, Loveno and Croce. The first is a former fishing village extending northwards 1km (0.5 mile) along the shore; above is the glamorous **Loveno**, home to the wonderful 18th-century **Villa Mylius Vigoni**, a 25-minute uphill walk from the Menaggio landing stage. Now an Italian/German conference centre, its spectacular park is open to visitors when no seminars are being held (tel: 0344-36111 or 232; access on year-round guided tours only: 2.30pm Thu only, except Aug, reservation compulsory; www.villavigoni.it). **Croce** (443 metres/1,453ft) enjoys panoramic views of Lake Como and Lake Piano to the west, particularly from its splendid viewpoint of La Crocetta (505 metres/1,657ft), a 25-minute walk from the hamlet. Croce is also home to the renowned **Menaggio and Cadenabbia Golf Club**, one of the oldest in Italy (www.menaggio.it).

Varenna

Arrive by boat, with ancient **Varenna** ⓬ slowly coming into view as the 13th-century campanile of San Giorgio chimes a welcome and you will never want to leave. This absurdly

pretty spot is not only a delight to look at, but also a wonder to look out from: standing on a rocky promontory, it has an enviable view of all three branches of the lake. Once there, the passarella is a scenic walkway hugging the rocks along the lakeside. The oleander arcades along the promenade are just the spot to enjoy a gelato, while a short walk up narrow, crumbling steps takes you to the main square, Piazza San Giorgio and the **tourist office** nearby (tel: 0341-830 367; www.varennaturismo.com; Apr–Sept Tue–Sat 10am–1pm, 3–6pm, Sun and holidays 10am–1pm).

Further along are the enchanting gardens of the neoclassical **Villa Cipressi**, now a hotel, with exquisite grounds sloping down to the lake. The adjacent **Villa Monastero** (tel: 0341-295 450; www.villamonastero.eu; Mar–Dec, opening times for both house and garden vary greatly, check website; museum only open when there are no conferences), a former Cistercian monastery built in the 13th century, is used as a conference centre, but its gardens are open to the public, and a museum inside the villa holds antiques and furniture belonging to the villa's former inhabitants.

A steep 20-minute climb up Mount Fopp from Villa Monastero or the landing stage reveals stunning views and the chance to explore the old town of **Vezio** and its semi-ruined 7th-century **Castello di Vezio** (tel: 348-824 2504; www.castellodivezio. it; Mar, Oct Mon–Fri 10am–5pm, Sat–Sun 10am–6pm, Apr–May, Sept Mon–Fri 10am–6pm, Sat–Sun 10am–7pm, June–Aug Mon–Fri 10am–7pm, Sat–Sun 10am–8pm). A falconer gives demonstrations in the grounds. A shorter walk south of Varenna takes you to a hamlet that is home to the Fiumelatte (River of Milk). This claims to be the shortest river in Italy (just 250 metres/820ft), its creamy-looking waters inexplicably flowing only between March and October.

Bellagio

Bellagio ⓭, the "pearl of Lario", lies at the tip of the triangle formed by the two southern branches, the Triangolo Lariano. Its location and scenic waterfront complete with ice-cream-coloured grand hotels and steep cobbled steps that serve as alleyways, bring out the poet in everyone who comes here – not least Pliny the Younger, Shelley, Flaubert and Mark Twain.

Two Serbelloni villas

Now home to the **Grand Hotel Villa Serbelloni** (see page 77) and its Michelin-starred restaurant, Mistral, the jet set flock here – as do day-trippers. Away from the jacaranda-lined waterfront, the tiny Borgo (the medieval part of town) and maze of stepped streets lined with delis, eateries and silk shops is a delight to explore. Peering down on the town is the Romanesque church of San Giacomo and its tower, survivors from Bellagio's medieval fortifications. The **tourist office** is at the landing stage on Piazza Mazzini (tel: 031-950 204; www.bellagiolakecomo.com; Apr–Oct

Neo-classical statuary is popular in the gardens around the lake.

A steep street in Bellagio.

Mon–Sat 9am–12.30pm, 1.30–5.30pm, Sun 10.30am–12.30pm).

On the hilltop stands the **Villa Serbelloni** with splendid views of all three branches of the lake and the mountains from its park. It is run as a study centre and is not to be confused with its namesake, the Grand Hotel Villa Serbelloni, below.

The two were once linked. In 1907, the hotel, then known as Grand Hotel Bellagio, bought and converted the then abandoned hilltop mansion; the hotel later changed its name in honour of the former residents, the Serbelloni family.

The villa is now owned by the Rockefeller Foundation and closed to visitors, but there are guided tours of the garden on Tue–Sun mid-Mar–Oct at 11am and 3.30pm leaving from the medieval tower in Piazza San Giacomo (tel: 031-951 555; groups of 6–30 only; booking ahead essential). If you cannot do the tour but want the view, take the road running alongside the park to Punta Spartivento and the small harbour at the very tip of the headland, which is a lovely spot for a dip. Head south along the lakeside promenade and past the lido (tel: 031-950 597) to Bellagio's other magnificent residence, **Villa Melzi** (tel: 031-950 204; late-Mar–Oct daily 9.30am–6.30pm) and its neoclassical chapel, museum and outstanding Mediterranean gardens. Further around takes you past the hamlet of **Loppia**, the landing docks of the old Lake Como gondolas, to the village of **San Giovanni** ⓮ (30 minutes on foot from the centre) and the **Museo degli Strumenti per la Navigazione** (Museum of Navigational Instruments; tel: 031-950 309; www.bellagiomuseo.com; daily 10am–1pm or by appointment), a collection of telescopes, compasses and marine chronometers. Other walks include one to **Pescallo**, a charming fishing village 10 minutes west of the centre on the Lecco side of the promontory.

The Triangolo Lariano

This triangle stands between the two southern legs of the lake. From Bellagio at its northern tip, the triangle opens southwards onto a wealth of delightful hamlets, historical sites

The appealing Bellagio waterfront.

and walks, ending in the five Brianza lakes and the town of Erba. Two roads run through it, the Lariana (the coastal road from Bellagio to Como) and the Valassina, running directly through the middle from Bellagio to the Brianza lakes. Outstanding views of the Alps to the north and the Pianura Padana to the south can be found at the peak of **Monte San Primo** (1,686 metres/5,528ft) – if you don't mind a steep two-hour climb. The Valassina is home to holiday resorts such as **Canzo**, at the foot of the rocky peaks of the Corni; viewpoints of **Monte San Primo, Piano del Tivano** and **Piano Rancio** become ski resorts in winter.

Where the Larian Triangle mountains and the plains meet in Alta Brianza are five lakes stretching from Como to Lecco, described as little drops left behind by Lake Como. Tiny **Lago Montorfano** ⓯ (7km/4 miles from Como) is overlooked by the prestigious golf course Villa d'Este and is perfect for swimming; **Lago di Alserio** (5km/3 miles from Erba) was once connected to **Lago di Pusiano**

(4km/2.5 miles from Erba), and both are found in the **Parco della Valle del Lambro** ⓰ and are ideal for afternoon picnics and strolls; **Segrino**, too is in Como province, while **Annone** is in the prealpine Lecco province. The green Brianza plains were a resort for noble Milanese families; today the area is more industrial – a fifth of all Italian furniture is made here.

Lago di Lecco

Lake Como's southeastern fork is less popular than its twin, perhaps due to its starker atmosphere with the craggy Grigne range looming over the rather prosaic villages.

The western shore between Bellagio and Lecco (20km/12 miles) has little by way of diversions once you leave Pescallo, but the eastern shore has a few interesting stops before reaching Lecco. The ancient settlement of **Lierna**, just south of Varenna, is the last alluring spot on this shore before the modern places such as the industrialised town of **Mandello del Lario** and former silk town **Abbadia Lariana**. Boats zigzag their way between

FACT

Cyclists can make a pilgrimage to their patron saint, Madonna del Ghisallo. The church stands at Passo Rancio (755 metres/826yds) and houses an exhibition of cycling memorabilia. With a café and parking area, it also makes a popular stopping point along the panoramic route from Erba to Bellagio.

The elegantly solid Villa Melzi.

Bellagio and Mandello throughout the year, adding in Lecco only during the summer season.

Lecco ⑰ itself is most famous as the setting of a classic book by Italy's cherished Romantic novelist Alessandro Manzoni. "Lecco is built on the shore of the branch of Lake Como that extends southwards," begins *I Promessi Sposi* (The Betrothed), but today there is little to inspire romance. Once the home of the Goths and Lombards, the commercial town has retained a few interesting historical sights. The reconstructed bridge, **Ponte Vecchio** (originally built 1336–38), indicates Lecco's past as a medieval site of importance; other medieval remains such as the **Torre Viscontea** survive around the Piazza XX Settembre and Piazza Cermenati. The tower, once a prison, is now the **Museo Civico del Risorgimento e della Resistenza** (Civic Museum of the Risorgimento and the Resistance). There is also **Pescarenico**, an old fishing village, and nearby, the **Villa Manzoni** art gallery (Tue–Fri 9.30am–6pm, Sat–Sun 10am–6pm) and the 18th-century **Palazzo Belgiojoso**, containing the Natural History and History museums, as well as a Planetarium (www.museilecco.org; museum Tue–Fri 9.30am–2pm, Sat–Sun 10am–6pm, free; Planetarium Mon, Tue, Sat 9.30am–noon, Fri until 9pm).

Lecco's attraction really lies in its scenery: look up above the factories and traffic and you'll see it is surrounded by mountain peaks: the harsh Grigne and Monte Resegone on one side; on the other the gentler Corni di Canzo and Monte Barro. Several interesting excursions head into the hills, including hikes into the stunning southern Alpine valley known as the Valsássina. The tourist board (Piazza XX Settembre 23; tel: 0341-295 720; www.provincia.lecco.it; Mon 9am–12.30pm and Tue–Sun also 2.30–5.30pm).

Ramo di Colico – Alto Lario

Heading along the northern limb of the lake, the scenery becomes increasingly dramatic, with the dazzling villages and patrician villas giving way to wild mountains. This branch is dotted with popular campsites, caravan

Lecco and Monte Resegone.

parks and watersports centres making the most of the Breva, the mild but constant breeze. Inland, good hiking and cycling exertions are rewarded with traditional trattorias and stunning vistas.

The main draw on the rough western bank is **Gravedona** ❶❽, which, together with Dongo and Sorico, formed the medieval republic of the Tre Pievi. On the lakefront is the imposing **Palazzo Gallio**, built in 1586 for Cardinal Tolomeo Gallio, while the **Santa Maria del Tiglio** (daily summer 8.30am–7pm, winter until 5pm) is an important Romanesque church with several 12th-century frescoes. The neighbouring churches of **San Vicenzo** (1050) and **Santa Maria delle Grazie**, built by Augustinian monks in 1467, are also worth a look.

A little further south, **Dongo** ❶❾ is today known chiefly as the site where Mussolini and his Fascist officials were stopped from fleeing to Switzerland by partisans (before being taken to Mezzegra and shot; see page 42). The events are remembered in the **Museo della Resistenza** (Como Resistance Museum), housed in the neoclassical Palazzo Manzi.

On the eastern shore, **Bellano** ❷⓿ is famed for its spectacularly steep gorge called **Orrido di Bellano**, which was formed by the waters of the Pioverna gushing through the rocky passage. A suspended footbridge takes you close to the water (though it is not for the faint-hearted).

The final stop on Lake Como is the northernmost town on the eastern shore. Industrial **Colico** is at the foot of Mount Legnone. Built by the Spanish in the 17th century, it has since been destroyed by foreign troops, plagues and the flooding of the Adda River. Around 5km (3 miles) south, perched on the peninsula, is the medieval **Abbazia di Piona** (tel: 0341-940 331; daily 9am–noon, 2.30–6pm; www.abbaziadipiona.it), occupied today by Cistercian monks.

Heading north into the lower **Val Chiavenna** and the Alpine passes leading to Switzerland and Austria is the reclaimed marshland of Piano di Spagna, one of the largest nature reserves in Lombardy.

Nets hanging in a shed beside the lake.

Como's misty light has filled the dreams of many a poet.

COMO BOAT TOUR

Slowly cruising past grand villas and their citrus-scented gardens is the best way to enjoy the lake.

Laglio harbour.

The best way to appreciate Lake Como is, of course, by boat – not least because you escape the congested lakeside roads during high season and weekends. From the water you get the sense that nothing much has changed since the Romans first succumbed to the lake's charms. And although some of the palatial homes built by centuries of the rich and super-rich can be visited or stayed in, many remain resolutely private, meaning that the only way to get a glimpse of them and their magnificent grounds is by boat.

Como is the main departure point, with boats taking a zig-zag route up the western leg to the Centro Lago. From Bellagio, the "pearl of the lake" and its centre, you can head up north (Alto Lago) to Colico, or down the eastern leg (Ramo di Lecco) to Lecco.

The western shore of the western leg (Ramo di Como) has long been a magnet for high society, with a wealth of sumptuous villas owned by the Italian elite and international superstars. Just up the road from Cernobbio's historic noble residence-turned-hotel, **Villa d'Este A** is the Versaces' weekend retreat of **Le Fontanelle B** in Moltrasio; further up in the gorgeous village of Laglio is George Clooney's summer home, the lemon-faced palazzo Villa **Oleandra C**, half-hidden by its oleander-lined gardens. On the opposite shore, in

Torno, is the **Villa Pliniana D** (1574–77), anoth notable patrician house. One of the best exampl of Manneristic architecture on the lake, it can on be viewed from the water. Back on the weste shore, in Ossuccio, is the opulent **Villa Balbian E**, one of the five oldest homes on the lakefro and residence of Como's Taroni silk king Miche Canepi. Its 18th-century owner, Cardinal Ange Maria Durini, built the resplendent **Villa Balb anello F** on the nearby Lavedo promontory.

Further up in the Centro Lago is perhaps Lal Como's most famous villa, Tremezzo's **Villa Carlotta G**, a sight to relish as you approach its neoclassical white facade with scissor staircase and terraced formal gardens. Other notable waterfront villas are Bellagio's **Villa Melzi H**, the tumbling gardens of **Villa Monastero I** and cypress tree-filled **Villa Cipressi J**, both in beautiful Varenna.

Of course, a trip around the lake reveals much more than its wealth of grand houses. Once past **Isola Comacina K**, the

Como harbour.

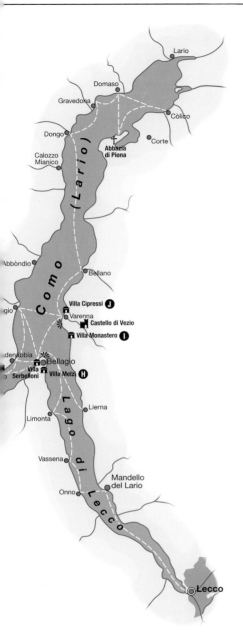

Moorings at Bellagio.

Sailing on Lake Como.

ly island and the setting for a magical annual ework and boat display, and the enchant-g Centro Lago, the scenery and atmosphere anges. The eastern branch becomes wilder as e rugged Grigne mountain range looms into ew, while the northern reach, popular with atersports and camping enthusiasts, becomes creasingly Alpine.

Several types of boat, all run by the Gestione Navigazione Laghi (tel: 800-551 801, www.navl aghi.it), tour the lake linking the major villages of each leg. You can choose to board a *battello* (ship), *servizio rapido* (hydrofoil/fast service), or *autotraghetto* (car ferry; centre of the lake only); buy tickets before boarding. Cruises touring the entire lake in around eight hours are also available from Como or Lecco, with a restaurant and bar on board. Every Saturday from June to September, evening "romantic" cruises set sail from Como, Lecco and Colico.

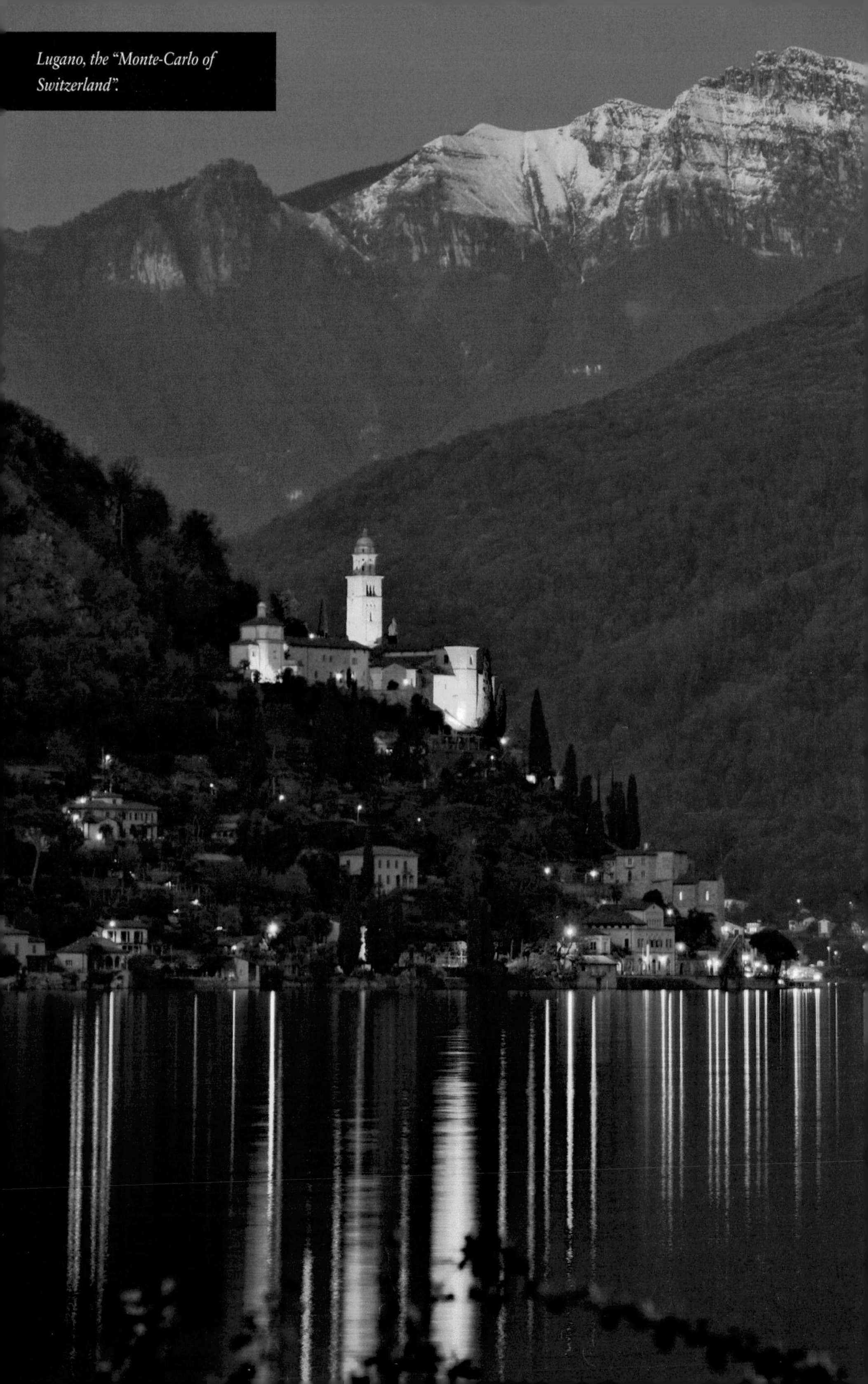

Lugano, the "Monte-Carlo of Switzerland".

LUGANO

One of the smallest and prettiest of the lakes, Lake Lugano is enfolded by mountains; steep wooded hills rise sheer from the water, precluding development along most of its shore. Lively, stylish Lugano, in Switzerland, is the only large town.

Also masquerading as Lake Ceresio, Lake Lugano lies deep in the mountains, shared between Switzerland and Italy, the long tongue of Swiss Ticino snaking through the middle with Italy on either side. About two thirds of the lake lies within Swiss territory; only the very eastern tip is Italian, plus the enclave of Campione d'Italia, a little lakeside town that remains proudly and typically Italian. In 1847, a dam was built across the middle of the lake, from Melide to Bissone, taking the motorway and railway across the water en route to Como.

Lugano

Set on a sweeping bay at the north end of the lake, **Lugano ❶** was built on trade and finance but has thrived for the last couple of hundred of years on tourism. Its lakeside promenades, café-lined piazzas, luxury shops and galleries have earned it the nickname "the Monte-Carlo of Switzerland". The town is thought to date back to the 6th century, but is first mentioned in 724, control bouncing between Como and Milan until it fell to the Swiss in 1512.

Work on the triumphant **Lungo-lago ❹** (waterfront) began in 1865, creating the broad walkway with its avenue of shady linden and horse chestnut trees fronting the arcaded shops, hotels, villas and open-air cafés. The **Frecciarossa** (Red Arrow)

Parco Botanico San Grato in bloom.

road train (tel: 89 20 21; www.trenitalia. com) runs tours of the city which loop around the bay along the Lungolago, between the two funiculars that stand like bookends at either end of the bay. At the western end of town, the **Paradiso Funicolare Monte San Salvatore ❸** cable railway (Lugano-Paradiso; tel: 091-985 2828; www.montesansalvatore.ch; mid-Mar–mid-Sept, every 30 minutes, first trip 9am, in summer last trip at 11pm) takes you up to 912 metres (2,992ft). At the other end, the **Monte Brè Funicolare ❻** cable railway (Via

Main Attractions
Lugano Waterfront
Monte Brè
Morcote
Monte Generoso
Villa Heleneum

Altarpiece from Lugano Duomo.

The bold lines of the Lugano Arte e Cultura complex (LAC).

Ceresio 36, Ruvigliana; tel: 091-971 3171; www.montebre.ch; Mar–Sept 9am–7.30pm, June–Aug Fri–Sat until 11pm, Oct–Dec 9.30am–5.30pm, closed Jan–Feb) goes higher to 925 metres (3,061ft), up to the village of Brè, an open-air museum of frescoes donated by enthusiastic visiting artists. Take time to wander, hire a mountain bike to come back down or just settle for lunch or dinner in one of the good restaurants that take advantage of the superlative views.

Two fine churches

To the west of the city centre, the **Chiesa di Santa Maria degli Angeli** Ⓓ (Piazza Bernardino Luini) is the city's most beautiful church, built from 1490–1515 as part of a Franciscan convent. The interior is covered with glorious Renaissance frescoes, many of them by Bernardino Luini, a pupil of Leonardo da Vinci, including his version of *The Last Supper* and the *Passion and Crucifixion of Christ*. In the city centre, the **Cattedrale di San Lorenzo** Ⓔ (Via Cattedrale) began life in 875, but was largely rebuilt in the 13th and

14th centuries, was heavily restored a century later and gained a new Renaissance facade in 1517. It has several 14th–16th-century frescoes inside. The Chapel of Santa Maria delle Grazie was dedicated in 1473 in thanks for the end of a bout of plague but refurbished in Baroque style in 1774.

Liberty mansions and art collections

Several of the city's magnificent Liberty (Art Nouveau) mansions open their parks to the public. Some are also used as museums and galleries. **Villa Saroli** Ⓕ (Via Stefano Franscini 9; grounds open all year, house open only for exhibitions; free), built in 1904, is home to the city **Museo Storico**, while the exuberant grounds contain an orangery and numerous flowering trees, from dogwood and magnolia to ancient camellia and rhododendron bushes.

The new **Museo d'Arte della Svizzera Italiana** (Via Canova 10; Tue 2–5pm, Wed–Sun 10am–5pm; Piazza Bernardino 6; Tue–Wed, Sun 10.30am–6pm, Thu–Sat 10.30am–8pm; www.masilugano.ch) opened in 2015 over two

locations effectively merging the former Museo Cantonale d'Arte and City of Lugano's Museo d'Arte. Spreading over both the medieval Palazzo Reali in the historic centre and the new lakefront **Lugano Arte e Cultura** (**LAC**) G cultural complex, it houses a permanent collection of art by Swiss-Italian and Italian artists of the 19th and 20th centuries, as well as temporary 20th-century art exhibitions and also showcases the region's art history.

Luxury shopping

Piazza Riforma H is the space at the centre of a web of pedestrianised streets that make up Lugano's city centre shopping heaven. Head along Via Nassa for designer boutiques and Swiss watches, Via Pessina for mouthwatering delis,

Via Canova for art and antiques, or just stay in the square with a cup of hot chocolate and watch the world go by.

South of Lugano

South of the city, the lake winds around the bulk of **Monte San Salvatore**. This peninsula has some of the prettiest countryside and most desirable real estate on the lake – luxurious mansions change hands for millions of Swiss francs – and you have to drive through Paradiso to reach it. The main road to Como follows the shoreline as far as **Melide** ➋, where it crosses over to the Campione d'Italia (see box).

There are plenty of healthy outdoor activities here, but the main attraction is **Swissminiatur** (Melidetel: tel: 091-640 1060; www.swissminiatur.ch;

TIP

Much of Lake Lugano lies within Swiss territory; just over a third of the shore at the eastern end of the lake belongs to Italy, plus the enclave of Campione d'Italia – so don't forget to take your passport with you.

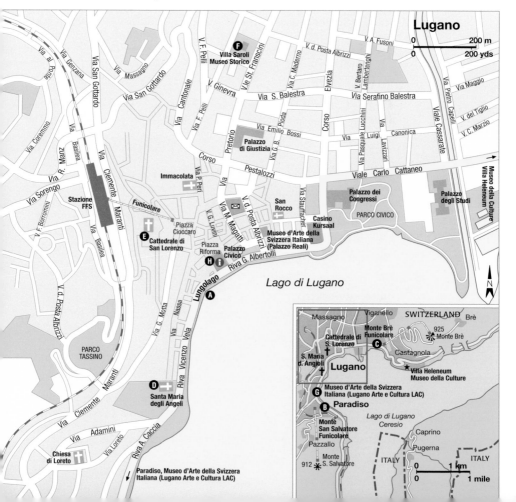

FACT

Born in Calw in Germany, Herman Hesse (1877–1962) became a Swiss citizen in 1924, living in Lugano. As well as creating the literary masterpieces for which he was awarded the Nobel Prize in 1946, he took up painting and grew flowers and vegetables for pleasure.

mid-Mar–mid-Oct daily 9am–6pm). This is delightful for adults and children alike, showing the country's highlights from its chateaux to the Alps in miniature, complete with a 3.6km (2.6-mile) model railway.

A steep road leads up to **Carona** ❸ (602 metres/1,975ft), which straddles the back of Monte San Salvatore. The panoramic views have inspired numerous artists to settle here, decorating their houses and the local churches and making Carona one of the prettiest painted villages in the region.

A walking and cycle path, the romantically named **Sentiero dei Fiori** (Path of Flowers), leads up to the San Salvatore cable car. Just outside the village, the **Parco Botanico San Grato** (tel: 091-943 1888; open all year) sprawls along the ridge, its terraces a picture at any time, but magnificent in April and May when the azaleas and rhododendrons burst into bloom. There are several walks of different levels of difficulty through the gardens, a restaurant, children's playground and a maze.

Back down at lake level, at the end of the peninsula, the **Parco Scherrer**

(Morcote; tel: 091-996 2125; mid-Mar–Oct 10am–5pm, July–Aug until 6pm) is another very different botanical garden, with each area representing a part of the world, from a floral Temple of Nefertiti to a Siamese teahouse.

Morcote

Known as "the pearl of the lake", **Morcote** ❹ itself is one of the prettiest villages in the Italian Lakes, the arcaded waterfront lined with cafés and the narrow streets and tiny piazzas behind meandering up the steep hill to the 15th-century church of **Santa Maria del Sasso**. Here you'll find fine 16th-century frescoes, a 17th-century organ and monumental cemetery.

Herman Hesse

Take the road up the other side of the peninsula to join the main road, signposted to **Ponte Tresa**. There are two very different stops en route. The first is to pay homage to the Nobel prize-winning writer and artist at the **Fondazione Hermann Hesse** ❺ (Torre Camuzzi, Montagnola; tel: 091-993 3770; www.hessemontagnola.ch; Mar–Oct

Swissminiatur.

daily 10am–5.30pm, Nov–Feb Sat–Sun 10am–5.30pm). Hesse moved to the area in 1919, living in the Camuzzi Tower, where the museum is situated, then transferring to the nearby Pink House with his third wife in 1931. Hesse wrote some of his most popular works here, including *Siddharta* and the Glass Bead Game. He is buried in the cemetery of San Abbondio in Gentilino.

Chocolate Museum

Chocolate is almost as Swiss as the cuckoo clock, so a stop at the **Museo del Cioccolato Alprose 6** (Alprose Chocolate Museum; Via Rompada 36, Caslano; tel: 091-611 8856; www. alprose.ch; Mon–Fri 9am–5.30pm, Sat–Sun 9am–4.30pm) is entirely justifiable. It is best to visit during the week when the factory is working, the smell of chocolate is all-pervasive and the tasting opportunities are increased.

The south

At **Ponte Tresa** (a steamer-landing and curious border village with both a Swiss and an Italian side), the road crosses the river and goes back into Italy, skirting the lake through Lavena and Brusimpiano to **Porto Ceresio**. A detour south along the Valceresio to **Besano 7** leads to the **Museo Civico dei Fossili di Besano** (Besano Museum of Fossils; Via Prestini 5; tel: 0332-919 200; www.montesangiorgio.org; Tue–Wed, Fri 9.30am–12.30pm, Thu 2.30–5pm, Sun 2.30–6pm). Here you can see findings from one of Europe's most important Triassic fossil beds (dating from c.230 million years ago). **Monte Giorgio 8** is a Unesco World Heritage site and to date has yielded 22 species of animal and 54 species of fish. More fossils can be found in the museum in remote **Meride 9** (tel: 091-646 0854; Tue–Sun 9am–5pm; www.montesangiorgio.org). Both museums organise guided walks on the mountain itself.

South of Besano, the fabulous privately owned **Villa Cicogna Mozzoni 10** (Viale Cicogna 8, Bisuschio; tel: 0332-471 134; www.villacicognamozzoni.it; Sun and holidays Apr–Oct 9.30am–noon, 2.30–7pm) was originally built in the 1430s as a hunting lodge. In the mid-16th century, it was converted into a country residence with lavishly

The picturesque village of Morcote.

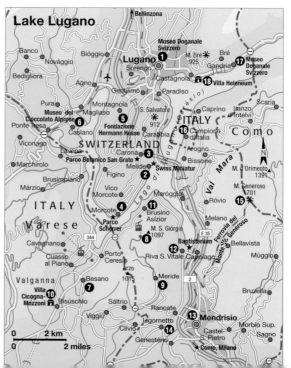

The rack railway up Monte Generoso offers spectacular views.

Around Monte San Giorgio

Back at the shore, the road starts working its way across the border and around the bulk of Monte San Giorgio. At **Brusino ⑪**, a cable car, the **Funivio Brusino Serpiano** (tel: 091-996 1130; www.serpiano.ch; Apr–Sept Wed–Sun 9am–6pm) whisks you up the mountain to **Serpiano** for fabulous views, walks, a spa visit or some fossil-hunting.

At the bottom of the next loop south, the **Baptisterium** (Baptistery) at **Riva San Vitale ⑫** is one of the oldest surviving churches in the lakes region, dating from the 5th century. The 12th-century font and frescoes seem young in comparison.

Wine-tastings and art

Heading south, the route winds through the gentle wine country of the Mendrisiotto, which provides the odd

Lugano ferry.

frescoed rooms. The formal gardens are on seven levels, linked by a double staircase lined by cypress trees, while a huge English-style park stretches over the hill behind.

stop for a tasting. (Merlot is the varietal of choice around here.) **Mendrisio ⑬** is renowned for its particularly beautiful medieval centre. One of the finest buildings, a former Serviti (Servants of Mary) convent, is now the **Museo d'Arte** (Art Museum, Piazza San Giovanni; Tue–Fri 10am–noon, 2–5pm, Sat–Sun 10am–6pm; http://museo.mendrisio.ch). World-class temporary exhibitions of modern art are held here alongside the permanent works.

Just west of town, in **Ligornetto ⑭**, the **Museo Vincenzo Vela** (tel: 091-640 7044; www.museo-vela.ch; Oct–May Tue–Sun 10am–5pm, June–Sept and Sun until 6pm) was the villa and studio of 19th-century sculptor Vincenzo Vela. Beautifully restored by local architect Mario Botta, it houses many of Vela's haunting plaster models together with works by his son, Spartaco, and brother, Lorenzo Vela. If shopping is more your thing, the **FoxTown Outlet Mall** is near at hand (www.foxtown.ch).

The east shore

Head back up to the lake to **Capolago**. Allow yourself plenty of time here for

CRUISING

While there is more than enough to occupy you on shore, it would be a crying shame to ignore the lure of the lake itself.

The Società Navigazione del Lago di Lugano (tel: 091-971 5223; www.lakelugano.ch) runs regular ferry services along the north shore from Paradiso to Gandria, Lugano to Ponte Tresa and Lugano to Campione d'Italia, all with stops en route. In addition, there are morning, lunch and afternoon cruises.

The Lugano Holiday Card (www.luganotourism.ch) is a free passport-sized card available to anyone who spends at least one night in the Ticino region. The card offers discounts on a variety of guided tours, transport, cultural and sporting events in the Lugano area.

a trip on the rack railway up **Monte Generoso** 🅕 (www.montegeneroso.ch; closed for redevelopment until 2017). The 40-minute train ride reaches a height of 1,701 metres (5,590ft) and offers unparalleled 360° views across the lake region and on to the Alps, with the Eiger, Matterhorn and Jungfrau all visible on clear days. As well as a restaurant and café, there are 51km (32 miles) of walking trails and an astronomical observatory at the top; you can also take a guided visit to a cave where bears' bones some 35–40,000 years old have been found. This is one of 50 caves found on the massif so far. And if none of that grabs you, strap on a helmet and take to a mountain bike or paraglider.

The main road from Lugano to Como runs along the shore for a while, crossing the lake to the city at **Bissone**. Just north of here, a spur loop leads into **Campione d'Italia** 🅖 (see box), a corner of Lugano that is forever Italy.

There is no road along much of the shore from Bissone to Ostano – the fastest way to get to the north shore from here is to take the causeway and head back through the city. The alternative is a beautiful but winding drive through tiny back roads and steep-sided switchback valleys in the Italian foothills of Monte Generoso.

North shore

The north shore is a busy, wealthy area lined by waterfront mansions and restaurants both heavily used by Lugano city commuters. Most of the tourist sights are clustered together around the little town of **Gandria**, just inside the Swiss frontier and an ideal spot for the **Museo Doganale Svizzero** 🅗 (Museum of Swiss Customs; Cantine di Gandria, reached by boat; mid-Apr–mid-Oct daily 1.30–5.30pm; www.customsmuseum.admin.ch; free), a surprisingly interesting look at the increasingly inventive battle between customs officials and smugglers over the last century or so.

The **Sentiero dell'Olivo** is a 2km (1-mile) path from Gandria along the lake, aimed at reviving the cultivation of olives here. The Parco degli Olivi, part-way along the path towards the city, was once the estate of a German baroness. Now the terraced gardens are a glorious mix of wonderful-smelling Mediterranean shrubbery – bay, olives, marine pine, oregano, thyme and sage with a riot of daffodils and tulips every spring.

A further 200metres/656ft towards the city, with its own boat stop, **Villa Heleneum** 🅘 (garden: summer 6am–11pm, winter until 9pm; free) is a faithful reproduction of Versailles's Petit Trianon. Built in 1931, it is surrounded by fabulous exotic gardens filled with Japanese palms, kumquats, grapefruits, medlars and cedars. The villa is the former home of the city's **Museo delle Culture** (www.mcl.lugano.ch), a fascinating collection of cult figures and masks from Africa, Oceania and Asia. The museum closed in 2016 and the collection is being transferred to Villa Malpensata (Riva Caccia 5) in Lugano.

FACT

Not so extinct – the prehistoric Wollemia nobilis conifer, which reaches 35 metres (115ft) high, was thought to be long extinct before a cluster of 100 trees was found in a deep Australian gorge in 1994, its location a carefully guarded secret. As part of the preservation effort, one precious tree now grows in the grounds of the Villa Heleneum.

Along the Sentiero dell'Olivo.

Lago di Varese.

VARESE

Tucked into the triangle between Maggiore, Lugano and Como, the rolling hills and fertile river valleys of the Varesotto became the back garden of the great aristocratic families who built their villas here.

I t was in quiet Varese that the warring, squabbling nobles came to find peace amidst the reedy lake beds and the rustling woodlands. It was here that they built monasteries and villas with lush gardens. Varese today still offers visitors a feeling of stillness, whether they come as pilgrims or campers, trudging up the hills on bicycles or taking the easy way up by cable car.

Varese

People have lived in **Varese** ❶ since the 5th millennium BC. The first town was founded here as a military garrison by the Romans. Today, it has a population of over 80,000, making a living from shoes and leatherwork, tourists and industry. For a very short while, in the mid-18th century, it was the feudal property of Francesco III d'Este, duke of Modena, who built the long, low strawberry-pink **Palazzo Estense** ⒶerrVol, topped with an imperial eagle, as his summer palace in 1787. The palace now houses the town hall and is not open to the public, but you are free to wander through the neatly manicured gardens, said to be modelled on those of the imperial residence of Schönbrunn in Vienna.

The Estense Palace gardens lead straight into the far larger and wilder gardens of the **Villa Mirabello** Ⓑ

Palazzo Estense gardens.

on the hill behind, home to some rare plants and majestic trees including a centuries old Lebanese cedar. The villa now houses the city's main museum, the **Museo Civico Archeologico** (Piazza della Motta 4; tel: 0332-255 485; Tue–Sun June–Oct 10am–12.30pm, 2–6pm, Nov–May 9.30am–12.30pm, 2–5.30pm), which features local prehistoric finds and Roman remains.

Historic centre

In the city centre, **Piazza Monte**

The Garibaldi Memorial in the Piazza del Podestà

The 17th-century bell tower of Basilica di San Vittore.

Grappa is unappealing, with great slabs of 1920s Fascist concrete at odds with the gentle city around it.

Across the main road, in the historic centre, the 16th–17th century **Basilica di San Vittore** was designed by Pellegrini (*il Tibaldi*) and built by Giuseppe Bernascone. The neoclassical facade was added later by Viennese architect Pollack. Inside, there are a number of fine paintings including a scandalously topless Mary Magdalene by Il Morazzone (1627). The free-standing campanile (bell tower) beside the basilica was added by Bernascone in the early 17th century. Next door, the 12th–13th century Romanesque **Battistero di San Giovanni** stands on an early 6th–7th century church and

contains fine 14th-century frescoes and its original 7th-century font.

The war memorial arch opposite the basilica leads through to the **Piazza del Podestà** ⓓ, where the monument **Il Garibaldino** celebrates a famous victory for the Risorgimento when Garibaldi and his Alpine Hunters defeated the Austrians at the Battle of Biumo in Varese on 26 May 1859. This in turn leads to the arcaded pedestrian street of **Corso Matteotti**, lined by upmarket boutiques and tea shops.

Villa Panza

In Biumo, on the northern edge of the historic centre, the extravagantly named **Villa Menafoglio Litta Panza** ⓔ (Piazza Litta 1; tel: 0332-283 960; www.fondoambiente.it; Feb–mid-Dec Tue–Sun 10am–6pm, last entry 5.15pm, guided visits on prior booking) was built in the mid-18th century by Marquis Paolo Antonio Menafoglio. It was extended in 1830 by neoclassical architect Luigi Canonica, during which time the more formal Italian gardens were

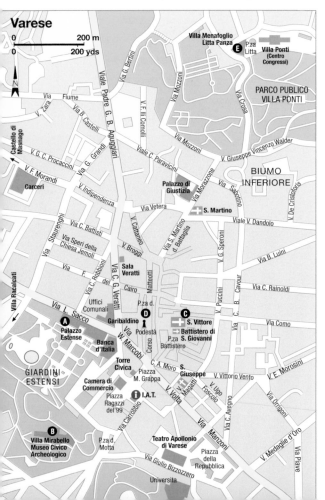

Varese

also redesigned in keeping with the then fashionable softer English landscape gardens.

While the house and garden are both undoubtedly beautiful, the property is chiefly famous for its world-class collection of modern art (**Collezione Panza**; for opening times, see villa) , begun by Giuseppe Panza di Biumo in the 1950s. Take the free audio guide or you won't have a clue what you are looking at. This is art of the square-monochrome-canvas-neon-tube-and-lots-of-background-explanation variety, but like it or loathe it, it fits in fascinating counterpoint with the flamboyance of the villa itself.

Next door to Villa Panza are two other grand 18th–19th-century houses, the **Ville Ponti**. They are used as a conference centre and are usually closed to the public but the gardens are open.

The road west from Varese towards Gavirate and Laveno passes the splendidly decorative **Villa Recalcati**, in Casbeno, built in the 18th century as a private residence, transformed into the Grand Hotel Excelsior in 1874 and now the seat of the provincial government and prefecture.

North of Varese

Just northwest of the city, the **Sacro Monte** ❷ is one of nine holy mounts in the lakes region (see box). The first chapel to Santa Maria was built by Sant'Ambrogio in the 6th century. A 15th-century convent and church was joined in 1604 by the processional way of 14 chapels, representing the mysteries of the rosary. Overseen by architect Giuseppe Bernascone, many different architects, sculptors and artists worked on the project. The result is an awe-inspiring work of devotion. Walk up past the chapels if you are feeling fit, or drive or take the cable car to the top to see the view, and visit the sanctuary and village of Santa Maria del Monte, which also has fine views and restaurants. The **Museo Baroffio** (tel: 0332-212 042, www.museo baroffio.it; mid-Mar–Oct Thu, Sat–Sun 9.30am–12.30pm, 3–6.30pm or by appointment, May–Sept also

Chapel IV, Sacro Monte.

HOLY MOUNTS

The Sacri Monti, or "Sacred Mountains", are an unusual feature of the lakes. Linking shrines and tiny chapels filled with life-size terracotta figures and frescoes, they are devotional routes which evoke the symbolic journey through the Holy Land. At the end of the 15th century, Christians were too fearful to go on pilgrimages in Muslim-controlled territory so, ingeniously, the Holy Land, Jerusalem and Palestine were recreated at home. After the Council of Trent (1545–63), the emphasis shifted to a vigorous defence of Catholicism, which provoked a new wave of Holy Mounts dedicated to Christ, the Virgin and saints. "Sacro Monte" is a misleading term, as it is not a mystical spot found in nature, but one created there.

*Arcumeggia is like an
outdoor gallery.*

Tue–Wed 3–6.30pm) displays the pilgrim offerings.

Beyond this, the **Parco Regionale Campo dei Fiori ❸** (tel: 0332-435 386) culminates in Pico Paradiso (Paradise Peak; 1,227 metres/4,026ft), home to an astronomical observatory. The once splendid Grand Hotel Campo dei Fiori, designed by Giuseppe Sommaruga in 1910–12 and a fine example of Liberty style, has long since ceased to be a hotel, and now makes a perfect mast for satellite TV stations and mobile-phone companies in the region. Elsewhere on the mountains, there are waymarked trails through forests of beech and chestnut, with fine views, and glimpses of the wild flowers that give the park its name.

In Casalzuigno, on the northern side of the Campo dei Fiori, **Villa della Porta Bozzolo ❹** (20km/12 miles northwest of Varese; tel: 0332-624 136; Mar, Sept Wed–Sun 10am–6pm, Apr–Aug Tue–Sun 10am–6pm, Oct–Nov Wed–Sun 10am–5pm; www.fondoambiente.it) is an opulent mansion now run by the Fondo per L'Ambiente Italiano (FAI), the Italian equivalent of Britain's National Trust (see box). Originally built in 1500, it was transformed in the late 17th and early 18th centuries into an aristocratic villa. Gianangelo III della Porta planted the avenue of cypresses that links the formal parterres near the house with the more natural gardens on the hill above. There are also historic farm buildings, including stables, cellars and a wine press.

A switchback mountain road leads through the Valcuvia district from the town to the "artists' village" of **Arcumeggia ❺**. In 1957, a holiday home for artists was opened and since then, Italian artists, including Aligi Sassu, Innocente Salvini and Aldo Carpi, have painted over 150 murals depicting daily life and religious themes on the exteriors of the village houses.

West of Varese

On the edge of Varese, the **Castello di Masnago ❻** (Via Cola di Rienzo; tel: 0332-820 409; Tue–Sun June–Oct 10am–12.30pm, 2.30–6.30pm,

Nov–May 9.30am–12.30pm, 2–5.30pm) is an architectural hotch-potch, but it has a series of fine 15th-century frescoes depicting lifestyles of the period, vices and virtues included. It is also the home of a modern art collection. About 3km (2 miles) beyond this, the ruined 11th-century **Torri di Velate** is not open to the public, but is seen as a symbol of the city of Varese.

Lake Varese

The main road continues along to Gavirate, the main town at the northern end of **Lago di Varese** ❼. Laid out in a wide basin at the foot of the Campo dei Fiori and surrounded by rolling hills, this is one of the smallest lakes, measuring only 8.8km (5.5 miles) long and 4.5km (2.75 miles) wide. Fed by underground springs, it is rich in freshwater fish stock like tench, carp, eel and pike. The road dips down to the lake through the reed-beds every now and then, but it is encircled by a walking and cycling track popular with picnickers and joggers.

In **Gavirate** ❽, the restful 12th-century **Voltorre Cloister** is all that remains of an old Cluniac monastery, while in the centre of the lake, on its only island, **Isola Virginia**, a small museum marks a Neolithic and Bronze Age settlement (tel: 0332-255 485; boat service from Biandronno, Apr–Oct Sat–Sun).

A short distance to the southwest are two more small lakes, **Lago di Monate** ❾, said to have some of the clearest waters in Italy, and **Lago di Comabbio** ❿, renowned for its floating vegetation, including water chestnuts, and for being shallow enough to freeze in winter.

South of Varese

South of the city, head across the plain to **Castiglione Olona** ⓫ (www.castiglioneolona.it), originally a Roman fortress before the Viscontis, Torriani and Castiglione families left it with a rich legacy of medieval and Renaissance art, including a masterly cycle of 15th-century frescoes on the life of John the Baptist in the Baptistery of the **Collegiata**

Fifteenth-century frescoes in the Castello di Masnago, near Lake Varese.

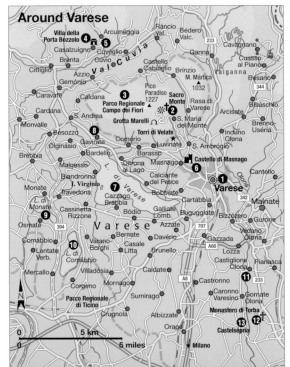

Picnic on Lago di Comabbio.

(Apr–Sept Tue–Sun 10am–1pm, 3–6pm, Oct–Mar Tue–Sat 9.30am–12.30pm, 2.30–5.30pm, Sun 10am–1pm, 3–6pm; www.museocollegiata.it) and secular scenes, in the **Palazzo Branda Castiglioni** (Museo Civico; Apr–Sept Tue–Sat 9am–noon, 3–6pm, Sun 10.30am–12.30pm, 3–6pm, Oct–Mar Tue–Sat 9am–noon, 3–6pm, Sun 3–6pm), both by Masolino.

The **Palazzo Castiglioni of Monteruzzo** (Corte del Doro) is now home to an ultra-modern and innovative **Museo d'Arte Plastica** (Plastic Art Museum; same hours as above).

A little further down the road, the **Monastero di Torba** ⓬ (Torba Monastery, Gornate Olona; 15km/10 miles south of Varese; tel: 0331-820 301; www.fondoambiente.it; Wed–Sun Mar–Sept 10am–6pm, Oct–Nov 10am–5pm) was a late Roman outpost with defensive walls from the Goths and Longobards (5th–6th centuries) that became a Benedictine monastery in the 8th–13th centuries, and features rare 8th-century

frescoes in the tower. It was made a Unesco World Heritage site in 2011.

Virtually nothing remains of nearby **Castelseprio** ⓭ (Via Castel Vecchio 58; tel: 0331-820 438; www.castelseprio.net; Feb–Nov Tue–Fri 8.30am–7.30pm, Sat 8.30am–7pm, Sun 9.45am–6pm, Dec–Jan Tue–Fri 8.30am–4pm, Sun 9.15am–2.45pm; free), once a Roman fort, then a significant medieval citadel until its destruction in the 13th century. Now an archaeological park, its fame resides in one little church, **Santa Maria Foris Portas** (Feb–Nov Tue–Fri 8.30am–7pm, Sat 8.30am–2.30pm, 5.30–7pm, Sun 9.45am–2.30pm, 5.30–6pm, Dec–Jan Tue–Fri 8.30am–6pm, Sun 9.15am–2.45pm; free) – *foris portas* means 'outside the gates'. The church is thought to date from the early 9th century and is decorated with superb Byzantine-style frescoes, unlike anything else in the region. Concealed for centuries until their discovery in 1944, these unique artworks have elevated the church to Unesco World Heritage status.

Palazzo Branda Castiglioni.

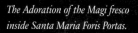
The Adoration of the Magi fresco inside Santa Maria Foris Portas.

LAKE MAGGIORE

"When a man has a heart and a shirt, he should sell the shirt in order to visit Lake Maggiore," said Stendhal. The luxurious lakeside villas, verdant gardens and jewel-like islands have been attracting visitors for centuries.

Milano • Brescia • Verona

t may be called Maggiore (Major or "the greatest"), but Lake Maggiore isn't the biggest of the Italian Lakes. That honour goes to Garda. In fact, to most of the locals, the lake is known as Verbano, a throwback to its Roman name that has never quite been shaken off. Nevertheless, it is still a very large lake, up to 65km (40 miles) long by 12km (7.5 miles) wide, with a total area of 212 sq km (82 sq miles). At its deepest, near Ghiffa, it is 372 metres (1,221ft). Like the other great lakes, it was created by glaciers, leaving a long narrow footprint through steep-sided mountains. The northern fifth of the lake is in Switzerland, the western shore is in Piedmont and the eastern shore in Lombardy.

The western shore

Arona ❶ is a giant bronze and copper statue by Giovanni Battista Crespi of **San Carlo Borromeo** (Apr–Sept daily 9am–12.20pm, 2–6.15pm, Oct Sat–Sun 9am–12.30pm, 2–6.15pm, Mar, Nov Sat–Sun 9am–12.30pm, 2–4.30pm, Dec Sun 9am–12.30pm, 2–4.30pm; www.statuasancarlo.it), the éminence grise of the Counter-Reformation. You can climb up through San Carlone (Big St Charles), as he is cheerfully known, and peer out across the lake through his eyes – or indeed his nose. Flaubert was far from entranced: "Big, nasty, easily painted,

big ears sticking out from the head," he noted in his diary.

Arona is a busy, rather industrial town, but it has a pretty lakeside promenade on the main square with a fine view across to the Rocca Borreomeo. Napoleon once stayed in the elegant 18th-century **Villa Ponti**, built into the battlements of the Rocca and now used for art exhibitions and concerts.

Stresa

From here, the road winds north, hugging the lake shore through the

Main Attractions
Statue of San Carlo
  Borromeo
Monte Mottarone
Isola Bella
Isola Madre
Villa Taranto
Ferrovia di Centovalli
Santa Caterina del Sasso

Statue of San Carlo Borromeo, Arona.

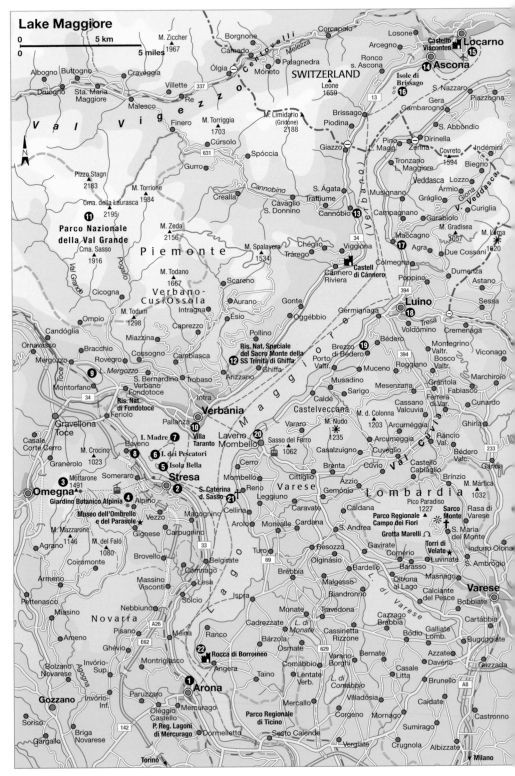

Lake Maggiore

0 ———— 5 km
0 ———— 5 miles

SWITZERLAND

M. Ziccher 1967

Borgnone

Corcapolo

Losone

Arcegno

Castello Visconteo

Locarno 15

Ascona 14

Cámedo

Palagnedra

Ronco s. Ascona

Ólgia

Moneto

Isole di Brissago 16

S. Nazzaro

Albogno

Buttogno

Craveggia

Villette

Leone 1659

Gera Gambarogno

Piazzogna

Druogno

Sta. Maria Maggiore

337

Rezzo

Brissago

Piodina

Pino L. Magg.

Dirinella

S. Abbóndio

Malesco

Finero

M. Torriggia 1703

M. Limidário (Gridone) 2188

Giazzo

Zenna

Covreto

Indémini

Cúrsolo

631

Tronzano L. Maggiore

1594

Biegno

V a l   V i g e z z o

Gurro

Spóccia

S. Ágata

Traffiume

Veddasca

Lozzo

Ármio

Pizzo Stagn. 2183

Cannobino

Crealla

Cávaglio S. Donnino

Cannóbio 13

Musignano

Campagnano

Gráglio

Giona

Curiglia

M. Torrione 1984

M. Gradisea 5057

M. Lema 1620

Cma. della Laurasca 2195

Maccagno

Garabiolo

Parco Nazionale della Val Grande 11

M. Zeda 2156

S. Spalavera 1534

Chéglio

Viggiona

Agra

Due Cossáni

Cma. Sasso 1916

Cólmegna

P i e m o n t e

Trárego

Castell di Cánnero

Poppino

Dumenza

Astano

M. Todano 1667

Scareno

Cánnero Riviera

Sessa

Cicogna

V e r b a n o - C u s i O s s o l a

Aurano

Gonte

Germignaga

394

Luino 18

Cremenaga

Ompio

M. Todum 1298

Intragna

Ésio

Oggébbio

Voldómino

Tresa

Candóglia

Miazzina

Caprezzo

Pollino

Brezzo di Bédero 19

Bédero

Montegrino Valtr.

Viconago

Ornavasso

Bracchio

Rovegro

Cossogno

Cambiasca

Ris. Nat. Speciale del Sacro Monte della SS Trinità di Ghiffa 12

Porto Valtr.

Bosco Valtr.

394

Rogglano

Marchirolo

Mergozzo

L. Mergozzo 9

S. Bernardino Verbano Fondotoce

Trobaso

Ghiffa

Arizzano

Muceno

Musadino

Sarigo

Mesenzana

Gràntola

Fabiasco

Montorfano

34

Ris. Nat. di Fondotoce Feriolo

Intra

Caldé

Cassano Valcuvia

Ferrera di Var.

Cunardo

Gravellona Toce

Pallanza

Verbánia 10

Villa Taranto

Castelveccana

M. d. Colonna 1203

Arcuméggia

Ghirla

Casale Corte Cerro

I. Madre 7

Laveno Mombello 20

Vararo

M. Nudo 1235

Arcuméggia

Ránclo Val.

M. Crocino 1023

Baveno 8

I. dei Pescatori 6

Sasso del Ferro 1062

Casalzuigno

Cuvéglio

Castello Cabiáglio

Bédero Valc.

233

Granerolo

Mottarone 1491

Isola Bella 5

Somerano

Cerro

Brenta

Cúvio

Brínzio

M. Mártica 1032

Omegna 3

Stresa 2

Mombello

Cittíglio

Ázzio

Gemónio

L o m b a r d i a

Giardino Botanico Alpinia

Alpino 4

S. Caterina d. Sasso 21

Reno

Leggiuno

Caravate

Caldana

Pico Paradiso 1227

Sarco Monte

Rasa di Varese

M. Mazzarone 1146

Museo dell'Ombrello e del Parasole

Vezzo

Magognno

V a r e s e

S. Andrea

Parco Regionale Campo dei Fiori

S. Maria del Monte

Agrano

M. del Faló 1080

Gignese

Carpugnino

Arolo

Monvalle

Cardana

Gavirate

Grotta Marelli

Torri di Velate

Indúno Olona

Coiromonte

Brovello

33

Turo

Besozzo

Comério

Luvinate

S. Ambrógio

Armeno

Belgirate

69

Olginásio

Bardello

Barasso

Varese

Pettenasco

Massino Visconti

Comnago

Lesa

Brébbia

Malgésso

Biandronno

Qlirona al Lago

Masnago

Calciante del Pesce

Bobbiate

Miasino

Ameno

Nebbiuno

Sólcio

Ispra

Monate

Travedona

Cazzago Brabbia

Bódio

Cartábbia

Bolzano Novarese

Ghevio

Pisano

A26

Méina

Ranco

L. di Monate

Bárzola

Cassinetta Rizzone

Varano Borghi

Bodio Lomb.

Galliate Lomb.

Buguggiate

Soriso

Invório Sup.

E62

Montrigiasco

Cadrezzate

Osmate

Bernate

Azzate

Davério

Gazzada

Gozzano

Paruzzaro

Rocca di Borroneo 22

Comábbio

Varano Borghi

629

Casale Litta

Brunello

Caidate

A8

Arona 1

Angera

Taino

Lentate Verb.

L. di Comábbio

Mercallo

Villadósia

Castronno

Invório Inf.

Oleggio Castello

Mercurago

Corgeno

Mornago

Sumirago

Albizzate

Gargallo

Briga Novarese

142

P. Reg. Lagoni di Mercurago

Dormelletto

Parco Regionale di Ticino

Sesto Calende

Verglate

Crugnola

Torino

Milano

N o v a r r a

S. Cristina

S a n t a

M a g g i o r e

V a l   G r a n d e

Pogallo

Feriolo

Cellina

Varese

little resort towns of Meina, Lesa and Belgirate to **Stresa** ➋, the largest resort on the lake, its shore lined for kilometres by hotels from the ultra-grand to the decidedly prosaic. Known for centuries as "the pearl of Verbano" in brochure-speak, it has immense charm but surprisingly little else in the way of sights – one of those places that was taken up by early travel writers and became trendy with travellers on the Grand Tour and has managed to trade on reputation ever since. Only a few fragments of the **castle walls** remain, in the grounds of **Villa Pallavicino** (tel: 0323-31533; www.parcozoopallavicino. it; daily mid-Mar–Oct 9am–7pm, last entry 5pm), just south of town, a wonderful combination of botanical garden and zoo, with children's playground, restaurant and picnic areas. A little road train connects the park with the Piazzale Imbarcadero (by the ferry).

North of the town centre is the cable car (closed at the time of writing, check reopening times at the tourist office) up **Monte Mottarone** ➌ (1,491 metres/4,892ft), a real outdoor playground, with mountain biking and rock-climbing in summer, and skiing in winter – and fabulous views across to the Alps, although there is no viewing platform at the top station.

Halfway up Monte Mottarone, is the **Giardino Botanico Alpinia** ➍ (Piazzale Lido 8; tel: 0323-927173; www. giardinobotanicoalpinia.altervista.org; Apr 9–Oct 9 daily 9.30am–1pm) which, as well as lake views, has a superb collection of tiny plants and flowers which flourish at high altitude across the world. The garden can be reached on foot or by minibus from Stresa. If driving to Lake Orta, a bizarre extra stop might be at the Museo dell'Ombrello e del Parasole (Via Golf Panorama 2, Gignese; tel: 0323-89622; www.gignese. it/museo; Tue–Sun 10am–noon, 3–6pm), home to over 1,000 umbrellas and parasols.

A trio of islands

Just offshore, in a ribbon heading north from Stresa, are three islands, two of them home to some of the finest palaces and gardens in the lakes

Isola Bella.

FACT

San Carlo Borromeo (1538–84) was the son of Count Giulio and Margherita de'Medici, the Archbishop of Milan, and one of the presiding influences over the Council of Trent, but he also devoted himself genuinely to serving the poor throughout his life, particularly during the plague epidemic of 1576. He would probably have hated the statue and the glass coffin in which he lies in Milan Duomo.

region. Ferries run to all three from Stresa and Pallanza (buy a joint ticket to save queuing time).

The largest and closest island to Stresa is **Isola Bella** ❺ www.borromeo turismo.it; mid-Mar–late Oct daily 9am–5.30pm), named after Isabella D'Adda, wife of Carlo III (1586–1652). The count decided to transform the rocky islet into a monumental Baroque palace with gardens. Its 10 formal tiers of planting, that involved rebuilding the entire island, are meant to mimic the decks of a ship. Work began in 1632 but the final touches were only added to the palace itself in 1959.The house is still full of treasures, gilt and stuccowork but is rather lifeless. However, the garden is a towering pyramid of fountains and walkways, topiary and colour that constantly delight – a perfectly preserved 17th-century Baroque Italian garden.

Nearby, the **Isola dei Pescatori** (Fishermen's Island) ❻ is a much humbler affair, simply an island inhabited to this day by a fishing community, although there is a strong sideline in tourism and restaurants. It is a

charming place to wander, with fine views, excellent fish restaurants and a couple of small swimming beaches.

A little to the north, near Pallanza, work on **Isola Madre** ❼ (tel: 0323-932 483; www.borromeoturismo.it; mid-Mar–late Oct daily 9am–5.30pm) began in 1501 with Count Lancellotto Borromeo. This is a much less formal garden, more English in style, with white peacocks roaming the lawns and spectacular displays of camellias, rhododendrons and azaleas in season.

Next to the great house, Europe's largest Kashmir cypress, a victim of storms, is clinging perilously to life and is spending years in traction, in an attempt to weld it back to strength. Within the palazzo itself are rooms filled with puppet theatres and marionettes, part of the family's obsession with dolls.

Back on the shore

Just north of Stresa is **Baveno** ❽, a quietly elegant resort town, renowned for its pink granite, which has been quarried for export around the world

to adorn buildings from Bangkok to New York. It is also known for its string of elegant waterfront villas, most of which are still in private hands, and best admired from the water. Just north of here, the coast road swings across to join the motorway at **Gravellona Toce**, a rather grim area that is very useful for everyday shopping, ringed with supermarkets and shopping malls.

Lake Mergozzo

A side road leads off to little **Lago Mergozzo** ⑨, once a gulf of Maggiore that got cut off and now reputed to have some of Italy's cleanest water (motor boats are forbidden). Mergozzo village is an enchanting place filled with ancient stone houses. It is near here that the pinky-grey Candoglio marble used to build Milan Duomo was quarried. About an hour's walk from the village, along a mule track, in the tiny hamlet of **Montorfano**, the 12th-century church of San Giovanni is a Romanesque jewel, untouched by time, with fine panoramic views.

The sedimentary reed-beds which cut off Lake Mergozzo from the main lake and still filter the water are now protected by the 360-hectare (890-acre) **Riserva Naturale di Fondotoce** (open access), which nurtures a rich variety of bird life, native and migratory, and flora, including water chestnuts. It is best explored on foot or bicycle. The nearest place to hire a bike would be in one of the coastal towns such as Stresa; many hotels offer bikes to their guests and there are plenty of agencies to choose from.

Verbania

Verbania was rechristened by Mussolini as part of his linguistic campaign to revive the glories of ancient Rome; it comprises several resorts bunched around **Pallanza**. It is a pretty place for a walk with a good Friday market, but the main reason for visiting are the glorious gardens of **Villa**

Taranto ⑩ (tel: 0323-404 555; www.villataranto.it; gardens: mid-Mar–Sept daily 8.30am–6.30pm, Oct–Nov 9am–4pm; villa closed to public). The gardens were the brainchild of a Scot, Captain McEachern, who bought the villa, in the centre of Pallanza, in 1931, and began importing plants from across the globe, including nearly 1,000 which had never before been cultivated in Italy.

Altogether, there are nearly 20,000 varieties here, making it a garden of botanical importance as well as great beauty. During the annual Tulip Week (late April), every fifth adult ticket has a stamp offering them a free plant.

National parks

From Intra, just up the road, one of the few access roads leads deep into the heart of the 117 sq km (45 sq mile) **Parco Nazionale della Val Grande** ⑪. This is one of the last truly wild areas in Italy, its racing waters and plunging falls, oak, beech and alder woodlands protected by high mountains that provide a safe haven for animal life, from

Traditional artisan's sign, Mergozzo Village.

Ancient stone houses in Mergozzo Village.

FACT

Ernest Hemingway's World War I novel, *A Farewell to Arms* (1929), tells the story of an American soldier wounded while fighting for the Italian army. After convalescing in Milan, he inadvertently deserts while escaping the Germans, but is reunited with his love in Stresa, where they stay at Des Iles Borromées Hotel (where Hemingway himself often stayed) before fleeing by boat across to Swiss Locarno.

chamois and roe deer to the humble hedgehog.

Those who don't want to go quite so far could content themselves with a walk in the **Riserva Naturale Speciale del Sacro Monte della SS Trinità di Ghiffa** ⑫ (Via SS Trinità 48, Ghiffa; tel: 0323-59870). One of the many Unesco-listed sacred mountains in the region, this one, started by San Carlo Borromeo was never finished, with only three chapels in the woods offering a vision of what might have been. Nevertheless, the setting is wonderful and the 200-hectare (490-acre) reserve offers several excellent trails.

The road now heads north along the so-called **Cannero Riviera**, towards the Swiss border (don't forget your passport), passing two small ruined castles that stand on islets near **Cannobio** ⑬. Originally fortified in the Middle Ages to control trade with Switzerland, they became the base of the piratical Mazzarditi brothers, before the Visconti removed the troublemakers and destroyed their lairs in the early 15th century.

Ascona

If you are heading for the northern end of the lake, take your passport as here you cross into Switzerland.

Ascona ⑭, perfectly set at the junction of the Alps and the lakes, grew rapidly from a small fishing village into a popular resort during the Belle Epoque. It was a paradise not only for seekers after sun but also for seekers after truth. This was the home of Rudolf von Laban's nudist School of Natural and Expressive Dance, which became the focus of a cultural movement that brought artists, philosophers and pacifists from C.G. Jung to Isadora Duncan flocking to the area to share ideas and beds. Their ideas are celebrated in the **Museo Monte Verità** (Casa Anatta; tel: 091-785 4040; www.monteverita.org; closed for restoration but the park is open to the public).

In town, all life centres on the lakefront Piazza Motta and network of cobbled alleys just behind it. Churches worth a visit include the church of **SS Pietro e Paolo** (1530-4), with three magnificent altar paintings by local boy Giovanni Serodine (1594–1630), who also decorated the town's most famous house, the **Casa Serodine** next door (not open to the public), built in 1620; the high medieval **Oratorio SS Fabiano e Sebastiano** hosts the **Museo di San Sebastiano** (Museum of St Sebastian; Via delle Cappelle; tel: 091-791 3521; Apr–Oct Wed–Sat 10am–noon, 8–10pm), which now houses a museum of religious art; the **Collegio Papio** (just off Viale B. Papio; Mon–Fri 7.30am–12.30pm, 1.30–6pm), with a 14th–15th-century biblical fresco cycle; and the richly frescoed **Santuario della Madonna della Fontana** (on the northern slope of Monte Verità; daily 10am–noon, 3–5.30pm and for regular concerts).

The **Museo Comunale d'Arte Moderna** (Via Borgo 34; tel: 091-759 8140; www.museoascona.ch; Tue–Sat Mar–June, Sept–Dec 10am–noon,

Church of SS Pietro e Paolo, Ascona.

2–5pm, July–Aug 10am–noon, 4–7pm, Sun 10.30am–12.30pm) mixes a fine permanent collection including works by Marianne von Werefkin, Paul Klee, Ben Nicholson, Richard Seewald and others, with temporary exhibits.

Locarno

Just around the bay, **Locarno ⓯** is the grander of the two Swiss resorts, the regional capital since the Middle Ages, with life revolving around the splendidly arcaded **Piazza Grande**, home to open-air concerts in the summer, and to the International Film Festival. The city is a shopper's heaven, with a Thursday market in the Piazza Grande, a splendid Christmas market and many specialist and designer shops for browsing.

The 13th-century **Castello Visconteo** (Via B. Rusca 5; tel: 091-756 3170/80; Apr–Oct Tue–Sun 10am–noon, 2–5pm) stands in the heart of the Old Town, built on the remains of an even older fortress. Although much of it was destroyed by the Confederation in 1532, enough of

it remains to house the **Museo Civico**; this archaeological collection includes some lovely Roman glass and pottery, an exhibit on the 1925 Treaty of Locarno, part of the ongoing efforts to secure a lasting peace in Europe after World War I, and some fine 15th-century frescoes. The city art gallery, containing works by 19th- and 20th-century artists, is housed in the late 18th-century **Casa Rusca** (Piazza Sant'Antonio; tel: 091-756 3185; Apr–mid-Dec Tue–Sun 10am–noon, 2–5pm). Those lucky enough to be there in spring should also stop at the **Parco delle Camelie** (Via Respini; tel: 091-791 0091; daily Mar–Sept 9am–6pm, Oct–Feb 9am–4.45pm; free except during Locarno Camellia exhibition), when the camellias are in full bloom.

The undoubted star, however, is the **Santuario of the Madonna del Sasso** (daily 7am–6pm), reached by cable car (Viale Balli 2; tel: 091-751 1123; daily 8am–7.30pm) from the town centre, or you can take the hard pilgrim walk up. In 1480, a vision of the Virgin appeared on the spot

The Santuario of the Madonna del Sasso can be reached by cable car or a steep path.

Thursday market in the Piazza Grande, Locarno.

The two garden-islands of Isole di Brissago.

to a Franciscan monk. Seven years later, the first pilgrimage church was built, although this palatial affair is a Baroque incarnation. Inside, look for Bramantino's Flight from Egypt (1520). From here, a cable car swoops higher still to the **Cardada plateau** (1,350 metres/4,430ft; www.cardada. ch), where a stroll through the woods leads to a chairlift up to **Cimetta** (1,672 metres/5,486ft). The views from here are fabulous.

Back down at the lake, **L'Astrovia** (Planets Way) is a walking and cycling track that wanders along the Maggia and Melezza rivers for 6km (4 miles), with the solar system laid out at a scale of 1:1 billion, offering a novel way to study the stars and get some exercise.

Island gardens

Off to the west snakes the line of the **Ferrovia di Centovalli** (Centovalli Railway; see page 234). Take a boat across to the **Isole di Brissago** ⓰ (Parco Botanico del Cantone Ticino, Brissago; tel: 091-791 4361; www.iso-lebrissago.ch; mid-Mar–Oct 9am–6pm), two islands which together make up

one of the great gardens in the lakes region. The smaller of the two islands, Isola Piccola, has remained in its natural state while the larger, Isola Grande, has been planted with an exotic mix of flowers from across the world, from edelweiss to the agave, which flowers every 10 years and then dies.

The eastern shore

Crossing back into Italy at Zenna, the quiet resort of **Maccagno** ⓱ stands at the mouth of the Giona River, popular with tourists for its sandy beaches. It is split into distinctive upper and lower towns, the lower section a higgledy-piggledy heap of fishing cottages, while above, with the views, stand the grander palazzi and porticoes and the little sanctuary of the Madonnina della Punta. The **Museo Parisi-Valle** (Via Leopoldo Giampaolo 1; tel: 0332-561 202; www.museoparisivalle.it; June–Sept Thu–Sun 10am–noon, 3–7pm, Oct–May Fri–Sun 10am–noon, 3–6pm; free) is a fascinating modern art collection with over 2,000 works from the 1930s to 1990s by over 70 artists. Behind the town, the beautiful,

forgotten Val Veddasca winds up to the village of Indemini, back across the border in Switzerland.

Luino

South, through the quiet resort of Colmegna, **Luino** ⑱ is the most important town along this stretch of the lake, with a gracious waterfront, several fine churches and palazzi lining the little Napoleonic harbour. Luino was a Roman garrison town and the birthplace of Bernardino Luini (c.1480–1532), who became one of the region's pre-eminent artists. The town has had a major market every Wednesday for the last 500 years. Behind the town, **Monte Lema** (1,620 metres/5,310ft) has fabulous views across both Lake Maggiore and Lake Lugano and hiking trails. There is a cable car up the mountain from the Swiss side.

A little further south and a great deal higher up the mountain in **Brezzo di Bedero** ⑲, the **Collegiata di San Vittore** is a church with a long and motley history and sections from the 5th to 19th centuries on show, although most of it belongs to the 12th. It has magnificent views, fine frescoes and several treasures, including four rare 12th–14th-century Antiphonaries (musical manuscripts), and hosts a major music festival every summer (Stagione Musicale della Canonica; tel: 0332-511 707; July and Aug).

Laveno Mombello

One of the largest towns and main ferry ports on the eastern shore, marked by having a railway station and a car ferry across to Intra, **Laveno Mombello** ⑳ is made up of several villages which joined together in 1927. Today, in addition to tourism and the weekly market (Tuesdays), which brings people from all the surrounding villages, it lives on ceramics and fishing. The **Museo Internazionale Design Ceramico** (Via Lungolago Perabò 5, Cerro; tel: 0332-666 530; www.midec.org; Tue 10am–12.30pm, Wed–Fri 10am–12.30pm, 2.30–5.30pm, Sat–Sun 10am–12.30pm, 2.30–5.30pm, June–Sept 3–6pm) celebrates the still thriving local ceramics industry, which was founded in 1856.

Frescoes at Santa Caterina del Sasso.

Dario Fo.

I AM NOT A MODERATE

Nobel Prize-winning satirist Dario Fo (born 1926) grew up in Leggiuno-Sangiano near Lake Maggiore. The story of his failed bid to become mayor of Milan is told in a documentary, *I Am Not a Moderate* (Fo's campaign slogan). A self-confessed anarcho-Marxist, Fo is most famous for his sharply farcical plays *Accidental Death of an Anarchist* and *Can't Pay? Won't Pay!* He credits the old folk in his home town with teaching him the "art of spinning fantastic yarns". Fo delights in provoking the authorities. In 2004, Forza Italia sued Fo for defamation after his satirical play, *The Two-Headed Anomaly*, used the premise that part of Vladimir Putin's brain was transplanted into Berlusconi's head. Dario Fo is also a director, a stage and costume designer, as well as a composer.

A thrilling, but perfectly safe bucket-style **cable car** (tel: 0332-668 012; www.funiviedellagomaggiore.it; Mon–Sat 11am–5pm, Sun 10am–5pm) swings up **Monte Sasso del Ferro** (1,062 metres/3,484ft), from where there are superb views across the whole lake – it's a fifteen-minute ride. At weekends, hang-gliders and parachutists swoop like butterflies from the heights.

The southern shore

About 10km (6 miles) south of town, near Leggiuno, the **Eremo di Santa Caterina del Sasso** ㉑ (Via S. Caterina 5, Leggiuno; tel: 0332-647 172; Mar, mid-Sept–Oct daily 9am–noon, 2–5pm, Apr–mid-June daily 9am–noon, 2–6pm, mid-June–mid-Sept daily 9am–6pm, Nov–Feb Sat–Sun 9am–noon, 2–5pm, 23 Dec–6 Jan daily 9am–noon, 2–5pm) has become one of Maggiore's most famous landmarks. Under the cliff and only visible from the water, it can either be reached by a long flight of steps or by means of an elevator dug into the rock.

In 1170, Alberto Besozzi was shipwrecked during a storm but was so grateful to St Catherine of Alexandria for saving his life that he came to live in this remote cave. It grew into a monastery in three parts – the South Convent with its Gothic frescoes (1439) in the chapterhouse and a Danse Macabre in the loggia; the Small Convent (1315), home to the main church; and the Chapel of the Rocks, named after five huge boulders that crashed through the rafters around 1700 and remained suspended in the roof timbers for the next 200 years. The hermitage is still a working monastery.

Finally, virtually opposite Arona, looking across the water at "Big St Charlie" (see page 223), you come to the **Rocca Borromeo** ㉒ (tel: 0331-931 300; www.borromeoturismo.it; mid-Mar–mid-Oct daily 9am–5.30pm; charge), the formidable fortress built by the Borromeos to guard the southern approaches to the lake. The castle dates mainly from the 14th-century era of the Torriani and Visconti, and there are fine frescoes (1314) in the Sala della Giustizia. The Borromeos refurbished it in the 17th century.

Rocca Borromeo.

LAKE MAGGIORE EXPRESS

This train ride is a perfect way to explore the hills and breathtaking scenery around the lake.

Two countries, two trains and a boat make up a tri-angular day trip that has become a Lake Maggiore classic. Take a day or a more leisurely two days, start from Ancona, Stresa or Locarno and choose which way round you go according to where you want to spend more time. Whichever option you choose, the Lake Maggiore Express is a perfect way to explore the beauties of the upper lake. The journey is possible mid-Mar–mid-Oct Thu–Sun.

A scenic tour

From Stresa, take the mainline train north past the wild country of the Parco Nazionale della Val Grande to Domodossola. Here, you link up with the scenic Centovalli Railway (100 Valleys Railway), which winds east through the hills via Santa Maria Maggiore (where you cross into Switzerland), heads back to the lake at Ascona, then follows the lake shore round to Locarno. Take time to explore this delightful Belle Epoque retreat before hopping on a ferry back down the lake. Run by the gloriously acronymed Swiss FART, the Centovalli railway has been operational since 1923, a twisting triumph of technology climbing across bridges and viaducts,

Poster for the Stresa–Mottarone line (1928).

puffing through tunnels and winding around precipitous hills through chestnut forests and ravines including the 75-metre (250ft) Isorno Gorge near Intragna, where bungee-jumpers have been flinging themselves from the rail bridge since 1993.

Chimney sweeps

Bizarrely, the most famous traditional export of the Centovalli region is chimney sweeps, who fanned out from here across the globe to rid it of

Centovalli railway.

soot. There is a museum dedicated to the spaz-
camini in Santa Maria Maggiore, and in 1997
e first Sweeps' Parade was held. Since then, this
s grown into a huge international event, hosted
different towns in the valleys and attracting
ndreds of chimney sweeps from across the
rld who descend on Centovalli to celebrate
eir vocation. A statue of a chimney-sweep boy
nds at the entrance of Malesco on the road from
nta Maria Maggiore.

For more information, contact the Associazione
izionale Spazzacamini, Piazza Risorgimento 28,
nta Maria Maggiore, tel: 0324-905 675.

omodossola

omodossola is an ancient city with a fabulous
turday market that first received its charter in
7. There are lovely old streets to explore, and just
ove the town, on the once fortified Monte Matta-
la, the Sacro Monte Calvario (tel: 0324-242 010),
e of the nine Unesco-listed Sacri Monti of Pied-
ont and Lombardy (see page 217), was built in
57 by Capuchin friars, with a processional way
lowing the stations of the cross up the hill.
Domodossola is most famous as the Italian end
the Simplon (Sempione)
nnel, built by Hermann
iustler and Hugo von Kag-
that connects the railway
tween Switzerland and
ly. There are actually two
nnels: the first, 19.7km (12
iles) long, was opened in
06 in Brig in Switzerland.
he second (19.8km long)
as only opened in 1922. For
early 50 years, it was the longest
nnel in the world.

cona's harbour.

Piazza del Mercato, Domodossola.

Information

www.lagomaggioreexpress.com
Centovalli Railway, Viaggi Fart SA, Locarno (CH);
tel: 091-756 0400, www.centovalli.ch.
Navigazione Lago Maggiore, Arona; tel: 0322-233
200, www.navlaghi.it.

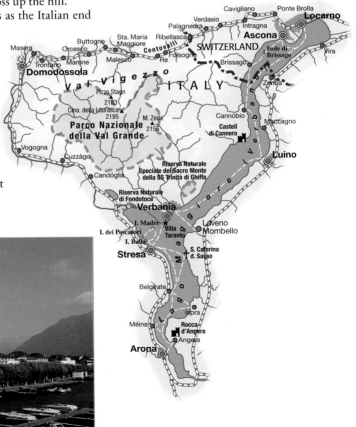

GARDENER'S GLORY

A perfect climate and oodles of millionaires have made the lakes lush with lavish gardens.

The lake villas are a testament to the whims of wealthy owners, the finest enjoying bewitching waterside settings, which often juxtapose manicured formal gardens with untrammelled views of distant mountains beyond.

Giardino Botanico Andre Heller bloom.

Set in the foothills of the Alps and sheltered by mountains, the lakes enjoy balmy sunshine and frost-free nights, particularly around Garda and Maggiore, where a Mediterranean microclimate prevails. The meeting of the Mediterranean and Alpine climates makes for an extraordinary exoticism, with plants ranging from camellias and azaleas to Kashmiri cypresses, Amazonian water lilies, Japanese maples, African palms and Chinese bamboo. Giant rhododendrons and hydrangeas are as common as bougainvillea, roses and magnolia. Beyond the laurels and cypresses, the well-tended topiary and water gardens are the exotica of palms, hibiscus and the lemons so associated with Lake Garda.

The same diversity underpins the landscaping: nothing less than a history of European garden design in miniature, combining the French preoccupation with perfect geometry with a Dutch tradition of topiary and an English love of lawns, woodland and bubbling brooks and communion with nature that epitomised the Romantic ideal.

Lotus pool at Villa Carlotta.

Isola Bella, an island tower of flowering terraces.

VILLA GARDENS

The formal Renaissance garden was inspired by Roman ideals of structure and symmetry. Set in the foothills of Varese, **Villa Cicogna Mozzoni** is a frescoed Renaissance villa enveloped by Italianate gardens, including formal box hedges, fountains and a grandiose water stairway. In Verona, **Giardino Giusti** presents a succession of box hedges, parterres, fountains and whimsical statuary fading into a forest of greenery.

Villa Melzi, on Lake Como, was the first garden in the lakes to be designed along "English" lines. The neoclassical villa enjoys an intimate mood created by an ornamental pool framed by cedars, maples, camphor and myrrh. A whimsical grotto opens onto enchanting Japanese water gardens, while on the terraces above, neoclassical statuary gives way to gently rolling lawns.

Villa Carlotta, also on Lake Como, is awash with colour, its planting evoking an exotic map of the world:

Statue in the garden of Villa Melzi.

Andre Heller scattered his gardens with ethnic masks.

JUST GARDENS

Villas do not have a monopoly on gorgeous gardens. South of Lake Garda, the Parco Giardini Sigurtà has gentle parkland and seasonal gardens dating back to the 17th century.

In Gardone, Western Lake Garda, the Giardino Botanico Andre Heller is an established botanical garden enlivened by provocative installations by Heller, an Austrian artist.

In sleepy Varenna, on Lake Como, Villa Monastero is a former Cistercian convent reborn as a cultural institute, with beguiling gardens. After admiring them, slip away to the lakeside terraces of the neighbouring patrician hotel, Villa Cipressi, or retreat to the even more palatial Villa d'Este.

On Lake Maggiore, the Isole di Brissago are a brace of botanical islands, while halfway up Monte Mottarone, above Stresa, Giardino Alpinia pays homage to the tiny Alpine plants of the world.

Villa del Balbianello, Lake Como.

ars of Lebanon, Egyptian papyrus, Japanese maples and ana trees. Formality merges into informality, with the a bordered by a profusion of pink and white azaleas and eatrical staircase climbing to the lemon terraces. arby, **Villa del Balbianello** has the most seductive ting of all, its 18th-century gardens studded with resses, magnolia and plane trees, framed by wisteria-d views accentuated by artfully sited urns and arches. On Lake Maggiore, the battle between the classical and antic aesthetic is played out on twin islands. If **Isola** dre's floating botanical garden feels Romantic, with its of haphazard planting, **Isola Bella** els in Baroque theatricality, the ship-ped terraces crowned by a four-tiered y studded with shells and topped by rubs, gods and a heraldic unicorn. n nearby Pallanza, Captain Neil Eachern devoted his life to his beloved a Taranto, importing exotic plants n the tropics, from coffee, cotton and to Amazonian water lilies, lotuses and ptian papyrus, creating not only a ightful spot but a botanical marvel. All of the gardens listed here are n to the public.

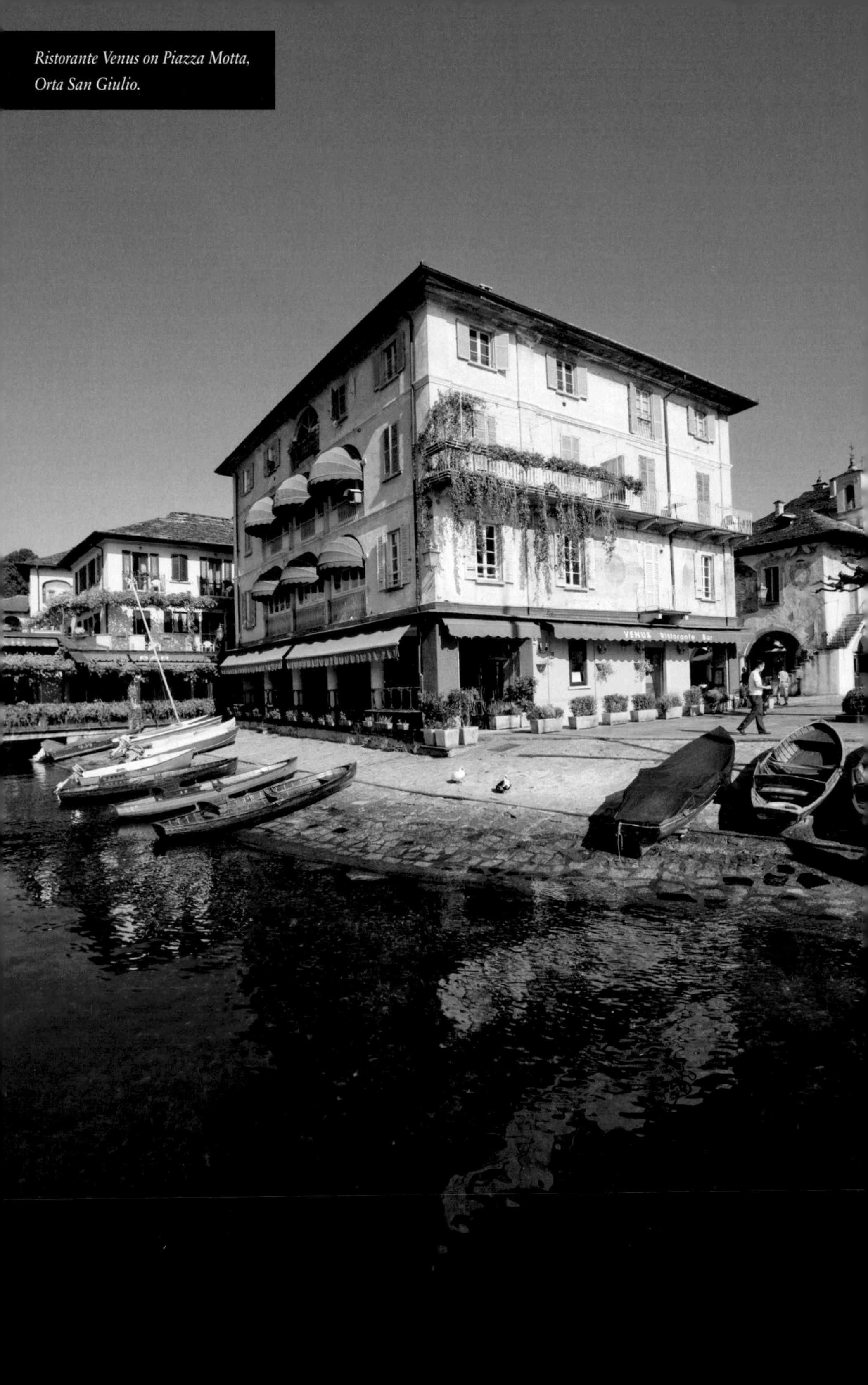

Ristorante Venus on Piazza Motta, Orta San Giulio.

LAKE ORTA

Little Lake Orta is often described as a shimmering, sleeping beauty. Mystical and romantic, with its understated charm it plays Cinderella to the bigger lakes.

J ust over 10km (7 miles) west of Lake Maggiore, as the crow flies, this is the only one of the major lakes to lie totally in Piedmont. Orta is framed by low hills at the south end of the lake and higher mountains at the north end. Cradled between is this bewitching area, with probably the most picturesque medieval village of all the Italian lakes.

Honoré de Balzac described the surrounding Piedmontese hills as "a green treasure chest" enclosing this "pearl" of a lake. Still known as Cusio, from the Roman Lacus Cusius, referring to the Usii tribe – its modest dimensions of just 12km (8 miles) long and less than 3km (2 miles) wide – make it of manageable proportions.

Picture perfect

The lake's main attraction, Isola di San Giulio, is a tiny island with passing steamers, a pretty harbour, porticoes, pergolas and slate-roofed houses. Dragons and serpents were said to have terrorised all who dared to venture across the waters, until the arrival of St Julius (Giulio) who cast them out 1,600 years ago and, in celebration, built his basilica. Now it is the jewel of the lake, with a reverential, peaceful air.

Standing opposite the little island, the medieval town of Orta San

Looking across to the basilica on Isola di San Giulio.

Giulio is utterly picturesque and the perfect base for exploring or just gazing and enjoying. The hub of activity is a charming lakeside piazza, overseen by the Palazzotto frescoed town hall and, from the waterfront, little boats ply back and forth across the lake.

Like the main lakes, there are built up areas and Omegna, at the head of Orta is a busy town as well as being the headquarters of Alessi, the guru of stylish Italian designer kitchenware.

Main Attractions

Ristorante Al Sorriso
Sacro Monte di San Francesco
Orta San Giulio
Isola di San Giulio
Alessi HQ
Santuario della Madonna del Sasso

Interior of Villa Crespi, near Orta San Giulio.

The western shore is delightfully sleepy and untouristy, overseen by the towering Madonna del Sasso, perched high on a rocky ledge. And on the eastern shore is the Sacro Monte, a station on the Way of the Cross tracing the history of St Francis. Both look out from their respective sides to the Isola di San Giulio, bathed in mystical, soft light – the jewel of the lake.

In the south

The gateway to Orta and its beauties is **Gozzano ❶**, to the south of the lake. Of Roman origin when it was probably a military stopover, it stands at the intersection of the roads running up either side of the lake to Domodossola and the Simplon Pass. This is an industrialised area which contributed in the 1970s to the pollution of the lake and destruction of its fauna. Since then, however, the lake has been reoxygenated, the water is clean and teems with fish. The manufacture of textile fibres, especially artificial silk at the Bemberg factory, is today the chief industry in the area.

In the centre of town, the parish church of **San Giuliano** (the Greek brother of Giulio) has a pleasing Romanesque bell tower. Inside, there are some fine Baroque carved wood choir stalls, and in the crypt a silver and crystal urn is said to hold the saint's skeleton.

Just to the west of Gozzano is the tiny village of **Soriso**, whose restaurant **Al Sorriso** (with two "r"s, meaning "smile"), has two Michelin stars.

On the eastern shore

A few kilometres to the north, on the eastern side of the lake, the old town of **Ameno ❷** has been a tourist destination since the 18th century. Overlooking Monte Rosa, it lies at 500 metres (1,640ft) above sea level and is a great base for summer treks through beautiful scenery, or for enjoying winter sports in the cold months. It is peppered with lush gardens surrounding aristocratic villas, often second homes to wealthy families from Milan and Turin. In June and July a festival of

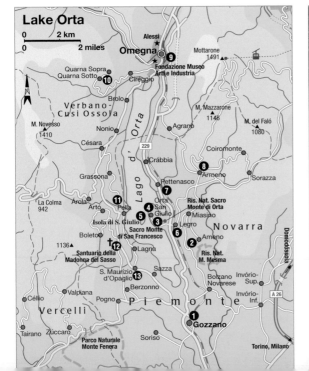

blues music is a popular event on the social calendar.

Well worth a visit is the Casa Calderara, former home of the painter Antonio Calderara (1903–78), now a museum. The **Collezione Calderara di Arte Contemporaneo** (Via Bardelli 9, Vacciago di Ameno; tel: 0322-998 192; www.fondazione calderara.it; mid-May–mid-Oct Tue–Fri 3–7pm, Sat–Sun 10am–noon, 3–7pm; free) showcases paintings and sculptures by contemporary European, American, Chinese and Japanese artists, including many by Calderara himself. He drew great inspiration from the romantic, misty landscapes of Lake Orta and its surroundings.

Sacro Monte

Just to the west is the **Sacro Monte di San Francesco** ❸ (Orta San Giulio; tel: 0322-911 960; www.sacro monteorta.it; daily Oct–May 9am–4.30pm; June–Sept 9.30am–6.30pm; free). Spectacularly set on wooded hillside above the lake, with views across to the Isola di San Giulio, this

Unesco World Heritage site, one of several in the region, is a devotional path comprising a series of frescoed chapels illustrating the life of St Francis of Assisi. Twenty-one chapels built between 1591 and 1750 alternate Baroque and Renaissance styles with 376 terracotta sculptures and 900 frescoes depicting his life and times. Of all the Sacri Monti, this is the only one dedicated to St Francis – all the others are devoted to Christ.

The **chiesa dei SS Francesco e Nicolao** (church of SS Francis and Nicholas) is similar to the lower Basilica of St Francis of Assisi, built between 1602 and 1607. The original church of St Nicholas was built in the 10th century, and the wooden *Pietà* on the major altar dates from this time.

Within the reserve of the Sacro Monte are also Monte Mesma and the **Torre di Buccione**. The tower dates back to Roman times, but although little remains of the original, there is a splendid view over the lake and Monte Rosa from the 23-metre (75ft) -tall lookout.

The Trenino tourist train – a less taxing way to negotiate the steep streets of Orta San Giulio.

Terracotta sculptures, Sacro Monte di San Francesco.

TIP

The Trenino: this great little tourist train is a good way of negotiating Orta San Giulio's steep terrain. It is also very useful for transporting luggage to hotels as the centre is traffic-free. The *trenino* runs daily Mar–Apr and Oct 9am–5.30pm, May–Sept until 7pm and Nov–Feb Sat–Sun 9.30am–5.30pm (€3.50) from Piazza Motta to the Sacro Monte and Legro.

Cliff-hanging villas, Orta San Giulio.

Orta San Giulio

From the Sacro Monte, it is about a 15-minute walk down to **Orta San Giulio** ❹ on a lush promontory on the east bank. Frescoed peach and cappuccino-coloured houses with galleries, wrought-iron balconies and gates cluster along the cobbled alleyways of this gorgeous little medieval town. Romantic, peaceful and car-free, it oozes charm and, everywhere you go, you will hear the sound of lapping water.

The main lakeside square is the **Piazza Motta** – also known as *Il Salotto* (the drawing room), enclosed by arcades on three sides and lined with terrace cafés, restaurants, shops and traditional hotels. A market has been held here since 1228; according to city charters, Wednesday was the day that judgements were carried out and that remains market day. This is where you can catch the *trenino* up to the Sacro Monte.

Opposite the Ristorante Venus, the 16th-century town hall, **Palazzo della Comunità**, is now a gallery with temporary exhibitions.

A couple of minutes' walk just to the north of the piazza along the main shopping street, Via Olina, **Casa Bossi**, now the town hall, has a beautiful garden overlooking the lake. Just on the left is the gourmet shop, Rovera (Largo de Gregori 15; tel: 0322-90123; closed Sun) – an Aladdin's cave of salamis, local specialities and wines.

The **Salità della Motta**, a stepped lane, leads from the piazza past elegant palazzi including the late Renaissance Palazzo Gemelli and the **Casa dei Nanni** (House of Dwarfs). This is Orta's oldest house, dating from the 14th century, and takes its name from the four dwarf-sized windows. You pass other houses in a variety of architectural styles leading up to the 15th-century Baroque church of **Santa Maria Assunta** (daily 9am–6pm).

Above the town, along the Via Panoramica (also known as the Strada Nuova), is the Moorish fantasy **Villa Crespi**, a luxurious hotel complete with minaret, with a two Michelin-starred restaurant (see page 76).

Isola di San Giulio

All roads lead to the water and views across to the pearl of the lake, **Isola di San Giulio** ❺. From the water's edge at Piazza Motta, rowing-boats and motor boats ply back and forth from 9.50am (Apr–early Oct). The lakeside walk to the south leads past beautiful villas in flower-filled gardens, arriving finally at **La Spiaggia Miami** (Miami Beach), Orta San Giulio's only sandy little beach where you have to pay an admission charge for access. Sun-loungers and parasols are for hire and the café bar/kiosk serves a delicious iced coffee – with or without a splash of Baileys liqueur.

As you approach the perfect little island, try to imagine how it appeared in the 4th century. Then it was a rocky wilderness, allegedly inhabited by dragons and hideous reptiles, to which no boatman would be persuaded to ferry the Christian preacher, Giulio, who wanted to build his 100th church here. Legend has it that Giulio spread his cloak over the water and, using his staff as a rudder, aquaplaned across the lake.

He quickly dispatched the sea of hissing, venomous reptiles, built his church and became a saint.

Boats land just by the island's centrepiece, the **Basilica di San Giulio** (daily 9.30am–noon, 2pm until last boat, closed Mon morning in summer, earlier closing in winter; free). Founded in 390 and modified over the centuries before being largely rebuilt in the 18th and 19th centuries, this Romanesque church is sombre, the atmosphere hushed; the remains of San Giulio and his relics, including his staff and cup, are said to be in his sarcophagus in the crypt. The pulpit, sculpted from rich green-black serpentine stone from the nearby quarries of Oira, shows carved reliefs of winged creatures and monsters in deadly conflict, "Strife among Animals", redeemed by the four Evangelists. Covering the walls, columns and ceiling are fine frescoes, the oldest dating back to the third century.

Silence and meditation

There is only one street on the island – the cobbled Via del Silenzio, which

Villa Crespi's Moorish minaret.

Isola di San Giulio.

Frescoes inside the basilica, Isola di San Giulio.

then becomes the Via della Meditazione. This picturesque route leads past the **Benedictine convent** (Palazzo dei Vescovi; closed to the public), which is the cloistered home to 60 or so nuns who devote themselves to prayer, work and contemplation. It is only on Sundays at 11am that the religious silence is broken, when the nuns arrive at the basilica for Mass to sing Gregorian chants.

The Ways of Silence and Meditation, created by the abbess, have signs at regular intervals to encourage contemplation and self-renewal on "the island within": "In the silence you accept and understand", "Silence is the language of love", "Walls are in the mind", "The wise man makes a mistake and smiles".

The one shop on the island, housed in a 14th-century building, sells rosaries, ceramics, crafts and souvenirs, some crafted by the nuns.

Along the eastern shore

About 2km (1 mile) to the east of Orta San Giulio is **Legro** ❻, "the painted village". Just over 40 murals painted by contemporary artists decorate the buildings, most portraying scenes from older Italian films shot around the lake. A set from *Il Riso Amaro* starring Gina Lollobrigida is on display, but the most famous is the risqué "beautiful Matilde", played by Italian sex symbol Ornella Muti in *The Bishop's Bedroom* (1977). However, she is not instantly recognisable in this mural painted by German Dietrich Blicker in 1999 as the portrayal is of her naked bottom.

On the bank of the lake just to the north, **Pettenasco** ❼ is a busy tourist resort in summer, with all kinds of accommodation ranging from campsites to hotels. It has Roman origins – Roman finds have been unearthed in the heart of town. But it is also known as a centre of woodcarving excellence, a tradition that has now been extended to include metal and plastic products. Worth a look for those interested in wood-turning tools and associated machinery is the **Museo dell'Arte della Tornitura del Legno** (Museum of the Art of Wood-Turning; Via Vittorio Veneto;

mid-May–mid-June and Sept Fri–Sun 3–6pm, mid-June–Aug daily 10.30am–noon, 4–6.30pm; www.museotornituirapettenasco.it; free).

To the east, **Armeno** ❽ is a lively, modern town, known for its tradition of hoteliers and restaurateurs. Thousands of people have left this area to work in the kitchens, hotels and restaurants of the world. The **Museo degli Alberghieri** (Museum of Hoteliers; Via dei Prati 3; July–Aug Fri–Sun, 2–7pm; free) charts the tools of the trade; hoteliers, simple cooks, grand chefs, unknown waiters and chefs' assistants have brought back mementoes and souvenirs of their lives gathered during their travels throughout the world.

Head of the lake

At the northern head of the lake, **Omegna** ❾ is a bustling town and the largest on Lake Orta. It lies on the two banks of the Nigoglia, one of the lake's outflowing rivers. Curiously, this is the only river in Italy that flows north towards the mountains, joining the Strona River which then flows into the Toce and thence to Lake Maggiore, which is at a slightly lower altitude than Lake Orta. The feisty local people are nicknamed "the wolves" (the animal which appears on the old coat of arms) from the motto: "*La Nigoglia la va in su e la legge la femo nu*" – the Nigoglia goes upriver and we make the laws.

The heart of the Old Town is the pedestrianised Via Felice Cavallotti, just around the corner from the well-stocked **tourist information** office (Piazza XXIV Aprile 17; tel: 0323-867 235). There are some good shops here and along Via Alberganti, also known as Via dal "Buter", in memory of the traditional butter and cheese market that was held along this street.

Design central

Household articles are especially good buys in this area as the town is the home of design guru Alessi as well as Calderoni, Bialetti and Lagostina – all well-known names in an Italian kitchen – and the area around has several factory outlets. For an insight into local craftsmanship, look at the

Mural of a Il Riso Amaro film poster, Legro.

River Nigoglia, Omegna.

The pretty village of Pella.

Fondazione Museo Arti e Industria "Forum" (Museum of Art and Industry; Parco Maulini 1; tel: 0323-866 141; www.forumomegna.org; Tue–Sat 10.30am–12.30pm, 3–7pm, Sun 3–7pm; free), which showcases world-famous design objects like the Bialetti Moka, Lagostina pressure cooker, Calderoni cutlery, as well as Alessi's distinctive designer household goods. The museum shop is hard to resist, and there is also a café.

Just to the north of Omegna is the **Alessi headquarters and factory shop** (Via Alessi 6, Crusinallo; tel: 0323-868 611; www.alessi.com). The iconic designer of kitchen and home items began life in the 1920s as a humble metal workshop turning out nickel, aluminium and silver-plated brass utensils and dishes. By the 1970s, the workshop had been converted into an international design factory producing some of the world's coolest and funkiest products. Alessi is now a global household name. Pasta pots, lemon squeezers like spaceships, fly swats, the original Alessi coffee pot – all pieces are designed to be fun as well as useful and are beautifully crafted. The vast factory shop sells the entire Alessi range. It's worth noting that items designated with a green spot are available at a reduced, or "seconds", price.

Western shore

On the northwestern shore of the lake are the towns of **Quarna** (**Sopra e Sotto**) ❿. In the higher town (Sopra), there are splendid views over the mountain pastures from the castle. **Quarna Sotto** (Lower) is famous for its production of brass and wind instruments, which it has been producing since the middle of the 19th century. The **Museo Etnografico e dello Strumento Musicale a Fiato** (Ethnographic Museum of Musical Wind Instruments; Via Roma 7; tel: 032-382 6001; mid-June–mid-Sept Tue–Fri 2–7pm, Sat–Sun 10am–noon, 3–7pm) has a display of over 300 working wood and brass instruments and the tools used in their production. In the town, the workshops of Rampone & Cazzani (tel:

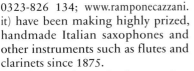

0323-826 134; www.ramponecazzani. it) have been making highly prized, handmade Italian saxophones and other instruments such as flutes and clarinets since 1875.

Going south on the less touristy western shores of the lake, you pass through the sleepy villages of **Nonio** and **Cesara**. The San Clemente church in Cesara is picturesque with its Romanesque bell tower. Inside on the walls of the choir is a painting of St Clement with St Peter and John the Baptist, which is attributed to a disciple of Gaudenzio Ferrari.

Opposite the Isola di San Giulio is the pretty lakeside village of **Pella** ⑪. This is a pleasant place for a stroll and an ice cream, with views of Isola di San Giulio. You can take a boat trip across to the island and to Orta San Giulio (tel: 347-723 7854; Mon–Fri 10.10am–6.20pm, Sat–Sun 9.30am–7.20pm).

Madonna del Sasso

Towering above the village 2km (1 mile) away, perched on a granite outcrop, is the **Santuario della**

Madonna del Sasso ⑫ (usually 3–6pm in summer, other times, tel: 0322-981 156). This sanctuary, which includes the Baroque church, bell tower and the hermitage, was built during the early 18th century. Inside the buildings there are some fine frescoes and a 17th-century crucifix; outside there is a version of Rome's *Bocca della Verità* (Mouth of Truth) where, so legend says, you are liable to lose your hand if you put it into the stone lion's mouth and tell a lie. Truth to tell, the highlight is the view from here, encompassing almost the entire lake.

Tap city

Inland to the south, **San Maurizio d'Opaglio** ⑬, known as "tap city", and the surrounding area are famous for an economy based on the manufacture of tap fittings and bathroom appliances. The **Museo del Rubinetto e della sua Tecnologia** (Tap Museum; Piazza Martiri 1; tel: 0323-89622; Fri–Sun 3–6pm) is mainly a homage to Giacomini, the area's largest tap company.

Fireworks on Lake Orta.

LAKE ORTA FESTIVALS

Since 2005, the **Amenoblues Festival** (www.amenoblues.it) has been held in Ameno in June and July – now a highlight on the calendar for everyone interested in Italian blues. In June, there are classical music concerts on the island – part of the Cusio music festival, **Festival Cusiano di Musica Antica** (Cusio Festival of Ancient Music; www.amicimusicacocito.it). Throughout August, the world's finest pyrotechnicians paint the night sky on Lake Orta, with the **Fiori di Fuoco fireworks competition**, perfectly mirrored in the lake. Two piers which jut out into the lake allow fireworks to be launched in total safety, as well as guaranteeing maximum visibility from all points around Orta San Giulio.

MILAN

The fashionable powerhouse that drives the Italian economy and clothes the world, Milan is also a very beautiful city with an illustrious past, magnificent galleries and splendid restaurants.

ounded by the Celts in the 4th century BC and one of the greatest cities in Italy ever since, deputising for Rome as the empire crumbled, and now undisputedly the wealth behind Italy's economic engine, Milan presents a strange mix of traditional values and flash cash, the newest style and good old home cooking. It is often ignored in favour of the more obvious charms of the nearby lakes, but although it is a busy industrial city, it is well worth exploring, with some fascinating architecture, masses of superb museums, excellent restaurants and, of course, La Scala.

The Duomo

Start in the heart of the *centro storico* beside the **Duomo ❶** (daily 7am–7pm; www.duomomilano.it; free). The first church on this ancient Christian site dates back to the 3rd century. It was replaced twice before the decision was taken to build this vast Gothic wedding cake confection in 1386. It took five centuries to complete, and it was not until 1966 that the last bronze panels were hung in the great west doors. With 135 spires and over 3,400 statues and acres of stained glass set in gleaming pinkish-grey Candoglia marble, it is 158 metres (518ft) long, 93 metres (305ft) wide at the transept and 108 metres (354ft) tall – the third-largest Roman Catholic church in the

world (after Rome and Seville) and a cathedral that truly proclaims the wealth of the city. On top of the tallest spire, the gilded copper Madonnina, made in 1774, has become the symbol of Milan. A lift (entrance outside; charge) allows you to walk on the roof amid the gargoyles for a magnificent view of the cathedral and the city.

Inside, 52 pillars, one for each week, separate out the five aisles. High in the roof arch hangs a crucifix containing a nail supposed to come from the True Cross. On the second Sunday

Main Attractions

Duomo
Galleria Vittorio Emanuele II
Teatro della Scala
Quadrilatero d'Oro
Pinacoteca di Brera
Castello Sforzesco
Basilica di Sant' Ambrogio
The Last Supper
Museo Nazionale della Scienza e della Tecnologia
Pinacoteca Ambrosiana

On the roof of Milan's Duomo.

Milan

0   500 m
0   500 yds

† CIMITERO †
MONUMENTALE
22

Piazzale
Cimitero
Monumentale

San Antonio
di Pádova

Via Carlo Farini

Via M. Quadrio

Via G. de Castillia

Stazione Porta
Garibaldi FS

Garibaldi FS

Via Ceresio

Piazza
S. Freud

Viale L. Sturzo

Gioia

Corso Como

Centrale

Grattacielo
Pirelli
(Pirelli Tower)

Piazza
Duca
d'Aosta

Stazione
Centrale

Via Procaccini

Via P. Lomazzo

Via G. B. Niccolini

Via Donato Bramante

Piazza
L. Einaudi

Via E. Cornalia

Via G. B. G. Pirelli

Via Fabio Filzi

Via E. Filzi

Via V. Pisani

Via F. Manuzio

Via Paolo Sarpi

Via Luigi Canonica

Via G. Giusti

Piazzale
A. Baiamonti

Viale Pasubio

Viale F. Crispi

Via A. Volta

Via A. Varese

Via Melchiorre Gioia

Via Marco Polo

Via G. Galilei

Piazza
S. Gioachino

Via F. Casati

Via Viale Tunisia

Viale Monte Grappa

Bastiani di Porta Nuova

Piazzale
Princ. Clotilde

Via V. Veneto

Piazza
della
Repubblica

Via P. Castaldi

Via Vittorio Veneto

Via F. Melzi d'Eril

Piazza
E. L. Morselli

Santa Maria
Incoronata

Largo
la Foppa

Solferino

Via San Marco

Via di Porta Nuova

Monte
Santo

Viale
Monte
Santo

Repubblica

Via A. Manin

Bastioni di Porta Venezia

Viale Elvezia

Moscova

Moscova

12
Arena

PARCO

Arco della Pace

Porta
Sempione

Via Legnano

Chiesa
Anglicano

Largo
Statuto

Via San Marco

Corso di Moscova

Via A. Appiani

San Angelo

Via F. Turati

GIARDINI

Palazzo
Dugnani

Museo Civico di
Storia Naturale

Piazza
Sempione

Bertani

Piazza
Sempione

SEMPIONE

14 Torre
Branca

13
Triennale

Acquario
(Aquarium)

Napoleone III

Via Gadio

Largo
C. Treves

San
Simpliciano

Palazzo
Crivelli

V. Fatebenefratelli

San
Marco

Via Montebello

Via F. Turati

Turati

PUBBLICI

Piazza
Cavour

Via Palestro

Palestro

Villa Reale
Galleria d'Arte
Moderna

Museo
d'Arte Antica

11 Castello
Sforzesco

Roccetta

Via Gadio

V. Moliere

Viale E. Alemagna

Viale E. Alemagna

Piazza
Lanza

V. Tivoli

V. Mercato

Foro Buonaparte

Via Borgonuovo

Pinacoteca
di Brera

ORTO
BOTANICO

Archi di
Porta Nuova

Palazzo
dei Giornali

Via Manzoni

Teatro
Manzoni

Montenapoleone

Museo Bagatti
Valsecchi

Via Senato

Palazzo
del Senato

Via Venezia

Palazzo
Rocca
Saporiti

Ferrovie Stazione
Nord Milano

Via Vincenzo Monti

Via G. Boccaccio

Cadorna

Largo
Cairoli

Cairoli

V. Dante

Teatro
Dal Verme

Via G. Verdi

V. Alessandro

Museo
Poldi-Pezzoli

Palazzo Morando
Costume Moda
Immagine

San Pietro
Celestino

Palazzo
Serbelloni

Corso Venezia

Prefettura

Santa Maria
delle Grazie

17

C. Magenta

Palazzo
delle
Stelline

Via A. Lamarmora

Via G. Carducci

Palazzo
Litta

Corso Magenta

Via Meravigli

Palazzo
Clerici

La Scala

Via S. Margherita

Museo
Manzoni

Galleria
Vittorio
Emanuele II

C. G. Matteotti

San Babila

San Babila

Palazzo
Durini

Conservatorio di
Musica G. Verdi

23

Stadio San Siro

Via G. Dogani

Sant'
Ambrogio

15 Museo
Archeologico

Palazzo
Stanga

Piazza
degli Affari

Piazza
S. Ambrogio

Cordusio

Via Orefici

Duomo

Via Mazzini

Piazza
del Duomo

Duomo

Palazzo
Reale

Piazza
Fontana

Piazza
San
Stefano

San Vito

Corso Europa

F. Corridoni

Corso di Porta Vittoria

Sant'Ambrogio **16**

Museo Nazionale
della Scienza e
della Tecnologia
Leonardo da Vinci **18**

Università
Cattolica

Sant' Agostino

San Bernardino
a Monache

Palazzo
Borromeo

Piazza
Borromeo

Piazza
Mentana

Pinacoteca
Ambrosiana **21**

San
Giorgio

Palazzo
Trivulzio

Missori

V. Torino

Via Laghetto

Via S. Antonio

Museo del
Novecento

Teatro
Lirico

Palazzo
Greppi

Torre
Velasca

Palazzo
Sormani

GIARDINO

GUASTALLA

Palazzo
di
Giustizia

Santissimi
Barnaba
e Paolo

Via della Pace

V. E. de Amicis

Via Olona

V. Ariberto

Via C. Correnti

Via S. Vito

Palazzo
Stampa

Circo
Romano

Palazzo
Annoni

Sant'
Eufemia

Piazza
S. Nazaro

Porta Romana

Policlinico

Via M. Fanti

San
Vincenzo
in Prato

Anfiteatro
Romano

San Lorenzo
Maggiore **20**

Piazza
d. Vetra

San Paolo
Converso

Via Santa Sofia

Santa Maria
d. Visitazione

Teatro
Carcano

V. Curtatone

Corso Genova

Viale Papiniano

Porta
Genova

PARCO
DELLE
BASILICHE

Via Molino delle Armi

Via
C. D. Fante

Via G. Mercalli

Santa Maria
del Miracoli

Piazza
Card.
A. Ferrari

Crocetta

Via Orti

Porta
Genova
FS

Viale G. d'Annunzio

Via Arena

Corso di Porta Ticinese

Museo
Diocesano

Sant'
Eustorgio **19**

Porta
Ticinese

V. Vigevano

Darsena

Alzaia Naviglio Grande

Santa Maria
delle Grazie
al Naviglio

Piazzale
XXIV Maggio

Ripa di Porta Ticinese

V. Ascanio Sforza

Corso S. Gottardo

→ Pavia

V. San Luca

V. San Celso

Via
M. Burigozzo

San
Celso

Via S. Martino

Via C. Crivelli

San Pietro
dei Pellegrini

Corso di Porta Romana

Via Bianca di Savoia

Via della Commenda

Corso Italia

Corso di Porta Romana

Via Vigentina

Viale G. Galeazzo

Viale Col di Lana

Piazzale
Lodovica

Viale
Viale Bligny

Largo Isabella
d'Aragona

Beatrice d'Este

Viale A. Filippetti

Via Carlo
Vittadini

Viale Bligny

Viale Sabotino

Porta
Romana

→ Fondazione Prada

in September, it is collected, using a strange lift designed by Leonardo da Vinci, and displayed to the public for two days.

There are several fine tombs, including the 11th-century stone sarcophagus of Bishop d'Intimiano, the 16th-century tomb of Gian Giacamo de' Medici by Leone Leoni and, in the crypt behind the High Altar, the glass-encased tomb of the high society saint, San Carlo Borromeo, canonised for his work among the poor during the plague. Look out also for the bizarrely anatomical 16th-century statue of San Bartolomeo, who was flayed alive and stands in the south transept with his skin flung over one shoulder. In the north transept is a superb 12th-century gold candelabra.

Piazza del Duomo

Outside the main doors, a brass line set in the paving marked with the zodiac is a huge **sundial** (no longer accurate since a shift in the earth's magnetic field). A separate entrance in the piazza leads to the Palaeo-Christian Baptistery **of San Giovanni alle Fonti**

(charge), where Sant'Agostino was baptised by Sant'Ambrogio in AD 387. On the south side of the piazza, the huge **Palazzo Reale ❷** (Royal Palace), built in 1778 by Piermarini, was once home to the Spanish then Austrian governors.

The adjacent **Museo del Novecento** (Museum of the Twentieth Century; Piazza del Duomo 12; tel: 02-8844 4061; Mon 2.30–7.30pm, Tue–Wed, Fri, Sun 9.30am–7.30pm, Thu, Sat 9.30am–10.30pm, free entrance two hours before closing and Tue from 2pm) brings together around 400 works of 20th-century art, including pieces by the likes of De Chirico, Kandinsky and Kounellis, in a swanky gallery.

Opposite, on the north side of the Piazza del Duomo, is the **Galleria Vittorio Emanuele II ❸**, built in 1877. Its architect, Giuseppe Mengoni, was killed falling from the scaffolding shortly before it was completed. The soaring spider's web of iron and glass became the symbol of Milan and it remains fashionable to gather in "*il salotto*" (the salon) for coffee, cake and shopping.

The bronze west doors of Milan Cathedral are intricately decorated with scenes from Roman history.

Piazza del Duomo.

WHERE

Fondazione Prada's new premises in Largo Isarco, south of Milan, were designed by architect Rem Koolhaas, who transformed an old factory into a cutting-edge Museum of Contemporary Art (www.fondazioneprada.org). Interestingly, the museum's café, Bar Luce, was designed by film director Wes Anderson.

Piazza della Scala

Walk through the Galleria into Piazza della Scala, where a statue of Verdi stands in front of the neoclassical facade of the **Teatro alla Scala ❹** (La Scala). Said to have perfect acoustics, this grandest of opera houses was commissioned by Empress Maria Teresa of Austria to replace the Royal Ducal Theatre which burned down in 1776 (it opened two years later). Its architect was Giuseppe Piermarini and it was built on the site of the 14th-century church of Santa Maria alla Scala. Owners of boxes at the old theatre paid for the new one in exchange for a private box here. There are four tiers of these. The theatre seats 3,600.

The season begins each year on 7 December, the Feast of Sant'Ambrogio, patron saint of Milan. Check the internet for tickets well ahead of time (www.teatroallascala.org).

The **Museo Teatrale alla Scala** (Largo Ghiringhelli 1, Piazza della Scala; tel: 02-8879 7473; daily 9am–12.30pm, 1.30–5.30pm, last entry 30 minutes before closing; www.teatroalla

scala.org) has an extraordinary collection of theatrical memorabilia, from portraits, costumes and *commedia dell'arte* figurines to Verdi's pianos and office, many manuscripts, and beautiful board games played by the fashionable clientele during intervals. **Laboratori Ansaldo**, the Costume and Scenery Workshops, are open for guided tours (tel: 02-4335 3521; Tue, Thu for individuals; booking essential).

The **Gallerie d'Italia – Piazza della Scala ❺** (Via Manzoni 10; www.gallerieditalia.com; Tue–Sun 9.30am–7.30pm, Thu until 10.30pm), showcases a wealth of 19th-century artworks, mostly by Lombard artists, from Canova's stunning bas-reliefs to Boccioni's pre-Futuristic works. Arranged across two historic *palazzi* – works of art in themselves – the beautifully displayed collections include some fine studies of Milan's Duomo.

The Fashion District

Walk up the elegant shopping street, **Via Alessandro Manzoni**. To the right at the end of Piazza Belgioioso

Piazza della Scala.

is the home of the author Alessandro Manzoni (1814–73), now **Museo Manzoniano ⑥** (Via Morone 1; tel: 02-8646 0403; Tue–Fri 10am–6pm, Sat 2–6pm; free).

In 1850, Gian Giacomo Poldi Pezzoli started building a rich collection of fine and decorative arts, as well as more than 300 paintings from the 15th–18th centuries. The results are now on display to all in his home, a 15th-century *palazzo*, the **Museo Poldi Pezzoli ⑦** (Via A. Manzoni 12; tel: 02-794 889, www.museopoldipezzoli.it; Wed–Mon 10am–6pm).

A couple of streets up, at the corner of Via Croce Rossa, Giuseppe Verdi lived at the **Grand Hotel et de Milan** for several years. He died on 27 January 1901 and 28,000 people lined the streets for his funeral.

To the right, Via Monte Napoleone, known to cognoscenti as Monte Napo, marks one border of the **Quadrilatero d'Oro** (Golden Rectangle, see page 260), the heartland of designer Milan. The fashion may be next year's, but the buildings include some of the finest neoclassical mansions in the city.

The wonderfully quirky **Museo Bagatti Valsecchi ⑧** (Via Santo Spirito 10; tel: 02-7600 6132; Tue–Sun 1–5.45pm; www.museobagattivalsecchi.org) displays the private collection assembled by Fausto and Giuseppe Bagatti-Valsecchi. In the late 19th century, the aristocratic brothers had the dream of living in a true Renaissance *palazzo* (albeit with modern plumbing). The resulting collection of 15th- and 16th-century furniture, art, weaponry and even domestic utensils is as much a tribute to Victorian eclecticism as it is an elegy for the Renaissance era.

For a timeline of historic Milan, head towards the **Palazzo Morando Costume Moda Immagine** (Via Sant'Andrea 6; tel: 02-8844 6056; Tue–Sun 9am–1pm, 2–5.30pm; free), which tells the story of the city from the 1700s to the 1900s through a collection of paintings, sculptures, objets d'art and period costumes.

Brera

North of the Fashion District, Brera is one of the younger, funkier inner-city

The Grand Hotel et de Milan was once home to the 19th-century composer Giuseppe Verdi.

Museo Bagatti Valsecchi

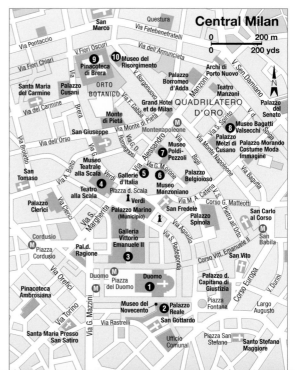

A quiet backstreet in Brera.

Pinacoteca di Brera.

areas, home to the art college, some excellent cafés and restaurants, art galleries and antiques shops – and the superb **Pinacoteca di Brera** ❾ (Via Brera 28; tel: 02-7226 3264; www. brera.beniculturali.it; Tue–Sun 8.30am–7.15pm, last entry 6.40pm, Thu until 10.15pm). Started in 1803 to house works taken from disbanded religious orders, it has grown into one of the world's great galleries, with works by Piero della Francesca, Van Dyck, Raphael, Lotto, Titian, Rembrandt and Canaletto, to name but a few.

Also housed in the same huge building, a 14th-century monastery with additions by Ricchino (17th century) and Piermarini (18th century), are the **Museo Astronomico di Brera** (tel: 02-5031 4680; Mon–Fri 9am–4.30pm; www.brera.unimi.it; free) and the **Biblioteca Nazionale Braidense**, a public library founded by Maria Teresa of Austria.

Behind the palace are the lush gardens of the **Orto Botanico** (Via Brera 28; tel: 02-5031 4696; Feb–June, Sept–Oct Mon–Fri 9am–noon, 2–5pm, Sat 10am–5pm, July–Aug, Nov–Jan

Mon–Fri 9am–12.30pm, Sat 10am–4pm; www.brera.unimi.it; free), also founded by Maria Teresa in 1774.

Just round the corner, the **Museo del Risorgimento** ❿ (Via Borgonuovo 23; tel: 02-8846 4177, www.museodelrisorgimento.mi.it; Tue–Sun 9am–1pm, 2–5.30pm) tells the history of Napoleon, Garibaldi and the Unification.

Castello Sforzesco

The city's rulers generally chose to live outside the hubbub of the centre. A semicircle of grand boulevards is all that ever got built of Napoleon's grand monument to himself. Earlier rulers did better. The original 14th-century fort was built by the Visconti. A century later, the Duco Francesco Sforza family replaced its ruins with the huge **Castello Sforzesco** ⓫ (Piazza Castello; tel: 02-8846 3703; castle daily 7am–7pm, museums Tue–Sun 9am–5.30pm; www.milanocastello.it; castle free, museum charge), turning it into one of Europe's most ostentatious courts with the help of artists of the calibre of Leonardo.

The tower by the main gate was built in 1901–4, replacing (eventually) the Filarete Tower which blew up in 1521. Inside, it has three courtyards, the parade ground, the Renaissance Rocchetta Court (public area) and the Ducal Court (private residence). It is now home to several magnificent collections of fine and applied arts, including sculpture, furniture, tapestries, ceramics, musical instruments, weapons and Egyptian art. Highlights include Michelangelo's *Pietà Rondanini* and Leonardo da Vinci's ceiling in the Sala delle Asse.

Behind the castle, the languid English-style **Parco Sempione**, once the castle's gardens, covers a vast 47 hectares (116 acres). On the north side of the park, the overblown, neoclassical **Arena** ⑫ (Viale G. Byron 2; tel: 02-341 924) was built in 1806 by Luigi Canonica. It holds up to 30,000 spectators, has been flooded to stage mock sea battles and hosted Buffalo Bill's Wild West Show.

On the southern side, the **Triennale** ⑬ (Viale Alemagna 6; tel: 02-8909 3899; www.triennale.it; Tue–Sun 10.30am–8.30pm, last entry one hour before closing) is the nearest thing this design-conscious city has, so far, to a design museum, with a permanent collection and excellent touring exhibitions.

Next to it, the **Torre Branca** ⑭ (Viale Alemagna; tel: 02-331 4120; www.museobranca.it; Tue, Thu–Fri 3.30–7pm, 8.30pm–midnight, Wed 10.30am–12.30pm, 3–7pm, 8.30pm–midnight, Sat– Sun 10.30am–2pm, 2.30–7.30pm, 8.30pm–midnight, winter shorter hours) is a 108-metre (356ft) tall steel tower designed by Gio Ponte for the fifth Triennale in 1933.

Roman Milan

A couple of blocks south of the castle is the huge **Museo Archeologico** ⑮ (Corso Magenta 15; tel: 02-8844 5208; Tue–Sun 9am–5.30pm, last entrance 30min before closing; free after 2pm Tue), with Roman, Greek, Etruscan, early medieval and Indian collections.

Further to the south again is the **Basilica di Sant'Ambrogio** ⑯ (Piazza Sant'Ambrogio; tel: 02-8645 0895; Mon–Sat 10am–noon, 2.30–6pm, Sun 3–5pm; free), built on the site of the 4th-century church of the martyr and Milan's patron saint, Sant'Ambrogio (St Ambrose). The basic design of the red-brick church set the fashion for Lombard Romanesque, while inside its capitals are a riot of imaginative design, much of it pagan in tone.

The bell tower dates from the late 11th century, but the crypt, containing the tombs of SS Ambrogio, Protaso and Gervaso, is far older. The Byzantine bronze serpent is supposedly the one made by Moses in the desert and will supposedly come back to life on Judgement Day. The church has always attracted gifts, from the 9th-century golden altar to the reliquaries in the Treasury, housed in the Chapel of San Victor in Ciel d'Oro, part of the 4th-century basilica.

A lift whisks you to the top of the Torre Branca for spectacular views right across the city, while the Just Cavalli Café at the bottom is one of the trendiest meeting points in Milan.

Fountain in front of Castello Sforzesco.

The Last Supper

When the monks went in for supper, did they admire the genius of the painting on the wall? Or was Leonardo's masterpiece simply the dining-room decoration?

In 1494, Leonardo da Vinci was commissioned by his patron Duke Ludovico Sforza to do a painting of the Last Supper for the refectory wall of the Dominican monastery in Santa Maria delle Grazie. The huge painting (measuring 46 metres/15ft by 88 metres/29ft), was to take him, on and off, four years to finish. It has become one of his greatest masterpieces, one of his most fragile works and one of his greatest enigmas.

The fragility comes down to Leonardo's love of innovation. Instead of using the lengthy but durable process of painting on wet plaster that makes a true fresco, Leonardo decided to seal the stone wall with pitch, gesso and mastic, then use tempera (egg yolk and vinegar) with oil paint. This would allow him to use a greater range of colours and to rework portions of the painting if he wished. Unfortunately, while it looked gorgeous, it didn't last.

Leonardo's controversial masterpiece The Last Supper.

By 1517, the painting had already begun to flake off. Within 60 years, in 1556, Giorgio Vasari was describing some of the figures as unrecognisable. A door was cut in it in 1652 (chopping off Christ's feet), and for a while a curtain was hung over it, which only trapped the moisture and made matters worse.

A clumsy attempt to restore it in 1726 used oil paints, and another in 1770 started overpainting the whole thing before it was halted by public outcry. The refectory was used as an armoury and a prison, and in 1821 an attempt to move the painting nearly destroyed it. More attempts to clean it didn't help, and in 1943, the refectory was bombed. Eventually, from 1978–9, a careful scientific effort began to remove everyone else's work, restore and stabilise the original piece, headed by Pinin Brambilla Barcilon. The results are spectacular, although inevitably controversial. *Il Cenacolo* is now heavily protected from the environment, with visitors restricted to one group of 25 every 15 minutes.

The painting is divided into four groups, with Jesus softly illuminated as the tranquil central figure. The disciples gesticulate with typically Italian vigour, with the exception of the recoiling Judas, depicted in shadow clutching his bag of silver. With confusion all around, Jesus calmly reaches out for his bread, his other hand open as a gesture of sacrifice.

Above the main painting, four lunettes pay tribute to the duke, his wife, Beatrice and their children.

Looking for Leonardo

Somewhat out on a limb geographically, Milan's single most famous sight is Leonardo da Vinci's fabulous painting of *The Last Supper*, known to the Italians as *Il Cenacolo*. It "hangs" on the refectory wall of the church of **Santa Maria delle Grazie** ⓱ (Piazza Santa Maria delle Grazie 2; tel: 02-9280 0360, www.vivaticket.it; www.legraziemilano.it; Tue–Sun 8.15am–6.45pm, visit last 15mins; book at least a week ahead in low season, at least a month or two in high season). On the opposite wall is a painting of the Crucifixion by Donato Montorfano (1495). Once inside, you will have only 15 minutes to admire the work, so do your homework first.

A couple of blocks south, the **Museo Nazionale della Scienza e della Tecnologia Leonardo da Vinci** ⓲ (Via San Vittore 21; tel: 02-4855 5558; Tue–Fri 9.30am–5pm, Sat–Sun 9.30am–6.30pm, summer Tue–Fri 10am–6pm, Sat–Sun 10am–7pm last entry 30 minutes before closing; submarine: guided tours from 10am; www.museoscienza.org) is an extraordinary museum of science and technology with plenty of things to press and pull for children, a submarine to tour and full-sized models of Leonardo's scientific inventions.

Early Christians

Walk east along the Via dei Amicis, then cut south through the ruins of the **Amfiteatro Romano** to the **Basilica di Sant'Eustorgio** ⓳ (Piazza San Eustorgio 3; tel: 02-5810 1583; daily 10am–6pm; church free, museum charge). This is one of the city's oldest and most beautiful churches, built on a palaeo-Christian burial site (accessed from the cloister) outside the city walls. Rebuilt in the 12th century, it supposedly houses some of the bones of the Magi, brought here by St Eustorgius (San Eustorgio), 9th bishop of Milan, in the early 4th century. Frederick Barbarossa stole them in 1162, but some were returned in 1903 and they now live in a simple Roman sarcophagus in a side chapel. The artistic highlight is the **Portinari Chapel**, gloriously painted by Vincenzo Foppa

WHERE

Tourist Information
Galleria Vittorio
Emanuele II (corner
Piazza della Scala), tel:
02-8845 5555; Mon–Fri
9am–7pm, Sat 9–6pm,
Sun 10am–6pm. Also at
the Central Station and
at all airports. City
Sightseeing (www.city-
sightseeing.com) run
hop-on, hop-off open top
bus tours (ticket validity
24 or 48 hrs; multi-
lingual commentary)
from Piazza Castello and
various other points
around the city.

*Basilica di
Sant'Ambrogio.*

Exhibits inside Pinacoteca Ambrosiana, Milan's oldest museum.

Navigli, the canal district.

(1455–68). The cloisters' **Museum Diocesano** (Diocesan Museum) has many treasures.

The Canal Quarter

Just south of here is the district of **Navigli** ("canals"), where you can see the last of the many canals which once crisscrossed Milan. These days the warehouses have been transformed into clubs and restaurants, and this has become one of the centres of the city's nightlife.

Walk back north along Corsa di Porta Ticinese, where a line of 16 Roman columns stands in front of the octagonal 16th-century **Basilica di San Lorenzo Maggiore** ⑳ (Corso di Porta Ticinese 39; tel: 02-8940 4129; Mon–Sat 8am–6.30pm, Sun 9am–7pm; church free, cappella charge). This began in the 4th century as a square church, and was rebuilt in the 11th century, before it was given its Renaissance make over. The church has fine early medieval frescoes, and the 4th-century **Cappella di San Aquilino** still has its original mosaics. Before heading

north, wander round to **Piazza della Vetra** to see the Lego-block back of the church. This seemingly peaceful place was the city execution ground until the 19th century.

Heading back towards the Duomo, the **Pinacoteca Ambrosiana** ㉑ (Piazza Pio XI 2; tel: 02-806 921; www. ambrosiana.eu; Tue–Sun 10am–6pm, last entry 5.30pm) is Milan's oldest museum, founded in 1618 by Cardinal Federico Borromeo. Art gallery and library rolled into one, it contains a truly extraordinary range of masterworks, including 35,000 manuscripts and more than 700,000 printed works, 2,500 of them printed before 1500. The collection contains Cardinal Borromeo's favourite work, Caravaggio's *Basket of Fruit*, and also reflects the founder's preference for Flemish and Venetian art. However, later bequests have broadened the Pinacoteca's appeal by including medieval Lombard sculpture, German old masters and Tuscan Renaissance masterpieces. Foremost among the Venetian masterpieces is Titian's *Adoration of the Magi* and Rococo

works by Tiepolo. Renaissance works include a luminous Botticelli Madonna and Raphael's cartoon for the *School of Athens*. Other treasures include a 5th-century copy of the Iliad, as well as the Codex Atlanticus, complete with over a thousand pages of scientific and technical drawings by Leonardo da Vinci.

Cimitero Monumentale

One of the grandest and strangest monuments in Milan is the vast, striped **Cimitero Monumentale** ㉒ (Piazzale Cimitero Monumentale; tel: 02-8846 5600; Tue–Sun 8am–6pm, last entry 30 minutes before closing; free), built in1866 by architect Carlo Maciachini. Many graves include monuments and sculptures by top artists, and people buried here include Toscanini and Manzoni.

Sporting Milan

To the Milanese, sport is right up there with fashion and food. Cosily two of Italy's top football teams – Internazionale and AC Milan – share the **Stadio San Siro** ㉓. The **Museo**

Inter & Milan (Stadio San Siro, Via Piccolomini 5; tel: 02-404 2432, www. acmilan.it; www.inter.it; www.sansiro.net; 9.30am–6pm; variation possible on match days) has tours of the stadium and plenty of memorabilia. Tickets for matches are available through the teams' websites.

San Siro is also the Milanese home of horse racing, and even those not interested in the races may want to stop at the **San Siro Racecourse** (27 Via Ippodromo; tel: 02-482 161; daily; www.ippodromitrenno.it; free) to see the world's largest equestrian statue. In 1482, Leonardo da Vinci was commissioned to build the giant bronze horse, but the plaster cast, 16 years in the making, was destroyed during French invasions. The present-day version was created by the "Leonardo da Vinci's Horse Incorporation" founded by an American pilot, Charles Dent. Sculptor Nina Akamo made the vast statue on the basis of Leonardo's many drawings. Cast with 12 tonnes of bronze, it was inaugurated in 1999, 500 years after the original was destroyed.

The Cimitero Monumentale is an open-air art gallery.

MILAN STYLE – THE LITTLE BLACK BOOK

Follow the fashionistas to Milan, one of the four corners of the fashion universe.

Fashion has always been fundamentally important to the Italians – they invented the term *"bella figura"* and brought in Giorgio Armani to design their police uniform, so perhaps it is no surprise that their richest city should become so central to the fashion world. We all know the names – Elsa Schiaparelli, Roberto Cavalli, Missoni, Ferragamo, Bulgari and Versace – but how to get the look? Women need hair – lots of hair, to toss in the breeze – figure-hugging shapes, whether jeans or evening dress, shoes with pointy toes and high heels, and plenty of make-up. Men need a light-coloured silk suit without a tie and a moody frown. Both sexes need oversized dark sunglasses, black leather jackets and tight trousers.

Whether shopping or window-shopping, the first stop for the fashionista or wannabe alike has to be the Quadrilatero d'Oro, the "golden rectangle" near the Duomo. Bounded by Via Montenapoleone, Via della Spiga, Corso Venezia and Via Manzoni, this tiny area of small streets comprises probably the richest and possibly the wackiest shopping area in the world, every window perfectly displayed with the latest trends from the biggest names – homegrown Italian talent Dolce & Gabbana, Gucci, Fendi, Valentino, Prada, Max Mara, plus international superstars such as Parisians Saint Laurent

Versace fashions.

and Chanel, Brit Paul Smith, and Kenzo fro Japan. Everyone is here; no one can afford to m the party. And it isn't just clothes – there are ba galore, shoes to die for (some look as if they wou kill you if you tried to walk in them), watches a jewellery, clothes for children and even for pe And then there are the cafés.

With fashion weeks held twice a year to hig light the new season's designs, the fashion wor descends on Milan for a feeding frenzy of catw shows, cocktail parties and gossip. The A-list e tors and celebrities are courted for their ability get the publicity shots, the buyers for their bulgi wallets. Every hotel in town is stuffed, every mo starving. Most shows are invitation-only, but t glamour rubs off on those determined to get a fo in the door.

Many of the designers have factory stores send their seconds and end of ranges to out warehouses for a fraction of what you norma pay. Stock turns over fast, and it can be hit or m as to whether they have your size, so you need keep going back.

Shopping at the Galleria Vittorio Emanuele II.

MILAN ON A BUDGET

Designer shopping is often more affordable outside Milan. As well as the outlet malls listed below, most of which offer free shuttle buses, Alessi has a huge factory shop on Lake Orta, and there are designer discount shops along the Alto Adige Valley in Trentino.

Serravalle Designer Outlet
Via della Moda 1, 15069 Serravalle Scrivia; tel: 0143-609 000; www.mcarthurglen.it.

The Place Outlet
Via Cesare Battisti 99, Sandigliano; tel: 015-249 6199; www.theplaceoutlet.com.

Foxtown
At the Mendrisio exit of the A2 (15 km/9½ miles from Lugano; bring your passport – it's just over the Swiss border); tel: +41 (0)848-828 888; www.foxtown.ch.

Franciacortia Outlet Village
Rodengo Saiano near Brescia; tel: 030-681 0364; www.franciacortaoutlet.it.

Armani Factory Store
Provinciale per Bregnano 12, Vertemate, Como; tel: 031-887 373.

OUT-OF-TOWN OUTLETS

DMagazine, Via Bigli 4, Milan; tel: 02-3664 3888; www.dmagazine.it. Daily 10am–7.30pm. Discounted clothes from the major designers in the heart of the fashion district. One of three Milan branches.
Diffusione Tessile, Galleria San Carlo 6; tel: 02-7600 0829. Mon 3.30–7.30pm, Tue–Sat 10am–7.30pm. Heavy discounts on all the Max Mara brands.
Eldorado Stock House, Via Montenapoleone 26; tel: 02-7600 6027. Tue–Sat 9.30am–7.30pm. In the heart of the fashion district, with men's and women's fashion and constantly changing stock from D&G and Moschino.
Il Salvagente, Via Bronzetti 16; tel: 02-7611 0328. Mon 3–7.30pm, Tue–Sat 10am–7.30pm, Sun 11am–2pm, 3–7pm. Huge warehouse operation offering last year's collections from multiple designers at up to 50 percent discounts.
Vestistock, Piazzale Lavater, corner of Via Ramazzini 11; tel: 02-2953 4502. Daily 10am–7.30pm. Includes Armani, Versace, D&G, Prada, Cavalli, Missoni and many more.

Handbags galore at Dolce & Gabbana.

Gucci show during Milan fashion Week.

TRANSPORT

GETTING THERE AND GETTING AROUND

The Italian Lakes are easy to reach from the rest of Europe, with several airports located nearby. While renting a car will give you flexibility to explore the smaller towns and villages away from the tourist centres, there is a very good network of public transport – trains, buses, boats – in the region, which will allow you to take a slower pace; the boats especially are a great way to get around. If you do drive, do so with extreme caution; Italians drive fast, and the roads are narrow, with many hairpin bends.

GETTING THERE

By Air

The lakes are well served with airports. Milan has three airports, with city-centre **Linate** (**LIN**) ideal if you want to explore the city as well as the lakes. Further north, Milan's **Malpensa** (**MXP**) airport makes for a convenient gateway to the western lakes. **Bergamo's Orio al Serio** (**BGY**) can also be used for Milan as well as being ideal for Lake Iseo or Lake Como; Brescia or Verona airports are the best for Lake Garda, but even Venice is within easy access. Despite being in Switzerland, **Lugano** (**LUG**) airport is another useful gateway to lakes Lugano, Como and Maggiore. Verona has two airports, the tiny **Verona-Villafranca** (**VRN**) and **Verona-Brescia** (**VBS**) which is 50km (31 miles) southwest of Verona but close to Brescia and Lake Garda.

Airport transport

Bergamo (Orio al Serio) Buses run from the airport to the centre of Bergamo from 5.17am–12.31am (tel: 035-236 026, www.atb. bergamo.it) or to Milano Centrale

train station roughly every half-hour from 4.25am–10.20pm (tel: 035-330 706, www.orioshuttle.com). A shuttle service links the airport to Milano Centrale station every 20–30 minutes from 4.05am–1am (1 hour; www.terravision.eu). Another service heads to Brescia every 1.5–3 hours from 5.10am–11pm (tel: 02-3008 9000, www.autostradale.com) for €12. Taxis to Bergamo city centre, a 10-minute journey, cost approximately €25–30 (tel: 035-451 9090).

Brescia-Montichiari (G. D'Annunzio) The airport is mainly used for cargo traffic and seasonal charters serviced by Meridiana and Windrose Airlines. Transport for Mantova (APAM; www.apam.it) operates a twice-weekly (Mon, Fri) shuttle bus service between the airport and Brescia's Santa Eufemia metro station.

Milan (Linate) A shuttle bus service (tel: 02-3008 9000, www.autostradale. com) leaves for Milano Centrale train station roughly every half-hour from 7.45am–10.45pm (also stops at Milan Lambrate railway station) and from 5.30am–10pm from Milano Centrale to the airport (25 mins). City Buses Nos. 73 (ATM, tel: 02-4860 7607; www.atm.it) leave Arrivals for Piazza San Babila underground station every 10 minutes from 5.35am–12.35am (25 minutes, €1.50 from newsstands). Linate and Malpensa airports run a shuttle service operated by Air Pullman (tel: 0331-258 411, www.malpensa shuttle.it). A taxi to the city centre will set you back around €40 (tel: 02-8585).

Milan (Malpensa) Two shuttle bus services to Milano Centrale station run every 20 minutes from 5.05am–12.10am, 7.10am–11.30pm from the airport to the station (50 minutes;

Airlines

Aer Lingus
www.aerlingus.com
Air Canada
www.aircanada.com
Air France
www.airfrance.com
Alitalia
www.alitalia.com
American Airlines
www.aa.com
British Airways
www.britishairways.com
Delta Air Lines
www.delta.com
easyJet
www.easyjet.com
KLM
www.klm.com
Lufthansa
www.lufthansa.com
Ryanair
www.ryanair.com
SWISS
www.swiss.com
United Airlines
www.united.com

www.terravision.eu; tel: 0331-519 000; www.stie.it). The Malpensa Express train connects Terminal 1 with Cadorna railway station and Milano Centrale in 29–43 minutes (tel: 800-500-005, www.malpensaexpress.it) from 5.26am–1.30am. Taxis wait outside arrivals (tel: 02-8585). Alibus buses (tel: 0323-552 172, www.saf duemila.com) run to towns around Lake Maggiore from the airport.

Verona (Valerio Catullo) Trains run every 20 minutes to Verona train station (10–15 minutes) from Verona airport (www.aeroportoverona.it). The 15-minute journey by taxi will cost around €20 (tel: 045-532 666). The

Aerobus (www.atv.verona.it) runs to Verona's Porta Nuova train station at 5.35 and 6.30am, then every 20 minutes until 8.30pm and every 40 minutes until 11.10pm, costing €6. In winter, special bus services from Verona and other airports take skiers directly to the slopes, but must be pre-booked (www.flyskishuttle.com).

By Rail

Given the range of low-cost and scheduled flights to the lakes, flying is advisable. However, Milan and Como are well served by trains coming from Switzerland, Germany and France, including Eurostar connections to London via Paris. If arriving from elsewhere in Italy, there are good connections from Turin, Bologna, Florence and Rome, as well as from within the lakes. Routes and prices vary greatly, so it is wise to plan your route at major train stations or with specialist agents such as Voyages-sncf.com (for further information, tel: 08448-485 848, https://uk.voyages-sncf.com).

If you want to do it in real style, try the Venice-Simplon Orient Express (www.belmond.com/venice-simplon-orient-express) from London or Paris to Venice.

By Road

Travelling to Italy by coach is a tough option, with Eurolines (tel: 08717-818 177, www.eurolines.co.uk) offering a 22-23-hour Milan service daily from London Victoria for no less than a bud-get air fare. However, bargain fares can often be found if booked in advance.

Driving yourself is another option, if you are prepared for the hazards of driving along narrow winding mountain roads, although it is probably cheaper to rent a car on arrival. Once across the Channel, the fastest route from France is to follow the Alpine route through Germany and Switzerland and arrive at Lake Lugano. Note that motorways en route as well as in Italy are toll roads; ensure you choose the correct lane to pay in cash, with credit card, or the frequent-user Telepass card.

You will need 5-star insurance and international markers if driving your own vehicle.

GETTING AROUND

Bicycle

This is popular cycling territory in spite of the steep gradients and hairpin bends. Bikes can be rented quite cheaply in most cities and resorts, and tourist offices carry maps of recommended cycling routes. Many serious cyclists make a pilgrimage to Madonna del Ghisallo, the patron saint of cycling, in Lake Como.

The Lakes region has three "bike hotels", which cater for the keen cyclist, offering secure rooms for your bike, repair shops and professional guides. See www.italybikehotels.it for a full list.

Boats

The best way of all to see the lakes is by boat, allowing you to enjoy the scenery without the hazard of navigating the roads, and at significantly lower cost. All main towns have passenger ferry connections, and many are also linked by car ferry: Lake Como (Cadenabbia–Bellaggio–Menaggio–Varenna), Lake Maggiore (Intra–Laveno) and Lake Garda (Maderno–Torri del Benaco and Limone–Malcesine). Cruises, some in paddle steamers, can take up a full day and are a wonderful way of seeing the whole lake. Bear in mind boat services are greatly reduced in winter.

For information on lakes Como, Maggiore and Garda, visit www.navigazionelaghi.it; for Lake Iseo, see www.navigazionelagoiseo.it; for Lugano, see www.lakelugano.ch, and for Lake Orta, see www.navigazionelagodorta.it.

Bus

The bus network around the lakes is very cheap and efficient, although in less touristy villages services can be infrequent at weekends. Local tourist offices provide timetables and information; tickets usually need to be purchased before boarding at newsagents and any shop displaying a biglietti sign.

Car

There is an excellent network of motorways (toll roads) and main roads linking the lakes and the major cities surrounding them. However, sheer volume of traffic, the terrifying speed of Italian drivers and the tunnels and hairpin bends mean that you cannot relax for a second. The Italian websites www.autostrade.it and www.quattroruote.it contain useful traffic information.

Car hire is expensive, but if arranged in advance a little cheaper. Major chains such as Avis, Budget and Hertz can be found in the airports and main towns. You must be over 21 and have a credit card for the deposit.

Insurance4carhire.com (tel: 0844-892 1770) is a cheap annual scheme which will save hundreds of pounds in comparison to the daily insurance offered by the car-hire companies.

To drive in Italy, you must carry a valid passport, full photocard driving licence (and international driving licence if a non-EU licence-holder), registration documents and insurance. It is compulsory to carry all your vehicle documents when driving, as well as emergency equipment such as spare bulbs, a fluorescent jacket and a warning triangle in case of breakdown.

A breakdown service (tel: 116) is available from the Automobile Club d'Italia (ACI).

Rules of the road

Drive on the right, overtake on the left and observe the speed limits: in built-up areas 50kmh (31mph), outside built-up areas 90kmh (55mph), on dual carriageways 110kmh (68mph) and on motorways 130kmh (80mph).

On-the-spot fines for speeding offences are particularly heavy. The police can impose the fine and collect one-quarter of the maximum fine, and must give a receipt for the amount paid.

Dipped headlights during the day are compulsory outside built-up areas and when there is snow or rain and generally poor visibility. Rear fog lights may only be used when visibility is less than 50 metres (164ft) or in case of strong rain or heavy snow.

As always, do not drink and drive; the penalties are severe.

Fuel

Service stations are open from 6.30/7am to 12.30/1pm and from 3pm to 7.30pm, but outside these times many have automatic pumps.

Try renting a bike.

Service is available 24-hours a day on motorways.

Contact: UK: www.theaa.co.uk; Republic of Ireland: www.aaireland.ie; Italy: www.aci.it.

Parking

Parking is a nightmare almost everywhere during the summer, with the lake shores cramped by the mountainous terrain and the city centres overcrowded. Locals park on every patch of spare land along the lake roads; drive a small car and be prepared to do the same. Unless you are planning to do a lot of touring, consider using public transport, which is excellent.

Taxis

Taxis are expensive, and supplements apply between 10am and 6am, Sundays, holidays, and per item of luggage. Fares are based on distance once outside city boundaries. As in any city, use only official metered taxis.

Trains

Travel by train is cheap, efficient, and between major cities, fast. The main types operating between major cities are Eurostar, Intercity and Interregionale, while the local Regionale trains stop at every city in the region and are very slow. The Europe-wide InterRail pass (www.interrail.net) can be good value if you're planning to travel extensively by train over several weeks. Note that all tickets must be stamped at the yellow machines before boarding, or you will be fined.

For more information, see www.trenitalia.com.

Boat on Lake Garda.

Getting Around the Lakes

Lake Como

Trains run from Milan to Como and Lecco, as well as the length of the eastern shore. Como has three stations, with trains on the FS line (www.fsitaliane.it) from Milan arriving in Como San Giovanni, a short walk or bus ride from the city centre. Regional trains on the FNME line (www.ferrovienord.it) pass through Como Borghi station and terminate at Como Lago Nord station on the lakefront, across from the bus station at Piazza Matteotti.

On the lakefront in front of the Piazza Cavour is the landing stage for boats offering trips on hydrofoils, car ferries, ships, and full day or evening cruises, with food, live music and drinks (www.navigazionelaghi.it).

Lake Iseo (including Franciacorta and Val Camonica)

Lake Iseo is easily accessible from Como, Bergamo and Brescia, with onward rail connections to Lake Garda. A delightful train route runs from Iseo to Brescia (through Franciacorta wine country) and takes 30 minutes.

However, a car is advisable if you want to explore the surrounding hills, the wine country and the prehistoric art in Val Camonica.

Navigating Lake Iseo is more straightforward than navigating Lake Garda (tel: 035-971 483, www.navigazionelagoiseo.it). As well as "three island" cruises, there are themed cruises, as well as an evening option with dinner.

Lake Garda

Prices on Lake Garda tend to be more competitive than elsewhere, apart from the high cost of ferries and hydrofoils. On the other hand, compared with the quiet refinement of Lake Como, for instance, Lake Garda offers more family holidays and sports facilities.

Desenzano is the main rail link on the lake, with frequent connections to Brescia, Verona, Milan and beyond. Lake Garda is the one lake where a car is optional, with a week's holiday happily spent on day trips pottering around on the water, or visiting resorts, villas and gardens.

Car rental is advisable to appreciate the rugged drives round Western Lake Garda (especially from Salò to Riva), as well as exploring the wine-growing hinterland of Valtenesi.

Navigating the lake: due to its size, when travelling longer distances it makes sense to catch the ferry on the outward voyage, stopping at various ports en route and visiting those, and to catch the faster hydrofoil back, which is less romantic but twice as fast.

For the purpose of fares and routes, the lake is divided into "Upper Lake" (including Riva and Malcesine) and "Lower Lake" (from Desenzano south). Work out the scope of a day trip carefully, as the cost of the "full" lakes pass is almost twice the cost of a "half" lakes pass, and you may only need the latter. For routes, timetables and fares, tel: 030-914 9511 (outside Italy), free-phone 800-551 801 (inside Italy), www.navigazionelaghi.it.

Lake Lugano

A car is crucial here to explore beyond Lugano city. There are ferries along the lake, but they are not as frequent as in some of the other lakes. For details on the ferries, see page 212. The train runs into Lugano along the northwest arm of the lake, leaving to the south over the Bissone causeway and down the southeast shore.

Lake Maggiore

Lake Maggiore has a complex network of local and long-distance ferries covering the full length of the lake that take people to villages and towns along both shores as well as to the island gardens that adorn the centre of the lake. The main line from Milan follows the western shore north, heading off into Northern Europe through the renowned Simplon Tunnel at Domodossola, from where the scenic Centovalli Railway twists its way back down to the lake.

Lake Orta

Lake Orta's main town, Orta San Giulio, is closed to traffic. Car parks are located along the Via Panoramica above the town. It is possible to drop off luggage at hotels by car, but only very small cars will be able to make their way through the narrow streets. Alternatively, the *trenino* is a convenient tourist train that goes from the Via Panoramica and car parks to Piazza Motta in the heart of town.

The journey by boat from Orta San Giulio to the Isola San Giulio takes five minutes (boats depart from 9.55am, Oct–Mar reduced hours; tel: 0345-517 0005, www.navigazionelagodorta. it). There are also less frequent boat services to other towns on the lake. If travelling by car, the best option is to park in Pella on the west bank of the lake, opposite Orta San Giulio, where you can park close to the boat landing-stage.

A – Z

A HANDY SUMMARY
OF PRACTICAL INFORMATION

A

Accommodation

The lakes provide a huge variety of places to stay, from 19th-century villas fit for a queen to 16th-century farmhouses, city-centre designer hotels and campsites. The area is popular with Hollywood film stars, so if you can afford luxury you will not be disappointed. That said, there are options to suit every budget, and below we give contact details for the various types of accommodation. During the peak season of July and August, booking ahead is a must.

Booking

Reservations can be made by the tourist offices, but they are often very busy, and you may be handed a photocopied list of rooms in the area and left to fend for yourself. To avoid hassle, book directly before you arrive, and ensure you have written confirmation of your reservation.

Agriturismi

Away from the lakes, the option of staying in a converted barn or farm building is increasingly common and is an excellent choice for exploring the hinterland and for more active holidays, such as walking, fishing and cycling. Farmers offer self-contained apartments, but rooms with or without en suites can be found.

An extensive list is available on www.agriturist.it, www.agriturismo.it, www.agriturismo.net or from the head offices of:
Agriturist, Corso Vittorio Emanuele 101, 00186 Roma, tel: 06-685 2337, www.byfarmholidays.com.

Via Manin 20, 58100 Grosseto, tel: 0564-417 418.
Terranostra, Via XXIV Maggio 43, 00187 Roma, tel: 06-4899 3208; www.terranostra.it.
Turismo Verde, Via Mario Fortuny 20, 00196 Roma, tel: 06-3240 111.

Alpine Huts

An excellent and highly economical way for hikers to explore the mountains, these shelters are basic but often provide hot meals and a warm atmosphere. The Club Alpino Italiano (Via Petrella 19, 20124 Milano) owns nearly 600 huts in the mountain districts. Information and itineraries can be found at The Touring Club Italiano (Corso Italia 10, 20122 Milano, tel: 02-852 6800). Consult www.touringclub.it or www.cai.it for full details.

Bed and Breakfasts

Standards in B&Bs vary (they are usually deemed 1-star or 2-star hotels), but are nevertheless best way to experience life in an Italian family home. As with youth hostels, this option may be no more economical than staying in a budget hotel, and cash is often the only method of payment available. Consult www.bbitalia.it or www.bbitalia.com, which lists more than 13,500 B&Bs in all categories, from basic to luxurious.

Camping

Campsites fill up fast, so booking well ahead is advisable. The cheaper ones are tucked away in peaceful spots away from the main tourist areas, so access to a car is often a must. Chalets and mobile homes are offered on larger campsites in addition to tents; the sites are usually well equipped with pools,

mini-supermarkets and games areas. Campsites tend to be closed in winter. A list of campsites with a location map is issued by Confedercampeggio, Via V. Emanuele 11, 50041 Calenzano (Florence), tel: 055-882 391, www.federcampeggio.it. Try also www.camping.it, www.campeggi.it and www.faita.it. Eurocamp (UK tel: 01-606 787 125, www.eurocamp.co.uk) offers family holidays in permanent tents and self-catering chalets in the lakes.

Hotels

As is to be expected, the nearer you are to the lakes, the higher the prices. Prime spots on the lake will be vastly more expensive than accommodation with less dramatic views, and especially in more rural areas. Breakfast is usually included, so if you prefer to eat more cheaply, it is worth asking if you can pay for the room only. As always, single travellers are penalised by often having to pay a hefty supplement for their single room.

Hotels are classified as follows: 5-star de luxe, 5-star, 4-star, 3-star, 2-star and 1-star. The term *pensione* (or pension), that describes a small 1-or 2-star hotel, is now only rarely used in Italy. *Locande* (inns), the most basic accommodation, are common outside touristy areas, but the name has now been adopted by chic and pricey city-centre hotels and is interchangeable with *albergo* and *hotel*.

A further option is motels, some of which come with pools, tennis courts and even beaches. A full list is available through the Italian Tourist Board (www.enit.it).

Private Home Stays

Accommodation in private homes is available in most cities and towns in Italy through contacting the local tourist office and asking for *un elenco di affittacamere* (list of persons letting rooms). As they are not official establishments, the tourist office does not grade them but will recommend the best ones.

Villa and Apartment Rentals

This is a popular, and often more economical way of staying by a lake or in a city centre, and is a good way of sampling local produce – and life – at the shops and markets. With rentals offered from a few nights to around a month, many holiday-makers split their time between two or three areas. Rental accommodation is increasingly listed privately on the internet and is often far cheaper this way, but a large number of companies offer extensive choices, often as part of a package:
Italian Breaks
Tel: +44 (0)20-8666 0407
www.italianbreaks.com
Owners Direct
www.ownersdirect.co.uk
Holiday Homes in Italy
Tel: +44 (0)845-229 7057,
www.holidayhomesinitaly.co.uk
Summer in Italy
Tel: US and Canada toll free: 1 800-509 8194 UK toll free: 0800-047 0248 International: +41 91-220 0567 www.summerinitaly.com.

Youth Hostels

Run by the AIG (Associazione Italiana Alberghi per la Gioventu'), affiliated to Hostelling International (HI), these are an excellent way of holidaying economically if travelling alone or with a family, and are much more sociable. A dorm bed costs around €18–25, a family room €15–20 per person.

In addition to the official HI hostels, a growing number of independent hostels offers accommodation at similar prices and often these are in more central locations; check www.hostelworld.com.

Self-catering kitchens and/or budget cafés are provided, as are discounted facilities such as bike and canoe hire. Like campsites, these are often tucked away from the main tourist drag and can therefore also mean a hop onto public transport to sightsee.

Strictly speaking, you need to be a member of HI to use the facilities at HI hostels, but it is not always required. Join your home organisation before you leave, and you can then also book ahead through its Booking Network.

Australia, tel: 02-9261 1111, www.yha.org.au.
England and Wales, tel: 0800-019 1700, www.yha.org.uk.
Ireland, tel: +353 1-830 4555, www.anoige.ie.
Italy, tel: 06-487 1152, www.aighostels.com.
New Zealand, tel: 0800-278 299, www.yha.co.nz.
Scotland, tel: 0345-293 7373, www.syha.org.uk.
US, tel: 240-650 2100, www.hiayh.org.

Admission Charges

For entry into villas and gardens, expect to pay in the region of €2–8; for museums and art galleries, €4–12.

B

Budgeting for Your Trip

Italy is one of the priciest countries in Europe, and Milan the dearest city in Italy, so a trip here will never be a bargain. However, there are ways of keeping costs down, such as shopping at factory outlets for designer clothes and staying in family-run guesthouses rather than grand hotels. Expect to spend €100–180 on a standard double room in a 3-star hotel, although prices will be highest on the lakes in July and August; Milan, so hot its residents flee to the lakes at this time, will be cheaper.

Getting around by public transport is cheap: a one-day travel card in Milan, for example, will cost €4.50. Taxis and car rental are not advisable if your pockets are not deep: a taxi journey of 7km (4.5 miles) costs around €25, more than twice the cost of a single train ticket from Milan to Como. A day's car hire will set you back around €80, with a litre of petrol roughly €1.70.

An evening meal can cost €25–60 (more if somewhere grand), while a pizza and a beer costs around €15. An alcoholic drink (beer or spirits) costs double the price of a soft drink, at around €3–4; local wine not much more.

C

Children

Italians love children, and you will find that they are accepted

– even doted on – even in smart restaurants. You can expect reduced entry for kids to museums and other attractions; admission is often free for under-6s. You will also pay less for kids' tickets on trains, and you are likely to be charged a small fee (20–30 percent of the room price) for a cot or bed for a young child in your room.

In summer, beware of soaring temperatures: the sunscreen sold in Italy is often a lower factor than you might choose for your children, so it's best to come prepared.

Climate

Differences in altitude and microclimates on the Italian Lakes means you should come prepared for extremes. Milan can be swelteringly hot, especially in August when temperatures rise well above 30°C (90°F) and the humidity is high – which is why the only people around are tourists; locals have fled to the cooler lakes.

The lakes' microclimate keeps them mild in winter and pleasant in summer, but a day trip up into the mountains can see the temperature drop significantly even in July and August. It is therefore advisable to pack sweaters and jackets as well as sun cream in your day-bag to cope with the extremes in altitude.

When to visit

The best times to visit are in May, June and September when the temperature is balmy, not baking, and the evenings cool. July and August can get very hot, but things cool down off-season (October–Easter) when rain and heavy fog roll in and icy winds sweep down from the Alps. Midwinter is ski season in the northern areas of Trentino and

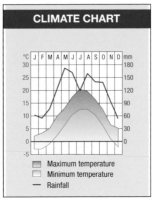

CLIMATE CHART

TRANSPORT

it's also a good time for a bargain city break.

What to wear

The Italian Lakes and Milan are known for their fashion and glamour, so it is worth packing something smart/trendy for dining out (although jackets and ties are rarely required for men) and for shopping. Bare legs are frowned upon when visiting religious buildings, and all visitors should have their shoulders covered.

The sun can be deceptively strong in high summer, so sun hats, long sleeves and high-factor sun lotion are recommended. Rain is a feature of winter, but it is wise to pack a raincoat and umbrella whatever time of year you go.

Shoes should be suitable for walking, especially on cobbled streets and for climbing steps, and have good grip to reduce the chance of slipping on boats.

Crime and Safety

Italy is a safe country and violent crime is rare, but petty crime is quite common, especially in tourist hotspots. As in all big cities around the world, watch out for pickpocketing and bag-snatching, and do not leave valuables in the car (if you really must, do not leave them on display). Crowded streets, busy tourist areas and train and bus stations are notorious targets, so it is wise to take basic precautions: keep a firm hand on your bag and camera and leave your valuables (including credit cards and extra money) in the hotel safe.

As always, take out adequate insurance coverage before leaving. If you are the victim of a crime or lose anything of value, it is essential to make a report *(denuncia)* at the nearest police station *(questura)* as soon as possible and get documentation to support your insurance. Be prepared to wait.

For help in an emergency, dial 113 for the local police, or 112 for the Carabinieri, the national police force.

Customs Regulations

Duty-free and tax-free goods are no longer available to EU residents, but there are no limits on how much you can buy on journeys within the EU, as long as you can prove it is for personal use. There are guidance levels:

Policeman in Verona.

3,200 cigarettes or 400 cigarillos or 200 cigars or 3kg of smoking tobacco;

10 litres of spirits; 20 litres of fortified wine; 90 litres of wine; 110 litres of beer.

Duty-free is still available to those travelling outside the EU, and allowances are as follows:

Australia: A$900 worth of goods (A$450 for under-18s and sea crew members) including gifts; plus 2.25 litres of alcohol; and 50 cigarettes, or 50 grams of cigars or tobacco products for each passenger aged 18 years or over. Check with the Australian Customs Service before you go: www.customs.gov.au.

New Zealand: NZ$700 worth of goods (children are eligible for this allowance provided the goods are their own property and a child would reasonably expect to own and use them); plus 50 cigarettes, or 50 grams of tobacco or cigars, or a mixture of all three weighing not more than 50 grams, 4.5 litres of wine or 4.5 litres of beer plus three bottles (or other containers) each containing not more than 1125ml of spirits or liqueur are also allowed. Check with New Zealand customs before travel (www.customs.govt.nz).

US: Each US tourist is allowed duty-free US$800 worth of goods purchased abroad. A flat rate of 3 percent is assessed on the next US$1,000 worth of goods purchased.

Luggage and passports are examined on entering and leaving Italy. Free entry is allowed for personal effects. Technically, professional photographers have to carry an ATA Carnet (issued in the UK through the London Chamber of Commerce, 33 Queen Street, London EC4R 1AP, tel: 020-7248 4444) for temporary importation of equipment.

A maximum of four litres of wine or one litre of spirits over 22 percent, 200 cigarettes and a quantity of cigars or pipe tobacco not exceeding 250 grams per person may be brought into the country duty-free. If you arrive in Italy after visiting other countries, you are allowed to carry up to €500 worth of souvenirs and only a verbal declaration is required.

D

Disabled Travellers

Italy is not easy for disabled visitors, but is making slow progress in improving transport, accommodation and buildings.

New trains and buses are low-level, and more museums now have lifts, ramps and adapted toilets, and recent laws require restaurants, bars and hotels to provide spacious and specially adapted toilets. The new legislation does not, however, necessarily cover access to the facilities.

Accessible Italy, Via C. Manetti 34, 47891 Dogana, Repubblica di San Marino, tel: +39 378-941 111 or 378-0549-941 111, www.accessibleitaly.com, a not-for-profit organisation, offers tours to foreigners with disabilities as well as listings of accessible wedding locations.

For US visitors, the **Society for Accessible Travel and Hospitality** (sath), 347 5th Avenue, New York, NY 10016, tel: 212-447 7284, www.sath.org, provides access information for a large number of airlines.

In the UK, **Disability Rights UK**, Ground Floor, CAN Mezzanine, 49-51 East Rd, London, N1 6AH, tel: 020-7250 8181, www.disabilityrightsuk.org, has comprehensive disability information.

Access at Last is a 'one-stop-shop' for accessible accommodation and services with a worldwide database of places to stay: www.accessatlast.com

A – Z

LANGUAGE

Emergencies

112 Police *(Carabinieri)*
113 Local Police *(Polizia Statale)*
115 Fire Brigade *(Vigili del Fuoco)*
116 Roadside assistance
(Soccorso Stradale)
118 Ambulance *(Ambulanza)*

E

Electricity

Italy uses 220v and two-pin plugs. Adaptors for British three-pin appliances can be purchased from airports or department stores in the city. Confusingly, outlets can be for small or close-set pins or wide and large pins. Some plugpoints may have overlapping holes to accept either older or newer types, but it may be sensible to have an adaptor for both types. You will need a transformer to use 100–120v appliances.

Embassies & Consulates

Embassies and consulates in Italy

Australia: Embassy, Via Antonio Bosio 5, 00161 Rome, tel: 06-852 721.
Consulate General, Via Borgogna 2, 20122 Milan, tel: 02-776 741; www.italy.embassy.gov.au.
Canada: Embassy, Via Zara 30, 00198 Rome, tel: 06-854 441.
Consulate General, Piazza Cavour 3, 20121 Milan, tel: 02-6269 4238; www.canadainternational.gc.ca.
Ireland: Embassy, Villa Spada, Via Giacomo Medici 1, 00153 Rome, tel: 06-585 2381. Consulate General, Piazza San Pietro in Gessate 2, 20122 Milan, tel: 02-5518 7569; www.dfa.ie/irish-embassy/italy.
UK: Embassy, Via XX Settembre 80a, 00187 Rome, tel: 06-4220 0001. Consulate General, Via S. Paolo 7, 20121 Milan, tel: 02-723 001; www.gov.uk/government/world/italy.
US: Embassy, Via Vittorio Veneto 121, 00187 Rome, tel: 06-46741. Consulate General: Via Principe Amedeo 2, 20121 Milan, tel: 02-290 351; http://italy. usembassy.gov.

Italian embassies abroad

Australia: Embassy, 12 Grey St, Deakin, Canberra, act 2600, tel: 02-6273 3333, www.ambcanberra. esteri.it.

The perfect souvenir.

Consulates: Melbourne, tel: 03-9867 5744 and Sydney, tel: 02-9392 7900.
Canada: Embassy, 275 Slater St, Ottawa, ON K1P 5H9, tel: 1613-234 2401, www.ambottawa.esteri.it. Consulates: Montreal, tel: 514-849 8351 and Toronto, tel: 416-977 1566.
Ireland: Embassy, 63–65 Northumberland Rd, Dublin 4, tel: 31-660 1744, www.ambdublino. esteri.it.
New Zealand: Embassy, 34–38 Grant Rd, PO Box 463, Thorndon, Wellington, tel: 04-473 5399, www.ambwellington.esteri.it.
UK: Embassy, 14 Three King's Yard, London W1K 4EH, tel: 020-7312 2200, www.amblondra.esteri.it. Consulates: London, tel: 020-7235 9371, Edinburgh, tel: 0131-220 3695, and Manchester, tel: 0161-236 9024.
US: Embassy, 3000 Whitehaven St NW, Washington DC 20008, tel: 202-612 4400, www.ambwashingtondc. esteri.it.
Consulates: Chicago, tel: 312-467 1550, New York, tel: 212-737 9100, San Francisco, tel: 415-292 9210.

F

Festivals and Events

January

Milan – Epiphany: Costumed parade of the Three Wise Men, from the Duomo to Sant'Eustorgio.
Brescia province – Musiche dal Mondo: Major series of classical concerts and recitals running from December to March (www.brescia tourism.it).
Salò, Garda: Classical musical performances (every Sunday afternoon in the resort).
Ascona, Lake Maggiore (1 Jan): Firework display.

February/March

All Italy – Carnival (dates vary): celebrated in February or March. Verona Bacanal del Gnoco.
Franciacorta Carnival, Erbusco – Allegorical floats parade in the heart of sparkling wine country; similar ones take place in Bergamo, Varese, Bormio, Schignano and Arco, as well as in Pisogne and Clusane on Lake Iseo.
Milan – Carnevale Ambrosiano: Celebration of the city's patron saint, with children's costumed parades and *chiacchiere*, special biscuits.
Milan – Fashion collections: invitation-only shows held during Fashion Week at end Feb/early Mar.
Mid-March: Cantine Aperte, "Open Wine Estates". A chance to visit many estates in Lombardy and other regions for tastings (www.brescia tourism.it).

April/May

Easter is celebrated throughout the region with parades, markets and fairs.
Trento – 15 April: Motorbike Blessing – Trento's archbishop blesses around 1,000 motorbikes in the Piazza Duomo.
Mid–end May: Open *palazzi*, with guided tours in Trento and its suburbs (www.cultura.trentino.it).
End Apr–beginning May: Trento Film Festival (www.trentofestival.it).
Orta San Giulio – 1–31: "Ortafiori" Flower Festival. Camellia flower show.
Omegna – 31 May: Madonna del Lago procession at 8.30pm, Bagnella.

May

Brescia – mid-May: Mille Miglia, the country's best-known vintage car rally, from Brescia to Rome and back, with concerts and events staged en route (www.1000miglia.eu).
Stresa – May and June: International Organ Festival.
Lake Maggiore – 17: Locarno – Strawberry Festival.
25–8: Ascona – International Street Artists Festival.
27: Brissago – Fish Festival.

June

Erbusco, Franciacorta – Festival d'estate Franciacorta: wine and food festival (www.franciacorta.net/en/festival/).

Brescia – Brescia con Gusto: Three-day food fair around Brescia's courtyards and city squares, with tastings of oil, cheeses, sardines and lake fish.

Como – Until Aug: Lario Jazz and Rhythm 'n' Blues festival; famous artists performing in different villages around the lake (www.provincia.como.it).

St John's Day/Sagra di San Giovanni: The Isola di Comacina commemorates the destruction of its 12th-century city with a huge firework display.

Lake Lugano – Estival Jazz Lugano – end June–early July: free concerts in Mendrisio and Lugano.

Lake Orta – Mid-June: Week-long Festival Cusiano di Musica Antica. **Festival of Ancient Music** in Orta San Giulio.

Amenoblues Festival, Ameno – June and July: A highlight in the blues jazz calendar (www.amenoblues.it).

Trento – mid-end June, Festival of San Vigilio: The town celebrates its patron saint through historical re-enactments (www.festevigiliane.it).

Verona – Opera season begins in the famous open-air Roman Amphitheatre. Until Sept (www.arena.it).

June–Sept Provincia in Festival: Music, theatre, dance and cinema (www.provinciainfestival.it).

June–Aug: live music in Piazza Grande in Locarno.

July

Firework displays: at Limone, Salò, Sirmione, Riva and in Omegna (Lake Orta) in August; Locarno and Muralto in Lake Maggiore, and also Lake Como (Festival dei Fuochi) in late June and especially in Gravedona (midsummer feast, 14 Aug).

Trentino – The Sounds of the Dolomites: "Music in the Mountains", free open-air festival (www.visittrentino.it; www.fassa.com).

Gardone Riviera – Stagione al Vittoriale. Summer season at the Teatro del Vittoriale, in the amphitheatre of the Vittoriale, D'Annunzio's home: music, dance, theatre and recitals (www.anfiteatrodelvittoriale.it).

Bogliaco di Gargnano – Cento Games: Sailing regatta with some of the boats from the Centomiglia del Garda (www.centomiglia.it).

Lake Garda – Palio delle Bisse: Night regatta with a folkloric gondolier-style

rowing competition in memory of Venetian rule.

Lake Ledro – Match Race Isaf: America's Cup in miniature, but female. (Lake Regattas are held throughout the summer on Lake Garda; see www.fragliavelariva.com for details).

Desenzano – Fish festival, with free wine tastings. Settimana della Tinca, Clusane – a week of feasting on the local lake fish, organised by Operatori Turistici Clusane.

Salò – Classical outdoor concerts staged in Piazza Duomo in July and August; also held in Lake Como Aug–Sept.

Como – Stagione Concertistica in Villa Carlotta: classical music concerts in a stunning setting.

Lake Orta – mid-July: Sagra del Pesce di Camogli, Omegna – two-day sea and lake fish festival.

August

Como – 16: Pognana Lario, Sagra degli Gnocchi – Food festival celebrating gnocchi, prepared by all the women of the village.

Centro Lago – Regatta of the Lucie, the Como standing rowing boats. Lake Orta – First week: Miasino Classic Jazz Festival (www.prolocomiasino.it).

Last two weeks: World Fireworks Championship.

Lake Maggiore – 10 days in early August: Locarno International Film Festival (www.pardolive.ch).

September

Ascona – Sept and Oct: Settimane Musicali concerts held by international ensembles in town

Passengers on a tram in Milan.

and around the lake (www.settimane-musicali.ch).

Weekly free classical music concerts are also held throughout the year.

Lake Garda – Centomiglia Regatta: Europe's most important sailing event starts in Bogliaco but races to Riva, Sirmione, Desenzano and Salo (www.centomiglia.it).

Arco – Aug and Sept: Rockmaster, free-climbing world championships staged on Europe's largest open-air wall: 18 metres (59ft) in height, 650 sq metres (7,000 sq ft) to be climbed and 2,000 mobile grips (www.rockmaster.com).

Iseo – Fiera dei Vini: wine fair in Rovato, near Iseo, held first weekend of Sept.

Pisogne – Festa del fungo e della castagna: Autumn festival on Lake Garda devoted to mushrooms and chestnuts, with stands selling local produce of every description (www.bresciaatavola.it).

Trentino – Traubenkur – bizarre grape juice cure.

Milan – Spring fashion collections: invitation-only shows held in October Fashion Week.

MVM Milan Fashion Fair (milan-ovendemoda) end of September, based on women's ready-to-wear, Fiera Milano City (www.fieramilano.it).

Val di Fiemme and Val di Fassa – Marcialonga Running Coop: September version of the most famous Italian Nordic skiing race, which shares the same starting and finishing lines: Moena and Cavalese (www.marcialonga.it).

Como and area – End Aug–mid-Sept: Palio del Baradello, Historical re-enactment of Barbarossa's

entrance to Como in the 12th century (www.paliodelbaradello.it).

Sept/Oct: Miniartextil – International review of contemporary textile art (www.miniartextil.it).

Lake Maggiore – First weekend: Locarno Triathlon – the only medium-distance triathlon in Switzerland (www.3locarno.ch).

Mid-Sept: Locarno-Monti Wine Festival.

October/November/ December

October: Lake Garda Marathon: Begins in Limone on the western shore and finishes in Malcesine on the opposite shore, via the northern shore of Riva del Garda, Arco and Torbole (www.lakegardamarathon. com).

Lake Garda – Desenzano: October Wine and Chestnut Festival to celebrate the grape harvest, on Lake Garda.

Pucia e Schisa: October barrel race in Erbusco, Franciacorta, plus food and wine fair.

Clusane, Lake Iseo – Vino Novello celebrates local wine and fish dishes.

Milan – "Oh bej Oh bej": A local holiday in honour of the city's patron

saint; huge Christmas market.

7 Dec: La Scala official opening, with the opera season running until July (www.teatroallascala.org).

Christmas Cribs *(Presepi):* processions and Christmas cribs on display in churches all over the lakes, with a fabulous one set over the water in Desenzano, by the Porto Vecchio.

Como – Città de Balocchi celebrates Christmas with a series of children's events and fireworks on New Year's Eve in the main square (www.cittadeibalocchi.it).

Lake Maggiore – 26 Nov–6 Jan: Locarno on Ice (www.locarnoonice.ch).

Lake Maggiore – Dec: Mercatini di Natale Christmas markets.

G

Gay & Lesbian Travellers

In large towns, and especially in Italy's gay capital of Milan, homosexuality is accepted, and the growing gay scene reflects this (see www.arcigaymilano.org and www.listalesbica.it). However, this is a Catholic country, and attitudes

Catching up on the news.

become conservative and even homophobic outside tourist areas, where even heavy petting in public is viewed harshly. The age of consent in Italy is 14. The website www.gay friendlyitaly.com is a guide to the gay scene across the country.

H

Health & Medical Care

The public health system in Italy is generally excellent and is managed provincially by asl (Azienda Sanitaria Locale), which can provide information on how to find the nearest hospital, clinic or any other medical service you may need. Private hospitals and clinics in Italy are very good, but are expensive if are not covered by medical insurance.

First Aid Service *(Pronto Soccorso)* with a doctor on hand is found at airports, ports, railway stations and hospitals. If you need an ambulance, you can call 118 from anywhere in Italy. As with any emergency abroad, call your local consul or embassy.

European citizens must have an EHIC (European Health Insurance Card) to be entitled to emergency medical treatment in Italy. They can be applied for in the UK online (www.ehic.org.uk), at the post office (www.postoffice.co.uk) or by phoning 0845-606 2030. There are similar arrangements for citizens of other European Union countries, and Australians are entitled to the same reciprocal arrangement via the Medicare system. Visitors from outside the EU are strongly advised to take out adequate holiday and medical insurance to provide full cover during their stay abroad.

No vaccinations are needed to travel to or from Italy, and tap water is drinkable. It is a good idea to pack high-factor sunscreen (against the sun in summer and to protect from snowburn when skiing) along with mosquito repellent. It is also advisable to cover up as much as possible – the cooling breezes on the lakes mask the sun's intensity.

Medical services

Pharmacies

The staff in chemists' shops *(farmacie)* are extremely knowledgeable about common illnesses and can dispense many more medicines without prescription than in other countries. Pharmacies are identified by a cross, often red or green and usually in neon. Normal pharmacy opening hours are Mon–Fri 9am–1pm and 4–7pm. Every *farmacia* posts a list of the local chemists who are on emergency duty on the door or listed in the local paper.

Hospitals
Milan – Ospedale Maggiore Policlinicio, Via Francesco Sforza 35, tel: 02-55031.
Lake Maggiore – Italian Red Cross (ambulance):
Varese, tel: 0332-813 163; Angera, tel: 0331-930 332; Luino, tel: 0332-510 444; Stresa, tel: 0323-33360; Verbania, tel: 0323-405 000.
　　There are accident and emergency departments at the following hospitals:
Bergamo – Ospedali Riuniti di Bergamo, Via Tito Livio 2, Bergamo, tel: 035-267 611.
Lake Como – Ospedale Sant'Anna, San Fermo della Battaglia, tel: 031-5851.
Lake Lugano – Ospedale Civico, Via Tesserete 46, tel: 091-811 6111.
Lake Maggiore – Arona, Ospedale SS Trinita', Via S. Carlo 11, tel: 0322-5161. Cittiglio (near Laveno Mombello), Ospedale di Circolo, Via Guglielmo Marconi 40, tel: 0332-603 000. Luino, Ospedale di Circolo, Via Forlanini 6, tel: 0332-539 111.
Trento – S. Chiara Hospital L.go Medaglie D'Oro 9, 38100 Trento, tel: 0461-903 111.
Varese – Ospedale di Circolo, Fondazione Macchi, Viale Borri 57, tel: 0332-278 111.
Verona – Ospedale Policlinico di Borgo Roma, Via delle Menegone 10, Verona, tel: 045-812 4848.

L

Left Luggage

There are left-luggage facilities at all airports and major railway stations with full security measures, but it isn't a cheap option. Most hotels are happy to store your luggage for you if you arrive early or have a late flight. Make sure your bags are properly secured.

Lost Property

Milan
Council Office: Via Friuli, 30, tel: 02-8845 3900.
Open daily 8.30am–4pm.

The eye-catching sign for a post office.

Train: Stazione Centrale, tel: 02-8845 3900.
Open Mon–Fri 8.30am–4pm.

M

Maps

Maps are found in stationery shops, large news-stands and petrol stations. Tourist offices usually provide free city maps. Stockists in London include: **Stanfords**, 12–14 Long Acre, London WC2E 9LP, tel: 020-7836 1321, www.stanfords.co.uk.
　　Insight Fleximap Lake Garda & Verona is a useful, waterproof map with all the detailed area and town plans you will need for your trip, as well as the lowdown on all top attractions and practical information.

Media

Italian newspapers are regionally based, with each large Italian town producing its own newspaper. A few newspapers, *La Stampa*, *Il Corriere della Sera* and *La Repubblica*, have a national following. English-language newspapers can be bought (at great expense) in major towns and tourism resorts.
　　Television is deregulated in Italy, so as well as the three national channels, RAI 1, 2 and 3, there are a huge number of other channels offering an array of chat, quiz and music shows. The main ones are Canale 5, Rete 4, Italia 1, La7 and MTV.

Money

Currency
Italy's currency is the euro (€), which is divided into 100 cents. The currency is available in 500-, 200-, 100-, 50-, 20-, 10- and 5-euro notes, and 2-euro, 1-euro, 50-cent, 20-cent, 10-cent, 5-cent, 2-cent and 1-cent coins.
　　Switzerland is outside the EU and uses the Swiss franc, divided into 100 cents. In practice, most people will accept euros.

Banks and ATMs
ATMs *(bancomat)*, are widely available and commonly used. There is usually a small transaction charge. Be aware that there is a limit to the amount you can withdraw each day (usually around €250). UK debit cards can also be used to buy goods in shops, with verification by pin at the checkout.
　　It is always wise to carry credit cards with you as a back-up, and while some places still insist on cash, this is slowly changing. At restaurants, petrol stations and budget hotels outside tourist areas, check beforehand if there is any doubt. With heightened fraud security, it's worth telling your credit card company when you are travelling and taking a contact number, or they may refuse payments from an unexpected place. Traveller's cheques are no longer widely accepted, as atms and credit cards have become the norm.
　　Banks offer the best rates of exchange, as many small exchange booths *(cambio)* charge up to 3 percent commission.

TRANSPORT

A – Z

LANGUAGE

O

Opening Hours

Shops and businesses usually open from around 8.30am–1pm and 3.30pm/4pm–7.30pm/8pm, although in the main cities and tourist areas some stay open throughout the day and, increasingly, Sundays too. In smaller towns, it is not uncommon for shops to close on Saturday afternoons and Monday mornings, while Sunday is still a day of rest for all but bars and restaurants.

Churches are generally open from 8.30am–noon and from 4–6pm; major Catholic churches (such as the Duomo in Milan) do not close in the afternoon.

Museums run by the government are supposedly open from Tue–Sat 9am–7pm (Sun 9am–1pm). Others are likely to close over lunch and will have reduced hours in winter.

Most things down on national holidays.

P

Postal Services

Main post offices in major towns are open all day; otherwise the hours are usually 8am–1.30/2pm Mon–Fri (11.45pm Sat). Note that some counters have different hours (eg registered mail, etc).

Stamps (francobolli) are sold at post offices and tobacconists' shops (tabacchi), as well as in some gift shops in tourist areas.

There is also a courier service available at major post offices for sending important documents worldwide guaranteed to arrive within 24/48 hours.

Courier services

The post office group runs its own courier service, SDA (www.sda.it), but American companies FedEx (tel: 800-123 800, www.fedex.com/it_english) and DHL (www.dhl.it) also operate here.

R

Religious Services

Italy is a Catholic country, with 88 percent of the population describing themselves as Catholic. In general, the Italians are very tolerant of other faiths, and accepting of the tourists

Public Holidays

Banks and most shops are closed on the following holidays, and banks may close early on the preceding day.
1 January (Capodanno) New Year's Day
6 January (Befana) Epiphany
March/April (Pasqua) Easter Sunday
March/April (Pasquetta) Easter Monday
25 April (Giorno della Liberazione) Liberation Day
1 May (Festa dei Lavoratori) Labour Day
2 June (Festa della Repubblica) Republic Day
15 August (Ferragosto) Assumption of the Blessed Virgin Mary
1 November (Ognissanti) All Saints' Day
8 December (Immacolata Concezione) Immaculate Conception of the Blessed Virgin Mary
25 December (Natale) Christmas
26 December (Santo Stefano) St Stephen's Day
Offices and shops are also closed in Milan on 7 December, the feast day honouring St Ambrose, the city's patron saint.

that visit their churches. However, behaving appropriately when visiting churches is important: wear respectful attire (your shoulders and knees should be covered), switch off mobile phones and keep noise levels down, especially during services.

T

Telephones

Mobile phones

European standard GSM mobile/cell phones are widely used. Americans will need a tri-band phone. It may be worth buying an Italian SIM card if you intend to stay for more than a few weeks; buy a "pay as you go" card, normally called scheda prepagata in any mobile-phone shop. It costs €25, €50, €80, €100 or €150. The major networks available are offered by Telecom Italia (TIM), Vodafone and Wind.

Global roaming SIM cards from operators such as Go-Sim (www.gosim.com) allow you to receive calls for free

in most countries and make them for considerably less than usual.

Public telephones

Coin-operated public telephones are becoming increasingly hard to find in the age of mobile phones, so you will need a phone card (carta telefonica), which is available from tobacconists, newsstands or post offices in various denominations. You can also make calls from some bars and from post offices by calling scatti (ring first, pay later according to the number of units or scatti used) or using a credit card.

For international calls, the cheapest time to telephone is between 10pm and 8am Monday to Saturday, and all day Sunday, although buying an international phone card can make calling abroad remarkably cheap in a country known for its extremely high tariffs.

Useful numbers

Directory enquiries: 12
International enquiries: 176
International reverse charges (collect): 170

When dialling Italy from abroad, dial the country code (00 39) and then the area code including the initial zero.

In Italy, when calling numbers either inside or outside your area, dialling must always be preceded by the area code including the zero.
Area Code (Prefisso Telefonico)
Area codes for some of the principal cities of Italy and in the lakes region:
Bergamo **035**
Brescia **030**
Como **031**
Florence **055**
Lake Garda **0365**
Lake Maggiore **0323**
Milan **02**
Rome **06**
Trento **0461**
Venice **041**
Verona **045**

Time Zone

Italy is one hour ahead of London and Dublin, eight hours behind Sydney, 10 hours behind Auckland and six hours ahead of New York and Toronto.

Tipping

Most Italian restaurants impose a cover charge (coperto) for linen, bread and service, but a tip of around 10 percent is appropriate for good service. There is no need to tip anyone else (drivers, concierges, maids) unless they have been especially helpful or if, in a hotel, your stay has been a long one. After dining, it is worth keeping the bill with you until you are at least 100 metres (300ft) away, to comply with Italian law – the restaurant owner (and possibly you) could otherwise face a heavy fine from the Guardia di Finanzia, the tax police.

Tourist Information

Tourist offices abroad

The Italian State Tourist Board, enit (Ente Nazionale per il Turismo, Via Marghera 2/6, Rome, tel: 06-49711, www.enit.it), provides tourist information for the whole country.
UK 1 Princes Street, London W1R 2AY, tel: 020-7408 1254.
US Suite 1565, 630 Fifth Avenue, New York, NY 10111, tel: 212-245 4822. There are also offices in Chicago, Los Angeles and Canada.

Tourist offices in Italy

Tourist information is available at the Azienda di Promozione Turistica (APT), the main tourist office in each provincial capital, and there are branches at major airports and stations. Most towns also have a tourist office (*ufficio di turismo*), while in smaller villages, the *comune* holds tourist information and some commercial banks and travel agencies publish tourist guides. Office hours for larger towns are usually Mon–Sat 9am–1pm and 4–7pm (sometimes Sun mornings). Smaller offices can be erratic, and in winter may even close.

The Touring Club Italiano (TCI), with offices in almost every major town, provides free information about the area and also produces excellent road and hiking maps. See www.touringclub.it.
Bergamo
Via Gombito 13, Città Alta, tel: 035-242 226.
Urban Center, Viale Papa Giovanni XXIII 57, Città Bassa, tel: 035-210 204.
Airport, arrivals terminal, tel: 035-320 402.
www.visitbergamo.net
Brescia
Via Trieste 1, Brescia, tel: 030-240 0357 (City). Piazzale Stazione; tel: 030-837 8559.
www.bresciatourism.it
Como
Piazza Cavour 17, Como, tel: 031-269712.
www.lakecomo.it

Lake Garda
Piazza Boldini 2, Gargnano, tel: 0365-791 243.
www.visitgarda.com
Corso Repubblica, Gardone Riviera, tel: 0365-20347.
www.visitgarda.com
Viale Marconi 2, Sirmione, tel: 030-916 114.
www.visitgarda.com
Largo Medaglie d'Oro, Riva del Garda, tel: 0464-554 444, www.garda trentino.it
Via Capitanato 6/8, Malcesine, tel: 045-740 0044.
www.tourism.verona.it
Piazzale Aldo Moro, Bardolino, tel: 045-721 0078.
www.tourism.verona.it
Lake Iseo and Franciacorta
Lungolago Marconi 2/C, Iseo, tel: 030-374 8733. www.iseolake.info and www.bresciatourism.it
Lake Lugano
FFS, Lugano, tel: 091-923 5120.
Piazza Riforma, Palazzo Civico, Lugano, Switzerland, tel: +41 58-866 6600.
www.luganoturismo.ch
Lake Maggiore
Piazza Marconi 16, Stresa, tel: 0323-31308.
www.illagomaggiore.com
Piazza Stazione, SBB Railway Station, Locarno, Switzerland, tel: +41 848-091 091.
www.ascona-locarno.com
Milan
Galleria Vittorio Emanuele II (corner Piazza della Scala), tel: 02-8845 5555. www.turismo.milano.it
Trento
Via Manci 2, Trento; tel: 0461-216 000.
www.visittrentino.it
Varese
Via Romagnosi 9; tel: 033-228 1913.
www.vareselandoftourism.it and www.comune.varese.it
Verona
Via Degli Alpini 9, Piazza Brà, tel: 045-806 8680.
www.tourism.verona.it
For a complete list of tourist offices throughout Italy, visit www.enit.it.

V

Visas and Passports

EU citizens need only a valid photo ID (passport, national ID card or driving licence) to enter Italy; no visa is required. All other nationalities need a valid passport unless you intend to stay for more than 90 days. You must then apply at any police

station (*questura*) for an extension of an additional 90 days with evidence to prove you have adequate means of support. As a rule, permission is granted immediately. Other nationals should consult their embassy about visa requirements before entry.

Don't forget that parts of the lakes are in Switzerland, so it's best to carry your passport with you as you travel around.

Police registration

You must register with the police within three days of entering Italy, although this is automatically done for you if staying at a hotel. The formality is rarely observed, but if you intend to stay for a longer period it is advisable to comply with regulations. You are legally required to carry a form of identification (driving licence, passport, etc) on you at all times.

W

Weights and Measures

The metric system is used for all weights and measures in Italy.

Websites

www.autostrade.it, www.rac.co.uk, www.theaa.com
Driving in Italy and planning your journey from A to B.
www.hellomilano.it
Good general site with listings information, advice and maps.
www.italia.it
Italian tourism official website.
www.italianlakes.com
A dedicated and informative site from an expat American couple, full of tips, advice and itineraries.
www.italymag.co.uk
This site focuses on living in Italy, with useful links and a discussion forum.
www.italia-magazine.co.uk
Aimed at travellers and expats, with features on living *la dolce vita* plus good links.
www.mediasoft.it/piazze
Virtually tour the squares of Italy.
www.museionline.info
Excellent database on Italian museums
www.parks.it
Useful portal about national and regional parks, plus event listings and itineraries.

LANGUAGE

UNDERSTANDING THE LANGUAGE

BASIC RULES

Here are a few basic rules of grammar and pronunciation: *c* before *e* or *i* is pronounced "ch", as in *ciao*. *Ch* before *i* or *e* is pronounced as "k", eg *la chiesa*. Likewise, *sci* or *sce* are pronounced as in "sheep" or "shed" respectively. *Gn* in Italian is rather like the sound in "onion", while *gl* is softened to resemble the sound in "bullion".

Nouns are either masculine (*il*, plural *i*) or feminine (*la*, plural *le*). Plurals of nouns are most often formed by changing an *o* to an *i* and an *a* to a *e*, e.g. *il panino, i panini; la chiesa, le chiese.*

Words are stressed on the penultimate syllable unless an accent indicates otherwise.

Italian has formal and informal words for "you". In the singular, *tu* is informal while *lei* is more polite. It is best to use the formal form unless invited to do otherwise.

BASIC PHRASES AND WORDS

Yes *Sì*
No *No*
Thank you *Grazie*
Many thanks *Mille grazie/tante grazie/molte grazie*
You're welcome *Prego*
All right/That's fine *Va bene*
Please *Per favore/per cortesia*
Excuse me (to get attention) Scusi (singular), Scusate (plural); (to attract attention from a waiter) *Senta!* **(in a crowd)** *Permesso;* **(sorry)** *Mi scusi*
Can I help you? (formal) *Posso aiutarla?*

Can you help me? (informal) *Può aiutarmi, per cortesia?*
Certainly *Ma, certo*
I need… *Ho bisogno di…*
I'd like… *Vorrei…*
Where is/are…? *Dov'è/Dove sono…?*
I'm lost *Mi sono perso/a*
right/left *a destra/a sinistra*
Go straight on *Va sempre diritto*
Can you show me where I am on the map? *Può indicarmi sulla cartina dove mi trovo?*
Can you help me please? *Mi può aiutare, per favore?*
I'm sorry *Mi dispiace*
I don't know *Non lo so*
I don't understand *Non capisco*
Do you speak English/French? *Parla inglese/francese?*
Could you speak more slowly? *Può parlare più lentamente?*
Could you repeat that please? *Può ripetere, per piacere?*
Please write it down for me *Me lo scriva, per favore*
here/there *qui/là*
yesterday/today/tomorrow *ieri/oggi/domani*
now/early/late *adesso/presto/tardi*
What? *Come…?*
When/Why/Where? *Quando/Perché/Dove?*
Where is the lavatory? *Dov'è il bagno?*
WC *il gabinetto*
Pull/Push (sign on doors) *Tirare/Spingere*
Entrance/Exit *Entrata/Uscita*

Greetings

Hello (good day) *Buon giorno*
Goodbye *Arrivederci*
Good afternoon/evening *Buona sera*
Goodnight *Buona notte*
Hello/Hi/Goodbye (familiar) *Ciao*
Mr/Mrs/Miss *Signor/Signora/*

Signorina
Pleased to meet you (formal) *Piacere di conoscerla*
I am English/American/Irish/Scottish/Canadian/Australian *Sono inglese/americano(a)/irlandese/scozzese/canadese/australiano(a)*
I'm here on holiday *Sono qui in vacanza*
How are you (formal/informal)? *Come sta (come stai)?*
Fine, thanks *Bene, grazie*
See you later *A più tardi*
See you soon *A presto*
Take care (formal/informal) *Stia bene/Sta bene*
Do you like Italy/Milan/Verona/Como? *Le piace l'Italia/Milano/Verona/Como?*
I like it a lot *Mi piace moltissimo*

Telephone calls

I'd like to make a reverse-charge (collect) call *Vorrei fare una telefonata a carico del destinatario*
Hello (on the telephone) *Pronto*
My name's *Mi chiamo/Sono*
Could I speak to…? *Posso parlare con…?*
Sorry, he/she isn't in *Mi dispiace, è fuori*
I'll try later *Riproverò più tardi*
Can I leave a message? *Posso lasciare un messaggio?*
Please tell him I called *Gli dica, per favore, che ho telefonato*
Hold on *Un attimo, per favore*

IN THE HOTEL

Do you have any vacant rooms? *Avete delle camere libere?*
I have a reservation *Ho fatto una prenotazione*

a **single/double room** *una camera singola/doppia*
a **room with twin beds** *una camera a due letti*
a **room with a bath/shower** *una camera con bagno/doccia*
for one night *per una notte*
How much is it? *Quanto costa?*
On the first floor *Al primo piano*
Is breakfast included? *E compresa la prima colazione?*
Is everything included? *E tutto compreso?*
half/full board *mezza pensione/ pensione completa*
It's expensive *E caro*
Do you have a room with a balcony/ view of the sea? *C'è una camera con balcone/con una vista del mare?*
a room overlooking the park/the street/the back *una camera con vista sul parco/che da sulla strada/sul retro*
The room is too hot/cold/noisy/ small *La camera è troppo calda/ fredda/rumorosa/piccola*
A double bed *una doppia/ matrimoniale*
Can I see the room? *Posso vedere la camera?*
big/small *grande/piccola*
What time is breakfast? *A che ora è la prima colazione?*
Come in! *Avanti!*
Can I have the bill, please? *Posso avere il conto, per favore?*
Can you call me a taxi, please? *Può chiamarmi un taxi, per favore?*
dining room *la sala da pranzo*
key *la chiave*
lift *l'ascensore*
towel *un asciugamano*
toilet paper *la carta igienica*

AT A BAR

coffee (small, strong and black) *un caffè espresso;* **(with hot, frothy milk)** *un cappuccino;* (weak, served in tall glass) *un caffè lungo;* **(with alcohol, probably brandy)** *un caffè corretto*
tea *un tè*
herbal tea *una tisana*
hot chocolate *una cioccolata calda*
(bottled) orange/lemon juice *un succo d'arancia/di limone*
orange squash *aranciata*
freshly squeezed orange/lemon juice *una spremuta d'arancia/di limone*
mineral water (fizzy/still) *acqua minerale gassata/naturale*
with/without ice *con/senza ghiaccio*
red/white wine *vino rosso/bianco*
(draught) beer *una birra (alla spina)*
a bitter (Vermouth, etc) *un amaro*
milk *latte*

(half) a litre *un (mezzo) litro*
bottle *una bottiglia*
sandwich *un tramezzino*
roll *un panino*
Cheers *Salute*

IN A RESTAURANT

I'd like to book a table *Vorrei prenotare una tavola*
lunch/supper *pranzo/cena*
We do not want a full meal *Non desideriamo un pasto -completo*
I'm a vegetarian *Sono vegetariano/a*
Is there a vegetarian dish? *C'è un piatto vegetariano?*
May we have the menu? *Ci dia la carta?*
wine list *la lista dei vini*
What would you recommend? *Che cosa ci consiglia?*
What would you like to drink? *Che cosa desidera da bere?*
a carafe of red/white wine *una caraffa di vino rosso/bianco*
fixed-price menu *il menù a prezzo fisso*
dish of the day *il piatto del giorno*
home-made *fatto in casa*
vat (sales tax) *iva*
cover charge *il coperto/pane e coperto*
the bill, please *il conto, per favore*
Is service included? *Il servizio è incluso?*
Where is the lavatory? *Dov'è il bagno?*

MENU DECODER

Antipasti – starters

antipasto misto m**ixed hors d'oeuvres: cold cuts, cheeses, roast vegetables**
buffet freddo **cold buffet**
caponata **aubergine, olives, tomatoes**
insalata caprese/di mare/mista/ verde **salad – tomato and mozzarella/ seafood/mixed/green**
melanzane alla parmigiana **aubergine with parmesan and tomato**
mortadella/salame **salami**
pancetta **bacon**
proscuitto **ham**
peperonata **grilled peppers drenched in olive oil**

Primi – first courses

brodetto **fish soup**
crespolini **savoury pancakes**
gnocchi **potato and dough dumplings**

il minestrone **thick vegetable soup**
pasta e fagioli **pasta and bean soup**
il prosciutto (cotto/crudo) **(cooked/ cured) ham**
i suppl" **rice croquettes**
la zuppa **soup**

Secondi – main courses

La Carne **Meat**
arrosto **roast meat**
al forno **baked**
alla griglia **grilled**
involtini **skewered veal, ham etc**
ben cotto **well done (steak)**
media cottura **medium**
al sangue **rare**
l'agnello **lamb**
la bistecca **steak**
la bresaola **dried salted beef**
il capriolo/cervo **venison**
il carpaccio **wafer-thin beef**
il cinghiale **wild boar**
il controfiletto **sirloin steak**
le cotolette **cutlets**
il fagiano **pheasant**
il fegato **liver**
il filetto **fillet**
la lepre **hare**
il maiale **pork**
il manzo **beef**
l'ossobuco **shin of veal**
il pollo **chicken**
le polpette **meatballs**
il polpettone **meat loaf**
la porchetta **suckling pig**
la salsiccia **sausage**
il saltimbocca (alla Romana) **veal escalopes with ham**
le scaloppine **escalopes**
stufato **braised, stewed**
il sugo **sauce**
la trippa **tripe**
il vitello **veal**
Frutti di Mare **Seafood**
affumicato **smoked**
alle brace **charcoal-grilled**
al ferro **grilled without oil**
fritto **fried**
alla griglia **grilled**
ripieno **stuffed**
al vapore **steamed**
l'anguilla **eel**
l'aragosta **lobster**
il baccalà **dried salted cod**
il branzino **sea bass**
i calamari **squid**
le cozze **mussels**
i crostacei **shellfish**
il fritto misto **mixed fried fish**
i gamberetti **shrimps**
i gamberi **prawns**
il granchio **crab**
il merluzzo **cod**
le ostriche **oysters**
il pesce **fish**
il pescespada **swordfish**
il polipo **octopus**

il risotto di mare **seafood risotto**
le sarde **sardines**
le seppie **cuttlefish**
la sogliola **sole**
surgelati **frozen**
il tonno **tuna**
la triglia **red mullet**
la trota **trout**
le vongole **clams**

I legumi/la verdura – vegetables

gli asparagi **asparagus**
la bietola **(similar to spinach)**
il carciofo **artichoke**
il cavolo **cabbage**
la cicoria **chicory**
la cipolla **onion**
i contorni **side dishes**
i fagioli **beans**
le fave **broad beans**
il finocchio **fennel**
i funghi **mushrooms**
l'indivia **endive/chicory**
la melanzana **aubergine/eggplant**
le patate **potatoes**
le patatine fritte **chips/fries**
i peperoni **peppers**
i piselli **peas**
i pomodori **tomatoes**
le primizie **spring vegetables**
il radicchio **red, bitter lettuce**
i ravanelli **radishes**
ripieno **stuffed**
rughetta **rocket**
spinaci **spinach**

la verdura **green vegetables**
la zucca **pumpkin/squash**
zucchini **courgettes**

La frutta – fruit

le albicocche **apricots**
le arance **oranges**
le ciliege **cherries**
il cocomero **watermelon**
i fichi **figs**
le fragole **strawberries**
frutti di bosco **fruits of the forest**
i lamponi **raspberries**
la mela **apple**
la pera **pear**
la pesca **peach**
le uve **grapes**

I dolci – desserts

al carrello **desserts from the trolley**
la cassata **Sicilian ice cream with candied peel**
il dolce **dessert/sweet**
le frittelle **fritters**
un gelato (di lampone/limone) **(raspberry/lemon) ice cream**
una granita **water ice**
una macedonia di frutta **fruit salad**
un semifreddo **semi-frozen dessert (many types)**
il tartufo (nero) **(chocolate) ice-cream dessert**
il tiramisù **cold, creamy rum and coffee dessert**
la torta **cake/tart**

zabaglione **sweet dessert made with eggs and Marsala**
zuccotto ice-**cream liqueur**
la zuppa inglese **trifle**

Basic foods

aceto **vinegar**
aglio **garlic**
burro **butter**
formaggio **cheese**
frittata **omelette**
grissini **bread sticks**
marmellata **jam**
olio **oil**
pane **bread**
parmigiano **Parmesan cheese**
pepe **pepper**
riso **rice**
sale **salt**
senape **mustard**
uova **eggs**
zucchero **sugar**

HEALTH

chemist la farmacia
antiseptic cream la crema antisettica
insect repellent l'insettifugo
sticking plaster il cerotto
sunburn scottatura del sole
sunscreen la crema antisolare
tissues i fazzoletti di carta
toothpaste il dentifricio
upset-stomach pills le pillole anticoliche

FURTHER READING

TRAVEL COMPANIONS

Desiring Italy, Susan Cahill (ed).
Writings by female authors (George
Eliot, Edith Wharton, Muriel Spark,
etc) on the beauty and culture of Italy.
Italian Days, Barbara Grizutti
Harrison. A witty and eloquent look at
Italy, revealing a fascinating insight
into a nation.

HISTORY, SOCIETY AND CULTURE

**A History of Contemporary Italy:
Society and Politics: 1943–1988,
Italy and Its Discontents, 1980–
2001 and Silvio Berlusconi: Television, Power and Patrimony**. Paul
Ginsborg – A masterly history of post-
war Italy and its politics is completed
with an account of the power of the
country's most powerful politician.
Alps and Sanctuaries, Samuel Butler.
The 18th-century traveller describes
his journeys around the lakes.
Mussolini, Nicholas Farrell. A
biography of the reviled Fascist dictator
that pulls no punches. It includes the
period of the Salò Republic, when
Mussolini's powerbase was on the
shores of Lake Garda.
The House of Gucci, Sarah Forden.
A biography of Maurizio Gucci, the
last family member to run the luxury-
goods fashion empire.
The Dark Heart of Italy, Tobias Jones.
Although flawed and obsessed with a
Berlusconi era that is now history, this
is an intriguing look at the underbelly of
Italy, from politics, crime and (lack of)
punishment to the Italian way of life.
How the English Made the Alps, Jim
Ring. The English love affair with the
Alps, from its beginnings in the early

Romantic movement, through to its
Victorian heyday.
La Bella Figura, Beppe Severgnini.
Incisive tour behind the seductive
face that Italy puts on for visitors by
a columnist for the daily newspaper
Corriere della Sera.

FICTION AND TRAVELOGUE

A Farewell to Arms, Ernest
Hemingway. The novel tells the story
of a wounded American soldier in
the Italian army who convalesces in
Milan, inadvertently deserts while
fleeing from the Germans but is
reunited with his beloved in Stresa, on
Lake Maggiore.
**Europa, Italian Neighbours, A
Season With Verona**, Tim Parks.
The novelist observes life in Italy
in a series of light-hearted and
affectionate tales.

FOOD AND WINE

Eating up Italy: Voyages on a Vespa,
Matthew Fort. Exploring Italy's regions
on an epic scooter trip, Matthew Fort
paints a contemporary portrait of Italy
through its food and the people who
produce it.
Truly Italian, Ursula Ferrigno. An
Italian cookbook with inspirational
recipes and a vegetarian focus that
features the healthiest northern
Italian cooking.

OTHER INSIGHT GUIDES

With comprehensive travel coverage
and cultural background information,

the **Insight Guides** series includes
titles on Florence, Sicily, Sardinia,
Tuscany and Venice.
   Insight Explore Guides provide a
series of routes to guide you through
the city or region. Titles include
Florence, Italian Lakes, Naples and
the Amalfi Coast, Rome, Sicily, Venice.
   Durable and weatherproof, **Insight
Fleximaps** combine clear cartography
with essential travel information.
Italian maps include Florence, Lake
Garda and Verona, Rome, Tuscany
and Venice.

Send Us Your Thoughts

We do our best to ensure the
information in our books is as
accurate and up-to-date as
possible. The books are updated
on a regular basis using local
contacts, who painstakingly add,
amend and correct as required.
However, some details (such as
telephone numbers and opening
times) are liable to change, and
we are ultimately reliant on our
readers to put us in the picture.
   We welcome your feedback,
especially your experience of using
the book "on the road". Maybe we
recommended a hotel that you
liked (or another that you didn't),
or you came across a great bar or
new attraction we missed.
   We will acknowledge all contri-
butions, and we'll offer an Insight
Guide to the best letters received.

Please write to us at:
**Insight Guides
PO Box 7910
London SE1 1WE**
Or email us at:
hello@insightguides.com

CREDITS

Photo Credits

Alamy 35, 36, 37, 41, 42, 43, 50, 53, 55, 83, 234B
Anna Mockford and Nick Bonetti/ Apa Publications 47, 130T, 151T, 162T, 190, 197T, 199T, 201, 203T, 231T
Aquaria 156BL
AWL Images 110
Bigstockphoto 27MR, 30, 58, 67B, 100T, 103, 105, 111, 126, 202, 235B, 236/237T
Cappuccini 156MR
Corbis 62, 68, 73, 75, 135TR, 234T
Dreamstime 10TR, 56, 59, 107, 113, 137, 149, 154, 159, 166, 229T, 237B
Fotolia 7ML, 11, 46, 104, 106B, 184, 223, 247
Fototeca ENIT 8T, 9ML, 31, 171, 172, 256
Getty Images 1, 4/5, 7MR, 9TR, 12/13, 16/17, 18, 26B, 34, 44/45, 80L, 80R, 86/87, 88/89, 90, 94, 95, 119, 120/121T, 145, 146, 158, 175, 186, 192, 197B, 198, 206,

207, 213, 221, 230, 238, 242, 246, 260/261T, 260B, 261R, 261L, 262
Glyn Genin/Apa Publications 6MR, 7TR, 24, 27TL, 28ML, 33, 38, 39, 51, 91B, 97T, 97B, 98, 100B, 101T, 102T, 102B, 106T, 121BR, 147, 150, 151B, 152, 176, 177, 179, 180, 181, 182T, 182B, 183, 248, 249, 251T, 251B, 252, 253T, 253B, 254T, 254B, 255T, 255B, 257, 258B, 258T, 259, 265, 269, 271, 273
iStock 6BR, 7B, 7TL, 10BL, 27BL, 48, 57, 60, 64, 66/67T, 66MC, 66ML, 79, 99, 101B, 116, 118, 120ML, 121ML, 144, 155, 156ML, 162B, 163, 185, 195, 205T, 211, 212B, 232, 236BR, 236BL, 243B, 272, 279
Leonardo 70, 157B, 157T
Neil Buchan-Grant/Apa Publications 6ML, 8B, 9BR, 9ML, 10BR, 14/15, 19T, 19B, 20, 21, 22, 25, 26T, 52, 71, 76/77T, 76B, 77ML, 77BR, 77TR, 78, 81, 82,

84/85, 91T, 109T, 109B, 112, 114B, 114T, 115T, 115B, 117, 120BL, 122, 123, 124B, 125, 127B, 127T, 129B, 129T, 130B, 131B, 131T, 132, 133, 134, 135ML, 135BL, 135BR, 136, 138B, 138T, 139, 141, 142, 160, 161, 164, 165, 169T, 169B, 173B, 174, 188, 189, 193, 194, 199B, 200, 203B, 204B, 204T, 205B, 208T, 214, 215, 216T, 216B, 217, 218, 219T, 219B, 220, 225, 227T, 227B, 236MC, 237T, 239, 240, 241T, 241B, 243T, 245T, 245B, 264, 266, 267, 270, 276
Photoshot 23, 29T, 32, 54, 65, 67T, 69, 72, 121TR, 124T, 231B, 235T
Public domain 28BL, 28TR, 63, 74
Robert Harding 120BR, 229B
Shutterstock 6BL, 7TL, 29B, 49, 61, 143, 173T, 208B, 212T, 222, 226, 228, 244
SuperStock 153, 167, 170, 187, 191, 210, 233
Terme di Sirmione 156/157T
TopFoto 40

Cover Credits

Front cover: Malcesine, Lake Garda *Shutterstock*
Back cover: (top) View over Marone, Lake Iseo *iStock*
Front flap: (from top) Isola Bella on Lake Maggiore *Shutterstock*;

Frescoes in Santa Maria della Neve *Neil Buchan-Grant/Apa Publications*; Ascona at night, Ticino *Shutterstock*; Spaghetti Con Le Vongole *Greg Gladman/Apa Publications*
Back flap: Malcesine *iStock*

Insight Guide Credits

Distribution
UK, Ireland and Europe
Apa Publications (UK) Ltd;
sales@insightguides.com
United States and Canada
Ingram Publisher Services;
ips@ingramcontent.com
Australia and New Zealand
Woodslane; info@woodslane.com.au
Southeast Asia
Apa Publications (SN) Pte;
singaporeoffice@insightguides.com
Hong Kong, Taiwan and China
Apa Publications (HK) Ltd;
hongkongoffice@insightguides.com
Worldwide
Apa Publications (UK) Ltd;
sales@insightguides.com
**Special Sales, Content Licensing
and CoPublishing**
Insight Guides can be purchased in
bulk quantities at discounted prices.
We can create special editions,
personalised jackets and corporate
imprints tailored to your needs.
sales@insightguides.com
www.insightguides.biz

Printed in China by CTPS

All Rights Reserved
© 2017 Apa Digital (CH) AG and
Apa Publications (UK) Ltd

First Edition 2008
Third Edition 2017

Every effort has been made to
provide accurate information in
this publication, but changes are
inevitable. The publisher cannot be
responsible for any resulting loss,
inconvenience or injury. We would
appreciate it if readers would call our
attention to any errors or outdated
information. We also welcome your
suggestions; please contact us at:
hello@insightguides.com

www.insightguides.com

Editor: Carine Tracanelli
Author: Natasha Foges, Melissa
Shales, Lisa Gerard-Sharp
Head of Production: Rebeka Davies
Update Production: AM Services
Picture Editor: Tom Smyth
Cartography: original cartography
Stephen Ramsay, updated by Carte

Legend

City maps

	Freeway/Highway/Motorway
	Divided Highway
	Main Roads
	Minor Roads
	Pedestrian Roads
	Steps
	Footpath
	Railway
	Funicular Railway
	Cable Car
	Tunnel
	City Wall
	Important Building
	Built Up Area
	Other Land
	Transport Hub
	Park
	Pedestrian Area
	Bus Station
	Tourist Information
	Main Post Office
	Cathedral/Church
	Mosque
	Synagogue
	Statue/Monument
	Beach
	Airport

Regional maps

	Freeway/Highway/Motorway (with junction)
	Freeway/Highway/Motorway (under construction)
	Divided Highway
	Main Road
	Secondary Road
	Minor Road
	Track
	Footpath
	International Boundary
	State/Province Boundary
	National Park/Reserve
	Marine Park
	Ferry Route
	Marshland/Swamp
	Glacier Salt Lake
	Airport/Airfield
	Ancient Site
	Border Control
	Cable Car
	Castle/Castle Ruins
	Cave
	Chateau/Stately Home
	Church/Church Ruins
	Crater
	Lighthouse
	Mountain Peak
	Place of Interest
	Viewpoint

Contributors

This new edition of *Insight Guide Italian
Lakes* was commissioned by **Carine
Tracanelli** and builds on a previous
edition updated by **Natasha Foges**, a
travel writer who has done an array of
jobs, from paparazzo's assistant to
Latin teacher, and regularly visits Italy to
soak up the atmosphere and satisfy a
craving for world-class pizza.

Past contributors include: **Rebecca
Ford**, who wrote The Making of the
Lakes; **Victoria Gooch**, who got to
sample the delights of Lake Como;

Adele Evans, who explored Lake Orta,
checked out the Grand Hotels, Skiing,
Wildlife and Economic Heartland; and
Lisa Gerard-Sharp, who wrote the
essays on the Master Builders,
Victorian Trailblazers, the Literary
Lakes; the features on Art and
Architecture, Celebrity Playground,
Spa Heaven and Gardener's Glory;
and explored Western Garda, Brescia,
and Lake Iseo, Franciacorta and Val
Camonica. The rest of the book was
written by **Melissa Shales**.

About Insight Guides

INDEX

Main references are in bold type

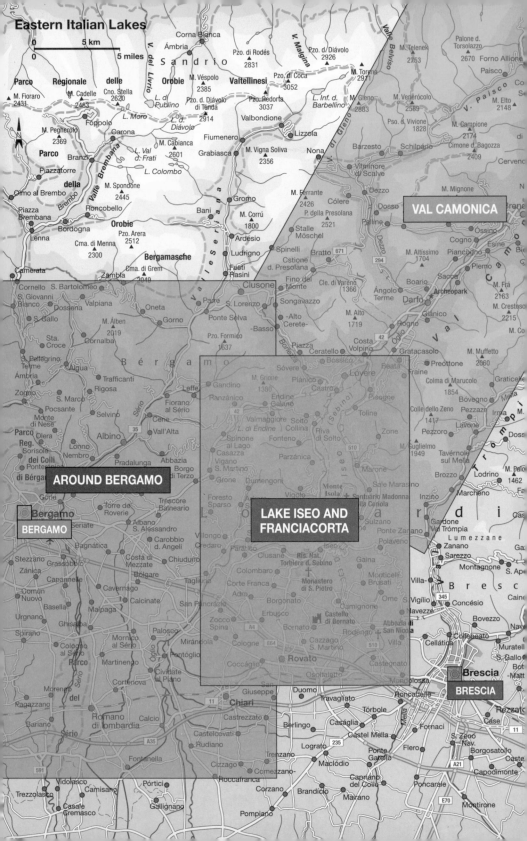